# THEY EVEN
# PAID ME

# THEY EVEN PAID ME

Raw reflections of a third generation
Kimberley cattleman.

## JANET WELLS

**National Library of Australia Cataloguing-in-Publication entry**
Creator: Janet Wells
Title: They even paid me : raw reflections of a third generation Kimberley cattleman / Janet R. Wells.
ISBN:  978-0-9942327-0-0 (paperback)
        978-0-9942327-1-7 (hardback)
        978-0-9942327-2-4 (ebook)
Subjects: Wells, John.
        Stockmen--Western Australia--Kimberley--Biography.
        Ranch life--Western Australia--Kimberley--History.

Dewey Number: 929.20994

Book Cover Layout: Marion Duke- O'Callaghan (Pickawoowoo Publishing Group)
Publishing Consultants: Pickawoowoo Publishing Group

This book contains the ideas, recollections and opinions of one man, developed over the course of his lifetime. This is not to suggest they are entirely factual, recalled with complete accuracy or aligned with the opinions of others. Aboriginal readers are cautioned that this book contains the names and images of deceased persons.

Some names have been changed to protect privacy however they reflect real people and events.

**Publisher Details**

A Touch of Silk

PO Box 433 Capel 6271

Western Australia

Available globally through Ingram Distribution and all good bookstores.

# DEDICATION

This book is dedicated to the memory

of John's father, William George Wells,

and to his loyal, lifelong friend Willie Lennard,

who taught him so much.

# CONTENTS

# FOREWORD

I am both honoured and delighted to have been asked to write a foreword to this book. Janet has worked tirelessly over many years gathering yarns of her husband, John Wells the ringer, head stockman, station manager and 'odd job' man to finally pull together this captivating story of a genuine Kimberley character best known as "Wellsy".

Accounts of a then young man preceded my meeting him in person almost fifty years ago. It soon became evident why this distinctive third generation Kimberley character earned his reputation within the pastoral community. A firm though especially judicious boss John showed incredible empathy towards his Aboriginal subordinates, clearly an exception rather than the rule of the day.

As the reader will discover John's exploits border on the legendary which Janet has exceptionally captured in this illuminating portrayal.

Gathering the stories was a painstaking exercise especially early in the developmental stages when collecting material involved a virtual clandestine approach. I first became aware of Janet's remarkably meticulous determination in assembling material for this book when spotting her sidling up to a group of blokes around a campfire, or esky, and intensely listening to unfolding yarns and recollections. Janet's objective of composing this book then took a new turn as the focus shifted to ensuring events were accurately depicted and characters sensitively portrayed. Wellsy is a stickler for correctness and authenticity.

Readers may be surprised by many revelations, reasoning some events must surely be fiction however you can be assured this is a real life story of a real life bloke who loved the Kimberley, loved his horses, loved his dogs and particularly loved his mule called Cheeky.

'They Even Paid Me' is a manifestation of John's philosophy to 'enjoy what you are doing to the best of your ability'. It is full of surprises, fascinating anecdotes and faithful reflections of the personal journey of a dinkum Kimberley character who has actually 'been there and done that'. It is a book you won't want to put down until finished.

Peter Kneebone, Derby WA August 2014

# PREFACE

They say a dog resembles his master. I say a man resembles the land from whence he came, in my case the Kimberley region of Western Australia. A land of rugged beauty, a land of extremes. Sometimes harsh, always hot. Either 'wet', or 'dry', never in between. Where rivers are swirling, raging torrents, or wide and waterless. It is a land of tumultuous thunderclouds, or endless empty skies. There is nothing moderate about the Kimberley. It is raw, vibrant, untamed. It's landscape, ancient and wildly magnificent, encompasses all that is sought after in today's over urbanised world. Here no effort has been spared by the forces of nature that formed it's vistas, it's jagged ranges, it's savage scenery. As raw, energetic and some would say, as untamed, as the land that nurtured me, moderation is not a part of my make-up either.

Lying well to the north of the Tropic of Capricorn the Kimberley is bounded by the Indian Ocean to the west, Timor Sea to the north, Great Sandy Desert and Tanami Deserts to the south and the Northern Territory to it's east. The region is three times the size of England, taking up one sixth of the total area of Western Australia and is geologically one of the world's oldest land masses. It was one of the first areas of the continent inhabited by indigenous Australians.

Explored by Alexander Forrest in 1879, the first land leases in the Kimberley were granted in 1883 and pastoralists began to bring sheep into the region. Cattle arrived two years later, driven across the top end from the Eastern States and the first cattle stations were established.

Despite the size of the region, two thousand and sixty-one square miles, or four thousand and twenty-one square kilometres, there are few towns in the Kimberley and a relatively small population overall. The three main towns were Broome, Derby and Wyndham, with smaller settlements at Fitzroy Crossing and Halls Creek, which emerged during the gold rush. Later the town of Kununurra was established with the building of the Argyle Dam.

My stamping ground was in the West Kimberley and most of my working life was spent on cattle stations where Derby was the nearest town from where we collected our supplies. Derby had one main street in those days, comprising a police station, post office, butcher's shop, bakery, hospital and a native hospital, two or three hotels, a school, general store, shipping agent, outdoor picture theatre and a handful of other small enterprises. The population within the town barely reached four figures.

My father and grandfather were both West Kimberley cattlemen. Dad managed Cherrabun and later, Meda Station, for Emanuel Brothers, who then owned several properties in the Kimberley. My grandfather, Billy Wells, managed Oscar Range Station and later Brooking Springs. My great uncle, George Poole, was manager of GoGo, another Emanuel owned property, until his untimely death of appendicitis, in the 'wet' of 1924. Without including George Poole, my grandfather, father and I, managed West Kimberley cattle stations for absentee owners, for a combined period of seventy years between 1900 and 1988. The remaining eighteen years were all spent working on cattle stations, but not as managers. Station life was in my blood.

When I was growing up there were still both sheep and cattle stations in the Kimberley, but like 'the farmer and the cowboy' in the musical Oklahoma the two did not see eye to eye. Their differences went beyond the style of hat they wore, the sheep men in low crowned, narrow brimmed hats, the cattlemen in wide brimmed, more shade giving head gear. The sheep men tended to look down on the cattlemen, who were thought uncouth, and perhaps we were. The nature of our work did not lend itself to genteel riding and gentlemanly behaviour. Our lives depended on our wits and ability. There was no room for error in the game we were in. But Australia was then 'riding on the sheep's back' and there was no doubt who was the more well to do. Over the years sheep numbers in the Kimberley declined and more and more properties changed over to cattle. Now there are no sheep stations in the region at all, nor have been for several decades.

Pastoral leases in the Kimberley were up to a million acres in size. They were largely unfenced, with few improvements and were managed from a single homestead. A station homestead generally included a manager's house, kitchen, store, workshop, men's quarters, blacksmith's shop, large native camp, a meat house and various other assorted buildings. There would also be a good vegetable garden, a chook yard, goat yard, horse paddock and a set of timber yards close by.

Because of the distances involved station hands, stockmen and contractors, would camp out on the job rather than return to the homestead at night. They could be out for weeks on end during the 'dry' time. Weekends were unheard of. During the monsoon, or 'wet' season, the homestead would be almost deserted. Station hands would head into town for a break, the natives would go 'walkabout' and little was done at the homestead, other than a few maintenance jobs. A caretaker would be left to keep an eye on things while the manager and his family went on holiday.

My parents managed Meda Station for twenty years, until Dad's retirement in 1964. They were sent there from Cherrabun to take over after the manager, Gordon Smith, was killed in a mustering accident. I was four months old at the time. Meda was my home from infancy to adulthood. My mother, a nurse from northern New South Wales, came to the Kimberley in 1939 to open the first Australian Inland Mission Hospital at Fitzroy Crossing. My father was managing Cherrabun Station at the time. They married in 1942 and I am their only son. Although I have a younger sister we have, for the most part, led independent lives. Both my parents worked extremely hard. They were highly regarded throughout the Kimberley, by both blacks and whites alike.

My father took his job very seriously and was utterly dedicated to his employers. He was sparing in all things, including words, and saved Emanuels from every expense possible. For example, Dad would never have both butter and jam on his bread. It would be one or the other, he considered it extravagant to have both. Once, when the station was running low on meat, he gave a bloke a single bullet and told him to go and shoot a killer. 'You've only given me one bullet' the man pointed out. 'I only want one killer' Dad told him. 'What if I miss?' the fellow asked. 'Don't.' Dad replied. Dad was renowned for his honesty. He was tough and physically strong, but he had a gentle streak in him. He loved nature and although he said very little, his kind gestures frequently exposed his softer side.

I think my father was proud of me, more so as time went by, but he was not a man to say so. Rather he showed it in other ways, no less meaningful. I suspect he and I are very much alike. As the years roll on the more like him I seem to be. This makes me wonder if he too may have made mistakes and been a bit wild in his youth.

As he was already forty years old when he met my mother none of us know, which perhaps is just as well.

My mother, who was fifteen years younger than Dad, was a stoic woman. She would be up well before daylight, every day of the week, working tirelessly. She did most of the cooking for the station, including the native camp, as well as tending to the health needs of everybody. She was a very practical woman who prided herself on her common sense approach to life and it's difficulties. Whilst my father was away in the stockcamp, Mum saw to the smooth running of the homestead in his absence, as best she could, and despite suffering severe migraine headaches she did a mighty job.

As a child I was a bit of a handful. I used to take off and go bush, giving Mum a lot of additional worry. Somehow she managed to rear me, keeping me safe and well, even though in today's pampered society some of the measures she took to accomplish this might seem a little harsh.

Later, when I was a bit older, I was allowed to go out all day with the blacks, because Mum fully trusted them to look after me. This really says something about the relationship between my parents and the natives in those times. They, likewise, absolutely trusted my mother and father. Each year as the time approached for my family to go on holiday, I remember how it was kept a secret from the native camp, so that the blacks wouldn't start wailing, grieving and carrying on. It was easier if we didn't leave the station until after they'd gone on 'walkabout'.

My parents never had much money. School fees had kept them broke and, despite being thrifty, they left Meda without very much at all, although Emanuels did help Dad with the purchase of a Holden ute and later paid him a small pension, which helped make ends meet. They moved into a small corrugated iron cottage in town and Dad went to work at the Derby Meatworks, reading brands, until he was seventy-six years old. Mum did a refresher course and returned to nursing, working at Derby Regional Hospital for fifteen years. Much of that time she was 'sister in charge' of outpatients, before finally retiring in 1980. Both my parents, despite the years of toil in a harsh environment, lived to their early nineties.

Much has changed on cattle stations over the years and throughout the

Kimberley. A good bitumen road now stretches the length of the state, bringing grey nomads and overseas tourists deep into the region. A communications revolution has seen distances shrink and the hazards of isolation all but disappear. Mustering on stations is now mostly mechanical, stockcamps relatively comfortable, with mod cons never dreamt of in my day. Many of today's station hands are back-packers. The cattle, mostly Brahman, are quiet, educated and contained in paddock systems. Broome, though firmly on the map, is unrecognisable with it's modern, luxurious sophistication. The entire region has been 'discovered' and is now one of the world's best known tourist destinations.

The Kimberley my parents knew is long gone and much of the life I knew has all but vanished also. Deals are no longer sealed with the shake of a hand. A word given is not necessarily a word kept. Hardly an aboriginal stockman is employed on a white owned station and the extensive 'blacks camp', with all its diversity, is now a thing of the past.

Unlike the wild enduring landscape that is the Kimberley, which cannot be obliterated no matter the number of 'adventure tourists' and four wheel drive vehicles exploring its heart; the life, vigour, and dare-devilry of the 'ringer' is a tale that needs to be told, or it will disappear without trace, as completely as the dust covered ashes of a long extinguished branding fire. To that end this tale is as honest a story as I am able to tell. I have read too many accounts of cleanly lived lives, in tough circumstances. Accounts that are perhaps not quite sterile, but which have certainly been sanitised to some degree. For the real picture to be drawn, of what my working life was like, I have left all the smudges and blotches in place. The reader may judge as he likes, think what he pleases, but at the end of the tale he will, at the very least, have some idea of what station life was like.

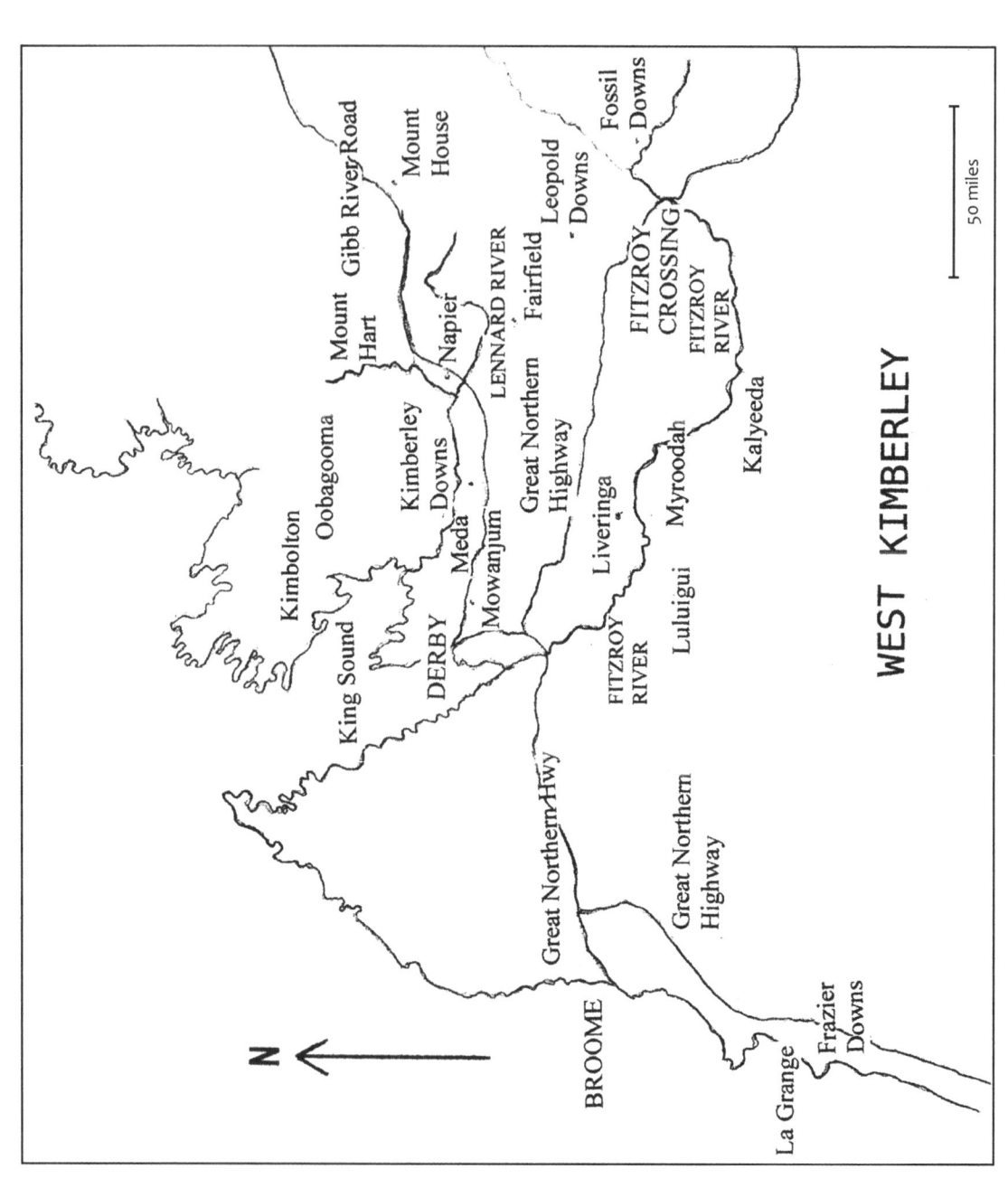

WEST KIMBERLEY

# PART ONE

# CHAPTER ONE
# WILD CHILDHOOD

*May I wander the paths I knew as a child,*
*In the only land I love,*
*Where my heart is young and my thoughts are wild,*
*And the stars shine bright from above.*

I don't know how far back I can remember, but when I was a little boy on Meda I used to just take off, so Mum got a couple of dog chains. She locked them together and then padlocked one end around a steel aerial pole and the other around my waist.

When I was first put on the chain I was just like a wild animal. I tried to break it but it would hurt my ribs and hips. I found out I couldn't break it, so then I tried to bite it. Then I'd get stones and I tried to hit the chain until it broke, but I never seemed to be able to break it. I screamed and carried on until, eventually, I just became one of the dogs. We'd lie down and go to sleep until we were let go again. The dogs and I spent a good few hours together amongst the creepers under the homestead verandah.

I never felt I had a harsh upbringing, or a deprived childhood. I always felt very fortunate, and I had more grannies than any other kid in Australia.

When Mum was busy cooking in the station kitchen, which was most of the time, one of the native women would be told to mind me for the afternoon, or morning. They'd take me for walks down around the billabong. One native in particular, Maudie, would show me things. Lots of things. Maudie knew where goannas were in a hole and having a sleep, or where lizards lived in fence posts that had a hollow down the centre. Sometimes she'd get a fishing line and put it up on top of the post, secure it and then we'd sit under a shady tree and wait. She'd watch till the lizard stuck it's head out and she'd give the line a pull. We'd miss it quite a few times, but eventually we'd get one and she'd catch it and show it to me. Then we'd let it go again. A month or two later she might take me back there and we'd catch it again. For some reason the blacks on Meda didn't seem to want to eat these lizards.

One day we were down the billabong. It was the wet season. I was playing in some water near a little creek where nice green grass was growing along the edge. I spotted a caterpillar on the grass. It was about three inches long, all hairy and woolly looking. Maudie saw me and said 'Ah don't touch that 'Shohn, you bin get an hitchy', but I took off with it, Maudie running after me. I put the grub in my pocket and kept going with this thing and I ran home. I thought it was absolutely marvellous, this big furry caterpillar. It wasn't long afterwards that the itches started. Maudie took the caterpillar from me and killed it. Soon after I found myself in a bath with stuff added to the water to get rid of the itch. I learnt that you don't ever touch one of those things.

## Catching water goannas

The blacks would show me how to catch water goannas in the billabong, with bushes held in front of my face. Maudie never went in to catch one, but sometimes the old girls would take me. They'd strip off and just have a petticoat on. They'd break some bushes off and they'd be sitting in the water with these bushes in front of their faces. When you're little you find it hard to spot the goannas, but after you've been with them a while you learn how to pick them up fairly quickly. They'd just have their heads sticking out of the water and if you moved they'd dive again. When the old girls saw one of these water goannas they'd move forward, in a way that looked as if the wind was blowing the bushes across the water, towards the goanna. When they got near, all of a sudden the goanna would disappear. They had grabbed him from beneath and pulled him under. They used to reckon that was pretty good. I did too. They'd light a fire then and cook him up.

Also on the billabong there were mussels, about two and half inches long. These old girls would find where they'd made their tracks on the edge of the mud. They'd get in the water and feel around for them and find them. When they'd got twenty or thirty of them they'd pop them in a billycan, light a fire, boil them up and eat them. I used to eat them too.

There were lots of crabs in the wet season round the billabong, so the blacks and I would go down there catching them and cook them up as well. They were pretty good too. The jabirus and brolgas used to get a lot of them though.

## Lily roots and nelgros

At other billabongs, a little further from the homestead, lilies would grow in the water. Some of them had a nice orange flower, in other places there'd be some with big blue flowers. The blue ones had quite large bulbs and the native women would get in the water and gather these. They'd break them off and put them in a bag they'd carry with them. The orange lily flowers would all go to sleep in the night time and wake up when the sun came up. They were bright orange, smaller than the blue ones, but they'd cover the billabong and look really good when they were all open in the daytime. The bulb on these water lilies is a bit less than an inch round. The native women, these 'grannies' of mine, would collect both sorts. They would put them in the ashes and roast them, or boil them. When they were cooked we'd take the rough skin off them and eat them. They taste a bit like sweet potato and are quite nice.

The gins, when I was little, also taught me to eat 'nelgros'. They're like an onion grass. The blacks would know where they grew and after the plant had withered and died they'd dig about and gather them up till they had quite a few. Then they'd light a little grass fire and lay the bulbs on it and roast them.

## Catching bream and eels

When I was a kid the billabong at Meda rarely went dry, though in latter years it silted up a bit. It always had water in it when I was a child and lots of bream, catfish, cobbler and eels lived there. The blacks and I would take an empty forty four gallon drum down there, roll it down, and into the water. We'd take the bung out, so water could run in and eventually the drum would tip and stand itself upright. Then we'd put the bung back in, sit on it and fish off it. We had sticks with a line about three foot long. We'd put a bit of meat on a tiny hook and catch bream. Sometimes we'd fish off the bank and if there'd been a flood we might get a small barra.

One day I was down there in the middle of the day, sitting on the drum. I had no shirt on, just a pair of shorts. I got a stick and chucked a line in. You never touched the line, just held the stick. When something hit it you flicked it, pulled the fish off and put it in the bag. This day I was sitting there on the drum and not getting anything. All of a sudden I felt something. I flicked it quickly, but it didn't come out of the water. It was too heavy. I knew I had something big. I pulled it and up came the head of a snake. Jeez I got a fright. Such a fright I let the line go and all. The blacks said to me 'No, no Shohn, dat not joordu, (snake) Dats eel, jad'un.' It frightened the daylights out of me that did.

## Fishing down the river

On their days off I would go walkabout with the blacks. They showed me where things lived, where they went and their tracks. Or they'd take me down to the river, fishing for barramundi. They would give me a fishing line. Sometimes we'd catch a pink fish which was good eating. These fish weren't very big, but if we got one the blacks would cook it straight away and we'd eat it. Sometimes they would get a turtle. That too went straight on the fire to be eaten. I'd eat pretty well whatever they had.

When you are a kid you always want to be next to the water. When we were at the river I could go down to get a pannikin of water for myself, but I wasn't allowed to stay there, or sit there. Every now and then I'd try. I'd sit and fish right next to the water. Some of the blacks would get a bit angry.

"Shohn, you gotta get back up here. Linguida will get you." (meaning saltwater crocodile.) If I dawdled they'd say, "I'll get 'im shtick an' belt you in a minute." When they said that they meant business and I'd get back up the bank pretty smartly. They were frightened that if I got taken by a saltie they'd be in serious trouble from Dad.

They didn't often belt their kids, but when they did belt them they didn't care what sort of a stick they used. It might be a green one about three foot long. They'd just break the twigs off it and the kid would cop it. It didn't matter if he got hit by the sharp bits, where the little branches had been taken off. That didn't bother them one bit. So when they threatened the stick I knew a belting from them wouldn't be very nice, and I'd do as I was told.

## Hell Fire Jack and a catfish barb

We were fishing at The Rocks near Number One for barra, and we weren't getting much. I used to get bored fishing. Quite often I'd go for a long walk up the river. Previously I'd found where there was a kingfisher's nest, high in a tree hollow. Because nothing much was happening this day, I decided to go and check it. I was barefoot. As a kid I nearly always went barefoot. We all did. On my way up the river I trod on a dead catfish, partially decomposed on the bank. I tried to pull the spike out, but it was jagged and barbed. You can't pull the barbs out as easily as they go in I discovered. When I couldn't get it out I decided to keep walking. I went on to the kingfisher's nest, climbed up the tree and had a look. The nest had a chick or two in it, so I climbed down again. I tried to pull out the catfish barb several times but I couldn't. I walked back to where our fishing camp was. Jack McMahon, or Hell Fire Jack as he was known, asked me what was wrong.

"Give us a look," he said. He tried pulling it out, but I was too touchy. He told me to soak it in the water for a while, so I sat there with a fishing line, my foot in the river. Later he said to me, "Give us a look at it again." That time he didn't mess around. He grabbed my foot and just reefed it out. It hurt like hell. We stayed there fishing for another couple of hours, then we went home. My foot had started to throb by then. Mum wasn't very happy about it. She said, "I'll just clean it up for you." She got a syringe, filled it with Dettol, shoved it into my foot and squirted the antiseptic into the wound. Gee whizz! I tell you what, that really lifted me! It hurt like bloody hell and I thought I was going to die.

I was due to get on the boat to Perth, with Dad, the next day. The ship was leaving Derby mid afternoon. When we got to town I was taken in to see the doctor, then down to the jetty and onto the boat. I was given some tablets. When I woke up I was given some more. I didn't know what day it was when I woke up. I'd slept for about two and half days and didn't know anything, but I got out of it and never had any further problems.

## Cherabin

Sometimes we'd go following waterholes, if the natives thought certain things would be in them at certain times of the year. Often we'd get cherabin. It was the blacks who taught me to take a four gallon tin bucket, with holes in it. To tie a rope onto it and fasten it to a tree, then, with a bit of meat wired into it, lower it down into the water. Later on I'd have these planted all over the place. I'd drop a bucket in and come back a week later and check it. I'd take home five or six big cherabin, which I'd give to the blacks. They reckoned they were pretty good tucker, but I didn't like them much when I was a kid. Only the Meda blacks, who walked the May River, were hunting them so you could catch big ones in those days. Poulton's Pool and Bull Camp, were quiet hidden places then, so there were always plenty of cherabin to be had.

## Sugar bag

At other times we might go collecting sugar bag. The blacks would look out for certain trees, beefwood, bloodwood and coolibah trees in particular, because they often had a hollow up the middle of them. They'd watch to see where the tiny bees would go. I don't know how, but the blacks knew where to cut into the tree. They'd get a long thin bauhinia branch and fray the end of it, so it was like a brush. They'd poke this down the hollow, into the sugar bag, then lick the honey off the frayed end. They used to find this stuff in there which they reckoned were eggs, but I thought it was pollen. It was powdery stuff. Lots of little round balls, heaps of them, stuck together with wax. They'd get that and eat it too. I found if I ate it, it would make me feel sick. Although it was quite nice, it was too rich. They work hard those tiny Kimberley bees. Only in crook years, when cattle were dying around waterholes, did the blacks leave nearby sugarbag alone. This was because the tiny sting-less bees used to collect moisture from the decaying carcasses.

We'd also spend heaps of time collecting coongleberries. These grew on low, straggly, prickly bushes. Some bushes grew round berries, others oval shaped, and some plants were far sweeter than others. We got to know all of them and which were the best to eat. Somebody will make money out of coongleberries one day. They'll be a 'newly discovered delicacy'.

There was a plant like a wild passionfruit which also had little berries. They grew around the bores. We didn't go looking especially for them, but if we found some we'd grab them, squeeze them and eat the juicy centres, chucking the skins away.

Bush plums grew in the pindan country. They look a bit like olives and it took me a while before I acquired a taste for them, but the blacks liked them. They used to gather ripe fallen fruit off the ground, rather than pick them off the trees.

## Hunting and exploring on my own

As I grew older and wasn't minded anymore, I used to take off and do my own thing. I'd go out all over the place. Often I'd be away all day, chasing kangaroos with dogs, or catching goannas and bringing them back to the native women. Now and then I'd catch a snake. I'd kill it and bring it back in a bag to give to the blacks. In the native camp they'd be playing cards, a game called coontz, and I'd chuck the snake in amongst them. They'd jump up, cards scattered, yelling and screaming and banging into each other. They wouldn't be too pleased with me, but they always forgave me. They were very good to me, my old 'grannies'.

As I explored more I learnt where the ducks all nested. These were whistling duck. They'd come to the billabong in their thousands at the end of the year, when water was scarce, later nesting once the wet had set in. I reckoned I knew every ducks' nest around that billabong on Meda. Every white cockatoos' nest within half a mile of the billabong and the homestead, as well as mudlarks, willie wagtails, honeyeaters, kingfishers, scissors grinders, crows and brolgas' nests. It was pretty important business for me, keeping a check on the ducks' nests when I was a boy. In the August holidays I'd check up on the cockies, hawks and crows' nests. Birds that breed in the dry time. I knew where most of the nests were, and at what stage they were at. I spent countless hours watching them.

I used to check on the ducks' nests every few days during nesting season, climbing high up into the branches. Some of the trees I couldn't get up, but they all lent out over the water, so if I climbed up a neighbouring tree I could often look across and see in. One day I climbed up and had a look in from another tree and there was a king brown (snake) sitting on the eggs. The blacks had told me, 'don't get up there and put your hand in the hollow Shohn. You gotta have proper look first'. They'd tell me to either go up another tree and look in, or go up the same tree but along another branch till I could look back into the hollow. The day I saw the snake there I knew what the blacks had told me was good advice. They really did their best to make sure I would be all right, it was as if I was their own.

Quite often whilst checking nests, the duck would hear me climbing up and she'd fly out, or sometimes the duck would still be in there and fly out past me. I'd see nests with big mobs of eggs in them, or the duck's down would be covering them up. One day I'd go back there to check on it and the duck and all the eggs would be gone, so I knew all the little ones would be planted somewhere nearby in the long grass, or I might see them out on the billabong.

## Birds' eggs

As a schoolboy I obtained a permit from the museum to collect birds' eggs. When I was a bigger kid I sometimes went with the stockcamp. We might have a couple of hours off during the day and if I'd found a nest that was close enough to camp, I'd go back and climb up to look at it. The black fellas would come along as well. All the young blokes. One of them was Arthur Gore and another was Snowy Thompson. They used to shudder when I found a nest. They'd be telling me to get down. They were worried I'd fall. I'd say, "No. I've just got to get up here and see if there are any eggs in here."

"You'd better get down. You might fall down and Wudul will be angry." Wudul was blackfella name for 'the boss', meaning Dad. But I wouldn't get down, so then they'd say, "Well you get down Shohn, an' we'll climb up." I wouldn't. I must have caused them a fair bit of anxiety.

If Mum and Dad had seen what I got up to they'd have had heart failure. I used to spend hours testing the strength of a branch. I'd put a bit of weight on it, then try again, then with a bit more weight and a little bit more, till it had all my weight on it. Then I'd move onto another skinny branch and do the same, until I reached the nest. These nests would be way up high. Jabiru or kite hawk nests. I got quite a few kite hawks' eggs. They only lay two eggs, but they are as big as a double yolker chook egg. Part of the deal with the permit was that you take all the eggs in a clutch, not just one, so the birds will nest again. I couldn't get down holding two eggs, so I'd put one in my mouth. I'd have a job getting it in my mouth, then I'd have a job getting it out, once I reached the bottom. I'd hold the other egg in one hand. I couldn't put it in my pocket because I had to lean against the tree and I'd bust it. So I'd have it in one hand all the way down, re-testing the branches again as I went. I wouldn't be game to do it now. Even ten years later I wouldn't have been game enough.

I had all kinds of birds' eggs, but I lost most of them over time. Sometimes friends of my parents would come out to the station with their children. The girls would go through my room and look at my things, which were nothing to do with them. One girl in particular was terrible. She'd pick up really fragile eggs and I would get angry. Then I'd get a belting for my behaviour. I pretty much got a belting every time she came to Meda. My word she gave me some trouble and she never really changed, even as an adult she was a trouble maker. Later on I was bringing my eggs up on the ship and it hit a big wave. The box fell and a lot of eggs were broken. I was pretty upset about it and I gave it away after that, though I still took a keen interest in where birds were nesting.

## A snake comes up the tree

One day I wanted to get up a tree that was fairly hard to climb, to look in a nest. I remember the day well. It was the Christmas school holidays and an RFDS plane had gone missing in a thunderstorm the previous night. It had been on a mercy mission from Tablelands to Derby. When the flight never arrived in Derby it was assumed it had crashed. That night there was a storm coming up and the wind was already blowing at Meda. Dad had told me to go and switch off the engine (pumping water) and shut off the windmill. The next morning, after we'd heard that the plane was lost, Mum and Dad asked me if I'd heard anything when I'd gone over to switch the engine off the previous evening. I hadn't. Several people were missing. Jack Ruddock, the manager of Tablelands, was one of those on board the plane, which had been bringing in his sick daughter.

Things were pretty gloomy at home so after dinner I decided to take the bicycle and go around the billabong. I took two dogs with me, Buster and another blue heeler whose name I can't remember. I climbed up a coolibah tree and out onto a branch, so I could look back into a hollow where I knew there was a duck's nest. As it was a fairly hard climb I usually had a look around at other trees while I was up there. There were green berry like galls growing on some trees. If I saw them I'd get them and break them in half. There was a grub that lived in them and I'd eat these grubs. They weren't bad tucker. Afterwards when I started to climb down the tree the two dogs began to go mad, barking and howling, especially the young one. I couldn't work out what was wrong with them. I kept telling them to shut up, but they wouldn't. They kept looking into the bottom of the tree. I didn't take much notice at first, but they wouldn't stop. I couldn't see anything and couldn't work out what was the matter, so I started to come down the tree. When I looked again I saw a big king brown snake coming up the trunk, and I was coming down! The dogs were trying to warn me. There was nowhere I could go, so I thought I'd better jump out, which I did. Both the dogs were still hounding the snake. I thought he might fall off the trunk and bite one of them if they didn't cut it out shortly, so I grabbed a stick and gave one dog a good welt and that stopped them. It gave me a good fright, especially for the dogs, because I liked the dogs.

I jumped on the bike and took off for the homestead. There was a double gate with a chain joining them in the middle. I was in a hurry. I went to put the brakes on, which were back pedal brakes, but they didn't work. I smashed into the gate, the front wheel going in between the two. This gave me a bit of a shake up. I opened the gate and flew up to the house. I was lucky. I ran into Dad. I said, "Dad, Dad, there is a big snake down there. He was coming up the tree and he's as fat as can be. Come down and shoot him for me." So Dad was very obliging! Really I think he was pleased to leave the strained atmosphere at the homestead for a while. We hopped in the motor car and away we went with the dogs. We got down there and looked around and after about ten minutes we found the snake in a nearby coongleberry bush. Dad shot him. We opened him up and he had seven or eight big green frogs in him. They looked like they hadn't long been eaten.

It took a long time to locate the crashed RFDS plane. I had gone back down to school in Perth before it was found and I only heard about it in the news. Five people were killed in the crash. Jack Ruddock, his sick young daughter, the pilot, the nurse and a second nurse who had accompanied them for the ride. It had crashed on the Hawkstone Creek on Napier Downs Station during the violent thunderstorm.

## Getting tucker for the blacks' camp

We had a lot of old true 'Bush Black Fellas' living in the camp on Meda in those days. The likes of Old Nosey Paddy, Spider, Sambo and some good old gins. Sometimes Dad would let me take the .22 and a few bullets with me when I went out in the bush, and I'd try to get a kangaroo to bring home for the native camp. Sometimes, if I succeeded and the kangaroo was too heavy, I'd drag it halfway home, then leave it and tell the blacks where I'd left it. They would go and pick it up, take it home and cook it.

Mostly I went out on foot. Barefoot. When I was older I had a bicycle. I don't know where it came from, but I'd go everywhere on that bike. I'd take the dogs with me and we'd go out chasing kangaroos. One day we went out to chase kangaroos. I had my dog 'Oglebash' with me. He could run. We were chasing this kangaroo on the airstrip and the kangaroo was out wide of me. I was on the bike, pedalling flat out and I reckoned I was going to get it. The dog was on my left, the kangaroo was on my left also, but a fair way in front of me. We were racing along when the kangaroo decided to change sides. Oglebash cut across after it and hit the front wheel of the bike. There was dog and bicycle and me all mixed up in a heap. Jeez that took a bit of skin off. We never got that kangaroo!

Sometimes I'd go out with some of the blacks, at other times, by myself. When we were looking around, we'd come across cats that were wild. Once we'd disturbed them they would usually run up a nearby tree and the old girls would say, "Ah Shohn, shoot 'em jad'un pushy' cat," so I'd shoot it for them. They'd put it in a bag, and later gut it and cook it up. The blacks loved to eat pussy cat. I didn't!

## Fishing at Millulla with Willie

One of the greatest men I've known in my life was a native called Willie Lennard. When I was young I'd go hunting with Willie, with spears. We would go hunting kangaroos. Dad would lend us the gun to shoot a kangaroo or two for the native camp. I didn't want to get a second one because they were too heavy to take home. If we wounded a 'roo we didn't just let it go. Willie could run, so we'd chase the wounded animal. We would run and run and I'd reckon my lungs were going to burst. Eventually we'd run it down, get it and kill it. Then we'd sit and have a rest for a while. Then Willie would sling it on his back and away we'd go, home.

Willie wasn't a big man, but he was strong. He was a very keen fisherman. One day we were at a place called Millulla, or Mary's Well, a waterhole on the May River. Depending on whether or not there was a big tide this waterhole could be freshwater or salt. If the water was salt the blacks knew where to dig a soak to get fresh water. Good fresh water. They showed me where to dig a soak so I could get a drink. Maudie was the first person to show me this. Saltwater crocodiles lived in this waterhole where Willie and I were fishing. We didn't have a gun with us that day, but Willie had his spears with him. All of a sudden he jumped up, grabbed the spear and woomera and raced into the water. He speared into the water and followed it up. The spear had gone through something and stuck out the other side. He had a shark and the spear had broken off. Willie raced on in and grabbed the broken end of the spear in one hand and behind the spear head in the other. He lifted the shark out of the water. It was about three foot long. We took it home for a feed, but it was hard work carrying it all that way.

## Snake bites three dogs

Once we went up to Lily Hole and to May River Crossing, fishing. The natives and I were fishing in this billabong and that billabong, this waterhole and that. Eventually we began to walk back, but the old girls really wanted to get a goanna. They saw a hole in the sand and they went up there and dug this hole. They thought a goanna might be in there. One of the gins spotted a snake track, so that put a stop to the digging. The next thing the dogs were down on the other side of the river under a steep bank, where it was cool and shady. The snake was there and the dogs were 'into' it. The dog of Fat Jimmy's, a black dog, got bitten and then two other dogs got bitten. The blacks weren't too happy. They killed the snake. Some of the blacks would eat poisonous snake and other blacks wouldn't. I can't remember if they lopped this snake's head off and put him in a bag or not. We were going along heading home and there were pools of water along the steep bank. The black dog was going to one waterhole, lying down in it, then on to another. It was buggered. Then he would get up and try to follow us for a while, but he couldn't manage it. The next thing he was dead. One of the other dogs was doing the same thing. He staggered along with us for a while, but eventually we left him behind.

The third dog with us was a little black and white bitch called Sipsy, which belonged to Willie. I didn't like Sipsy getting bitten. She used to come chasing kangaroos with us, and she could run. She would never come up to the house, but if I was going hunting, somehow or other she knew. She would just appear, so we'd all go off together. Then when we got home she'd go back down to the blacks' camp. She was a good dog. This day, after she was bitten, she got really, really crook. I thought we were going to lose her as well. She got as far as the iron gate inside the horse paddock, but no further. No-one was feeling too happy, but in the end only the black dog died. Sipsy got home that evening and the other dog rolled up at the blacks' camp the next day. Each dog must have got a little less venom with each bite.

## My pets

The blacks were very good to me. If they killed a kangaroo that had a joey, they'd bring the joey up to the homestead and give it to me, so I was always rearing joeys. Not too many grew to adulthood, because once I started to let them out the dogs would often kill them. A few would grow up and stay around. For some reason the dogs didn't go for them and I think it was because those roos weren't frightened, so didn't run. Eventually they'd leave and go bush with the other kangaroos. In those days we'd see kangaroos all the time, not like in latter years when we hardly saw any. As a child I pretty well always had a pet kangaroo, or two, somewhere round the homestead. My mother didn't approve and, somehow or other, they always seemed to disappear in the end.

At times I'd have a pet cockie, but there were cats too. Even though the cats would be killing mudlarks, which upset me, I still used to protect the cats. They would have kittens. Kittens in the wood heap, kittens in the store, kittens in the fat room and in the spare room. If I found a litter I'd be shifting them, Mum would be killing them and we'd have a hell of a bloody blue over it.

I was always gathering pets. One 'wet' season brought very little rain and the billabong only had about thirty yards of water in length, maybe fifteen yards across. Birds were congregating there in their thousands, amongst them pied geese and they were all starving. We didn't usually get pied geese on the billabong at Meda, but this particular year was exceptionally dry. They were in a desperate state. I went down every day to pick up geese, brought them home and tried to feed them bread. Each morning I would find that a big mob had died overnight. I'd take them down to the rubbish heap, then go back to the billabong again and get another lot to replace them. I'd make trips and trips, back and forth, collecting these geese. My mother was nearly going mad. Every day she had to de-louse me and she used to get very agitated about it.

One day I went down to the billabong and there were two brolgas there, that were too weak to fly away. I taught them to lead, by the beak, and I led them up to the house. I put them on the lawn and put the sprinkler on for them. Those brolgas stayed at the homestead a long time. Mum went crook about it. She said they'd peck my eyes out, but they were still there when I went back to boarding school. I don't know what happened to them after that.

Once I caught a half grown goanna. He was alive and unhurt, so I put him in a bag and took him home. I thought I'd keep him for a pet, but where would I keep him? How would I keep him? I decided I'd make a harness. It went around his two front legs, across his chest and onto a fishing line. I let him live under the kitchen. There was nothing there for him to eat, so I would catch him, prise his mouth open with something and shove meat down his throat. He became quite savage. One day I had him on my lap, next to my stomach and I tried to open his mouth and keep it open, so I could put some fresh meat in. He wriggled and latched onto my belly. I had a hell of a job getting him off. Mum put Dettol on the bite. It still festered up a bit and it seemed to be itchy for months after. Scabs kept forming and were always itchy, but eventually it went away. After this I thought I'd better let the poor bugger go, so I did.

I was always trying to gather up pets, but sometimes things went wrong. One day I saw a mudlark and I wanted to catch it for a pet. I picked up a little stone and I threw it at him. I hit it and broke his wing. I picked him up, took him over to the house and put him in a box, but shortly afterwards he was dead. I took him and buried him and I wasn't feeling very happy about it. Then it was smoko time. I went in for smoko and Dad said, "You bloody little murderer." That didn't make me feel very good. I didn't know that Dad had seen. When I threw the stone I never thought I'd hit it. I just thought if I could catch him I'd look after him. I never threw stones at mudlarks again and I still feel guilty over that incident.

## Imaginary, but not a friend

When I was a little boy, a large black cat used to sit watching me from on top of the wardrobe, which was a mob of kerosene boxes with a curtain across the front. It had big orange eyes and it would just sit and stare at me. I was frightened of it. I don't know where the hell it came from, but I told Mum about it once. She told me not to be so silly. I only ever saw it on Meda, in that one place. It watching me and me watching it. It never followed me. I suppose I must have been hallucinating, perhaps from eating too many nelgros with the blacks. I don't really know, but it seemed real enough and it was there pretty regularly, watching me. Anyway eventually it stopped being there and it never appeared anywhere else.

## Dust and thunder

We used to get some terrific thunderstorms on Meda. The homestead was built on an ironstone ridge which seemed to attract the lightning. Sometimes the lightning would hit right close to the house, the thunder would just about lift me clean off the bed. The storms would bang around for hours and I'd lie curled up in a ball on the bed with a pillow over my head. It was pretty frightening.

When I was a kid on Meda, the dust was absolutely unbelievable. In winter time, 'dry time' when the easterly winds blew, you could see the dust in the sky. The blacks used to say, 'Dat's all the dust breedin' longa dat Christmas Creek.' At the time we had goats, so even around the homestead there was not one bit of grass left. At the end of the year the dust storms were really something.

Meda had a flock of about seventy or eighty goats. They were kept for milk, milked night and morning, and also for meat in the 'wet' season. Goats were never killed at any time except during the 'wet'. If the men could get out in the 'wet' with horses, they'd muster up twenty or thirty head of cattle and bring them in close to the homestead for our meat supply. When we needed a killer, someone would get up a tree, the cattle would be driven up under the tree and one would be shot. The other cattle would be let go again. If it was too wet to go out and get cattle, two or three wethers would be killed instead.

When it rained a lot of the goats wouldn't come home, so the white kids and the black kids would be sent out to look for them. When we found them we'd have to bring them back to the homestead. Although we were on foot we'd pretend we were riding horses and we'd treat the goats as if they were cattle. You couldn't run, you'd have to pretend to gallop like a horse. We thought it was absolutely great. Sometimes we'd have to cross them over a watercourse and we'd have to work like hell, being stockmen, getting the goats into the water, because goats hate water. Once we got them in we'd race in amongst them, grab a billy goat and jump on his back. When we'd got them across the billabong we would take them up and put them in the goat yard.

Sometimes, especially if we thought no-one would see us, we'd go down to the goat's yard, catch the billy-goats and wethers and have a rodeo. Some goats were poly and some were horned. When the goats were made into wethers their horns grew longer. We had to be careful not to get hit in the face, with the horns, when we tried to ride them. We would have a great time until someone saw us, then we'd be in strife. We weren't supposed to knock the goats around.

One time when we were sent out to get the goats I went off in one direction on my own. I couldn't find them and was heading back when I came across the flock.

They were all in a circle. The goats were tightly bunched, with the billy-goats on the outside and there were about seven dingoes spaced around them. The wind was in my favour, so I sat under a tree and watched. Some dingoes, young ones I suppose, were playing. Every now and then a goat would venture out of the group and a dingo would fly in and try to separate it from the others. When this happened two or three billy-goats would rush at the dingo and hunt it away. All would be calm for a while, then the same thing would happen again. As a kid I didn't realise the significance of what I was watching, which was a pity because, years later, I bought a mob of goats, but without enough billies. Over time I lost the lot. The dingoes got them because there weren't enough billy-goats to protect the flock.

## Boabs

A lot of boab trees grew around the station. When boab nuts fall off the tree they often break open, revealing white pulp inside. This pulp has small kidney shaped seeds embedded in it. The goats used to eat the pulp and swallow the seeds, which would later come out the other end. As kids we would collect up these seeds in hankies or our pockets. When we had enough we'd find a shady tree and crack the seeds open with a stone. They were very hard with a shiny shell. Once we had a good half pannikin full we would eat them. They were really, really nice. As good as any peanut. We'd sit for hours cracking them, with no thought as to where they'd been.

You can also eat the pulp from boab nuts, but like the coongleberries, some trees are sweeter than others. As children we used to know which were the best. We used to get the pulp, wet it, put a bit of sugar in it, light a small campfire, cook it up and eat it. Or we would cut into a boab tree with a girth of three or four feet, using a tomahawk. We'd take out a wedge from the trunk. We'd discard the bark, which was no good. The next bit grew in rings and was a creamy colour. We used to chew on this, sucking out the moisture and spitting out the fibre. As with the pulp, some boab trees were no good, while others were quite sweet. Horses and cattle used to eat this stuff as well as us. Because horses have teeth both top and bottom, they would gnaw through the bark and make the initial opening. Cattle only have bottom teeth, so they would come along later and chew at a trunk which had already been opened up by horses. Sometimes stock would make huge holes in the boab trees. They seemed to really like eating this stuff.

Boab trees come into flower at the beginning of the wet season. They have lovely large cream coloured flowers, with lots of stamens and they smell really nice. We used to pull the stamens off and eat them. Not the pollen, because that was bitter. The other tree that was plentiful around the homestead was the bauhinia. This has attractive red seedpods which adorn the tree for months. But it was the bauhinia flowers, laden with nectar, that we sought. We'd pick them, pull out the stamens, then drink the nectar from the cup-like base of the flower.

As I roamed about the bush as a kid, for all that Mum might worry about me, there was never any reason for me to go hungry.

*Me aged four months with my parents, George and Margaret Wells, outside the old Meda homestead. August 1943*

*Fat Jimmy 'Gunnanulla' showing me a dead goanna. Meda Station circa 1948*

*Aboriginal woman pulling a goanna out of a hole up a gum tree.*

*Me riding our pet goat 'Ginger'.*

*Dad takes me for a ride on his horse 'My Roan'.*

*Me on my first horse 'Felix' with Maudie's half brother Tony.*

*I show off our catch after fishing with 'Hellfire Jack' and Lucy McMahon. Meda Bullock Paddock, circa 1953*

*The old Meda homestead, where I grew up. Photo courtesy of D. Pollard*

*The 'dry weather' road from Meda to Derby, in flood. The billabong is on the right.*

*The 'dry weather' road from Derby into the Meda homestead during the 'dry' time.*
*Photo courtesy of D. Pollard*

# CHAPTER TWO

# TAMING THE BOY

*Take me to where I long to roam,*
*Where the spear grass grows so tall,*
*To the only place that I call home,*
*Where the king tides rise and fall.*

## Home schooling

I don't know what age I was when Mum started trying to teach me schoolwork. All I know is, I wasn't interested. What I was interested in was what was going on on the station. As soon as horses came into it I was away with the fairies. If the men were breaking in and they rode the colts down past the homestead, that was the end of lessons for me. I would be off. At other times if Mum had to go and do something in the kitchen, or attend to a problem down in the native camp, I'd shoot through and head down to the yards.

There was no School of the Air, or anything like it, in those days. There was no school house either, or governess. It was just Mum, and lessons were in the homestead. She did her best to teach me to read and write, but it wasn't very satisfactory for her. There were too many distractions. I don't even know how long she tried to teach me. It was all so unimportant to me I don't have any clear recollection of it at all, apart from the shooting through at every opportunity. I got into a lot of trouble over it, so that made me hate it even more. For starters, I didn't understand that you had to be able to read, write and do arithmetic to survive in the world. To me I already knew the things I needed to know. I couldn't see why I had to do lessons. The natives didn't have to. They weren't going to school. I just had my mind set on birds and lizards, cats and dogs, cattle and horses. Even from a kid I already belonged to that life. I was fully focused onto that, nothing else mattered to me.

Dad would sometimes take me out to the stockcamp. I thought that was really good, watching them bronco branding, letting cattle out or yarding cattle up. Dad would have his camp horse out there in the plant. He might be there cutting out for an hour or two, sometimes three. I wasn't bored. I watched it all. Beasts broke out and blokes chased them, put them back in the mob, or threw them. I was soaking up this kind of life. Taking it all in, from a very early age.

Dad was very quiet about things. He never said to me, 'Don't do that, this will happen to you, or that will happen to you'. Nothing was said. The only things I knew not to do was when the strap came out, or Mum got Dad to give me a belting for playing up while he was away. The blacks all protected me and looked after me. On the station nobody seemed to have too much time for kids, except the blacks. They might threaten to give me a belting, but they'd also tell me not to do something and why. They seemed to be friendly towards me, as well as protective. They have been all my life, especially those from Kimberley Downs, Meda and Derby. A lot of them could play the mouth organ or guitar. They'd sing cowboy songs. All that fitted right up my alley.

If I went out for a day with Dad, around the bores, it was a long hard day. Dad would cut across country, from one bore to another, instead of following a station track. Sometimes it would take hours and hours to do just five miles, it was that rough. Dad was saving petrol. He always tried to save the owners any unnecessary expense. I didn't really know the country at all back then, and although these trips seemed to take forever I just thought 'everything will be OK, because Dad's here'. On one such trip Dad decided to cut across from a new bore, called Geoff's, to the Meda River Crossing, out near Meda Well. There was no road. It was black soil, so it was up one bump, down the next. It took us about two hours to cover the distance. Jeez it was rough and slow. Hot too, being the middle of the day. We could have driven all the way back around Orange Pool and still been home earlier, but we were conserving precious fuel.

## Boarding in Derby

Mum trying to educate me didn't work. Eventually I was sent in to Derby to board with the Lovell family. Although they had several kids, I don't think any of them liked me much and I didn't feel much wanted. My mother was very religious. So was I in those days. Living with that family things were a bit different from what I'd been used to. In that household they smoked, drank and swore pretty freely. I got fed, my clothes were washed and ironed, so the basics were OK, but it was just a different sort of an attitude living there amongst them. But I was all right.

From there I attended Derby School, which was where the Masonic Lodge now is. Kids would come over and play after class was out, which I enjoyed. The other thing I liked was that old George Lovell had race horses. Early in the morning he'd go out and work them on the marsh, near where the Derby Caravan Park is now. We kids would go and watch. In the morning blokes would ride the horses out there and work them round a makeshift track on the marsh, where there were pegs in the ground to show how many furlongs they'd run. I thought it was pretty good. I really liked it.

Some weekends, I would go home to Meda and I always went back to the station for the holidays. I still didn't do much school work, even though I was in a proper class. I s'pose I must have done some learning during this time, but I clearly remember how far behind the other kids I was. I couldn't do times tables. I couldn't remember tables. I didn't have any interest in it and I didn't want to learn. I didn't mind play time and lunch time! We'd get out and play hockey, cricket or tag, but basically schooling, for me, was a waste of my parents' money.

Later I was shifted from the Lovell's, to board with a religious family called the Faulkeners. So I went from an environment of smoking, drinking and swearing, to one of God bothering, where I found I had to go to Sunday School as well as regular school. The Faulkener household was a different world again. I still had a reasonably Christian outlook on life, I suppose. I couldn't really help it with a mother like mine, but I still got up to pranks and messed around. I just didn't really fit in. I also missed George Lovell's race horses. I don't remember this part of my life very well at all. I suppose because there was nothing in it of any real interest to me, other than the good days when I could escape back to the station. They are the ones I remember best.

## Hollywood Primary School

Mum and Dad used to go down to Perth for holidays during the 'wet' season when I would be put into Hollywood Primary School, which was near where we stayed with my Nanna, in Nedlands. Hollywood was the first place I learned what cruel bastards humans can be. I was treated like the ugly duckling, hounded wherever I went. I was a misfit, ostracised by the other kids.

Looking back I think there must have been something really wrong with me. Part of it might have been the way my mother dressed me. Shorts pulled too high by a pair of braces, with no undies underneath. I was embarrassed to sit down cross legged. To top it off I had to wear a hat like my fathers. The other kids called me 'grandpa'. I learned never to go far from where the teachers were, or I'd get a bashing. I was too different and I was picked on because of it.

When I got out of school at the end of the day I used to run like hell to try and get home before 'they' got me. Sometimes Mum would come and pick me up, which was good, because I'd get home safely. If she didn't I'd get a touch up all the way home. I would try and take different routes home, but there would always be kids waiting in lane-ways to get me. It was terrible and the teachers never seemed to do anything about it. I had to endure it, but I hated it. I was always pleased when it came time for us to return to Derby.

## Scotch College

When I was nine years old I was sent to boarding school in Perth, where I got the living daylights belted out of me, for three years. Going to Scotch College was a really big shock, but looking back I feel I was very fortunate to go there. At boarding school I learned what life was all about and those first three years set me on course for the rest of my life. I changed. I turned it all round the other way and from that point on, I never backed down from anything, even if it might have been smarter to do so. But before this happened I had a lot of punishment to go through.

There were other boys from the Kimberley going to Scotch at this time, but I didn't know any of them. The stations we lived on were miles apart and although I may have known their names, I had never met any of them before. For me Scotch was a frightening place, filled with strangers. Many of them would become my tormentors. From the outset I was set upon and I really copped it.

I had a distinct drawl, still have, and was known as 'Naap Naap'. Because of my small head, other boys called me 'Vice-head' or 'Four-'b'- two'. I had basically grown up with the blacks and although I didn't realise it, I was a misfit in the city. I found schoolwork hard and was well behind the other kids. I wasn't good at writing, or spelling and I got 3% for arithmetic.

I spent my first winter sleeping in the school sanatorium. I seemed to catch every bug going. I suppose I'd never been exposed to winter colds and flu before. I seemed to get the lot. I was constantly cold, so if the sun shone I'd find a sheltered spot around some little corner and soak up the sunshine like a lizard. Despite this, although I had plenty of clothes, I never ever seemed to be warm. I wasn't acclimatised for cold weather like that. I'd grown up in the tropics and the only time I'd been to Perth was in summertime. No wonder I was always sick.

After I had been at Scotch for a couple of weeks my mother came to see me before returning to the Kimberley. I had already experienced what school life could be like by then. After Mum left that afternoon I went to have a shower. I had undressed and I was thinking about her heading back home to the station. Suddenly I decided I wasn't staying in that place. I wrapped a towel around my waist, ran out of the building and crossed the road to where my mother was waiting at the bus stop.

"I'm not staying here." I told her. "I'm coming home with you." It was no good of course. She took me back to my boarding house, handed me over and left me to get on with my new life as best I could. I had achieved nothing, other than to cause her to miss her bus. I felt very alone.

Boarding school became my life for the next six years. I only went back home to the Kimberley twice a year, for the Christmas and August school holidays. Easter and the May holidays were spent with an aunt and uncle who lived at Roleystone.

I think I believed more in God then than ever, but over time I began to wonder why He never came to help me when the bullies gave me knuckle dusters on my head, kneed me in the thigh, or corked my upper arms. The muscles in my thighs were perpetually sore and bruised. When I got another doing, it just hurt a bit more. Once I got kicked by a bigger kid between my legs. I thought he'd cut my dick off. He got me right between my backside and my ball bag and it hurt like bloody hell. I was just walking past and he decided to give me a boot. There was no need for that. Each morning they would do a roll-call when boys had to say where they would be after class. School, Swanbourne Beach, Cottesloe shops, Claremont Baths. I didn't like it because it meant other boys knew where they could find you. A couple of times when I returned from Claremont and hopped back over the low school wall, off the footpath, there would be two or three bigger boys waiting for me. They grabbed me from behind and choked me till I blacked out. When I came to, no-one was there.

Plenty of times I got stripped. Six or eight boys would grab me, just on the prep bell and they'd take my clothes off and dump them in a bin or hide them. I'd have to go back to the dormitory to get some more. I wasn't supposed to be there at that time of day, but I had to have some clothes on. Then I'd be in trouble from the master for getting to prep late. In the end I didn't even fight to try and keep my clothes. I knew I couldn't win. It was a bit like a horse being broken in. When you realise you can't do anything about it, you just accept it.

After a while I started to wonder about all this 'ask God and He'll help you' stuff. I got sick of all the punishment. All the time, no let up. I began to realise religion didn't help little boys in the real world. There was never any help for me, not from anyone. Even the teachers would deal it out to me. Once I remember a master picking me up by the collar and hanging me on a coat hook. Or they'd grab me by the hair above my temple, twist it, pull it upwards and march me along. Jeez, they were tough bastards. After three years of this I had grown a bit. I'd endured plenty of punishment. I'd discovered no-one would help me. God certainly didn't and nor would anyone else it seemed. I started to fight and I fought in earnest. I would take on anyone who I thought wanted it, no matter they were bigger and stronger. I copped a few good hidings but things improved greatly after that. Basically my whole life changed.

Once I started to fight, things got a lot better. Mum and Dad put me into boxing lessons, so I could learn to fight properly. But I got that way, that if it looked like a fight, it was for keeps. It wasn't for learning, or playing. It wasn't sport anymore. For me it was dinkum. It wasn't long before I was taken out of boxing class. I took it too seriously, because by then, fighting, for me, had become a question of survival. During the last three of my six years at Scotch, I got into a fair bit of trouble. I fought hard and often. I dealt out a good few beltings and I got a fair few too, but I didn't get as much punishment as I had from standing still.

Life at boarding school wasn't all about torment, fighting and punishment. Nor had I been completely abandoned by my parents, although sometimes it felt like it. Mum had arranged for a parcel to come from Boans Store once a week for me. In it there would be a couple of packets of biscuits, a tin of sardines, a bottle of Vegemite or peanut butter and a couple of other things for my tuck box. I got pocket money, threepence a week when I first went there, rising to three shillings and sixpence by the time I left. Sometimes Dad would give me extra money to come down to school with, but Mum wouldn't know about that.

I had a bicycle at Scotch and you could go to the purser for parts for your bike, if needed. I used to ride my bike over to my Nanna Wells' house in Nedlands most Fridays, or I would run. She used to cook me meals I liked. I think I was her favourite grandchild. Dad's sister, Aunty Nora, would usually be there visiting. She and her husband, Uncle Arch, had an orchard. Sometimes they would bring me fruit and cream from the orchard. Quite often Arch would come in to Perth on Fridays, to work at the metropolitan markets. After work he'd pick Nora up from Nanna's house and take her home.

We were allowed a certain number of free weekends a term and I usually used all of them. Sometimes Uncle Arch would take me up to the orchard, or I'd catch a bus, from Adelaide Terrace to Roleystone. My uncle would either pick me up from the bus, or I'd walk, in daylight or dark, the four miles to their place. I wasn't frightened to walk. It didn't bother me one bit. It was good and things were different in those days. I loved my weekends up there with them. My Aunty Nora was very good to me. She was a hard worker. She, and her son Alan, did most of the jobs on the orchard, with the help of an employee, Dick Craven, who lived on the property. There was always something for me to do and always plenty to eat. No fruit has ever tasted as good as it did then, straight from the tree. Even tomatoes had plenty of flavour in those days and kids would walk about eating them as if they were peaches or plums. They had pigs on the orchard, so windfalls didn't go to waste, a couple of milking cows, chooks, ducks, and heaps of bantams. Both my aunt and my older cousin, Alan, were good cooks, so we always had wonderful meals. It was a schoolboy's delight, to escape the boarding house, the classroom and the bullying, for a weekend of sheer enjoyment up there with them.

The only downside to these happy times was the presence of their worker, Craven. Even after all these years, I don't want to revisit that part of my childhood. He didn't confine himself to the fruit farm either, but would come to Scotch and ask to take me out for a couple of hours. Almost half a century passed before I told anyone what had happened to me. There seemed no point in speaking up at the time. Nobody would have believed me. Besides, those kinds of things weren't spoken of back then. But when the fellow turned up, decades later, at my father's funeral, he came back to my parents house with other mourners after the service and I finally put the record straight.

One of the good things at boarding school was a club called The Ramblers Club. It was run by a teacher, Mr McMillan, who had been up North, and who knew Mum and Dad. It was Mr McMillan who helped me obtain a permit from the West Australian Museum to collect birds' eggs. I did very well at Nature Study and I enjoyed those weekends. Often we'd go bird watching. We'd ride our bikes down to Bibra Lake, up to Kalamunda, or down to Penguin Island. Or he'd show us how to get the scale off pearl shell, or teach us about taxidermy.

I also enjoyed sport at Scotch. I could run a bit. Probably from chasing kangaroos with Willie, on the station. One afternoon they took any boys who were interested, and in a certain age group, to run in a mile race. I went. I ran the mile and I won, straight off the grass. After that about a dozen of us were selected to go into training with Austin Robertson, a former world champion sprinter and VFL football player. We had to run laps and he'd make us run at a certain pace and keep up with other blokes. It was gruelling and after training I'd be absolutely had it. I wouldn't be able to eat my tea that night. When we had our school athletics carnival, to see who would be selected for the interschool competition, I only came fourth. Aunty Nora had come to watch me compete, as she often did when the occasion warranted it. But it was a disappointing finish and after the race I could smell, or taste, blood on my breath. I've always felt, if I hadn't been so keen to do what Austin Robertson wanted, not pushed myself so hard and had a longer preparation, I might have done better. I was pretty fit, really. We used to run to Swanbourne beach regularly in the summertime. We'd stay body surfing for as long as we possibly could, then run back to school, getting there right on tea time. We'd chuck our towels and bathers in a bin, line up for the meal, then go and retrieve them later. In between tea and prep we'd often play some sort of game out on the oval. Although I enjoyed sport, was fit and keen, I didn't excel. Far from it, but there were others at Scotch who would later go on to become household names.

I remember one very sad day at Scotch. During the final term of 1954 one of the senior boys, a prefect and a really nice bloke, was involved in an accident down at Cottesloe. Before meals we all had to line up in a sunken area, then we'd go up a set of steps and on into the dining room. This is where we were assembled, before breakfast, on the morning it was announced that Ned Gmeiner had been killed. Everything went completely quiet. During breakfast all you could hear was the sound of knives and forks on plates. Not a boy spoke for the whole meal. For me it was a big deal because death had always been kept secret from me. I knew that natives died on the station, although that was kept hush hush too and was never talked about in the house. So this really shook me and I've never forgotten how so many boys were so eerily quiet that morning.

Some time after this I was confronted by death again, this time much closer to home, and personally far more shocking. I had gone to visit Nanna Wells one Friday afternoon. Aunty Nora was not there. Nanna told me that my cousin Alan was dead. I couldn't believe it. I had really looked up to Alan. He always seemed to me so big and strong. He was quiet, never saying much, but capable and dependable as he went about his business on the orchard, shifting water pipes and starting engines. He had a motorbike, which he used for getting about, and would go out dancing once or twice a week. Apparently he was a good dancer. He didn't drink, ever, and he had a girlfriend. It seemed to me he was a man who, in the quietest of ways, would do well in the world. Although I knew that he suffered from epilepsy, I never thought much about it. I knew he took tablets, that if he didn't he would have fits, but that was the extent of it. People didn't talk freely about such things then. It was all kept quiet. I later learned that Alan had suffered a fit whilst at a dance. He was in the toilet when it happened and as he fell he hit his head. People thought he must be drunk and left him there. It was a tragedy. I had difficulty coming to terms with the loss of a cousin I had admired greatly and I remember spending that first terrible night in the school san.

Over time I made a couple of good friends at Scotch. Graeme Hutton was one, others being Gaydn Rose, Gordon Thomson, Simon Hammersley and Gerry Petersen. Even so, when things were difficult for me, these blokes couldn't really help me much. My friends couldn't race around protecting me all the time. It didn't really work like that. Lots of things went on when these blokes weren't about, that people never saw or knew about.

What I learned through it all was that refusing to lie down slowed the bully boys, in some cases even stopped them, from attacking me in the first place. Standing up for myself and throwing a few punches of my own seemed to be very worthwhile. But fighting was not allowed, so I was often in trouble from prefects or the staff. I was either gated or I got the cane. It almost became routine. There was never any dust in my pants, it was always beaten out of me. If I felt I deserved it, I was happy to take the consequences. I always told myself it would only hurt for a little while. This didn't mean I meekly accepted the punishment if I thought it unjust, nor if I had little or no respect for the teacher meting it out. I clearly recall one occasion when a school chaplain ordered me to wait outside his room for some misdemeanour or other. I did and when he eventually came and took me inside, he reached for a cane from the top of a cupboard. I didn't have much respect for this bloke, a 'God Botherer', resorting to corporal punishment, so I refused to bend over. Instead I kept as close to him as I could. He would step away from me and try to take a swipe. I stepped closer, not giving him the room. This went on for a while before eventually he became furious. Spluttering with rage he ordered me out. "Out. Get out!" he yelled. So I went and that was the end of that.

When I got home to the station and got in trouble with Mum, she said 'I'll belt you John' and I said 'Righto.' When she went to get the strap I stayed there and waited for her. She didn't quite know what to do about that, so she said 'I'll get your father to do it when he comes home.' Again I said 'Righto.' It didn't shake a rivet anymore. I had taken that much at school it meant nothing to me. I never got the strap at home again after that.

A few kids had pets at school and I was one of them. At one time I had geese and later a rabbit which had got caught in a bracken fire. All his fur was singed, so I caught it and cared for it. I had it for a fair while. Later word spread that Wells was keeping a feral rabbit and I was afraid it would be destroyed. I didn't put it back in it's hutch, but let it go instead. It lived under the buildings at Scotch for a long time.

I also had racing pigeons while at Scotch. When it came time to go home for holidays I couldn't leave them at school, so I took them with me. On this occasion I was going up on a DC3 plane. We were flying out very early in the morning and I was to be taken, by taxi, to the MMA office in St. Georges Terrace, then by bus out to the airport. It was dark, still night-time, when I went down and got all my pigeons from their coop and put them in a box ready for the journey. I intended taking them in the cabin with me, but I knew I'd have to stop them cooing on the plane. I got some small elastic bands, caught a bird, put a couple of twists in the rubber band and slipped it over his beak. Then I put him back in the box and caught another one. I did the same thing and popped him back in. As I felt around for the next pigeon I found the first one lying on the bottom of the box. I pulled him out and to my dismay, discovered I'd smothered my best bird, the band having gone over his nostrils suffocating it. I'd learned the hard way not to do that again. I got all the other pigeons and put bands on their beaks, but kept them clear of their nostrils, then the taxi came. So with my little box, which was more important to me than anything else, I got delivered to the MMA offices where they weighed the box and my suitcase. I sat there for quite a while waiting for the bus, hoping the birds wouldn't start cooing. After a while I took my precious box and went and sat on the step outside until the bus came.

We took off in the dark. It was an all day trip from Perth to Derby and not a very nice trip on the DC3, being bumpy and the aircraft vibrating. I had the box on the floor, tucked under my legs. We stopped at some place on the way up and I thought the pigeons must be getting thirsty. I'd taken a couple of tobacco tins with me, which I put water in while we were off the plane. When I got back on board I took the bands off their beaks and put the tins of water in the box for them. I don't know whether they had a drink or not, but I shut the box up again and on we went. The hosties must have known I had the pigeons there. They would have heard them scratching and carrying on, but no-one ever said a word. Eventually we got to Derby and I got off and took my box of pigeons with me. When I got home Mum wasn't very impressed. The pigeons lived in the chook yard at Meda for years and years. I thought they were great. They had chicks and I'd let them out every now and then, but the hawks would be into them. In the end Mum got them caught, at night, and gave them away to people in Derby.

I think my mother must have wondered what I would bring home next. Once I arrived with a puppy, called Buster, which Aunty Nora had given me. I took him home on the ship. During the voyage I won a fancy dress competition with him, and was presented with a pewter tankard engraved with the name of the vessel, the Koolinda. Another time I took a bantam rooster, really pretty with golden feathers, some black with a teal sheen, and a bright red comb. The crewmen weren't too happy because it used to crow at all hours of the morning. It was kept in the stern of the ship where I could visit it anytime. Somehow it escaped while we were berthed at Port Hedland. He was going all over the place, on the ship, off the ship onto the jetty, then back on board again. I was afraid he was going to jump off the wrong side of the vessel and end up in the water, which would have been the end of him, but we caught him eventually, much to the disappointment of the crew. I got him home safely in the end.

## Oglebash

I don't know if I got into trouble more than other kids my age, or whether I remember those times more clearly. Probably a bit of each. What I do recall is the period, before I overcame my fear of 'the strap', when I had a friend and ally in the form of a dog, called Oglebash. A time during my youth, when no-one could lay a hand on me. I was a bit lucky to get Oglebash, though I wasn't so sure about that at the time. One evening I overheard a telephone conversation, between my father and a bloke in Derby, who had a dog he needed to find a home for. It had got into trouble for biting someone and although it was said to still be a pup, the police were going to shoot it, unless a home could be found for it out of town. The bloke wanted to know if Dad would take it. I only heard one half of the conversation and my Dad was a man of few words, 'Yes' or 'No' pretty much covered it, but I did hear him say 'Dog' which immediately aroused my interest.

"Is that man going to give you a dog?" I asked when he got off the phone, not having heard any of the 'why's and wherefores'.

"Yes" he said curtly.

"Can I have him?" I asked.

"No"

I was home for the summer holidays. It was hot weather and I was in Derby with Dad the day he went to pick up the pup. Dad went into the house yard and knocked on the door. There was a full grown dog tied up on the verandah. When the bloke came out Dad said, "I've come about the pup."

"That's him over there." The man said indicating the full grown dog.

"John, come and get your dog." Dad called over to me. So in I went to get him. The dog heckled up and growled at me. He seemed a vicious brute. I thought 'Jeez! He's not a pup. He's savage.' As I approached the dog kept snarling at me. I was dead scared of him, but I wasn't game to tell Dad I didn't want it anymore. I unhooked him, expecting to be bitten at any moment. We put him in the Land Rover and headed back out to Meda. I had to sit in the back with the dog. It was hot, 'wet' season, but no rain, so along the way Dad pulled up and we had a drink. Dad used to drive at about fifteen miles an hour. The road went in and out of every pole along the telegraph line for thirty miles. When we were stopped for a drink I thought the dog might be thirsty too. I got my hat, put some water in it and offered it to him. From that moment on he was my best mate. Jeez, he was a good dog. He was called Oglebash and I never got a belting while I had him. My mother didn't mind using the strap on me. If it was serious then Dad took over. But while I had Oglebash, neither of them were game to give me anything. When they came near me and the dog jacked up, that was it! He slept under my bed in the sleep-out and if I did anything wrong he would protect me. I didn't even have to take any medicine. I could please myself. No-one could control me. I reckon I could have gone anywhere with that dog and nobody would have ever laid a hand on me. He would be right there, everywhere I went. Oglebash was the boss and I thought it was great. Mum didn't. She ended up shooting him and that was the end of poor old Oglebash. With Mum it was on all the time. If she decided she didn't like a dog it was gone.

## Running over Willie

When I was about fifteen and home for school holidays I think Mum might have told Dad I should be taught to drive. In those days we had Land Rovers and a Thames truck on the station. Sometimes Dad let me get behind the wheel of the Land Rover. I didn't like learning to drive with Dad. He used to fire up quick. We'd be approaching a gate and he'd be saying 'brake, brake!' I'd be thinking everything was all right and under control. So it wasn't going all that well. After a while Willie used to let me drive. I expect Dad had told him to, so he didn't have to teach me himself. I used to drive about the place a lot with Willie. It was good, much more relaxed. Willie basically taught me how to drive.

One day we were out checking bores and waterholes. Another native, Billy Munroe, or Morndi as his own people called him, came with us. We came onto a big open plain and there was an emu with a mob of chicks. They were big lumps of chicks, strong, about three months old and I wanted one. We lapped the mob around with the vehicle, in the open, eventually splitting one chick off from the mob. Billy Munroe jumped out and grabbed it for me. It was a strong young bird and after a while we got sick of trying to hold it, so we put it behind the seat of the Land Rover. We drove on and checked a few waters.

When we arrived at Number Six Bore there was a beast 'down' near the trough. It was late in the year. We got out and had a look. The cow was buggered, at the end of her life, and she couldn't get up. We got the gun out and Willie shot her. We put a rope on her legs, then Willie told me to drive the Land Rover closer so we could drag it away. I hopped in the motor car to do as he said. I'd forgotten about the emu. By then the young bird had had a rest and not being knocked up anymore, managed to push the back seat rest down. As I drove forward it was trying to get out of the driver's side window. I was trying to knock it back in and it was scratching me. Being distracted I ran onto Willie. I jammed him pretty much under the vehicle. I felt shocked. I jumped out to have a look and Willie was saying 'back off, back off'. So

I did. Thankfully, he seemed to be OK. We dragged the beast away from the trough and we still had the emu! After this excitement we went on and checked a couple more bores, Norman Creek then back to Surprise. Willie seemed to be getting lamer and lamer. I decided it might be best to let the emu go. I knew if we took it back home Dad would want to know where we got it, and how. If he found out I'd hurt Willie he wouldn't be too impressed. I didn't even know where I was going to keep the emu, so we let it go free. When we got home and parked the Land Rover I said to Willie, "Wait here." I ran over to the kitchen and found Mum.

"I need a bottle of Aspros." She asked me what I wanted them for.

"I ran over Willie and his knee's sore."

Mum wanted to see Willie but I said, "No, I only need the Aspros." She agreed to give me half a dozen tablets, with instructions for Willie to take two straight away, two later and two during the night. I told Mum not to tell Dad. I don't know if she did or not, but nothing was ever said about it. I was very relieved.

## Narrogin Agricultural College

At the age of sixteen I left Scotch College and was sent to Narrogin Agricultural College, two hundred kilometres from Perth, out in the wheatbelt. I didn't want to go. By this time I had fought my way free of the endless tormenting I had endured during my earlier years at boarding school and things were pretty good for me. I was dead scared I would cop the same sort of punishment when I started as a new boy at Narrogin. When the time came for me to go to Ag. School, Tim Emanuel drove me out there, with Mum and Dad. On the way we pulled up on a creek, Shit Creek, not far from the college, where we got some water, boiled the billy and had lunch. (Many years later, when I recounted this at an old boys re-union, people were aghast at the thought of us lighting a fire in January to boil a billy. I don't know if total fire bans existed in those days, but even if they did, it would have been difficult for us to comprehend. We had been living in hot dry country my entire life and it had never stopped us from having a camp-fire, boiling a quart pot or cooking a damper. We knew how to make a fire safely, and put it out thoroughly.)

After we had had lunch we drove on into the Agricultural College where I was to spend the next two years. I was dropped off and shown where I would sleep. I sat on the end of the bed and waited, wondering what kind of punishment would be dealt out to me by the older boys. Presently a couple of the bigger lads came in. They asked me a few questions, where I was from, how I got there, that sort of thing. I answered them and said we'd pulled up for a picnic lunch and a cup of tea on a creek nearby. They thought this was a great joke.

"What? You got water out of Shit Creek?" they laughed. That was how I first came to know the name of that water course. They were enjoying themselves, taunting me, but I just sat there and took no notice. If they'd pushed it I was quite prepared to let them have it. I'd learned to stand up for myself and wasn't going to drop my strides for anyone, no matter how much stronger than me they might be. As for the boys making a big deal of our drinking the water from Shit Creek, it just showed me how little they knew. I'd drunk far worse water, many times, during my childhood in the Kimberley. Their teasing wasn't worth getting stirred up about.

Later, once I'd settled in at the college, we used to have a lot of fun down on Shit Creek. On one occasion we were waiting for the bus to take us in to town to the movies. It was summertime, still daylight after tea, so we were messing around outside. We went down to Shit Creek where a bunch of blokes were fooling about with bicycles. We had made crossings over the creek with planks, and places where you could hurtle down the steep banks on either side. It took a bit of skill to line it up right. One needed to get a fair bit of pace up, on the downward run, in order to get up the other side. Stupidly I decided it would be fun to take the plank away. For every action there's a reaction we're told, and in this case it was Clive Chapman hitting the other side of the bank, flying off his bike and ending up in a tangled heap. It was a spectacular crash and I was a bit worried. Clive was my friend. He didn't have any broken bones, but he was hurt. I didn't know whether he'd report me or not. If he did I knew I wouldn't be going to the pictures that night. But I was lucky. Nothing was ever said, we still got to go to the cinema and I learned something.

Whilst at Narrogin Ag College nobody seemed to want to put shit on me and, although I felt a bit wary at the beginning, everything seemed to go all right. I also had a really good teacher, who had a big influence on me. His name was Monty Butfield. All the boys liked him. He was tough but fair, a good bloke. I had matured a bit by then and I was good at sport, which I took seriously. I played football, hockey, basketball and athletics. I wasn't much good at the schoolwork side of things, but I got top practical student both years. I thought it was all pretty good and during my time there I never got into one fight. I still managed to get into other kinds of trouble from time to time, so punishment continued to be a normal part of my life.

Once a group of us boys were talking amongst ourselves, about what all boys our age talk about. Girls and sex! Monty Butfield must have overheard us and he was very cross. Each of us had to go to his room in turn, where we were given a good talking to and punished. When my turn came Monty put the fear of God into me, by telling me that he'd tell my parents, and the girls parents about it. He said it was very serious, even a police matter. I really thought I was in big trouble. He gave me six of the best there and then, told me I was gated, was to do lines and cut forty barrow loads of wood. So away I went. Over the coming days I began thinking about this, and I decided the punishment was unfair. I decided to go and see Monty. I knocked on his door.

"Who is it?" he called.

"John Wells." I told him. There was silence. After a bit he said, "Come in. Shut the door." He was marking and I stood for a fair while waiting for him to stop. This was part of the intimidation I suppose. Eventually he said, "Yes?" I told him I thought the punishment he had given me was too much.

"Do you?" he said and kept marking. He left me standing there for a long while. Presently he said, "Why's that?"

"Well, I think it's too much and something should be dropped off."

Monty didn't say anything. I stood my ground and waited. I watched him as he kept on marking. Finally he said, "So what do you think should be dropped off?"

"Well, I've already had the cuts, so it can't be that." I told him. "so I think it should be the lines." He kept me waiting a good while longer before he said, "All right then. That's it." So away I went. I was pretty happy with that. I didn't like being gated, but I hated 'lines' more. I'd already had the cane and as I was the one who cut the wood for the heater anyway, I couldn't care less about that. Forty barrow loads of wood was nothing. It was in my interest to keep the fire going. I used to have a hot shower as soon as I got up in the morning, sometimes after breakfast, at lunch time and after sport. That was how I kept warm. Chopping the wood was nothing to me. I reckoned I'd struck a good deal.

When I started at Ag. School I made a good friend, Milton Maurice Mincherton, who was off a farm up around Geraldton. Not long after, Monty decided to split us up. When we asked him why he said, "Because together you're a pair of little bastards, but on your own you're both crackerjack blokes." I was a bit surprised. He might have thought I was capable of getting into mischief but Milton was a pretty docile sort of a bloke. Anyway the two of us remained friends, despite being separated, and still are to this day.

First year students at Narrogin were known as 'melons' and over time it became fairly clear that the 'melons' of 1959 were quite a strong bunch of young fellows. A couple of senior boys, the same two blokes who had fronted me on my first day, thought they were pretty important. A bit of animosity developed, between us and the senior students, over some of their capers. It all looked like coming to a head. At one stage, if the staff hadn't stepped in, we 'melons' would have taken over from the senior boys. That could not be allowed to happen, because the entire pecking order and college system of seniority would have been out of balance. Monty Butfield stepped in and put a stop to it. I think Monty liked me. He was our football coach and for me football was deadly serious. I played to win and I didn't give up, no matter how tired I felt. Once I remember feeling a bit betrayed by Monty. He'd told me to 'rough up and bump' a player in a footy match I was in. During the third quarter I did, and the umpire chatted me about it. I laid off for a bit, then in the last quarter I had another go and decked him. I got into trouble for that, not only from the umpire, but Monty as well. I always thought that was a bit rough. I'd only been doing what my coach had told me.

## The Lees at Jingalup

For the last couple of years at Scotch and whilst at agricultural college I spent my May school holidays with Jim and Nancy Lee on Western Hills Farm at Jingalup, near Kojonup. Mr and Mrs Lee were a childless couple, who treated me as if I were their own. Mrs Lee, who had grown up at Cherry Tree Farm, between Katanning and Kojonup, had been a school teacher before her marriage. Her husband, Jim was a war veteran. He carried a limp from a shrapnel wound in his leg.

I used to catch a bus from Perth out to Kojonup where the Lee's would pick me up and take me out to their farm. I was never sent back to Perth by bus. They always drove me back to the city, would book into a hotel for the night, then take me back to school the following day.

When I was at agricultural college, Mrs Lee used to come up to Narrogin for the end of year presentation days. I think she thought of me as her son. Nancy Lee was a wonderful woman. She could do anything. She was a good cook, could drive the tractor, do seeding, ploughing, or work in the yard. Whatever had to be done, she was capable of doing it. No farm hands were employed on Western Hills. The Lees did all the work themselves. It was primarily a sheep farm, although they did have a small herd of cattle, including a milking cow. Some calves were bucket fed, and there were usually a few orphan lambs to rear. There were only small square bales of hay at that time, so when we had to feed sheep I would be up on top of the haystack, rolling the bales down to Jim. Shearing was done a couple of times while I was staying there. The shearing shed was mud brick, and things were pretty flat out then. Nancy cooked for everybody.

During quieter times Jim Lee showed me how to set rabbit traps and how to skin rabbits. To skin them we would cut them in certain places, put a foot on their head and pull the skin off in one piece. There were lots of rabbits in the area and I often used to go off rabbit trapping. Sometimes I'd go out at night, with a hurricane lamp, walking two or three miles checking rabbit traps. If I caught a rabbit I'd reset the trap. Those that were empty I'd leave, then go back in the morning and check them all again. Once caught the rabbits were skinned. The pelts were then stretched inside out over a 'U' shaped piece of wire and dried. When dry they were pulled off and added to the stack. A lot of rabbits in the area had myxomatosis. It used to upset me seeing blind rabbits around the place, being harassed by the crows.

I remember the Lee's had a couple of blue tongue lizards, that lived in the laundry. While I was staying on the farm they produced a couple of tiny little blue tongues. I thought that was really great. These lizards have live babies, they're not born from an egg. The Lees seemed very happy to have the blue tongues living there.

I really liked it at Western Hills. I never felt lonely there, despite it being just me and the old couple. I was with them everywhere they went. If Jim went somewhere, or Nancy went somewhere, I was taken along too. One day we drove out to Katanning to take delivery of a brand new Mainline Ford Ute. That was pretty exciting. They included me as if I were family. I couldn't have been treated better. It was a good place to go to for my holidays.

A lot of the boys at Narrogin Ag. College had family farms to go home to at the conclusion of their course, M.M. Mincherton being one of them. The blokes who didn't, myself included, took whatever opportunity came our way. I had loved my time at Narrogin. They were two of the best years of my life, but I was now eighteen and it was time for me to enter the workforce. As the end of the year approached people would write to the college asking for students to go and work for them. One day Monty Butfield took me aside and asked what my plans for the future were. I said I didn't have any. He told me of a farmer he knew, an ex Scotch Collegian, who was looking for an energetic young fellow to go and work on his farm at Pingorup. Preferably someone who played football and basketball. Monty thought I might suit him. It sounded all right to me. I loved sport and I wanted to work on a farm, so I agreed to go.

L-R George Wells, George Lovell, me, Bruce Lovell on 'Ginger' the goat
and Clive Lovell.

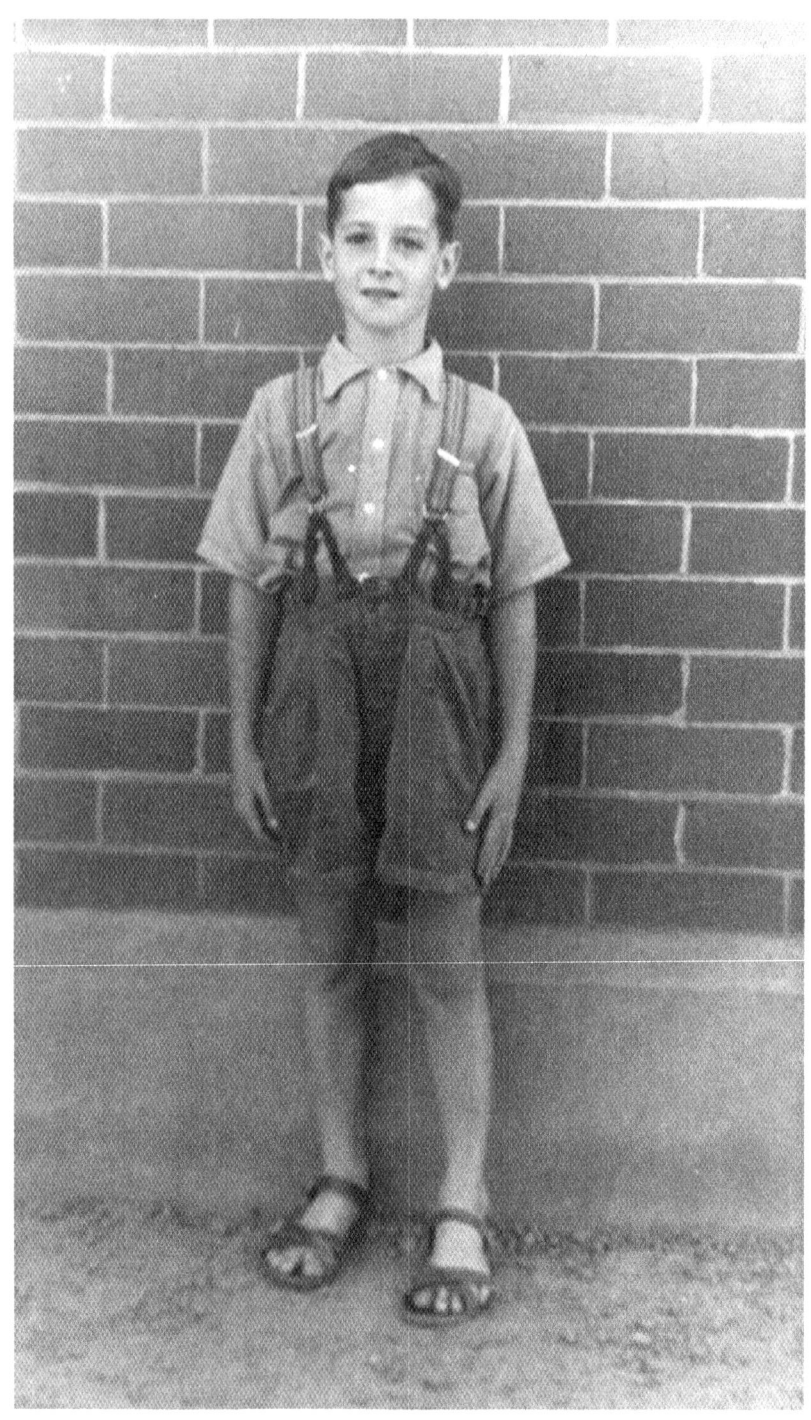

*Me at Hollywood Primary School aged seven or eight.*

*Pupils at the old Derby School in Hardman Street. I am on the extreme left. circa 1950*

*Me as a pupil at Scotch College.*

*Me with puppy 'Buster' at my Aunty Nora's orchard.*

*Me with my mother at Derby airport ready to fly back to school on a DC3 aircraft.*

*Happy times spent at Western Hills, Jingalup.*

*With my father and the station Land Rover.*

*Me as a pupil at Narrogin Agricultural College. circa 1958*

# CHAPTER THREE

# FIRST JOBS

*What's wrong with the world and it's people,*
*That the ones who have all the say,*
*Never came near the Kimberley,*
*Till others had paved the way?*
*What's wrong with this land and it's leaders,*
*That decisions are always made*
*With never a thought to the past*
*Hard slog with shovel and spade?*

## Farm hand at Pingorup

There were two houses on the farm I went to at Pingorup. One where my boss lived and one where his parents lived. My quarters consisted of a room in a shed, painted and with lino on the floor. The old man was a good bloke and a much more reasonable man than his son turned out to be. At first everything was OK, but as time went on it got harder.

In the mornings, before breakfast, I would milk a couple of cows and feed the pigs. Breakfast would be cooked and ready for me by the time I got to the kitchen. If my jobs took me a bit longer, my meal would be crispy. I got used to dried out eggs and dark crunchy bacon. The farmer would give me certain jobs to do each day. Fencing, root picking, ploughing, seeding, that kind of thing. I used to reckon I'd finish my work by five o'clock. At Narrogin Ag. I'd learnt how to slaughter sheep. This bloke would come and see me during the day. He'd tell me to yard the sheep when I got home. Then get a killer out of the mob, slaughter it, hang it for the night, then let the other sheep go. So much for me thinking I was going to finish work on time. This was on all the time. I wasn't very impressed with the man. He had an arrogant style about him and I found him to be cunning. After a while I started to get a bit frightened of him. One time I forgot to take any water with me when I went out to the paddocks to do some job or other. I didn't dare go back to get some. It was a hot day and I was perishing, so I drank the water out of the radiator of the truck. After a while I felt very sick. I ended up going home to get some water. When I got there I saw his father, who asked me what I was doing back there. I told him and he seemed all right about it.

Once I was given the job of putting up a fence in sandy country. My boss had drilled all the post holes a good while earlier. By the time I was put on the job the holes had filled in with sand, so I had to dig them all out with a jam tin. The posts were lying there ready to be put in. Having re-dug the holes, I put the posts in and ran the wires. The farmer expected me to do a mile a day, on my own. He told me I wasn't to have smoko and my lunch break was to be no longer than twenty minutes.

Another time I was told to fill bags up with oats, out of the big silo. The oats wouldn't run, so I'd hop in the silo and push it all down. Then I'd climb out, take that bag off, then do the same for the next. My eyes were watering and my nose running. I'd be sneezing and the itch! Jeez, talk about an itch. Anyway I did it, but I didn't like it. It was a hell of a job.

We did ploughing of paddocks and I'd be picking up roots, with a horse and cart. She was a good old mare, a half bred clumper. She was a very good horse, but on the dot of five o'clock she would head home. I don't know how the hell she knew, but if you weren't on that cart at five o'clock sharp you'd find yourself walking, because she just went. This amazed me. She would stay there all day and do her job unflinchingly. I'd say 'whoa' and she'd stop. I'd chuck roots on and when the cart was full we'd take them over to the edge of the paddock. The cart had a tip mechanism. Again I'd say 'Whoa'. I'd tip the tray up, she'd step forward. I'd push the tray down again, then back we'd go over the paddock and start again. This went on all day. She'd be as good as gold. Absolutely faultless. But if you were on the ground when it was time to go home, she would be gone. Somehow she knew it was time to go, and she'd be off.

My boss's father-in-law came to stay at the farm. I was working with him and we were doing more fencing. We'd stop at smoko time and I'd say 'John doesn't like us to stop for smoko.' 'Well I've brought smoko for us, and we are stopping.' he would tell me. So then we'd have half an hour for smoko. At lunch time I would eat my meal and I'd say 'We'd better get going' and he'd say 'No. We're having an hour for lunch break.' He'd find a good shady tree and, like in the stockcamp, we'd lie down and have a camp for twenty minutes, or half an hour, before we went back to work. Later we'd have a bit of afternoon tea and we'd knock off at five o'clock. It was great. He and the old mare were the two best things while I worked at Pingorup.

The farmer was always promising things, I suppose to keep me going. He promised me they'd put in a paddock of wheat and what they got off it would be mine, like a little incentive, or bonus. He said he'd have to ask his father first. Nothing further seemed to happen. Several times I asked him if he'd spoken to his Dad yet. The answer was always the same. 'No not yet.' This went on for a good while. Finally he told me he'd asked the old man who said he didn't want to be in that deal. So that was that. Next he told me we'd go shares in a big mob of turkeys. He said we'd have to buy material for the pens, build them, then we'd grow turkeys.

"Do you want to be in that deal?" he asked. I said, "Yes, all right, I'll be in it."

Later, when I asked him when we were going to start he said, "Dad says he doesn't want us to have turkeys." In the end he told me he'd give me three or four sows and whatever I made out of them would be mine. The prospect of this really pleased me. I'd done very well with pigs during my time at Narrogin, winning best baconer at the Narrogin Show in my second year. But of course it never happened. He was just dangling carrots.

I had been told my employer wanted someone who played sport, and in the beginning he did take me in to play basketball at Pingorup, or wherever the match was being held. Later on he hurt his back and couldn't play, so he decided he wouldn't take me in anymore and the lifts just stopped. Fortunately there was a bloke, who had the fuel depot in Pingorup, who was really good to me. He would come out to the farm, pick me up and take me to town so I could play basketball. If it wasn't a home game he'd take me further afield, to wherever the game was being held. He drove me a lot of miles. It was very good of him.

I continued to work on the farm and when winter came I was asked if I'd play football for the Pingorup club. I said I would, so the same bloke would come and pick me up, from the farm, on weekends and we'd travel long distances to play football. Sometimes I wouldn't get home till ten o'clock at night, to find my tea sitting in my bedroom, absolutely foul.

One time we were loading bags of super onto the truck, to take out for cropping. We'd been doing this for quite a few mornings, but this day I got over there first. There were two trolleys, a good one and a crook one. My boss always grabbed the good trolley. This day I grabbed the good trolley and began putting these bags of fertilizer on the truck. They weighed eighty pounds and I was battling to handle them, but it made it a lot easier having a good trolley. After a while John said, "This trolley's no good. Give me yours."

"No. I've been using the crook one all the time. You can have a turn on it." We ended up having an argument. I told him 'he could shove his bloody job and I'd be leaving at the end of my weeks notice.' He didn't take the trolley off me.

After the blue his father came and saw me, "What about stopping here?" he asked,

"No, I'm not staying." I said, "I get fed like a dog and treated like a dog. I have to do the washing up and drying up after meals at night, as well as my days work. My breakfast is very crispy toast, bacon that's like leather and eggs that are fried till they're rubbish. I'm not treated very well. The dogs live under the shed I live in, and the fleas from the dogs are in my bed and everywhere."

After I'd finished speaking my mind his Dad said to me, "What if I give you two pounds a week more and you eat at our place?"

I rather liked the old fellow so I agreed, but I said, "I don't really want my orders from John. I'd rather them from you." but he told me that was a bit awkward. He said, "Just see how you go." I stayed there for a while after that and things were better. At least the meals were better. But my boss was not a nice bloke. Eventually I couldn't put up with him any longer and I pulled the pin. I worked my weeks notice out and left.

After I left the farm at Pingorup I went over East with my mother, on the Indian Pacific train, to visit our relations in northern New South Wales. My maternal grandmother owned a house in Guyra, New England. She had lived in the district her entire life and my Mum grew up there, before going to Sydney to do her nursing training. Grandma also owned the two houses adjacent to hers. My aunt lived in one, with her husband and two children, my uncle in the other with his wife and their two boys. Although we had plenty of relations to catch up with I was not particularly interested in being over there. I had a serious girlfriend back in Western Australia who I'd met while attending Narrogin Ag. College. She was going to the Senior High School in town at the time, but later moved to Perth to do hairdressing. We had been going out for a couple of years and I was pretty keen. All I wanted to do was go back West.

## Scaffold rigger's offsider

Once I got back to Perth I needed to find employment. My girlfriend had an uncle who found me a job with Roberts Construction, working as a scaffold rigger's offsider. By this time Aunty Nora and Uncle Arch had left the orchard in Roleystone and were living in Queens Road, Mount Pleasant, so I boarded with them. I had a couple of mates who were butchers in Fremantle. Both boys had been at Scotch with me and the elder of the two later went on to Narrogin Ag. as well, so the three of us became good friends. I would go down on weekends and play football with them for Medina, where they also had a butchers shop.

My job as scaffold rigger's offsider was quite hard physical work, but I was very fit. In those days I didn't drink any alcohol whatsoever, and I didn't smoke. One of our first jobs was on a large brick storage building for Westralian Newspapers, in Fremantle, at the time. There were quite a few Italians working there. At lunch break they'd sit down with salami and baguettes, breaking the bread in half, salami in one hand, bread in the other, washed down with a bottle of wine. They were cheery sorts and it felt a bit like the stockcamp at lunchtimes. I liked it. If work was slow I'd be put onto wheeling barrows of concrete, for the brickies, until the scaffold rigger needed me again. I worked an eight hour day and it was good money. I was earning a lot more than at the Pingorup farm. I'd never had so much money in my life. I thought it was all pretty good. I had a Holden Ute and was using a fair bit of fuel driving to Medina and back, where I had footy training twice a week after work. I played football matches on the weekends, both home and away games, so I was totting up quite a few miles. Yet I always seemed to have money in my pocket, for the times I took my girlfriend out.

Although things were going pretty well for me down in Perth, back on the station there had been a terrible accident. Stumpy Fraser, the headstockman on Meda, had been killed in a horsefall at Euringa. Dad was pretty cut up about it and Mum suggested I go back north for a while and work for Dad, so I did.

## Youth in the stockcamp

When I got home to Meda, Dad put me in the stockcamp, full-time. He made sure he showed no favouritism towards me. In fact being the manager's son probably made my life harder. I didn't know a lot. I was on wages, which wasn't a lot. Six pounds a week, plus 'keep'. 'Keep' meant my tucker. I provided my own swag and slept on the ground under the stars.

## Waiting at Breezer

One day we were sent down to the bullock paddock to get some cattle for the Leprosarium. We left the homestead early in the morning and had ridden to a place called Breezer, a distance of some ten miles or so. We had about a hundred head of cattle in hand. A native bloke, Billy Munroe, was in charge. He said to me, "You stop here and mind these cattle, till we come back." So I stayed there while the rest of them rode off in search of more cattle.

There was a tank at Breezer, but it was empty at the time. They didn't start pumping the well until late in the year, when an engine was put on it. I was riding a horse called Baldy this day, watching these cattle. I waited and waited and waited and I began to get very thirsty. I thought 'These blokes won't be much longer'. I waited some more, but there was no sign of the other men returning. I kept looking for a dust, that would tell me they were coming. Nothing. My thirst was getting worse. I was badly needing a drink. Eventually I rode over to the well, which was about five hundred yards from where I was minding the cattle. A ladder went down into it. There was no windmill, only a dead tree to tie my horse to. I wanted to climb down the well and get a drink, but I thought, 'If I tie Baldy up, when I climb back out of the well, he might get a fright and pull away.' I knew if that happened, it would be the end of the cattle and the horse, with a saddle on. Dad would be very cross. I returned to the mob and tried to forget about a drink.

As the morning wore on I got thirstier and thirstier. I rode over to the well three or four times, with the intention of getting a drink. Each time I was needing one more, but I wasn't quite game enough to go down the well, in case something happened. I was only a young fellow, but I knew it was a big 'No, No' to leave the cattle to go and get myself a drink. Eventually I got desperate. I couldn't hold out any longer. I tied Baldy to the lone tree and I climbed down the ladder into the well. When I reached the water it was full of dead frogs, finches and maggots. I decided there was no way I could drink it. I climbed back out again, very cautiously, so as not to scare my horse. I rode back over to the cattle. I felt sure the men would be back soon.

I waited a good while longer. As the day wore on I returned to the well several times, but it was no good. I couldn't bring myself to drink the water. I minded those cattle for eight hours. Finally I could stand it no longer. I returned once more to the well. I climbed down the ladder, put my hat into the water, scooped some up and drank it.

Eventually the other stockmen came back to Breezer, bringing the rest of the cattle we needed with them. We headed off with the mob to Number One. It was mid afternoon by the time we got there. When we arrived, Dad was waiting for us. He must have thought we would be a lot earlier, because he had the billy there and our lunch. He was pretty angry. He took it out on me, although I had nothing to do with our being so long. It seemed pretty unfair, so I had a drink, but I wouldn't eat lunch. Instead I got on my horse and went back out to the cattle. It wasn't a very good day, but the experience taught me that no matter what people say about not drinking dirty water, if you need it badly enough you will drink it eventually.

## An incident at Sandy Creek

A little later, that same season, we were mustering at a place called Rarriwell. Long before, in the time of S.F. Emanuel 's father, Isadore, there had been a homestead out there. Rarriwell had once been a sheep station. This is where the trading name Rarriwell & Meda came from. When I was a kid, a scary old gin, called Lulu, was living in the native camp on Meda. Her finger nails stuck out about an inch. Poor old Lulu. She was as blind as a bat and as thin as a match stick. I'll never forget her coming up to the homestead saying 'Missus, missus! Gunanula 'n' Jimmy bin hit 'em me longa head.' It sounded like two people were hitting her, but it was only one. She was using both the black fella name and the white fella name for the one person. Goodness knows how ancient she was, but as a child she had grown up at the Rarriwell homestead.

On the Oobagooma side of Rarriwell we had a timber and wire netting drafting yard. We were camped nearby at a place known as Sandy Creek, really part of the Alexander Creek, on a red sandhill, no trees on it other than a single boab. Our camp was about fifty yards from the water. This was our drinking water, as well as water for our horses and the cattle. When horses go for a drink they don't drink from the edge. They walk out into the water and then have a drink. Cattle do the same. As they walk out into it they slosh, or backwash, the water up onto the banks, the waves making the edge wet.

Just on daylight I went down, with a towel and pannikin, to get some water to clean my teeth and wash my face. I got back from the water a fair way and after brushing my teeth, tipped the remaining water over my head and face. When I looked up I saw a bloke having a shit, right on the edge of the water, where the wet mud was. I was absolutely disgusted. I said to him, "You fucking, dirty, bastard." I walked back up to the camp. When the repulsive bloke returned he fronted me.

"What did you say?" he asked.

"I said, you're a fucking dirty bastard."

"Why's that?"

"Because you were having a shit right next to our drinking water."

"It wasn't in the water."

"No, but the horses and the cattle wash the water up there, and it runs back into our drinking water," I told him.

"You talk to me like that and I'll kill you." The bloke threatened.

"Well you come near me and you might be in trouble too." I replied. He started walking towards me so I went over to where I'd been sleeping. I had a star picket for my mosquito net. Everything was pulled down, so I grabbed the star picket.

"You come over here and you'll be wearing this star picket." I warned him. I wasn't much more than a kid at the time. He was a Koepanger type of a fella. His gin was the cook in the stockcamp and he drove the mule wagon. After this exchange he walked away, acting as if he'd forgotten, but I kept watching him. Then he'd try to sneak up on me, so I'd walk straight over and grab the star picket again. In the end I was walking around carrying it with me, because I started to get frightened of him.

"I'll get you bye and bye." He warned me. "You've gotta go to sleep sometime."

That really scared me. I did have to go to sleep sometime. After this he rolled up his swag, got his gin and started walking. I thought 'This is no good. He might just go a mile, hide in the other creek over on the Rarriwell side, have a sleep and keep out of sight for the day. Then in the middle of the night he'll come back and fix me up.' I thought 'I've gotta get out of this.' I decided to leave camp.

I really liked my horses. I didn't like anyone else riding them when I wasn't there, so I thought I'd take them with me. I caught one, a strong horse called Big Prince. He was prone to sores, so I used to really look after him. I had pieces of rubber, with holes cut in them, which I'd put on him to try and stop him from getting sores. I saddled him up ready, then tried to catch my other horse. I don't know if the horses sensed it, but things seemed a bit toey in the camp that morning. I couldn't catch the other horse. In the end I let Big Prince go. Instead I caught Baldy, my favourite, and I left.

I must have learned a bit by then, because I knew a short cut across country. I rode from Sandy Creek to the Meda River crossing. When I got there I could see the pair walking along the road in the distance. When I got to Euringa I cut across to Daley's and rode on to Number Four. From there I crossed the May River, rode through the horse paddock and on to the homestead. I got to the homestead at about one or two o'clock in the afternoon. Mum was away, but Dad was there.

"What are you doing here?" he asked,

"I've had a blue with Billy Williams." I told him. Dad wasn't very pleased.

"Well he beat you didn't he? Because you've left the camp and come home."

"Well, he told me I'd have to go to sleep sometime and I do." I replied.

Billy Williams never turned up at the homestead, nor did he go back to the stockcamp that day. Instead he and his 'wife' walked all the way into Derby. He didn't return to work on Meda until after I had left.

Dad put me onto checking bores for a while after that, which I didn't enjoy half as much as being in the mustering camp. I hadn't wanted to leave the stockcamp that day, I really loved it, but I didn't know what else I could do. We were supposed to go out moonlighting that night, at Wallamore. I had never been moonlighting before and had been looking forward to it, but because of what happened I missed out. They got a big mob of cattle that night too, so I've always regretted not being with them.

Moonlighting is when you go to a waterhole, with coachers, quiet cattle, and wait there on horseback, in the dark, for the bush cattle to come in for a drink. Cattle don't seem to be frightened of the smell of man, but everything is dead silent. You don't talk, light cigarettes, smoke, cough or make any sound at all. Presently the bush cattle will come in for a drink and man and horse quietly control them. It is done towards the end of the year when there isn't a lot of water around. The wild cattle settle down very well in the dark, amongst the coachers. Because the quiet cattle have been handled they aren't concerned about anything. There is no sense of fear, so the wild cattle reckon everything is all right. When you think you've got enough, you take them to a nearby yard and yard them up. The next day you brand them. When you let them out of the yard you've usually got a bit of a circus on your hands. Because it's daylight the wild bush cattle all realise what has happened to them and they aren't very happy about it.

## A fall at Bob's Yard

Dad allowed me back in the stockcamp after a while. George Dann, a coloured man, was headstockman and we were camped at Bob's Yard. I didn't really know much about ringing. I was just a big teenager, still learning, but keen as mustard. I was riding a grey mare called Sue. She was an older mare, a lot more experienced than me. She was smart and fully switched on.

Two beasts had been cut out of the mob, one to go in with the bullock mob, the other back into the cow and calf mob. The ground was as flat as a table top, apart from one dried up cattle track. The two cut out beasts split, so I rode between them. The mare's hoof went into a hole on the cattle track and she lost her footing and fell. We hit the ground. In those days, when I had a fall, I didn't have any idea what was happening from start to finish. All I would know, at the end of it, was that I'd had a fall. Later, as I got more experienced, I would know exactly what was happening all the way through. It was as if it was all in slow motion. This day, we hit the ground and the mare went over the top of me. All I knew was that, as the saddle went over me, I heard a sort of crackling in my head. That's all I can remember. When I came to, there were blokes all around me, some had dismounted, others were on horseback. I got up and I started to walk away, but I wasn't really with it. All of a sudden I realised something had happened. Then I remembered I'd had a fall. I went and found the mare, Sue. She had grazed the side of her face and shoulder, but apart from that, seemed OK. I got on her and went back to doing the job. We were taking a mob of meatworks bullocks to water, and as we were going down to the watering place I didn't feel real good. I was getting a headache, but I still reckoned I would go on down with the bullock mob. The headache started to get worse and worse. I began to get a bit frightened. I told the blokes I wasn't feeling good. I didn't just ride away, I let them know I didn't think I could go on. I rode back to the camp and unsaddled my horse.

That evening, after the rest of the stockmen had eaten their tea they caught their horses. They were going up to Bob's bore moonlighting. I really wanted to go with them, but I didn't feel well enough. I felt pretty sick. A fair while later, when they returned, I was still sitting up by the fire. I was too frightened to go to sleep and I was too frightened to go home. In the morning I woke up lying alongside the fire. I was very happy to be awake, to be alongside the fire and to still be around. I felt a bit groggy and a bit crook that day, but after that I came good fairly quickly.

## I'm given an outlaw

George Dann was running the camp when I was given a horse called Brownlock to ride. The blacks were very concerned, but I wasn't. I didn't know he was the station outlaw and had always been prone to buck.

I had been riding him, on and off, for a couple of weeks. I thought he was just an old pensioner I'd been given. He knew his job. One day, because I was young and still a bit slow getting ready, I left the camp a bit behind the other blokes. I was cantering towards the yard to catch up with the men, when suddenly Brownlock propped and was 'into it'. I was decked, no trouble at all. I was very surprised. I pulled the saddle cloth off and checked it for prickles. I couldn't believe he would buck me off for no reason. I couldn't find anything that might annoy him, so I hopped back on and everything was OK. About ten days later, after dinner camp, I caught Brownlock as my afternoon horse. I saddled him up and walked him around for a bit, then hopped on him. I was just sitting on him, when all of a sudden he started to unwind. He bucked for a while, and there was a big branch of a coolibah tree. I thought he was lining me up for it, so I leaned to one side to miss it and he got rid of me. After that Tommy May jumped off his horse and grabbed the reins of mine. He bossed Brownlock a bit, then hopped on and gave him a good larraping. When he'd taken the sting out of him he gave the horse back to me.

"You'll be all right now." He told me. A few of the blacks were not too happy about me being given a horse like that. They talked to Dad about it. I was only a young fella and I didn't know much at all. It never entered my head that a dirty horse had been given to Biddul's son. Biddul was Dad's black fella name.

## Trying my hand at bull throwing

We were at Bob's Yard. A mickey bull, about two year old, took off out of the mob. Kenny Oobagooma and I took off after it. I jumped off my horse and the bull went into the wings of the yard. The gate was shut. I thought 'This is good, wings on two sides and a closed gate ahead.' I went to grab him by the tail, but he whipped around on me. I didn't have much experience then. Well, none actually! I ran.

The bull was gaining on me. I thought he was going to get me, so I put my hands behind my backside and there were his horns. I'd grabbed one horn in my hand. He was close.

I knew he was close, but I didn't know he was that close. All of a sudden I had a bit more power and I got away from him. Fear is pretty handy sometimes. After that Kenny Oobagooma got him and pulled him down, so the mickey bull didn't get away. This was fortunate, because a bull who has had a win is twice as dangerous next time.

## My first thrown bull

We were mustering from Rarriwell, heading out towards George Wells Island. I was about nineteen years old, working in the camp under headstockman Dann. It was still early in the morning when all of a sudden we came onto some cattle. We were running these fresh cattle into our coachers when a bull took off towards Salty Creek. The other blokes seemed to have control of the rest of the mob, so I went after the bull. He was a big bull and he took off and ran along the creek, where there were paperbark trees growing on either side. I jumped off to get this bull and we ran round and around the paperbarks along the creek bed. I was pretty fit. I didn't smoke and I could run for a long time. Eventually I grabbed his tail, but I didn't really know the knack of pulling bulls down. I pulled him this way and I pulled him that way, but I couldn't get him off balance. If you make a mistake and end up on the ground, you're cactus. You're gone. A couple of the black fellas saw me and they headed over to help. They had about half a mile to gallop to reach me. I didn't know they were coming, but just as they got there I finally got the bull down. The blokes jumped off and helped tie it up. I needed a bit of a spell by then. I was pretty much buggered, but the bull was tired too. He was the first bull I ever threw, but I think I was lucky. If I'd got a bad bull I'd have got done that day.

Afterwards Tommy May gave me a good rev. He was a wonderful Aboriginal man who always seemed to watch out for me. My mother taught him to read and write and he later became a good artist. He calls me his brother. He wasn't very pleased with me that day.

"You berry chilly boy Shohn. You could get yourchelf killed." He told me and he was right.

## Mungiddygiddy

The following season, a different bloke was in charge of the stockcamp. We were out at Daley's, moonlighting. I was riding one of my best loved horses, Baldy, when a nobby bull took off from the mob. He was a good looking poly, shorthorn. He ran out onto blacksoil country, holey ground. I chased him, jumped off and after a fair sort of a struggle, I threw him. When I jumped off, Baldy left me and headed back to camp. I tied the bull up, using my belt as a bull strap. He was about the third bull I'd thrown in my life, but my first in the dark.

When my horse walked into camp, alone, a few of the natives became very frightened, thinking I'd had a bad fall and wondering how they'd find me at night. I walked back towards camp, feeling quite happy about things when I heard Tommy May coming. He was yelling out for me. He seemed very relieved that I was OK. He gave me a bit of a ticking off. Everything had worked out all right, but later I realised it had been a very silly thing to do. Chasing a cleanskin bull, in the dark, across blacksoil country, with no one there as back up in case I got into trouble when I threw him. I had come out of it unscathed, but really what I'd done was nothing short of suicidal. The blacks were always worried something might happen to me, and they were frightened Dad would be very angry if I got hurt. They did their best to protect me, but I suppose I was a bit headstrong at times.

In the morning we went to let the roan bull up and put him into the coachers. From Daley's we headed on towards Number Four, then cut across the May River to Number One Bore, where we watered the mob. After watering the cattle the nobby bull I'd thrown the previous night lay down and died. So my foolhardiness had all been for nothing. The assistant manager, who was also acting as headstockman that season, was not there when we headed to Number One. His wife would sometimes drive out to pick him up and take him home, which I suppose is what happened this day, because nobody seemed to be in charge. I had already learned that you don't, ever, put a big mob of cattle onto a trough at the same time, or they will scramble over each other and damage the trough. Usually the cattle would be pulled up some distance away, then be split into smaller mobs, each group being allowed to go in to water in turn. I wasn't in charge, far from it, but I knew the trough at Number One was new and Dad wouldn't be happy if it was broken. Nobody was saying we should pull up and split the mob and we were almost too close already. The cattle knew the water was there, they could smell it. So I took charge. I said we would split the mob, water them in three or four smaller mobs and block the rest.

There was a native boy in the stockcamp at the time, from up around Balgo or Billiluna. He was a jovial fellow called Mungiddygiddy. We were battling to hold the cattle back off water, when Mungiddygiddy decided he'd ride in for a drink. I told him he couldn't go for a drink right then.

I said, "We're battling to hold these cattle. Come back. We need you here. You can get a drink later." He took no notice and went in anyway and got his drink.

When all the cattle were watered the rest of the stockmen had a drink. I was riding a mule, that wasn't fully reliable, called Monty. I saw the native boy, Mungiddygiddy, go and break a green stick off a tree. I thought 'Oh. This doesn't look too good' so I stayed on the mule. I started to ride away and I thought 'I don't know what I'm going to do here.' I didn't want to run away so I just walked. The native boy kept coming closer, so I decided to take my stirrup leather and iron off. Mungiddygiddy walked up to me. He grabbed my mule by the cheek strap and tried to take control of it. I pulled Monty round, so his hind quarters were towards the boy, who let go. He shook the stick at me, so I raised the stirrup leather and iron. Mungiddygiddy told me he'd kill me by'n'by. I put my stirrup iron back on and sat on the mule for a long time. The native boy went and had dinner, caught another horse and went back out to the cattle. I went back into camp. I let Monty go. I didn't even wash the mule down. I went straight over and caught my fresh horse. I saddled him early and kept him with me while I ate my dinner. But nothing more ever happened and the native boy left Meda shortly after that.

I don't know what got into Mungiddygiddy that day. Before this incident I had always got on very well with him. He seemed to be my friend and would crack jokes with me. He had a horse fall once. The horse rolled on top of him, in the black soil, and it couldn't get up. I rolled the horse so that it could get up off him. Mungiddygiddy's finger had been dislocated in the fall. Being out of joint it was giving him gyp and he reckoned it was broken. I told him to give us a look at it. When he showed it to me I saw that it was facing the wrong way. I took hold of it and I gave it a good yank. It went back into place. After that he was jumping around a bit, but later he was OK about it and very happy it was fixed.

## A thirsty young man

Emanuels had sent bullocks down from GoGo, to fatten up ready for shipment the following year.

When they got to Meda they got hit with red water, an illness caused by ticks. It was decided to shift those not yet affected, from Emanuel's Paddock out to Charlie's Paddock, where there was better feed. We mustered them up one afternoon, ready to head off next morning for Langoora. From there it would be a long day through to Charlie's Paddock.

I was the last out of bed, the morning we left Langoora, and didn't have time to eat breakfast. I poured a pannikin of tea and saddled up. The tea was too hot to drink, so I chucked it out, put the pannikin down, hopped into the saddle and galloped down to the yard, in time for letting out. We let the bullocks out and were walking them back past the tank and trough. Everybody was filing off to get a drink of water. I wondered why. We had only just had breakfast, at least those blokes had. It seemed odd. I kept riding along with the bullocks.

I was riding a mule called Dolly. I was young and very keen. We were heading to Middle Bore. I was working like hell across the tail of the mob, trying to do the right thing. I was doing more work than anyone else and I ended up as thirsty as hell. When I swallowed, my tongue wouldn't come back. It was so dry it just stuck to the back of my throat. Eventually we got into Charlies Paddock. We were out in the middle of the plain, no water, full sun, midday and the cart with the dinner on didn't turn up.

I was really needing a drink by this time. With no sign of the cart coming I thought, 'I can't stand this any longer'. I got off the mule and lay down on the ground. Surprisingly I felt quite good, as if I could just doze off and go to sleep. The cattle were pulled up and being minded, while we waited for dinner. The blacks were quite concerned about me. They weren't happy with me dozing off.

"Come on Shohn, we can see dust coming. Cart 'n mules are coming and we'll have a drink," they encouraged me. I thought they were just trying to get me up, so I took no notice of them. Some of them were standing around me. Eventually a couple of them grabbed me and stood me up, so I could see that the cart really was coming. I got on the mule and rode over to the cart and they got the water off. Everybody else was needing a drink too. I got a pannikin and I had a big drink of water. One cup straight down. Phew! Did I feel sick? Up came the water. Straight back up again. I felt really ill and had pains in my stomach.

"Don't drink it. Pour it over your head and wet your shirt." Somebody suggested, so I did. Then I went and laid down and went out like a light. I woke up about an hour later. I got up and had another drink. I drank a big pannikin of water, but more slowly this time, then the sweat came out of me and I felt I wanted to vomit. I didn't have any dinner. I sat around while everybody else ate theirs. Then we caught our horses and went on with the bullocks to Middle Bore. That was the first real 'perishing' I'd ever had. I thought I was gone that day.

## Tim Emanuel drops in at Yabbagoody

We were tailing shipping bullocks on the trough at Yabbagoody windmill, when Tim Emanuel rocked up. He was the only son and heir of the owners. I was a junior stockman at the time. I was riding Baldy that day and I used to ride him without a bit. He could really gallop and he'd do everything without a bit in his mouth. I kept the bit tied onto my saddle.

When Tim arrived he came over to me and we talked for a while. Then he asked if he could borrow my horse to have a look at the bullocks. I said he could, but to hang on a minute while I put the bit in this horse's mouth. Tim seemed to be in a hurry. I hadn't put the bit in tight enough and he wanted to go.

"I'm not quite ready yet." I told him, but off Tim went. I was a bit worried. I thought 'Jeez, I hope these cattle don't get a fright and jump'. Baldy was a very good horse and I was afraid, if that happened, he might take off after them. Everything was all right, but when Tim got back I saw that the bit wasn't even in Baldy's mouth. It was hanging under his chin, so I was thankful nothing went wrong.

## Brickies' labourer

After working for Dad on Meda for eighteen months I decided to return to Perth, where I knew I could earn better money and thought I had a girlfriend.

I returned to the building site in Fremantle where Roberts Construction agreed to take me on again. I worked for a short time there, as a scaffold rigger's offsider, before being sent up to Kalamunda to work, as a brickies labourer, on the new high school. This was a bit of a shock. I didn't know anything about brickies labouring, other than wheeling barrow loads of mortar. I think they had just been holding onto me until the Kalamunda job came up, because they knew I could work. Anyway I had a job. I was back on good money again, but my long term girlfriend, unbeknown to me, had given me the arse. I went back playing football for Medina and in time found myself a new girlfriend.

There were no other brickies labourers on site to tell me or show me anything, and there were five bricklayers. I had to wet all the bricks fairly thoroughly, then cart them up and stack them for the brickies. Then I had to go back and make the mortar. After the first day the balls of my fingers and thumbs were pretty well raw. It was like electricity to touch a brick. Nobody told me that you needed to have a certain rubber pad for your fingers. I kept doing the job and after a few days I could hardly put up with it. I'd have hankies wrapped around my hands, or I'd take bits of rag to try and protect them, but it didn't really help.

One day a little Greek guy came to me and handed me two bits of tube.

"What do I do with these?" I asked.

"You put them on your fingers and it makes it easier for you to handle the bricks." He told me. By Jeez! It was really, really good. He brought me another couple of pairs that he'd made and once my fingers were protected they eventually got better and I was away.

I had to get to work a bit early to wet the bricks down, get them stacked ready for the brickies, then get the mortar mixed. I couldn't make the mortar too early or the brickies would whinge about it. I was kept flat out all the time, getting bricks and mortar up there for the five of them. This went on for a month, maybe six weeks. Always flat out. I was getting knocked up, though I was pretty fit with playing football and football training. We would stop for smoko, but I'd have to eat mine while I was working, because I didn't have time to sit down and eat it. I needed to catch up on my job. Then the same thing at dinner time. I'd bolt my dinner down and wet bricks, make more mortar and get it up there ready for them to start work again. One brickie, a Dutchman and an arrogant bastard, would be giving me revs, telling me to hurry up. One Friday at lunch time, I said to the little Greek fellow who'd made me the gloves, "I'm going to get my pay tonight and I won't be back on Monday." He asked me why.

"Because I've had enough of this. It's too hard. I'm flat out all the time. I'm battling to keep up and I get growled at."

"Oh don't do that." He urged, "When you get your pay tonight, tell the pay clerk that on Monday you're only keeping three brickies going, not five. Tell him if they want five brickies going they'll have to put on another brickies labourer."

"They'll just tell me to piss off."

"No they won't. You do that and they'll have another labourer here to start work on Monday morning." He told me. So I got my pay and then I told the paymaster that.

"OK." He replied casually.

I went and played football that weekend. When Monday morning came we had two brickies labourers there. Jeez it was easy after that. I could sit down and have lunch with the blokes. There were some younger fellows I got on all right with and the little Greek fellow. I'd still get to work a bit earlier because I had to get ready for the brickies to start work, but the job became a lot easier.

I did that job for five or six months. Then one day I had some business to sort out in Perth, so I asked for a day off. While I was in the city I met Paddy Le Lievre in London Court. We were talking and he asked me what I was doing. I told him I was a brickies labourer.

"Well what about coming back to the Kimberley and working for me?" He offered. Paddy was running Kimberley Downs at the time. I was on good money, so I ummed and erred for a bit.

"How much was your old man paying you on Meda?" he asked. "I'll pay you two pounds a week more."

"Dad was paying me ten pounds a week."

"Righto. I'll give you twelve." Really it was a joke, when I think about it and I must have been crazy to accept, but I did. It was a lot less than I was getting as brickies labourer, but I belonged to life on stations, so I agreed. It was winter time. I don't quite know why he was down in Perth at that time of the year. Really it was an absolute fluke that we ran into each other like that. Over the years I've often thought it 'was just meant to be'. Serendipity. One way or another I reckon I was destined to work in stockcamps on Kimberley cattle stations.

*Childhood behind me and ready to enter the workforce.*

*On Meda Station as a young stockman, with 'Baldy'.*

*Me in stockman's attire, at the homestead. circa 1960.*

*Willie Lennard reaches down to tip a bull's horns, while headstockman George Dann watches on. Photo courtesy of D. Pollard*

*Native stockmen scruff a calf at Meda as I watch on mule 'Skipper'.*

*Me riding mule 'Monty'.*

*L-R Tim Emanuel, Sydney F. Emanuel, Dan Luck and my father George Wells.*

# CHAPTER FOUR

# STOCKCAMPS

*Round the campfire at night you sat down for a bite,*
*Of brisket and damper, or bread,*
*And thought back on the day, of your work, which was play,*
*Before finally tumbling to bed.*

Stockcamps became my home for many years. I loved the life, the excitement, the camaraderie. For a young fellow with boundless energy it was all I could wish for. Money meant little to me then, as long as I had enough to get by, and material comforts seemed unimportant. It was a lifestyle I took to with relish despite it's discomforts.

Stockmen, in Australia, are often referred to as 'ringers'. They dislike being referred to as 'cowboys' which many stockmen consider derogatory. The term 'ringer' came about because of the circling technique used by horsemen, when trying to gain control of cattle.

Life as a ringer was not for the faint hearted or feeble, but for many young blokes in the first flush of manhood it was a thrilling, adrenalin charged existence. Ideally suited to that reckless stage of life when young fellows enjoy risk taking, have unlimited energy and are not yet saddled with the responsibility of family, stockcamps offered unbounded freedom from the mundane. Where better to burn up youth, with all it's invincibility, vigour and enthusiasm, than in cattle camps outback? Or so I thought. It wasn't until many years later, when I paused to consider such things, that I realised what a boon we were for profit seeking station owners.

## Gear 'n' kit

Your swag was made up of a canvas ground sheet and two blankets. If you were lucky you might have a mosquito net and two sticks. That was it. No sheets, no mattress, no pillow. If you had more, the headstockman would say 'get your bloody woman out of there', so you'd have to chuck anything else out, or you didn't have a job. I used to dig a hole in the dirt for my hip bone and leg bone, and that was my girlfriend for the night. Your clothes, stored in a flour bag, which you got for free because there were hundreds of them, was your pillow. For clothes you'd probably have two pairs of jeans and two shirts. No singlets, no undies, no socks. In winter you might have a jumper. So that was your pillow, which was all right at first, when the clothes were clean, but not so good after you'd been out for a while. Then you'd have dirty stinking clothes. They'd be covered in blood, and sweat, which pours out of you like nobody's business. Your 'pillow' didn't smell too good then. You never used undies or socks in the camp, just shirt, trousers, boots. Yeah we smelt – everybody did. Toiletries consisted of a toothbrush, tooth paste, soap and a towel. You might have a couple of bars of bought soap to begin with, but once that ran out it was station soap, which was pretty powerful stuff. Maybe a comb and razor somewhere in your gear, but you lived like a wild black fella so it didn't much matter. Most blokes took a bottle of Aspros with them. These were used for horse falls, cold 'chick' (sick), anything that went wrong with you. There was no First Aid Kit in the stockcamp, but there was usually a spare bottle or two of Aspros in the tucker box. The blacks used Apros a lot.

Apart from my 'pillow' I used to have another flour bag with a bit of medicine in it. The Aspros, a bottle of strychnine, some potassium citrate, anti bite tablets, later my tobacco and papers and maybe a couple of bandages. I'd also put any mail I got in the bag too. One day, when we were in at the homestead the teacher on Kimberley Downs, Kerry Lamb, asked me if I had a reference amongst my gear that he could copy. I'd been in the camp for a while by then and had learned to smoke. I said I did and I felt around in the flour bag where I thought the reference was. There was all this powdery stuff in there and I presumed the lid must have come off the bottle of Aspros. After I'd found the reference for him I built myself a smoke. When I put it in my mouth, it tasted bitter. I licked my fingers. They tasted bitter too. Then I remembered the poison. I looked in the bag and sure enough, the cork had come out of the strychnine bottle. My ticker started going like hell. I went up to the main house and told the manager's wife, Mary Campbell, what had happened.

"How long ago did this happen?" she asked.

"About ten minutes."

"And how are you feeling?"

"OK. Except I feel like I've run a hundred yards flat out and my heart is pounding."

"If it was that long ago I think you'll be all right." She told me.

I took her word for it and I was.

Some of the old fellows in the Kimberley used to take a little bit of strychnine now and then, for a bit of a kick. Just a tiny little bit off the end of a pocket knife.

## Tucker

Tucker in the camp would, in the main, consist of a four gallon tin of dried spud, the same of dried veggies, which gave you the farts, tomato sauce, pickles, flour of course, a few tins of sausages, or tinned dog and maybe some tinned butter. The butter was usually rancid, though we'd try to keep it cool by putting it in a trough, if there was one. Once it had melted and turned to oil it was no good any more. It was really crap stuff, so we'd use a bit of beef fat spread on our bread or damper instead, which was pretty good gear. Then of course there was salt beef. Always salt beef.

If we got a killer we'd have a big feed of rib bones and maybe a roast or two and steak. The cook would make up big stews, when there was fresh beef and the older it got the more he'd lace it with curry powder, to disguise the taste. Once a stew started bubbling, without being on the fire that is, it was too dangerous to eat, however much curry was in it. Then once the meat had gone off it was back to salt beef. You got really sick of it after a while and it made you constipated. When you were in the stockcamp, quite often your poos were just like sheep shit. Just little pebbles. You got used to this, but then there were times when the cook soon fixed that problem for you. You had to be careful not to offend the cook or he'd pull the pin, so you just had to dodge the crook tucker as best you could.

We always had bread, damper or sometimes Johnny cakes to go with the meat. The Johnny cakes were a mixture of flour and water made into a dough. The dough was made into patty shaped discs which were tossed onto the coals. They weren't bad if you were hungry, but it was all pretty basic.

## Blacks' tucker

During my ringing days there were always more Aborigines in the stockcamp than whites. Sometimes I was the only white man. The blacks really liked their meat. Meat and bread, or meat and damper. They were very good. They never complained about shit tucker, so long as there was meat.

Sometimes they'd eat calves balls, otherwise known as 'desert oysters'. We all did. They were all right too. Or they might catch a goanna or porcupine, or a croc. If they got a crocodile then we'd all have a feed of it, whites and blacks.

Depending where we were the gins might go fishing and bring back a turtle, or a mob of bream. They'd cook these up, but only the blacks would have them. They never seemed keen on getting a wild pig. I don't know why. However if we, whites, got a wild pig we'd skin it and cook it up. Then the blacks would hop into it as well. There were mobs of wild pigs on the Myroodah, Kalyeedah, Luluigui side and also up on Oobagooma. There were none on Meda, Napier or Kimberley Downs. I don't know why that was.

## Water

Long thirsty days were not uncommon in the stockcamp and we often had to go for long periods without a drink. Maybe from seven in the morning until three in the afternoon. If you were soft, in that climate, you couldn't go that long, so you had to harden up.

Quite often in the stockcamp we'd be living on a billabong that was getting a bit low and there might be half a dozen dead beasts in it. When you first saw it you'd think 'Golly! Is that the drinking water?' and you'd be half sick thinking about it. But once you'd checked it, you'd know if it was really crook or not, and mostly it was OK. It didn't smell or anything, it was only the thought of what was in it that put you off. We wouldn't take water from right alongside a dead beast, but we would drink that water. That would be our water supply, for washing, drinking and making our tea. We didn't boil it first, unless we were making a billy of tea, we just drank it as it was. Eventually you got to the stage where you'd drink almost any water. You stopped being fussy.

The exception was if water had algae in it. Then we'd shy off it and wouldn't use it. You can't. You'd be very ill. There was too much shit and piss and juices from dead cattle in it, and it had a smell about it that warned you off. When you came onto water like that it usually meant no drink for a few more hours. That was when the day became long and thirsty and any water seemed good at the end of it.

One time we went mustering on Kimberley Downs and had dinner camp at a billabong. Quite often, at the end of the year, we took canteens on a mule, or a canteen on one side and a packbag on the other, with our billy-cans, bread, meat, tea and sugar. On this occasion we didn't take a canteen with us. We got to the billabong, which we knew had water in, and we had two new blokes with us. We were mustering, with coachers, and we kept the cattle away from the water, off the wind side, so they wouldn't smell it. I said to the new blokes and some of the other fellows, "You'd better go in and get a drink of water here, because we're going to go on further." I went in with them, leaving four or five blokes with the cattle. I rode into the billabong and lent down and scooped up some water with my hat. There were a couple of dead cattle in there, but I didn't go near them. I had a drink and my horse had a drink. Then I had a bit more.

"Are you going to get a drink?" I asked the new blokes.

"No. We're not drinking that. The water's too dirty to drink."

"All right. Please yourselves." We returned to mind the mob while the remaining few blokes rode in for their drink. After that we went on for another two or three hours mustering, then we came back to the same billabong. This time the pair didn't wait for permission to leave the mob. They were off, straight to that same billabong and they couldn't drink enough of it.

## Cut prick

If we had to drink the water at Limestone Springs, on Napier Downs, blokes would tell you 'You'll get cut prick from this water' and they were right. When you had a widdle it was as if you were widdling razor blades. It used to really burn, probably from all the lime in it. Because of this we would try and have water with us, just for drinking, when we got to Limestone Springs. We didn't like it if we ran out and had to drink the water there, because we knew what was going to happen. It was crystal clear, but it did that to you and it wasn't very nice. I used to have a bit of trouble with my kidneys and I always carried a bottle of potassium citrate with me. If I got a dose of 'cut prick' I used take some and it helped. Dr Lawson Holman put me onto it, but he also told me 'to go to Tasmania and pick apples!', which was a piece of advice I never followed.

## Black dysentery

The water at Telephone Dam used to give us a dose of the shits. Black dysentery. Terrible it was. Really stinking. Mariarna also used to give us the dysentery, but Telephone Dam was the worst. We didn't need a crook cook to sort out our constipation when we were in that country. We all knew we'd get the shits when we were going there. We would try to take a 44 gallon drum of water with us. Robin Campbell would also bring a drum out, from the station for us, when we were camped. If we were out with packs we never had any good water with us. We just had to cop it. The water at Telephone Dam didn't taste too good either. You wouldn't have drunk it if there was any choice, but when you're thirsty you'll drink anything and hang the consequences. When we got the dysentery we used to take cornflour and water, make it into a thick mix and drink it straight down.

Quite a few of the waters had a smell about them. A bit like bad eggs. If you got the water from the tank it was all right, but if you drank it straight from the delivery pipe it smelt of sulphur. Blokes who were new in the camp used to complain about it, but amongst the older fellas, nothing was ever said. You just drank it. Blokes simply wouldn't drink that sort of water nowadays. There's no way. It just wouldn't happen. Work Safe wouldn't allow it in any case. But in those days it was just normal. Part of being a ringer. You don't complain, just 'toughen up'.

## Treats and comforts

Treats and comforts were few and far between in the stockcamps of those times, but what there were seemed all the better for their rarity. The goodies that occasionally found their way to us often came from unexpected sources. Seldom from the owners, with the exception of Bob Maxted, who often brought us such things as bacon, sausages, eggs, cigarettes and tobacco. But generally it was other kind hearted souls who thought to send out some treat for us all. One such person was the wife of travelling saddler Jim Kelly. When Jim was at Kimberley Downs doing leather work his wife would cook up big tins of biscuits for us. Or she might bake a large fruit cake and send it out to the stockamp. We didn't have anything flash in the camp, so we thought she was marvellous.

One time, towards the end of a long mustering season, I was getting very sour. I was knocked up, worn out from months of long hard days in the camp. The manager, Robin Campbell, must have read the mood amongst the stockmen and one day he brought out a carton of cold tinned fruit for us. By gee, we all thought that was great. It was like lollies to a kid and it jollied us along for a while longer, as we worked our way towards the end of the season.

## Campfires and cold nights

A campfire is a magic thing and of pivotal importance in stockcamps. It was everything to us. Our hot water, our stove, our warmth and our comfort. In the dark solitude of the night, or the chill colourless dawn, the campfire was like a friend to us. It was the focal point of our living space, pulling everyone to it. In the evening we ringers would gravitate from the shadows to within the fire's glow. There, perched on an upturned drum, or squatting on one heel with a pannikin of tea resting on our leg, we would absent-mindedly gaze at the embers, and ponder on the day just over. In our constantly tired state it was easy to become mesmerized by the gently flickering flames, playing around the edges of a piece of coolibah or woollybutt.

More relaxing even than watching wavelets lapping on a shoreline, the campfire's soporific effect soon saw us heading sleepily to our swags. We never sat up late in the stockcamp.

On cold winter nights, when even in the tropics inland temperatures can drop to near freezing, we would cut bushes to put around the wind side of the campfire, in order to keep it alight, and stop it from spreading. Sometimes we'd light fires alongside ourselves, to sleep by, or if it was unbearably cold, we'd take the tarpaulin down, lay it out flat, pull half of it over ourselves and all sleep in a line. Some of us had dogs in the stockcamp. I had two or three dogs and they'd camp with me. It was good on cold nights. When I wanted to roll over, early on, I used to pick up my belt and go whack, whack, whack on my swag. The dogs would all stand up and move away a bit and I'd roll over and get myself comfortable. Then the dogs would come back and settle down alongside me again. After a time I only had to stir and they would all move, so I could turn over, then they'd lie down again and we'd all go back to sleep. They made great blankets, as well as being good friends to me.

When the mosquitos were bad, especially early in the season when everything was still green, and there was a lot of water about, we'd burn coongleberry as a deterrent and light up cow dung on the wind side of our camp. Cow manure, or horse manure, it didn't matter which. The aromatic smoke wafted over us and kept the blighters away. Well sort of. It wasn't perfect, but it was better than nothing. If the mozzies were really thick we'd rub kerosene on ourselves to try and keep them off. Some of us had mosquito nets. I remember once, when we were at Mundooma, it was winter time and cold as could be. We weren't allowed big swags and as I was running the camp I couldn't just change the rules to suit myself. It was that damned cold I had a fire on either side of my swag. Then I put the mozzie net over me. I woke up during the night and remember seeing all these thin red lines going everywhere. I couldn't work out what they were. I was a bit confused for a while. They were very pretty. Then I realised it was my mosquito net smouldering.

We always made sure we had wood at our camp sites. Sometimes at the end of the season we would take wood out and leave it there, ready to use during the first mustering round early the following year, when we'd only have packs with us. If we ran short of wood at our camp site we would sometimes use one of the pack mules to pull up a big log, or small dead tree from a short distance away. Generally dry wood was plentiful and not a problem for us. If there was wet weather about we made sure we kept our matches dry, and had some dry grass and a bit of kindling safely stored out of the rain, so we could still light a fire. We always managed to have a campfire, no matter what the weather, although sometimes it might be a bit hard to light. I think a stockcamp without a campfire would be a dreary, heartless place.

## Barcoo rot

Ailments in the stockcamp were more often endured, than cured, and some were more prevalent than others. Barcoo rot was a common scourge amongst ringers. If we got scratched by wire, a stick, or anything that broke the skin, it would make an angry red line. That scratch, or any small wound, would turn into a festering sore. This was due to a lack of fruit and vegetables in our diet. When I was ringing on Kimberley Downs and Napier, we never saw fresh vegetables in the camp.

We must have been deficient in all sorts of minerals and vitamins, not that we ever thought about it, but I don't really think the dried veggies or dried spud helped us at all. We ate what was on offer and that was all there was to it. Normally a festering wound would be cleaned and dressed, but when you were in the stockcamp they were generally left open to the dust and dirt and the flies. In time they would form hard scabs which, until knocked, protected them a bit, though they would often ooze puss from under the scabs if touched. These sores would last for some weeks before finally healing. My mother used to give me vitamin tablets to try and prevent this happening.

By the time I was managing Meda, in the late seventies and eighties, times had changed and things were a bit better for the blokes. We had fresh vegetables in the camp and back at the homestead, a case each of apples and oranges was shared out, once a month, amongst everyone on the station. Over time Barcoo rot became a lot less prevalent.

## 'Q' fever

I used to get an illness in the stockcamp, a sickness where I would sweat like hell, and the next minute be freezing cold and shivering. I'd ache all over and feel really rat-shit. I used to think I was going to die. When I got back to camp, from drafting or mustering, I would get in my swag and pull everything over me, the ground sheet and all. Then the next minute I'd be chucking it all off again because the perspiration would be flying out of me. That's how it would go. It didn't last that long, but while I had it I felt terrible. It would hit me quite suddenly. I'd be good and then within half an hour, really crook. I might get it at dinner time and have it until about halfway through the night. Then in the morning I might feel a bit dopey, but generally I was pretty good. I seemed to get this illness at certain yards. Windjana, was one, the Kimberley Downs homestead yard another and at Napier. When we left the Kimberley I never got it. Not for years. But when Janet and I went back up there for a visit, it hit me again. We'd spent a few days out at Napier Downs and a night at Jubilee Downs. The next day I went down with it, just like the old days, very suddenly but not as severe. I've always assumed it was 'Q' Fever, which years later I did test positive for.

## Exhaustion

The other common ailment in stockcamps was exhaustion. I remember once when the stockcamp was at Windjana Gorge. It was raining like hell. The manager had sent us out early, thinking the 'wet' was over, but it wasn't. The rains came again and everything was wet, flyblown and all pretty terrible. All of our gear was sodden and even the saddles were 'blown'. Because of the risk of snakes, Tommy Hedley, another white ringer, and I were too frightened to crawl into a cave for shelter. A lot of king browns live in that country and I've always had a healthy respect for venomous snakes. In the end we were so tired from work, the cold and wet we decided 'Bugger it'. We dragged up our saturated gear and in we went. Never mind the snakes! The swags were miserable to be in, but we climbed into them anyway, forgot about the snakes and went to sleep. We were that tired nothing else mattered. We were past caring. I really believe some bosses thought of us as engines. You know, just fill 'em up with petrol and they'll keep on going. Never mind we were buggered. They always wanted just that little bit more. At the end of the season I'd be absolutely 'had it'. Not an ounce of fat on me. No bum, just arse bones. In camp I used to make up a sort of blancmange out of cornflour, water and heaps of sugar. I'd mix the cornflour into a paste, boil up the water and sugar and then mix it all together. I'd pour it into a pannikin and eat it. I reckoned it was great gear. It gave me a bit of energy to be going on with and was really good tucker.

Towards the end of the year my energy levels got so low that, sometimes, I would just sort of go to jelly. If I jumped off to throw a bull, once I'd got him down on the ground, I'd be shaking all over. The blacks would come along and tell me to get out of it and they'd take over. Again, if a horse wanted to buck at the end of the year, or we had to chase cattle over holey ground, the same thing would happen to me. I'd be shaking from head to foot at the end of it. It wasn't anything to do with fear. We did this sort of work all season, so I was well used to it. I was simply sapped of energy. Utterly drained. It probably wasn't a very safe state to be in, doing the kind of work we did. Not that anyone worried about that kind of thing in those days. It was at times like this when I reckon some bosses thought we had a fuel tank they could just 'top up'.

## Horses

Whilst in the mustering camp our lives revolved around horses and cattle. The horses were everything to us. Not only the means by which we could get the cattle together, but they were our friends, companions and workmates as well. Over the years much of the work our horses did has been taken over by helicopters, motorbikes, fixed wing aeroplanes, bull buggies and roadtrains. Years ago everything was done by the horses and mules, even the shifting from camp to camp. There was nothing else. Cattle stations ran, literally, on 'horse power'. For this reason horse numbers were necessarily high, and ran into the hundreds on most properties.

Whilst every horse was considered to be of some value, be they stallion, breaker, brood mare or gelding there was a certain 'horse hierarchy', some being viewed as more important to us than others. For starters once a horse had been broken in, it's status lifted considerably. From that point on, if it became sick, or injured, everything possible would be done to help it, although often there was not a lot we could do.

## Colts

All newly broken-in horses are called colts, whether they're male, female, gelded or in tact. A freshly broken filly is still called a colt. Confusing, but that's how it is. A 'colt' may also be described as a 'green horse', meaning it hasn't done much work and is still learning. Colts need to be treated with care. If they're asked to do too much too quick you can ruin them for life. It doesn't matter how well a horse is broken in, if his rider 'over cooks' him too early in his career he will turn out no good. For this reason there are certain jobs that a colt shouldn't be asked to do until he has had a bit of experience. Chasing bulls is one of them. Nor should you use a colt to chase horses, or gallop him excessively after cattle, or over holey ground.

When I became a headstockman I was fortunate in being allowed the pick of the breakers, ahead of the other stockmen. My choice would usually be based on conformation, strength and looks, but there were times when I would see something in a colt I'd shy away from, no matter how good looking it was. An example of this was when a station manager, Robin Campbell, took me down to see the breakers and choose a colt. I picked a good, strong, brown gelding.

"You don't want him John. He's got an enlarged hock." Robin pointed out. "The black filly over there is the one you want."

I admit she was a good looker, but there was something about her I didn't like.

"No I don't want her." I told him. "I reckon she could be a bit dirty." Robin tried to change my mind, but I wouldn't. I was stuck on the brown gelding. He became known as Sandover and he turned out an exceptional horse, eventually becoming a night horse. A good native boy, Benn Bibingnulli, took the black filly for his 'colt'. She used to buck a bit with him during her first two seasons, but gave it away over time. She wasn't a 'dirty' horse, which generally means kicking and striking, but I saw something in her that had warned me not to take her, though I can't explain what it was.

Because station horses were broken in in such a short time, they were sort of shell-shocked. They didn't quite know what was going on. I didn't like to give my colts too much work first up. They had to work, but not gut busting work. During their first mustering round they would begin to learn everything, from following a beast, turning, balance, when to pull up and when to pick up pace. After they'd done one round, usually six or seven weeks, and had had a spell, they'd come back into the camp and that was when you first discovered what they had learnt. You'd either be very pleased, or not so pleased, but it didn't matter either way, because it's like with kids. Some pick it up quickly. Others take longer. My mare Penny was a good example of this. She wasn't properly broken in, by me, because she went lame. When she next came in I basically put the saddle on her and hopped on. She accepted it, so I rode her to let cattle out. We were shifting them. We took them through a gate into another paddock and a cow broke out of the mob. I forgot I was on a green horse, so I pulled Penny round and gave her a kick. She bucked and fell over. She was lying on the ground with me still in the saddle. I gave her a minute or two and she stood up. That was the beginning of her working life. After that, for the next four years, when you pulled her round, her head would come round, but she'd keep going straight ahead. When I was at Frazier Downs I lent her to Father Chris Saunders to ride. She was still doing this, and earned herself the name 'Rubber Neck'. Eventually, over time she came good. I used her as 'coacher' whilst horse breaking at Mandora and she became a top gymkhana horse a year later. She wasn't 'Rubber Neck' any more. Over the years Penny became one of my best horses and I've had a lot of very good ones. So it doesn't matter if a colt is a bit slow to learn. With perseverance and patience some of them will develop all the skills you want in a really good stockhorse. It is the man who first takes a colt that usually determines how much ability that horse will have.

## Mustering horses

Each stockman would have his own string of mustering horses, either chosen or allocated to him by the manager or headstockman. Depending on the ability of the rider, and the amount of work he would do, he would usually have about three or four horses in his string. Some ringers, such as the Bear boys, would be allotted an extra horse because of their workload, whilst a raw young fella, or a dying old bloke who was reluctant to gallop much, might have one less in his string. Experienced ringers were expected to have at least one colt each.

It was the responsibility of the stockman to look after his own horses, wash them down after they'd been worked, feed them, hobble them, and generally care for them. Some stockmen were more diligent than others in this regard. Their horses were supposed to be worked in rotation and it was part of a headstockman's job to ensure that this was being done. Sometimes a good, willing working horse would be ridden out of turn, if a man had a mongrel, or lazy horse in his string that he didn't like riding.

The working horses were hobbled at all times, when not being used, and allowed to graze. Early in the year they got no supplementary feed, but as the season progressed and feed became scarce they would be given a milk tin of oats and one of bran, in a nosebag, morning and night. If we happened to be in camp at dinner time they would be given a nosebag then as well. They were hobbled out at night and any rogues amongst them might also wear a bell. This was so the horse tailer could locate them more easily before dawn, although we never used horse bells if we were mustering in a new area, because it would alert the cattle to our presence.

After each round, usually six or seven weeks, the working horses were spelled, and the ringers given a new string of fresh horses. The same bronco horses, or mules, and night horses were used for each mustering round.

## Bronco horses

Bronco horses were half draught horse and were used to pull cattle, one by one, up to a bronco panel where they could be earmarked, branded and castrated. They had to be strong horses. Bronco panels aren't used anymore and bronco mules and horses are a thing of the past. In my ringing days we used them all the time if there was no drafting yard.

Two bronco horses, or mules, would work in unison, a man on each. They wore a collar and harness. There was a ring on the near side of the harness, close to the rider's left leg, to which the end of the lasso rope was tied. A stockman would lasso a young beast. The bronco horse then moved behind the panel, so that the rope slid up a sloping rail and into a groove between two posts. The horse then pulled the lassoed beast up towards the panel. As it did so, another stockman would put a hind leg-rope on the offside hock of the beast. This was passed to another man who secured it to a timber peg in the ground, and tightened it. A leg-rope was then put on the off-side front leg and passed to another stockman to secure and tighten. Both caught legs were stretched, and the bronco horse would have the beast pulled tight against the panel. At this stage someone would call 'Righto', and the horse would swing to the left to slacken the rope. The head rope was taken off before the beast hit the ground. The animal was then branded, earmarked, castrated and if necessary the tips of his horns sawn off. Once done, the leg-ropes were taken off and the beast let up. By this time the second bronco horse would be bringing the next animal up in the same manner.

With a good team of experienced men, working a bronco panel ran like a well oiled machine. Each stockman had their allotted task and with a skilful man on the hind leg-rope, which was especially important, it was possible to do sixty beasts an hour. Everyone involved knew what they had to do, so did the bronco horse. This was the only job they did and they got very good at it. If the man with the lasso missed a beast the horse would know. It learned the length of the rope and the exact distance it had to go before the animal was pulled hard against the bronco panel.

## Camp horses

In years gone by bullocks were never yarded at night, but left to camp on an open flat, minded by singing stockmen on night horses. Likewise they were never drafted through a yard. All cutting out was done in the open using camp horses. A camp horse is a very special horse and kept for this job only. All they did was draft cattle out in the open. They had to be good, pliable, intelligent horses.

## Night horses

Of all the working horses our 'night horses' were the most highly thought of. They were the most trusted and were kept for a specific role. There would generally be four 'night horses' in the camp at one time and their main job was to get the cattle back if they rushed in the night. They might also be used to help yard up, or to bring the working horses up in the morning, but apart from this they were only worked at night time. We would catch them each evening, before sundown, to stop them from sneaking away and hiding, which my night horse, Calwyn, was a bit prone to do. We would tie them loosely to a tree, their saddles on, but with girth and surcingle loosened and the surcingle over the flaps, to stop any noise. They'd have bridles on and if there was no yard, their bits would be in.

If we were worried about the yard the cattle were being held in overnight, we would ride around it on a 'night horse', for an hour singing. This was to help settle the cattle. After an hour another bloke would take over on a different 'night horse'. We would take it in turns all night. When there was no yard and the cattle were camped out on the flat, three men on 'night horses' would do night watch in shifts, whilst the fourth horse was rested. In the morning they'd be used to take the cattle off camp and they'd feed them along for a bit, until the other blokes came and took over. The 'night horses' were then let go for the day.

During the night the 'night horses' might be lying down and if the cattle rushed in the night, taking the yard, the horses would hear and stand up. We'd go to them, check the bridle, tighten girth and surcingle and hop on. We might listen for a moment, to gauge what direction the cattle had gone in, then away we'd go in the dark. We basically left everything up to the 'night horse' and just hung on, because these horses knew exactly what to do and didn't need any interference from the rider.

Calwyn was my preferred 'night horse' and I had total trust in him. Although we had some scary rides together we ended up getting the cattle back every time.

## Coachers

These horses were used for breaking in and there were generally only one or two, used for this purpose, on the station. They were a quiet, steady and utterly reliable horse, used by a breaker both for protection, whilst working on a colt, and as reassurance for the young horse. Sometimes a coacher horse would boss the youngster. They were as near to bomb proof as any horse you'd find on stations at that time.

## 'In love' with the horses

I thought very highly of a lot of the horses I rode on stations. Although I loved the ringing game, there were times when I felt like pulling out, but I was too in love with the horses to leave them. My life was on their back and I totally trusted them. If one of my horses got hurt it was my pain as well. I was the bloke asking them to do the job, if something went wrong we were in it together and most of my horses did everything I asked of them. In some instances the effort they gave was colossal and they didn't get much in return. When I had to leave a station I was always concerned for the horses and what might happen to them after I'd gone. I owned a fair few horses of my own, which I would take with me, but if I'd had my way I'd have bought a lot more, just so I could look after them and make sure they weren't ill-treated.

Some horses have certain physical characteristics which can give an indication of their temperament. For example, a horse with big ears is often a quiet natured horse. Those with a black line down their back, known as a 'Mule Line', are generally tough horses with a lot of endurance. People say a horse showing the white of his eye is bad tempered, although I've never found this to be true, whilst horses with a Roman nose were often good quiet horses and strong. Dish faced horses could be good horses, but I found some to be giggle-headed. In the hot conditions of the Kimberley black, bay and brown horses were favoured above chestnut horses, whilst those with a lot of white on them, such as a prominent blaze, were avoided. Likewise horses with black hooves were preferred over those with white hooves, which were considered too soft for the conditions. Many stations were short of horses and could not afford to be fussy, but if horses had to be purchased or there was a choice, these were some of the attributes sought.

## Equine Ailments

### *Walkabout*

Unlike mules, horses were prone to sickness and often there was nothing we could do to help them. In such cases the kindest way out for them was to shoot them. The saddest illness of all to affect them was 'walkabout'. Walkabout was most commonly seen in the working horses, caused through 'saddle disease'. That is, the horses were often run-down and overworked, making them more susceptible to illness. When we were short of horses we lost more to walkabout. It was a rolling effect. Once we got our horse numbers up we saw less of the disease. Another contributing factor was stockcamps camping in the same spot for each round of mustering, so that the area became eaten out. A shortage of feed meant the working horses would sometimes eat whatever was available, even if it was poisonous.

The most common cause of 'walkabout disease' in horses is a small grey bush called 'crotalaria crispata'. It is low growing, with inconspicuous, yellow flowers and tends to flourish where ground has been disturbed, such as along a new fence line. On some stations it is prolific, causing ongoing devastation amongst the horses, with sad outcomes for many. Another species of 'crotalaria', commonly known as 'rattlepod', is a bigger bush with yellow pea flowers and plump pods, which rattle when dry. This plant is also toxic to horses, though less so than crispata. When eaten, crotalaria affects the liver, building up over a period of time, causing irreversible damage.

When horses get 'walkabout', often the first sign indicating something is wrong, is a tendency for a horse to be a bit dopey. This may well be mistaken for tiredness. Another early sign I noticed was a certain puffiness in the hollow next to their ears, and above their eyes. An affected horse will seem as good as gold one day and the next day you know he's got it. He'll start walking. He will just walk and walk, more or less straight ahead. It will not stop walking, even if there is an obstacle in it's path. It will simply walk into it, through it or fall over it. If an unbroken horse is affected by 'walkabout' it is possible to go up to it and put your hand on it's forehead and it will just stand and lean on it. This is true of even a six or seven year old unbroken horse. It will stay standing there, indefinitely, until you move aside and let him walk on. Sometimes they will fall into a wash-away, end up on their backs, and die there. Others walk into fences. If there's a flywire door through a breezeway, they'll come in one door, through the hallway, push the door over and walk out at the other end of the building. A horse with walkabout is really sad to see. There was nothing we could do to help them, other than destroy them before they met a slow death in a gully somewhere, or tangled up in a fence.

## Whitewood poisoning

Whitewood is a small tree which produces new shoots and comes into flower when humidity levels rise towards the end of the year, before the rains come. Horses tend to eat the new shoots, which they seem to like. If they eat a certain amount and you disturb them, they behave erratically. A horse that has eaten whitewood, if he is mustered up, might go along quietly for a quarter of a mile, but will suddenly break out of the mob and take off at a hundred miles an hour. He will gallop in a wide circle. If you get in his way, he will go straight through you, even if you're on horseback. If there is a fence in his way he will gallop clean into it, sometimes with devastating injury. If he is able to gallop unimpeded, the circle gets smaller and smaller, until he's galloping more or less on the spot. He will then start to stagger and eventually fall down. He will try to get up, but will fall down again. He will bang his head against the ground severely, over and over again. It's not very nice to witness. At this stage, if at all possible, it is best to get a couple of blokes to grab him and hold him down tightly. You have to hold his head, or he will keep banging it against the ground, causing himself injury. If you can hold him for almost an hour he will gradually relax and slowly recover.

Whitewood poisoning is not fatal, unless the affected horse runs into something, or strikes his head against something sharp or too hard. There would have been a lot of horses, across the length and breadth of the station, affected by whitewood that we didn't see. It was really only when we mustered them that we came across them in this violently intoxicated state. Mules don't seem to get whitewood poisoning. I have never seen a mule with 'whitewood poisoning' or 'walkabout'.

## Swamp cancers

These are like a cancer that grows on the skin. At first it might be a little cut. Swamp cancers mainly occur on the front of the horse's chest, neck or on their fetlocks. They tend to develop in the 'wet' season and grow very rapidly. Some horses come in at the start of the season with swamp cancers as big as a dinner plate. Such cases were hopeless. If the swamp cancer was small enough we would try to cut them out and put sulphur on them. We would endeavour to keep the flies off, but this was pretty difficult. If the cancer was on their legs we might put bluestone on, to burn it off a bit more. This treatment was pretty savage and we would often have to put a twitch on the horse to do the job. The horse would be watched closely and treated every day for months. We were sometimes able to cure the small swamp cancers, but the bigger ones were difficult to beat and often the horse had to be destroyed.

## Mules

Mules are by a 'Jack' donkey, out of a mare. Mules can't breed. If a mare has a foal, born into the working horses where mules are present, the mules will fight over the foal. Unless you can get it out of there, the foal generally ends up being killed while the mare tries to protect it, and the mules try to steal it. In the same way, if a mob of donkeys are living near where you have working mules, and there is a donkey foal in the mob, the mule will break his hobbles to go and run with the donkeys, and try to steal the baby donkey.

In my opinion mules are really great animals. In the early days, if it weren't for mules, the Kimberley would have been battling to get going. They were used for many tasks. There used to be heaps of mules on stations, and although they're a thing of the past now, they were once an integral part of station life and had many uses. There were pack mules, cart mules, mustering mules and bronco mules. A good bronco mule knew as much as the rider. A mule could do almost anything, but they were never used as night horses, as far as I am aware. Neither did I use mules for cutting out.

Mules are a tough animal, their life span longer than that of a horse and they didn't seem to get sick from 'walkabout' or be affected by whitewood poisoning. They were resilient and had greater endurance than the horses. Where our horses would do half a day's mustering, often the mules worked for a whole day, if necessary, without ill effect.

Admittedly mules were a bit harder to break in, and took a bit more time to educate initially, but overall they were more economical because, once broken, you had them for longer. If mules, out of good mares, were broken in at three year old, there would have been nothing wrong with having forty working mules in the stockcamp. Once you've got a good 'going' mule, you've got him for life. You could ride around Australia on him if you wanted.

A lot of blokes would live on mules because they were so hardy. If a mule didn't do what they wanted they would ride him more and more, in an effort to make him conform. If a mule developed a sore back he wouldn't turn to the sore side. Then he'd be considered more of 'a mongrel bastard of a thing' and be hated more by his rider. This wasn't the mules fault. It didn't make a good mule, because then you wouldn't be able to catch him, which caused further annoyance. In some stockcamps I've been in, a lot of mules never got a feed, so all round they didn't really get a very fair go.

When I was a kid on Meda we had mules you could pack. One in particular, Daniel, would set off with packs with no-one in charge of him. He'd go as far as the first dinner camp, pull up and wait until we came along. Later, after dinner, he'd go on to where our night camp was and wait for us there, standing in the shade of a tree until we came and took the packs off and set up camp.

Although mules have been badly condemned over the years they are not at all stupid. Certainly they are cunning and some mules could be really 'dirty', but often this was because they were out of a 'dirty' mare. Some station blokes only put 'mongrel', bad tempered mares with the Jack donkey. I've never understood why. What did they expect to get? If they had put good mares to the 'Jack' instead, there would have been a better chance of getting a good mule from her. As it was many station mules were ill tempered, intractable, and wasted a lot of our time. I've always said, if a mule ever tries to kick you and he misses, don't think it was you who got away. You didn't. The mule didn't want you, that's all. A mule very rarely misses his target. If he wants to kick you, he'll get you all right. But a good mule can be as quiet as any horse and there were mules that even kids could ride.

## Poker and mule races

We once had a quiet little mule in the stockcamp, called Poker. If a beast broke out and you went to turn him round, he'd go ten yards and stop. That's all he'd do. I got pretty sick of this mule, so I ended up getting a good stingy stick and I'd give him a real good touch up, down the shoulders and down the flanks. He ended up learning he had to do his job. Eventually I took him into town and raced him in the mule races. He finished the course. So he'd gone from doing ten yards then dead stop, to completing two and four furlong mule races.

Mule races used to be a big thing in the Kimberley when I was a kid. When I was a young man I rode in mule races for several years and I saw a lot of funny things. Some mules would go to the start, then when the starter let them go they'd turn around and go the opposite way. Others would take a short cut across the race course and you'd meet them at the winning post. Other, better educated mules, would stay on the race track until they got into the straight, then, when they heard the crowd cheering they would prop and go back the other way.

One time we took our mules to Derby for the Picnic Races and I won. Second place was awarded to a mule who had come down outside the running rail, along the inside of the racecourse. A couple of other mules cut across the middle, then came onto the track at the beginning of the running rail. They'd been a fair way back when they left the track, but after cutting across they got up with the leaders. So then there was a big argument. A fellow stockman, Tommy Hedley, came to me and said, "Can you tell the stewards that the mule they've given second place to wasn't even on the race track?" So I went and told them and they changed all the placings.

Several different stations had good pliable race mules. GoGo had two, Bindii and Prickle. Fossil Downs had a black mule called Crow and Lansdowne had a good galloping mule.

Meda also had quite a few good mules. When Dave Ledger was managing Meda he sold all the mules. When I heard about this I went and asked if I could buy them. He said they were already sold. I asked if I could better the price, but he said 'No'. Kimberley Downs had mules too, and when I was a young fellow, working for Robin Campbell, the station bought a mob of mules off Tablelands, which we broke in. There was a big black gelding mule amongst them, about six years old. (Despite being infertile mules have to be gelded or they become really savage and impossible to control.) I chose him before they'd even finished breaking in. I made a big mistake there. He was a good, strong, angry mule and he used to try to wipe me off on trees. I rode 'Indonesian' for a couple of years, then he disappeared. The natives told me later they'd seen him up past Inglis Gap, sixty miles away. Then he'd been seen further east still. He and two or three others were heading back home to Tablelands. In that same mob, there were some younger mules that turned out to be very good. One in particular was a big black ginny mule called Sabrina. Sabrina was about fifteen hands, really good looking, with a nice body and head. I reckon she was out of someone's good thoroughbred mare. Sabrina could really cover ground and she was a good mule with cattle. I reckon if she had been taken straight into the races when she was broken in, or a year later and forced to conform, she could have beaten anything. Another good mule was LayLay. She had a bit of age on her, but she was a good cattle mule also. Both Sabrina and LayLay went on to race and though they could beat my mule, Cheeky, at the station, neither would perform properly at the race track. Tin Lid also came from Tablelands. Michael Bear had him from a colt. He went in to race as a young mule and unlike the two ginny mules, Tin Lid took to the race track all right.

## Cheeky the mule

Cheeky was a very good mule and I ended up buying him when I left Napier. Ray Jorgenson broke him in and he pelted Jorgy, saddle and all, while being broken. Cheeky had a fair bit of character. I'd try and saddle him up and he'd chuck the saddle. I'd get a collar rope and eventually get it on him. Then he'd lie on the ground and he'd take it off. I'd be swearing and cursing with all the messing around he was causing, getting angrier and angrier. Finally I'd chuck the saddle cloth on him roughly. Then I'd basically chuck the saddle at him, and land it on his back. Instead of 'going off' he'd stand there, as good as gold, and let me saddle him up, as if to say 'Ha Ha. I made you cross and I've made you work hard. Ha Ha.' When I first saddled Cheeky and got on him, I'd gallop him for a hundred yards and back, to take the sting out of him. He rarely bucked with me, though he bucked other people off. With cattle he was absolutely brilliant. If a beast took off and you weren't watching he'd be gone. He'd turn on a thruppence.

After I left Napier I took him to Meda where Ledger was supposed to be looking after him. One day Cheeky came into the yard and a native boy recognised him as mine. He asked Ledger if he could ride him. Ledger told him he could. They got Cheeky saddled up and were riding out from the station, when a few hundred yards down the track Cheeky decided this was enough. He unwound, decked his rider and tried to wipe him out. After that Cheeky got left behind and wasn't ridden again.

Cheeky was a very good race mule and I had a lot of wins with him. I tell people I had seventeen runs, sixteen wins and one loss with him. The loss was the first race I ever took him to. It was up the length of the straight, two furlongs. Cheeky jumped out at the start, then he got 'stuck into it' and bucked. Eventually I got him going, but a Meda mule, called Sally, ridden by Bob Jack, beat him by a nose. So in that race he got knocked off. Then we had a four furlong race. I jumped him out in that and Cheeky won it. He raced for quite a few years and he won every year.

At the mule races in Derby they would hold a calcutta, when blokes would bid for a mule and whichever mule won, the bloke who'd bid for it got the cash. One time Tommy Hedley and I decided to swap mules. I rode his mule and he rode Cheeky. A lot of the people were too silly to realise that I wasn't riding the right mule. They all backed me instead of the mule and Tommy won on Cheeky. We weren't very popular for that caper.

One year a girl was loaned one of our horses which she fell off during a race. The horse bolted and I took off on another horse to fetch it back. It had gone out to Myall's Bore, where we were camped. I brought it back a couple of miles to the race course. By the time I got back with it they had already run the mule race. It didn't matter because Joe Rodgers had saddled up Cheeky, in my absence, ridden him and won with him.

They were a pretty serious business, these mule races, because you'd go to line up and you sort of knew that people were trying to cut you off at the start. There were no starting gates of course. We were just in a line and 'Go'. They were two furlong or four furlong races. I knew in this particular race, which was over four furlongs, that they were going to try and cut Cheeky off. By this time he was about eight years old and knew what the game was all about. We lined up. I noticed these people waited till I lined up, then they came either side of me, so before the starter said 'Go' I swung Cheeky around and went to the outside. The blokes followed me, so then I knew they were going to try and bump me. When you jumped Cheeky out at the start he jumped out like a race horse. One of the other mules was trying to keep him out, but I got in front with him, stayed in front and won the race.

Cheeky got that smart that when you got to the finish line you had to keep him on the track till everyone had pulled up. Otherwise he'd take a sharp right and shoot off, straight into the saddling paddock. If someone was coming up behind him he'd cut him off. I really valued Cheeky and had him for many years. In latter years, when I was managing Meda, if I had cause to sack someone and they had the shits on with me, they'd threaten to shoot Cheeky, because they knew how much I thought of him.

# Cattle

For most of us in the stockcamp the main purpose of having good horses and mules was so that we could get and hold more cattle. We took pride in the ability of our horses, almost as much as we did in our own agility and fearlessness. If there were cattle to be got, no matter how wild, I wanted them. Over time I built up a team of ringers who wanted them almost as much as I did. If it meant mustering by moonlight we did. Or galloping through darkness after a 'rush', we did. While mustering by day, we'd happily risk life and limb galloping over holey ground, or through the scrub, and around termite mounds. We'd negotiate our way up over rocky ridges and boulder strewn hillsides, if there were cattle to be got by doing so, crossing billabongs, washaways, creeks and watercourses if the circumstances called for it. We'd do almost anything in the pursuit of cattle. But mustering was not an unruly helter-skelter of man, horse and beast. There was a pattern, a method, rules and discipline.

## *Coacher cattle*

Coachers is a term used to describe a group of educated cattle already in hand, into which other cattle can be mustered. The coachers are held together by a couple of horsemen, whilst other stockmen run in newly mustered cattle to put in with the coacher mob. Usually the new arrivals will quieten and remain amongst the already settled mob, enabling the 'ringers' to go in search of more cattle to bring in. Sometimes a beast refuses to stay and will either burst through the mob and keep going, or try and break out of the mob and slip away. When this happens stockmen will try to put them back with the coachers. If they can't the beast might be thrown. If we couldn't get a bull, or bullock, to go where we wanted it would also be thrown, if at all possible. During my stockcamp days we threw a lot of cattle, many of them bulls and big mickies. It required skill and stamina, but whilst being dangerous and sometimes terrifying, it was a high adrenalin activity many of us enjoyed.

## Bull throwing

In my mid teens, because there was no money for full grown bulls, they were pretty well shot on sight. Young bulls, that is eighteen months to two year old, would be castrated then let go, but a lot of them didn't end up going in the shipping mob. Being cut late, they were a bit too stagy.

When you're holding cattle and a bull leaves the mob, if you're on an experienced horse, you jump your horse out and try to put him back into the mob. If he says 'I'm not going', you let him run more or less where he wants, but if it's into bad country, you try to manoeuvre him off it. Some bulls you can shoulder, but some you can't because they'll whip around and horn you or your horse. These are particular bulls. I can't tell you how I know, but I, and most stockmen know, when not to put a horse onto a certain bull. You never try to put a bull back on a young horse. A young horse will do it with heifers and smaller cattle, until he learns what you want of him, but it is very dangerous to handle full grown bulls off a young horse.

A bull who leaves the mob and won't be put back in would be thrown. There were two ways of doing this. Either you race your horse right up alongside him, grabbing his tail as you do so, with a half hitch around your hand, and accelerate your horse very quickly. When you can't hang onto the bull's tail any longer you give him one last reef. The bull's back end will come round towards the horse. Another horseman will be behind you. You yell out 'Righto' and then let go. As the bull hits the ground and rolls, the other horseman jumps off. He grabs the bulls upper hind leg, pulling it backwards and upwards. This is to prevent the bull from getting his bottom front leg on the ground and getting up. You will already be off your horse and will have raced up to help the other bloke. You'll put your knees into the bull's back, at the top of his shoulder blade, folding and lifting the upper front leg backwards, to roll him more. This ensures he can't get any traction from the bottom front leg. If he is throwing his head about and is a nobby bull, you put your right foot at the base of his ear to hold him still. If it's a horny bull, you put your foot at the base of his horn. The bull is held like this for a while until he stops fighting. The bloke on the hind leg will have a belt ready. He will quickly wrap it around the bull's hind legs, three or four times, and buckle it up, with no slack in it. We would wear wide, leather belts, with good strong buckles just for this purpose, both around our waist and over our shoulders and chest. The reason for wrapping it three to four times around the bull's legs was so that the tongue of the buckle wouldn't tear through the holes of the belt, thus loosening it. Depending on how many bulls and bullocks we'd thrown, if we had a belt spare, we might also strap his front legs.

The second method of throwing a bull is to run him, on horseback, until he begins to tire. When this happens his gait will change. You don't jump off straight away, because he's got too much run, but when his gait changes, you race your horse up as close as you're game enough to. So now you're riding right up behind him and you can jump off. You don't pull on your horses mouth to stop him. You put your hand on his neck and just get off, as if he's standing still. He'll just go 'boom' like Roy Rogers' horse. His back legs will go under him and he'll pull up. With him stopping he propels you, so when you hit the ground you're already running. You always keep your hat with you. Next you grab the tail of the bull and get a wrap around your hand with the hair. You run up alongside him. Most bulls get so angry they whip around the same side as you're on, to try and gore you. When this happens you pull his bum to his head. Now he's got all his weight on one side and down he goes. When he hits the ground he'll usually kick up. His leg will come up in the air and you grab it, flick the tail around under his hock and lay back on it. You have to half roll, so that he's on his back and can't get his front leg onto the ground. If he does he can stand up on you, so you have to keep him half rolled on his back, with his front leg just off the ground. While you've got him there, he'll fight you, but he's had a run and is tiring. After a while there will be a breathing pattern. The bull will struggle, then he'll stop to get his wind. Then he'll struggle again. You take notice of this. You wear a heavy leather belt round your waist, but not through the belt keepers. As you're taking notice of the breathing pattern, you take your belt off. Then when he stops fighting you deftly get the belt around his hind legs. Although one bloke can do this on his own it isn't really advisable.

Usually there were two of us. If you are on your own you only secure his hind legs. Although he can get up, even with his hind legs tied, you know that when he stops fighting you can let his legs go, get back to your horse, get on and be gone. The bull is lying there tied up. Then he will sit up, and nobody is there. He will just sit there.

He might try to stand up and he'll probably fall over a couple of times, till he learns he can't stand. But beware. If you go back for any reason, say you've dropped your pocket knife and think you'll go and retrieve it, he will spin around and can run fifty yards, flat out, even with his hind legs tied. So that can be a trap. Often we didn't tie the front legs, because the bull wouldn't be able to stand up at all. If he's left there too long, on the hot ground, he'd never get up again. He'd die. As the purpose of all this was to catch him to send to market, it would be a bit silly. So it would depend on how long we thought he'd be left, whether we'd tie his front legs or not.

When you go back to get the bull later on, there will be two of you. This is because he will jump up and chase you, so one bloke will be there, on a horse, to distract him. Or you both dismount and both annoy him. When the bull goes to turn he will fall over, so then you whiz in, grab him and deal with him. We would earmark him, take four or five inches off his horns, depending on the size, so he's not too knocked around and stressed. If you think you can get the bull back into the coachers and he'll accept it and stay in the mob, you do that. This is because it's better to try and get him to a yard and brand him, than to let him go with just an earmark. If another station gets him later, and he's not branded, they can take the ear off with the earmark in it, destroy the ear, slap their brand on him and then he's theirs. You've done all the hard work for nothing. Sometimes if a bull was too hard to handle, we would castrate him, making him into a stag. He would then be kept, in the hope that next year he'd remember what he got and be more civil, which is what quite often happened.

You can basically get any bull, sometime, somewhere. If luck has it you've got a bulling cow in the mob then he'll stay, tracking her. If you're close enough to the yards, he's in the yard before he realises he should have left an hour ago. These wild bulls, after you've had them a couple of days, become very quiet. Bullocks take a bit longer to steady down.

Once, we were getting control of a thrown bull when a horse went over the bull, just as it was standing up. Straddling the beast, it was pivoting around on the bull's back, the rider still in the saddle. For a moment the horse's front feet would touch the ground, then the bull would rock, so the hind feet would make contact with the ground, briefly. The bull was just too high for the horse to get off. Eventually it's hooves touched ground long enough for the bull to get out from underneath it. It was as funny as could be, for everyone except the man and horse, that is.

Although throwing bulls was almost an every day occurrence it was not a game. It was really highly dangerous. I was fortunate to have a team of competent men always willing to back me up, or me them. I hated to see any bull get away and would do my utmost to get him if I could. It was a high adrenalin activity, thrilling, sometimes frightening and for the owners financially rewarding.

## Cattle afflictions

### Ticks and red water

When I was a kid on the station a lot of coastal cattle, during the dry season, would be covered in ticks. There would be no hair on their flanks, necks or shoulders. On their necks there would be a slightly bloody, but mainly yellow discharge resembling egg yolk, caused by the ticks, that would crack where the wrinkles were. A lot of bull calves had so many ticks on their purse, we'd have to shave them off before we could castrate them. They would be just covered in them. Dad used to have wires with bags wrapped around them, soaked in diesel and kerosene, so the cattle could rub themselves on them when they came in for a drink. We must have lost a lot of cattle from tick. Many would become too weak to get a drink at a billabong to be able to walk out again. The tick really pulled them down and their skin was not good from this scourge. The tick caused a condition called 'red water', so named because the cattle would have blood in their urine. They'd fall away, (lose condition) fairly quickly and become very aggressive. Red water bullocks will charge anything that's moving.

When I was a youth working on Meda, a mob of GoGo bullocks were sent down to us, ready to be shipped the next year. After they arrived they started getting red water. My father decided to shift those still not affected to Charley's Paddock, which was thought to be clean (free of tick). You couldn't travel or shift cattle affected with red water, because they'd just bail up and charge anything that moved. They fell away very quickly and a lot of them died from it. Although there were dips on Meda, at Number One Bore and at 'The Dip' crossing, I never saw them in use when I was a kid.

There was a set of drafting yards and dipping yards at Myall's Bore, just outside Derby, where cattle were taken before being shipped. Because Myall's Bore yards were frequented regularly by drovers, stockmen and others, a phone had been installed for public use, behind a nearby boab tree. Once a lady and her family, including a couple of kids, were driving out to the airport when their car broke down. Knowing the telephone was near at hand, they began walking over to it to ring for help. A bullock, who was affected with red water, had been dropped off there because it was ill. It saw the group walking across and went for them. The family ran back to their motorcar, and clambered in. The bullock put a few dents in the vehicle for them, causing a big panic. After that they were too frightened to get out again and had to wait, in the heat, until eventually someone came along and helped them.

In the bullock paddock on Meda there was a small herd of shorthorn cattle, maybe fifty head, that always seemed to be fatter, shinier and clean of tick. This was when there were still ticks around, but there were none on them. I think they must have had some resistance in their breeding which kept them free of tick. I mentioned this to Tim Emanuel one day and he said another manager had said the same thing. That there was a mob of cattle down there that never had ticks on them. If we'd known more we should probably have got that little herd and bred a resistant strain from them. Tick seem to have more or less gone out of the Kimberley, though there were still a few on Meda in the early eighties. Brahman and Santa Gertrudis cattle don't seem as susceptible to tick, as shorthorns.

Horses can also be affected by tick, but not as severely as cattle. I believe this is because horses sweat and cattle don't. Mostly it was working horses, that became a bit run-down, who suffered from tick infestation. When this happened we would get warm water from the cooked salt beef and pour it all over the horse. The salt and melted fat in it made the ticks fall off.

## Buffalo fly

Buffalo fly used to tickle the cattle up. This biting fly would take the hair off around the cattle's eyes and on their dewlap, leaving bare patches susceptible to sores. When we were drafting cattle off a horse, often the horses were reluctant to go back into the mob, to bring out another beast, because of the buffalo flies. They would stamp their feet, their tail would be twitching and they'd be trying to bite themselves. The buffalo fly would also bite us, behind our ears and on our neck. It wasn't very good, but the job had to be done.

## Pink eye

As the season progressed and the country became drier and dustier cattle used to get a condition known as 'pink eye'. Sometimes we might have steers and mickey bulls in the mob, who we would be holding for up to six weeks, until we could take them back to a paddock. (There were very few paddocks on stations in my day, it was mainly open bush.) In situations like this, when they were exposed to dusty yards each night, 'pink eye' became a problem for them. In severe cases it could cause blindness. Bullocks who lost the sight in one eye would generally be used as killers (be shot for meat). This was because they were prone to get a fright, which in turn might lead to a 'rush'. It was best not to have them in the mob if we could help it. Horses suffered from 'pink eye' also, but we used to treat them with ointment, similar to that used for conjunctivitis in humans. The hotter and dustier the conditions became, the more prevalent 'pink eye' was.

## Calving

The gestation period for cattle is the same as for humans, nine months. Cows get in calf when on a rising plain of nutrition, which in the Kimberley generally meant during the 'wet' season when there was plenty of green feed. Calving would then take place towards the end of the following 'Dry', when feed was scarce and natural waters drying up. As the calves were nourished entirely by their mothers during the first weeks of their life, the lack of feed was not a problem for them, though wet cows fell away rapidly and were a sorry sight towards the end of the year. Once the monsoon starts the country comes away rapidly, germination commences almost immediately, and within days a green tinge is evident. In no time at all there is feed aplenty and stock begin to flourish.

Sometimes if we had significant 'winter rain', that is rain during June or July, normally our 'Dry' time, cows might get in calf then, if there was good green feed around. This would cause them to start dropping calves towards the end of the next 'wet' or the very beginning of the next 'dry' and everything would be out of whack for them.

Mustering when there are very young calves around can be problematic. They cannot keep pace with the rest of the mob and their mothers try to hang back. Helicopter mustering is particularly hard on small calves. If a calf is dropped off from the rest of the mob it will almost certainly be killed by dingoes. I always preferred to do several short musters, rather than one long muster, because it was easier on the weaker cattle and the calves, not to mention the working horses.

## Bogging

Towards the end of the season, especially in dry years, cattle can become very weak. Food is scarce and natural waters dry up, or recede, leaving treacherous muddy edges. Thirsty cattle enter billabongs to drink, only to become bogged when they try to walk back out. Losses can be high and death can be slow. If we came across a stricken beast and it was beyond help, we would put it out of it's misery. There is a place at the back of the neck, where you can insert your pocket knife, nick the spinal cord and kill a beast instantly. It is called pithing. It is safe, swift and humane and apart from shooting a stricken beast, is the best way to end it's life.

## Killers and strangers

Cattle that were shot for meat are called 'killers'. On cattle stations there was a loose understanding that if you had a 'stranger', that is a beast belonging to another station, on the place it was fair game to shoot it for a 'killer,' if it was at all suitable. This practice was justified because of a firm belief that your neighbour was doing the same thing. Even honest and otherwise respectable men would happily shoot a beast they knew was not theirs. Nobody liked to shoot one of their own bullocks, or spayed cows if they could possibly avoid it. The general rule was 'knock' someone else's if you can. When I got to manage stations, if I thought the neighbour was straight I wouldn't touch his cattle, but if I thought he wasn't, well that was another matter. If the station meat supply was running low I would either take a bloke with me and get a 'killer' myself, or send a reliable man to do the job. My men were well aware that there were a few rules, should it be necessary to kill one of our own. I didn't like them shooting pregnant cows, big bullocks, or quiet cattle. I was fairly choosy about what I killed, so if I went it might take me two or three days before I found one that was suitable. Often I'd get up early in the morning and travel out into the wild areas. If we saw a bullock that put it's head up and looked ready to take off, we'd race up and shoot it, 'bang', right behind the ear. We'd bleed it, drop the guts out, quarter it, but leave the skin on. We'd cover the meat with bushes, or small leafy branches, to keep the flies off and take it back to the homestead. Because some of the killers were nine year old, we'd hang them in our cool room for up to a fortnight before cutting them up. Leaving the hide on stopped drips of condensation from tainting the meat and turning it green. By the time we came to eat it the beef was really good and tender. Sometimes the bosses, or the owners, would say 'Don't you ever get a crook killer Wellsy?' as though I were killing their best, but I wasn't. I was killing what we couldn't get with the helicopter and we couldn't muster with horses.

In stockcamps we didn't have the luxury of hanging our meat till it was tender, though if we got a killer sometimes I would get the rump and roll it up in my swag by day, and hang it in a tree at night. I'd keep it as long as I could before it went green and it would be really good tucker. Generally though we would eat freshly killed meat, when we had the chance, no matter how tough it was, just to have a change from endless meals of salt beef. In those days it all seemed like good tucker to us. We definitely weren't difficult to please.

## Droving

Before roadtrains came into the country, sale cattle had to be walked in to the port at Derby for shipment. This was called 'droving'. In some cases it was undertaken by stockmen from the station, in others, especially over longer distances, by contract drovers. I was fortunate to see the last of the droving days and to have had the opportunity of taking bullocks 'on the road'.

If we went droving with packs there were usually two men with the horse plant. One would be the cook, one the horse tailer. Then there would be about six stockmen. If we took the truck with us, instead of packs, we still had two men with the horses, but the truck driver would be the cook

We would walk the mob first thing in the morning, in the cool, then steady them down a bit and let them spread out and feed along. Once it got warm we'd pull up for dinner camp. This was usually on a creek, or billabong, so the cattle could drink. Later, when the cattle began to move about a bit we'd get going again, but first we'd push them onto water for a chance to have another drink, because their next opportunity wouldn't be until noon the following day. After that we'd feed them along until we got to camp. The cook and horse tailer would have arrived before us and set up camp. There would always be a couple of trees at the camp site and the four night horses would be tied up to one of them. We'd come onto camp just on dark. A couple of the blokes would be sent in ahead of us to have a break, whilst the other three or four stockmen would bring the cattle in.

The cook and horse tailer would do 'first watch' on night horses, while we had tea and rested. After two hours, the next two blokes who'd come into camp early, would do their watch. Each man knew when it was his turn. He'd take his night horse, always ready saddled, tied up and waiting, and ride slowly out to the mob in a diagonal line. This was so as not to startle the mob. It was an unwritten rule, known and understood by every stockman, when camping with cattle. Another was never to cross between the cattle and the campfire, to avoid casting any shadow. All bungs on drums were loosened, and surcingles went over the saddle flaps of the night horses, so there would be no sudden noise should a horse shake itself, or a drum expand or contract. Whilst on watch stockmen would sing, or make some other noise, though never sudden or sharp, as they rode around the mob. The night horse sees and knows when a beast wanders out of the mob in the dark and will move about diligently keeping the herd together. They walk almost continuously. They hardly seem to need the man on their back, trying desperately to stay awake, crooning softly till his two hour watch ends. In the dark roan and white cattle are especially hard to spot, a red bullock being much easier. But the night horse has no difficulty. He is an invaluable and highly regarded member of the team.

When on the 'road' we would usually camp at the same 'camps' each trip, unless it was eaten out. We never made camp on 'drummy' ground as this would spook the herd. Occasionally we might come across a good looking 'camp' and consider pulling up there, but usually the older blokes, good old blacks, would tell you 'not to camp here boss, 'dis place no good', meaning it had hollow areas below the surface that might startle the cattle and cause a rush. All my droving trips were good, we had enough feed and we always had water. Other blokes sometimes had it harder, with no water for maybe two days. When this happened they would need to pull up a fair distance from the water trough, split the mob into small manageable groups and then take them in to water in stages, so they didn't break the trough.

When droving the manager would telegram, or phone, the stations through which the drovers would pass, notifying them of the date they would be entering and exiting the property. This was done for each station, until the drovers reached Crown Land. As the drovers and their mob approached, the manager, or one of his men, would ride out to meet them, check their waybills and have a look at the cattle. Although it was never said, this was to see that no strangers were in the mob and that they hadn't 'picked up' any that didn't belong to them on their way through. Droving bullocks was a big responsibility but it was also an enjoyable experience, one I would not have missed.

*Relaxing at Hawkstone camp. L-R Les Blake, sprawled across our 'kitchen table'! Phil Le Lievre smiling and me curled up fast asleep. circa 1962*

*Meda mule wagon. Photo courtesy of D. Pollard.*

*Native stockman on Meda bronco mule 'Skipper'. Photo courtesy of D. Pollard*

*Native stockman on Meda bronco mule 'Polly'. Photo courtesy of D. Pollard.*

*Native stockmen work a bronco panel. Billy Munroe on left.*

*A bull being pulled up to bronco panel by a mule, (out of picture). L-R Mickey Thomas, Ralph Clifton, unknown, Billy Williams, me on the bull's tail and Tommy May running in to assist.*

*Me on 'Cheeky' for his first mule race.*

*Willie Lennard and I getting a killer.*

*A bit of fun at Windjana Gorge. A native stockman practices for the rodeo.*

*The public telephone at Myall's Bore was in this boab tree. Photo courtesy of D. Pollard.*

*The rail track and long race to the Derby wharf. Photo taken during a locust plague.*

*View of old Derby looking from Loch Street towards the goods sheds and jetty.*

*Cattle in the long race, approaching the ship at Derby wharf. Note the tide is in.*

# CHAPTER FIVE

# KIMBERLEY DOWNS

*Take me to where the kite hawks wheel,*
*Over station paddock and plain,*
*Let me hear again the dingo's call,*
*And the curlew's sad refrain.*

## Paddy Le Lievre

Paddy Le Lievre was the manager of Kimberley Downs who persuaded me to leave my job as brickies' labourer, return to the Kimberley, and go back to the life of a ringer. I had known Paddy most of my life. His eldest son was a friend of mine and his wife, an Ah Chee, was a lovely lady held in high regard by everyone, including my mother. When Mum spoke about Edie Le Lievre she would always say 'She was a lady.' Paddy Le Lievre could seem gruff at times, but was well respected and liked by the blacks. He spoke in a way that others couldn't, without seeming rude or offensive.

One day he was dealing out stores when Edie, who was doing the cooking, yelled out to him.

"Pat can you send a bag of flour over?"

"Yeah" He called back, saying to a native bloke standing nearby, "Here, take this bag of flour over to the kitchen."

After a while the black fella, who was also called Paddy, was still standing around outside and nothing happened. When Edie yelled out again, "Pat where's that bag of flour?" Paddy Le Lievre said to the black fella, "Haven't you taken that bag of ----- flour up? Grease your arse and slip along. Hurry up or I'll knock you down." And the black fella turned to Paddy and said, "By Chris', I like t'chee you try!" Normally a black fella wouldn't have said that to his boss, but by then Paddy Le Lievre was old and pretty much buggered. The story went around the station and was much enjoyed by all for a long time.

When I first arrived at Kimberley Downs, or K.D. as the locals often call it, I slept in the house where Paddy and Edie lived. Also staying at the homestead that night was a bloke called Robin Campbell, his wife Mary and their two children, Bruce and Heather. I was told Robin would be taking over as manager and that Paddy Le Lievre was going across to run Leopold. This was the first I'd heard about a change of manager and it came as a bit of a surprise. The next morning I was run out to the stockcamp at Munjaweela.

Paddy's eldest son, Phil, was running the stockcamp. I was as fit as a buck rat in those days. Really mobile. I think Phil Le Lievre and the blokes got a bit of a surprise. If I jumped off for a bull, or a bullock, I'd chase it, on foot, for up to a kilometre and eventually I'd pull it down. They couldn't believe it. Phil used to be amazed.

"Well" I said, "I was a brickies labourer and nearly dead every day from work, then I went to football training two nights a week, and I played matches on weekends." I was in really good shape in those days. I hadn't yet started smoking and drinking at that time and the physical work on K.D. ensured I remained in peak condition.

## A bad day at the office

We were out mustering with Phil running the camp, and we came onto a billabong between the Barker River and the Lennard River, where we stopped for dinner camp. Phil used to give his cattle a drink of water at dinner camp. There were two bulls there. One was a big strong red bull, with sharp horns. They stayed in the mob while we had dinner, but I said to the blokes, "If that red bull goes, he's mine." After lunch I saddled up a mare called Darl'. She was a race mare, privately owned by Paddy Le Lievre. We were moving the mob off the water when this bull decided to leave. I was on the wrong side of the cattle when he decided to go, so I rode right around the mob. Being on a race mare I easily passed all the other blokes. I jumped off and grabbed the bull by the tail, wrapping the hair around my hand. I went to go to his left side to tip him over, but a native bloke, called Rastus, on a mare called Roma, had ridden up onto his right side. The bull flicked around to have a go at Roma and in doing so took my feet clean out from under me, sending me rolling over and over like a forty four gallon drum, the hair of his tail still in my hand. I don't think that bull even knew I was there. If he had registered I was, and had whipped around the other way I was 'gone'. Having lost my footing I had no hope of getting out of it. We lost that bull and never got him, ever.

Half an hour later a bullock broke out of this same mob and headed for a dry billabong. I was best positioned to put him back in the mob. He ran along the billabong, whilst I was above him on higher ground. Then the bullock headed across the dry billabong to the other side. As the ground was solid, I decided to cross twenty yards wide of him, hoping to turn him once we were on the other side. I asked the mare for a bit more pace to catch up a bit of ground, but where we were crossing, unbeknown to me, there was a crust and it was boggy underneath. The mares hooves broke through the crust and she came to a pretty sudden stop. I went over the top of her and landed on the rough, cattle trodden surface, scoring a good few grazes. The mare floundered about a bit and came out OK, her legs coated with mud. The bullock by this time had gained too much ground, so I let him go and returned to the main mob.

Later the same day we were crossing the Lennard River. We had quite a big mob of cattle at this stage. When we went into the river crossing, some cattle were turning off and following the bank down the river. There were supposed to be men there to keep them going straight across, so they couldn't sneak away, but there weren't. I was on the tail. As I neared the crossing I saw what was happening, so I galloped along the bank until I thought I was in front of them, with the intention of blocking them and turning them back. I rode the mare Darl' down a single file cattle pad into the dry river bed. These ramps were only wide enough for one beast at a time. When I got to the bottom I came across a two year old mickey sneaking along the bottom of the river bank. Just prior to this Phil and his crew, had been knocking down mickey bulls. Wild, totally uneducated cattle, cutting and earmarking them, but not de-horning them. This mickey had not long been knocked down, had his balls cut out and been earmarked. He still had his horns and he had the shits on. We spotted each other at the same time. I couldn't back the mare up the bank and as I tried to jump her forward, whack, he put the horns straight into her, behind her ribs. Once spotted I had no hope of getting us out of harm's way. Having done the deed the angry mickey continued on down the river.

When we had got the cattle over the crossing I got off and had a look at the mare. She had been badly gored. I pulled the saddle off her and carrying it, was leading her back towards camp when Paddy Le Lievre rolled up in the Land Rover. When he saw it was his mare he asked what happened and I told him. I didn't tell him Phil hadn't cut the horns off. Paddy just wheeled around and left. So I thought 'bugger the saddle'. I put the saddle down and led the mare back to camp. I washed her down, to get the mud from the billabong off her. I cleaned the wound as best I could with soap and water, putting kerosene in it as an antiseptic. There was nothing more I could do for her. I got another horse and rode back to pick up the saddle I had left. I was feeling pretty wretched. The next morning she was dead.

Despite Darl' having been Paddy's personal race mare, bought from down south, this incident was never ever mentioned by anyone. But it hurt. She was a good little mare, with a good mouth and good brakes. When something like this happens to a good horse, everyone feels it. If it's a mongrel bastard of a thing, like some horses I rode, that was a different matter. You were allotted your mustering horses and sometimes, when they were being run through the yard, the manager would ask 'who wants this?' There'd be dead silence. Someone had to take it, so if no one volunteered it would just be allocated to some unlucky sod. Then later, if it met a sad end it didn't really shake a rivet, but Darl' didn't fall into this category and losing her was a sad business for all of us.[1]

---

1  It was usual practice for everybody, who jumped off to do throwing, to all have a horn saw on their saddle. Once a beast had been thrown it was earmarked, castrated and de-horned. Apart from bullocks, horns were taken off at the butt. Bullocks tend to die if de-horned. The older the bullock the higher the likelihood of it dying, so we only used to tip them. For some reason, on this particular day, the de-horning was not being done. The ultimate cost of this shortcut was the loss of a very good mare.

## Horse tales

We had taken a mob of shipping bullocks into Derby and it was time for us to head back home. We were still at Myall's Bore when one of the horses went to 'have a go' at another horse, a good Billiluna horse, called Bob. Bob jumped away, and as he did so a minneriche stick went into the point of his shoulder and broke off. We pulled the stick out, but it left a nasty wound. On this droving trip, Phil Le Lievre was in charge. We had the manager of Tablelands nephew with us, who was fairly useless. He was to take the horses home, while the rest of us were given a day or two off in town. The least valuable blokes were usually the ones sent home with the horses. They had a pack mule with two or three swags on, and enough tucker for two days. The horse that had been staked in his shoulder, was to go with them.

The horse tailers left Myall's Bore early in the morning. When they got to Meda that afternoon Dad came across them at the Claypan. The staked horse was in a bad way. Dad told them to drop Bob off there and leave him, which they did. Over coming days Dad kept going down to the Claypan to check on him. He reckoned Bob was like a dead horse, all blown up and puffy, he told me later. He said if Bob had been his horse he would have shot the wretched animal to put him out of his misery, but being owned by another station he didn't like to. It was just as well he didn't.

The following year I went in with bullocks. Phil had left Kimberley Downs by then and it was my first time in charge of a mob of sale bullocks on the road. On the way in we met the Tablelands nephew heading out. He was still useless, so this time he'd been sent home with the horses for Gerry Ash, who'd taken a mob of 'shippers' in earlier, and here was the young fella riding Bob.

"How come you're riding that horse?" I asked.

"Well he's a Kimberley Downs horse and he was at Meda station for us to pick up. He's a fat horse, so I thought I'd have him for myself."

"Well it's not for you to be picking and choosing. He's not your horse to be riding. You've got your allotted horses in this plant, and they're still your horses. This one isn't your horse." He was a strange fellow. Anyway, he went on to Kimberley Downs and nothing was ever said about it, but I felt a bit annoyed after the ordeal Bob had been through.

Kimberley Downs had bought horses from Mount Vernon. One of them was a horse called Floater. I don't know who broke Floater in, but he was a horse with a reputation and they, the horse-breakers, wouldn't ride him out of the yard. He used to buck and carry on. When the colts were being allocated Robin Campbell said, "Who's going to take this horse?" Silence. So I said I would.

Because he'd never been ridden outside the yard I said to someone, "You wait outside the gate and if this horse wants to buck, you interfere with him for me." When I first rode him out Floater had a half hearted go, then I rode him to Six Mile and there was nothing wrong with him. But later I discovered, if you were chasing cattle, wanted pace and opened him out, next thing he'd prop and 'into it'. The saddle would move, so when that was over I'd hop off and check the saddle clothe for prickles. There'd be nothing. I'd get back on and he'd be fine. When he bucked something used to happen in my groin and it would be sore for days. We were out at Rarrigee and I was whingeing to Robin Campbell about this.

"Wear a pair of spurs and a put a crupper on him," he suggested. "Then when he decides to buck 'give it to him'."

"You must think my capabilities are better than they are." I told Campbell.

Floater had been broken in with a crupper and Campbell brought one out to the camp for me. It was Floater's turn to be ridden. I put the crupper on the saddle and under Floater's tail, then led him around for a bit. I thought he might unwind when I got on, so I was hoping someone would stay with me, but nobody did. I got on and, to my surprise, he fully accepted it. He never bucked. Even when I opened him out, he was good as gold.

The next season I was in charge of the stockcamp. We were out horse mustering and we didn't get enough horses. As two of my horses were in the mob, I took my favourite and I said to this black fella, "You can take Floater. Over in my swag there's a crupper. Go and get it and put it on that horse." So this fella led him away and saddled him up. Next thing I hear laughing and squealing and carrying on. Floater galloped over and there was no crupper on him, and no rider either. I said to the black fella, "I thought I told you to put a crupper on that horse?"

"I bin tinkin' you bin makin' joke longa me." He hadn't believed me.

"It's no joke. You gotta ride him with a crupper, or else he'll buck." And Floater was always like that. Once we had learned, he turned out to be not a bad horse, and a good looker too.

## Asked to be headstockman

I was twenty when I first ran the stockcamp. Paddy Le Lievre had left Kimberley Downs. Phil had stayed and had been running the camp for Robin Campbell during his first season as manager. Before Paddy left he went up to the races at Fitzroy Crossing and he brought a bloke back with him, called Ringer Gibson. Ringer was a white man and he came into the stockcamp with Phil and I. Before the end of the season Phil decided to leave and go over to Leopold to work for his father. Robin told me Phil was leaving and he asked me if I would run the camp for him. It was the end of the year and we were trapping. I told him I thought I was too young and not experienced enough. Campbell said, "Just run it for me until the end of the season. I'll pay you a couple of quid a week extra. See how you go. When you come back next year we'll have a talk about it. If I think you're good enough, and you're confident enough, I'll pay you eighteen quid." I didn't tell anyone about this conversation, but somehow Ringer Gibson got wind of it. He seemed pretty dirty on me. I presume he thought he was going to be running the stockcamp, not me. Anyway that was the first stockcamp I was fully in charge of. Ringer Gibson left soon after.

When I first took over I used to hear the blacks talking about me at night. How 'dat guddia 'im bin makim michtake.' After a while I told Campbell about this.

"Buy yourself a radio and put it under your pillow, so you can't hear them!" he advised, so I did.

## A mustering round with Gerry Ash

The following season, when I returned after the 'wet' I was sent out to muster the horses.

There had been three mustering camps on Kimberley Downs the previous year. One was run by Phil Le Lievre, who had now left, one by Alec Clarke who had also gone, and the third by a bloke called Ray Jorgenson, who had come from Milligidee with Campbell. There had been a major blue in Jorgy's camp the previous year and he had also left the station. Campbell told me he was going to start the season with only one mustering camp and he asked me if I wanted to run it. There was another bloke there at the time, Gerry Ash, who was a yard builder, as well as a stockman. When Robin asked me this I said 'No, give the camp to Gerry. He's older and more experienced than me.' So that's what happened. Campbell got me to do the breaking in, then I went into the stockcamp with Gerry. Also in the camp was a friend of Gerry's, called Keith Bolger, who later came to work for me on Meda as windmillman. We had a number of good smart native ringers with us also. Amongst them Windbag, George Ngumburra and Ringer Campton, whose wife Elsie had grown up with my Dad on Brooking Springs.

Amongst the horses I had just broken in were two we named Gerry and Bolger and these were allocated respectively to their namesakes. I took one of the other colts, and my working horses and mule from the previous season. Before we went out, after we'd drafted the plant off, GerryAsh said to me, "That mule Cheeky is not going to be your riding mule, he's going to be a pack mule."

I said, "He's isn't. He's never been packed in his life. He has been my riding mule since I came here. I've been on the books the whole time, so you can't just take him off me."

"Well I am." Gerry said. So I went and saw Campbell. He sorted it out, and Cheeky wasn't packed.

It was a very dry year and after the unusually light 'wet' we were starting mustering earlier than usual. It was still very hot. We left the station and camped out the first night. Everything was going OK. Next day we started mustering and had dinner camp at a place called Sixty-Seven, an abandoned artesian bore. After dinner we continued mustering, but we were getting very few cattle so we used the horse plant as coachers. We camped that night at Barnett's Tank. The following day we did another muster but still got very few cattle, so we decided to brand what we had. After lunch we were lying about in the shade having a camp, when Gerry started to scratch himself. He was really scratching. Chest, shoulders, neck. He scratched so hard he had skin under his finger nails and he had gone bright red.

My swag was nearby so I suggested he lie down on it.

I gave him some anti-bite tablets I had in my gear, that Mum had given me. Next thing he was vomiting all over my swag. He was sweating like hell. I was pretty concerned about him, I thought he might die. I went and saw Ringer Campton. I told him to grab my mule, Cheeky, and ride him to the station, that Gerry was very sick. I didn't know what was wrong with him. It seemed like an allergic reaction, maybe from a tick bite. When they'd fetched the horses, which were in a horse paddock nearby, Ringer said, "More better I take my mule Shohn. Your mule might not like me." He was probably right and his mule, LayLay, was a good, reliable mule too. When he'd saddled up and was ready to leave Gerry called me over,

"Tell him to hang on for a half hour." He did. During that time our headstockman began to improve and eventually he came good. With the drama over, I took my swag over to the trough and 'turned the washing machine' on. Once I'd washed it all out I let the water out of the cattle trough, re-filled it and rinsed my gear again. Then I had to dry it all out before night-time.

We stayed there at Barnett's Tank the next day, then moved on to Davies Bore. Pretty well all the billabongs where cattle should have been watering were dry. We had only picked up about twenty head. We threw a few mickies along the way and de-horned and castrated them. We got to Davies bore and the tank was empty, trough empty and although the pumpjack and engine was there, there was no belt. We took the pack surcingles and cut off the buckles, joined them together with rivets and eventually got the engine to start. We had a fair bit of trouble with the makeshift belt, which was stretching and slipping. In those days every stockcamp had a couple of tins of treacle in the tucker box, so we put syrup on the belt to make it grip. Eventually we got the engine started, but it didn't run for long before the belt jumped off again. I was perishing because I'd thrown a few mickies and spent a fair bit of energy during the morning. I got one of the buckets we were carrying with us, and put it under the delivery pipe to catch the water. When we got the engine going again I caught the water and dead fish came up in it. It really stank. It was putrid, so we didn't drink it. Eventually we got the engine going a bit better and caught a couple of buckets of good water for ourselves, then we had to try and keep it pumping, to get enough to water our horses.

We stayed at Davies bore and mustered around the area and got about sixty head. One afternoon we went over to Blina, camped there the night, then mustered back, picking up a few more cattle. Blina was a sheep station then. From Davies we headed on to Barnes'. As we were saddling up, preparing to leave, I noticed we were short of a couple of colts.

"Those two horses, Bolger and Gerry, are missing." I told the head stockman. Neither of these colts had been ridden yet. They hadn't had a saddle chucked on them since I last rode them, back when I was breaking them in. When I pointed out they were missing, Gerry didn't want to know about it. Although they were fresh broken colts, neither horse was particularly young. They would have been between four and six years old and were amongst a mob bought from Mount Vernon, at the same time as Floater. Gerry didn't seem very pleased with me for alerting him to their disappearance. I couldn't understand why, but he was definitely cross and he showed little concern as to their whereabouts. Strangely, neither horse was ever seen again.

We continued on towards Barnes', still not getting many cattle. We had dinner camp on a dry billabong. It was very hot and no rain.

"You watch the cattle over lunch." I was instructed.

"OK. I'll just whip in and get a drink first."

"No you won't." Gerry retorted. He seemed to have the shits on with me, since I'd told him about the missing horses, so this was a bit more punishment. Usually, before starting dinner watch you get sent in to get a drink of water, but this day I wasn't sent in, and I was perishing. The billabong had cracks in it where the mud had dried up. That's how light the 'wet' had been. I thought I might get some water if I dug a bit of the mud out. But no such luck. I just got muddy hands and no water.

After dinner camp was over we headed off again. After a couple of hours travelling, I think Gerry might have been feeling a bit guilty, because he sent me on ahead of the mob to see how things were at Barnes' Bore, and to check the yard. Before I even got there I could see that the windmill was broken. The wheel looked like a shuttlecock. At this bore dirt had been pushed up against the tank walls, so I walked up and looked in. The tank was empty. Half the floor was dry, the other half had little pools of water on it, a dead goanna was in one of them. I was thirsty after throwing the mickies, so I hopped in the tank and, lying on my stomach, sucked up water from the floor. Then I checked the yard. It was all OK. I rode back to the mob and reported the situation to Gerry.

We took the cattle on to Barnes' and yarded up. Then we took the horses and pack mules three or four miles further, to Mount North Creek, where there was a pool of good clean water. We camped there the night. Next day we rode back to fetch the cattle. We watered them at Mt North Creek also. This was the first drink, for some of them, since we'd left Davies Bore almost two days earlier. We had dinner camp at the pool and that arvo mustered on to Windjana Gorge.

It was getting dark by the time we reached Windjana and as we approached we could see a glow down in the gorge. We yarded up. There was a bullock yard and bronco yard at Windjana at that time. After yarding I galloped down to the light, expecting to find Robin Campbell there. He usually came out to the stockcamp about once a week, to check on us and bring stores. We hadn't seen him yet on this round and we were running short of tucker. When I got down there, instead of finding Robin, I discovered a group of young people, Warwick Rowell amongst them, who'd driven out from Derby to spend Easter at Windjana. They had only just got there and were the first to visit the gorge since the 'wet' ended. After talking to them for a bit, I watered my horse at the river, then I returned to camp. Next day we drafted and branded, then knocked a killer. The visitors camping nearby told us they planned to leave the following day. We told them that we had been expecting our station manager to come out with fresh stores for us. We had only been able to bring limited provisions with us, as we were using packs, and we were running low. Warwick said when they were ready to leave they'd give us whatever leftovers they had, which turned out to be heaps. In return we agreed to give them half the killer, so they had fresh meat to take back to town. So that's what we did and we lived off some pretty flash tucker for a few days after that. Eventually Robin came out with stores for us.

We mustered around Windjana for about a week before moving on to Police Camp, where there was only a barbed wire and picket holding yard. With the river on one side and scrub on the other it wasn't a great place to be holding cattle for long. Lots of scorpions lived in the sand at Police Camp, but you'd only see them after dark when they came out into the firelight. We did a couple of musters and then went on to within four miles of Rarrigee, where we had dinner camp. I didn't have to do a dinner watch that day, so after I'd eaten I had a twenty minute nap. Gerry called us back to work with his usual 'Righto, come on.'

There were still some horses, fresh broken, that hadn't yet been ridden. This was not very good. A real lazy jackeroo style. I decided to catch one of them, even though it wasn't in my string. I caught a filly and saddled her up. It took me a bit of time because three or four weeks had gone by since her last ride, which was back when I'd broken her in. I saddled her up, led her round for a bit and hopped on her. She seemed to be okay, so I trotted her along and caught up with the cattle, a distance of about three quarters of a mile. When I got to the tail of the mob the blokes yelled 'Watch Out', but it was too late. A very aggressive cow with a newborn calf came straight at us, me on this green horse. I pulled her round sharply and the cow didn't get her. Afterwards Gerry rode up to me.

"You've got the bar of the bit through that horse's cheek," he pointed out. I hopped off, managed to get it out and tightened the cheek straps up, but Gerry was very snaky and we had a few words.

At Rarrigee we picked up a few little mobs of cattle and did a bit better than we had on the rest of the round. It was a good set-up there, with a big drafting yard and a horse paddock around a swamp, where there was green feed all the time. It was a good place for cattle. When we arrived Robin Campbell was there with a couple of horses. He had ridden out from the station. After having had words with Gerry I didn't have too much to say, but after tea that night I said to Robin, "I think I'll pull the pin."

"Why? What's the matter?" he asked. I told him what had been going on.

I said, "It's a bit of a circus." Campbell told me not to pull out.

"After this round you'll be on your own again." He meant I'd be in charge of my own camp, so I stayed. Once we'd mustered Rarrigee we moved on to Traveller's. Robin stayed with us. He did the first couple of musters around Traveller's, then left and went home, taking his horses with him. Once we had arrived at Rarrigee, and from there on, we were getting a fair few cattle. It was very good country, with blacksoil plains on either side of the Lennard River and a lot of billabong country. After another couple of camps and a few more musters we headed home with what cattle we had. We made up the numbers for a shipment, from the paddocks. Soon after Gerry and his crew left, with the pick of the pack mules, to drove the bullock mob into Derby. I was put in charge of my own stockcamp and went back out mustering.

## A rush

We were mustering the paddocks to put another mob of sale cattle together. We had come from Mariarna, in the bullock paddock, to Telephone Dam where we counted off the bullocks. We were still a few short, so Robin told me to go back out and do a 'galloping muster' and pick up what we could. We had dinner then headed out to muster White Well Paddock. It was fairly fast and hard. We gathered up what bullocks we could, cutting out the cows and calves on the job, whilst keeping the bullocks together. It was about nine o'clock by the time we got back to camp that night, with a mob of about forty-five bullocks. It wasn't a lot, but we'd got enough out of the muster to make up the numbers for a shipment. Robin Campbell was in the camp that night. It had been a long day and I was pretty tired. I had my tea, took off my boots and went to bed.

During the night the cattle rushed, smashing the yard. I heard them go, but I thought the other blokes could deal with it. I'd put in a pretty solid day and reckoned it wasn't for me to go out again. There were other fella's to do it, including the boss. This was the first time I hadn't jumped up to grab a night horse when there was a rush. Usually I was one of the first to go, but I wouldn't be this time. The next thing I heard Robin yelling at me.

"John, here! I've got Calwyn for you." Calwyn was a night horse and a darned good one. Robin had him all ready for me to go. I don't know why he didn't just hop on him himself, instead of calling for me. But here was the boss, holding Calwyn, basically telling me to get going. I jumped up out of my swag, hopped on, no boots or anything, and away we went. I didn't know which way the cattle had gone, but a bloke was singing out 'Over here' so I headed in that direction and caught up with him.

"This isn't the main mob." He explained. Somebody else was yelling out, so off we went in that direction. It was dark. The middle of the night, but with a good night horse like Calwyn you basically just let him go. He knows his job and what he's meant to do. You don't steer him or interfere with his head at all, because he could be dodging a tree for you, and if you do you might turn him into it. The horse won't hit it himself, but he'll go that close your head might hit it, or you could get wiped off on a branch. He can see much better than you in the dark, so you have to trust him and let him go. A night horse has brains and ability. He makes all the decisions. If there is an antbed he might jump it, or dodge it, but either way you're not ready, because you can't see it. You don't know what is going to happen, you just have to put your faith in your horse and hang on tight.

There were a lot of antbeds where we were that night. As Calwyn swerved this way and that, my bare feet were skimming them on either side. First he'd swing one way, then back the other, dodging these termite mounds. As he did so my feet were hitting them left and right. There were also slender bushes with tall thin stems. As we galloped through them they got between my toes, ran the full length to the top, taking the skin off. Eventually we got the cattle, and we held them. By the time we'd blocked them up it was about one o'clock in the morning. We hung onto them till daylight, then other blokes came out and took over.

When there is a rush, the noise is quite something, and the horses tend to scatter. It takes a while to put them back together. Once the other blokes came out we were able to go back in for breakfast. After I'd got my boots and we had eaten, we rolled our swags, caught our working horses, then headed off with the mob to Six Mile, mustering along the way. My feet were absolutely burning and sore as hell, but although they hurt they didn't really bleed. They were covered in lymph. Clear yellow sort of stuff, which if you leave it, goes a bit like egg yolk. The sun was shining on one of my riding boots, making my foot burn even more through the leather on that side. We didn't wear socks in the stockcamp, so the rubbing didn't help either. In the end I took my boots off again, tied a piece of string through the 'pull on loops', hung them across the front of the saddle and rode on barefoot. When we reached Six Mile, Campbell stayed with the stockcamp and I rode on into the homestead. I washed my feet in warm water and Mary Campbell gave me some ointment to rub on them. No dressings or anything were put on them, but I did get a couple of days off and basically slept the whole time. After that I never took my boots off again to sleep, if we had cattle in hand. I had learnt my lesson.

## Droving bullocks from Kimberley Downs through to Derby

Once the paddocks were mustered and we'd put a mob of sale cattle together, Robin Campbell got me to drove them in to Derby to be shipped. It was the first time I was in charge of a mob of sale bullocks on the road and I turned twenty-one on that trip. We were at Johnny Hole camp, just on the Kimberley Downs side of the Meda boundary. No celebration of course. Nothing, but I think Mum gave me a shirt to mark the occasion. On our way in we met Gerry Ash and his crew heading back home.

Usually we had the shipping bullocks, three or four hundred of them, in hand two days before we left. We'd leave the Six Mile past the homestead and go onto Johnny Hole, where the mob were yarded overnight. The yard was built of bush cut posts and eight gauge wire. Next day we'd go on as far as Bull Camp, on Meda, where we'd night watch the mob before moving on to The Dip. Here we'd night watch the cattle again, as we would each night until we arrived at Myall's Bore Yard. From The Dip we continued, through Meda country, to Forrest Camp. It was difficult going from there, first over open red ground, then into wattle scrub from Native Well onwards. We wouldn't let the cattle stop to feed, but walked them on slowly through the scrub. In this area there is a cleared patch of ground, about four or five acres, at a place called Deep Well, where there is a tank and a trough. Here the mob were held off, split into smaller mobs of about fifty head and allowed onto the water trough in groups. On this occasion we had watered two mobs in this way without incident, when they got a sudden fright and jumped. We managed to regain control of them and finished off watering the remainder, although we never discovered what it was that had startled them. I never stopped there to water bullocks again, it gave me such a fright. From Deep Well we continued on through the scrub and came out at Goody Goody, where the mob was watered at a gravel pit nearby.

It was all open country in this area, with timbered points going out to the tidal area. Rice grass, which the cattle really love, is plentiful and we fed them out. We had a couple of dozen spayed cows with us on this first trip, which were for the Leprosarium. The Leprosarium was situated a few miles from Derby, close to the marsh, on land adjacent to Meda's bullock paddock. The people from the Leprosarium met us at Goody Goody, where we drafted out on the flat and they took delivery of their spayed cows.

Between two timbered points is a sandhill where there are a couple of trees. We would camp at this spot and tie our night horses to the trees. My girlfriend at the time, Dawn, would know roughly when we were due. She'd ask the natives at Numbla Nunga, the Native Hospital, to tell her when they 'saw a dust' and she'd come out to meet us. She'd bring us goodies, such as sausages, cordial and other treats we never saw in stockcamps. It was goodo. Robert Rowell might also come out, to tell us what time to be at Myall's Bore for dipping against tick. Depending on whether we were early or not we would feed out across the marsh in the direction of Yabbergoody, where in places there was an abundance of rice grass. Or we'd dawdle about the edges of the sandy rises and let the cattle eat their fill. At Yabbergoody there was a tank and windmill which was also used as a 'camp' depending on feed and water. From Yabbergoody we'd walk the mob through the scrub to Myall's Bore, where the bullocks would be watered, at the famously long trough, and then yarded. There was no need to split the cattle at this watering point and unlike the flimsy yard at Johnny's Hole, Myall's Bore yard was built of railway iron posts, set in concrete, with 4 x 3 mill timber. At Myall's Bore the stock inspector would come out to inspect the cattle and waybills, showing the number of head in hand, their origin and ownership. After the bullocks had been dipped we'd leave them to drain out a bit in the yard, while we had a drink of tea, some damper and beef. Later we'd let them out and feed them along slowly down to the dinner boab, on the marsh. In the afternoon we would head down the 'long race' to the jetty. The long race was a timber race which ran from the fuel depot down to the jetty, a distance of a couple of kilometers. At the mouth of the 'long race' was a heap of black rocks which sometimes caused the cattle to baulk. The mob would be put down the race in groups of about seventy to a hundred head, pushed along by a couple of stockmen, with another group of a similar number being brought along behind them by a further two stockmen, until the whole mob was finally safely in the jetty yards. From the jetty yards the bullocks were loaded onto the ship, on a rising tide. Once loaded, the ship would sail on that tide, and we would ride back to camp at Myall's bore. I always felt a bit sad at this time. I would become attached to certain bullocks during the trip and now they were gone. I really wanted to catch bullocks, it was what I lived for. Then once I had them, I got to like them and I didn't want to sell them. Nothing has changed!

## Salt beef goes missing

I was taking bullocks in one time and when we got to Yabbagoody, the owner came out and got two killers off us. I was a bit annoyed about it. He had a cattle station full of them. He could have gone out at any time to get one. Instead he waited until we got to Derby with a mob of shipping bullocks. These were his money cattle. Over the preceding weeks we had mustered them, held them, nursed them and walked them in. We'd got them onto open country, done the hard part and out he comes and takes two.

When he came to Yabbagoody that day he had his daughters and a couple of their school friends with him. It was lunch time and I was eating a lump of bread with meat on it. During lunch one of the night horses got away from his tree and started walking off. We had the cattle on camp at the time. I put my meat down on a 'bush plate', a dry cow dollop, and walked over, caught the horse and tied it back up again. When I came back and picked up my bread and meat and continued eating it all the kids were sniggering and looking at me. They thought it was a hell of a joke. The cow pat was all dried up. There was nothing wrong with it. It made a better plate than getting sand all over the tucker.

On the same trip, the day before we were to load the bullocks, while we were at Myall's bore, the owner came out again, wanting a third killer. We needed a bit of beef too for our trip home, so we knocked another beast for him and salted a hind leg for ourselves. The owner wanted all the fresh meat, so we had bones and the salt meat. We left the salt meat under some bushes beneath a tree, while we took the cattle down to the 'dinner boab' on the way to the jetty yards. We had rib bones for lunch and were going to have rib bones for tea. Later I sent someone over to get the corned beef and bring it back to camp, but it had gone. There were some Mowanjum blacks visiting our aboriginal stockmen in the camp, who I suspected knew something about the missing meat, and I let them know it.

"You blokes were there this morning when we killed a killer. You knew the salt meat was there and somebody has stolen it." Having said my piece I reckoned that was the end of it. The beef had gone and there wasn't anything I could do about it. But half an hour later Albert Barunga, a Mowanjum elder, came to Myall's Bore, doing a bit of a war dance.

"You bin reckon we bin steal 'im your beef." He accused me and made a fair sort of a 'carry on' about it. Things got a bit heated. Albert went and saw the owner in town, who then came out and smoothed things over. But we still didn't have any salt beef to go home with, and no fresh meat either.

## I apply a tourniquet in town

After we had taken bullocks in for shipping we were sometimes given a few days off to spend in town. On one such occasion I took my girlfriend to the open air picture theatre. There was a shop across the road, Aylings Store, where you could buy chips, cool drinks, magazines, country and western music, clothing and all sorts of other goodies. Before the movie finished I went across to buy a soft drink. Myrtle Kelly, the saddler's wife, was working behind the counter. When I entered she seemed a bit harassed. She told me a bloke had just broken the shop window trying to get a rifle that was on display.

"He has cut his wrist and is bleeding very badly."

"Where is he now?"

"He took off up the street, but he's badly hurt. I've rung the ambulance." I asked her to get me something suitable for a tourniquet. She passed me a tea towel and a sharpening steel and I took off after him. I could see a blood trail down the footpath as I ran and I soon found him lying between the footpath and the road. I put the tourniquet on loosely, then put the steel in and twisted it to tighten it up. I told him help was coming and tried to reassure him that he'd be all right. While I waited with him he started criticising the nurses at the hospital and he seemed quite aggressive towards them.

"You want to cut that sort of talk out. They do a damn good job." I told him. He kept on abusing them, so eventually I said, "That's enough. My mother is a nursing sister, so you'd better shut up right now," he didn't. I was getting pretty sick of it. "If you don't cut it out I'll take this bloody tourniquet off in a minute." I warned him. "You can bleed to death for all I care." But he kept on going. "Righto. If you're going to be like that I'm taking this off." I bent down and swiftly removed the tourniquet from his arm. When I stood up there was Dr Lawson Holman and the ambulance.

"What's going on here?" he asked. I explained what had happened and what I'd done. The doctor put the tourniquet back on, then took the bloke up to the hospital.

A great many years later, at the closing of The Leprosarium, Lawson Holman reminded me of the incident. It seemed the night I'd stood up as a champion for nurses had stuck in his mind, though fortunately he didn't seem to think any the worse of me for the action I took.

## Broome rodeo

One day, we'd come in from the stockcamp and were at the homestead. While we were there Robin Campbell told me my mother had been in touch and that there was somebody staying with them she wanted me to see. Because of this Campbell said I could have the weekend off. I drove into Derby and called in at Goldsborough Mort, where I heard that there was a rodeo on in Broome that same weekend. I thought this sounded pretty good, so having called on my parents and seen whoever it was that was staying there I decided to drive on down to Broome.

When I got there I nominated for the barebuck ride. I had never ridden in rodeo before.

I drew a horse, called The Giant. This was not a lucky draw for a novice like me. Nobody had ever ridden 'time' on him and this included seasoned rodeo riders. Being my first time and me not really knowing the finer points, blokes were telling me what to do.

"As soon as they open the chutes just hook your spurs into his shoulder." they said. I'm listening to all this advice and thinking, 'Yeah, righto. No worries.' There was an old bloke there, Jack Huddlestone, who had been listening to these young fellas. He came and spoke to me also.

"Wellsy, don't you listen to a bloody word they just said. You don't know what you're in for on this horse. You just hang on for dear life and get the feel of it. Don't try any fancy stuff."

"Yeah, righto Jack." I agreed, but then, I suppose after a few seconds, but it seemed like a minute or two, just before they opened the gate, I thought 'Oh bugger it. I'm here now. I might as well go the whole hog.' At that age nothing was impossible. We jumped out of the chute and in went the hooks. I lost timing, my legs came up and I ended up with my shoulders on the horse's rump. He gave a kick up which sent me up higher. As I was coming down, the last thing I remember seeing were my legs up in the air, and his hind legs coming towards me. I didn't know anything after that.

When I woke up there were all these feet around me and blokes had their hands on me asking if I was O.K. I didn't really have a clue where I was. Eventually I started to wake up. I'd landed right on the back of my head with the weight of my body pushing my head into my chest. After a while I felt a bit better and tried to get up. A couple of blokes helped me up, putting an arm under each of mine. We were walking along, them holding me up and they said, "Are you all right now, Wellsy?"

"Yeah, I'm right." They let go of me and I went 'whoomph', straight back down again.

"You'd better stay down there," they recommended. After that I heard them put an announcement over the public address system asking if there was a doctor. Presently one came. By this time I was sitting up. He looked in my eyes and felt my neck, then told me to stay where I was. After a quarter of an hour, or twenty minutes he asked how I was feeling. I told him I was feeling alright.

"See if you can stand up," he said. I did and I walked away. Within an hour I was in another event.

I didn't see stars when I got pelted. I don't think you're properly 'done' if you see stars, but next morning, Jeez, my neck hurt.

## I learn to smoke

While I was at Narrogin, unlike some of the other students who smoked regularly, although it was against the rules, I only had two smokes in two years. They made me feel sick and I was crook the next morning, so I never touched another cigarette until I was on Kimberley Downs.

I was running the camp. This day me and a black fella, called Singer, were going after some bullocks. The native boy didn't back me up. He wasn't really trying and we ended up losing them. I was pretty dirty on him so when I rode past him I had a go at him and told him he was a useless bastard. I kept this up for a while until Tommy Hedley butted in.

"For Chrissake Wellsy, leave the poor bastard alone. Have a smoke."

"You build it and I'll smoke it." I agreed, so he built it and I had a few puffs on it. My head spun round and I thought 'bugger the black fella, bugger the bullocks and bugger the bloody horses.' After that every time I got a bit 'hot' under the collar, I'd ride over to somebody and get them to build me a smoke. They'd build it for me, light it and give it to me. I'd puff away at it and think everything was all right. Later on we went to town and I bought a carton of Rothmans. I didn't know which cigarettes were which then, so I didn't know what to choose. Anyway I bought this carton of 'taylor mades' to take back out to the station, so I wouldn't have to ask other blokes to build smokes for me.

We were mustering on the Napier, Oobagooma boundary, at a place called Mundooma. There were wild cattle out there. Heaps of them and big bullocks. A fixed wing was booked to come this day and, for some reason, I put two packets of smokes in my pocket before we left camp that morning.

We had coachers in hand and two way radios to communicate with the pilot. The plane started bringing cattle in, a lot at once, pretty toey cattle. Then, before we got control of them, he'd hit us with another mob. The pilot was a young fella and he didn't know what he was doing. He was giving us these cattle in mobs of two and three hundred. He wouldn't give us enough time to get them controlled before he'd be running another mob in. I got on the two way radio to him, "Can you block the ones you're bringing in till we've got control of the first mob?" I asked. He never answered. I was trying to tell him what to do. To 'steady 'em back a bit to give us time to get control of these cattle'. Nothing changed. I'd have another smoke and another smoke, then I started cursing and swearing. We had these walkie talkie things, but the pilot wouldn't answer whenever I tried to talk to him. He just kept bringing in more cattle, so I abused him over the two way.

"If you come near enough and low enough I'll throw this bloody radio at you and hope you get hit." I kept smoking the 'taylor made' cigarettes and I smoked the lot in one day.

Eventually we got back to the yards. It was late when we yarded up, but we had a good number of branders, bulls and bullocks in the mob. The pilot had left earlier. When we were having tea in the camp that night I felt as sick as a dog. Really crook from all the cigarettes. I said to Tommy Hedley, "You can have the rest of this carton of smokes. I'm never going to smoke again." Tommy said he'd got a pair of new jeans that were too big for him.

"You can have the jeans and I'll take the cigarettes." He suggested, so we swapped.

About a year later we were mustering out around Hawkstone, Douglas' and Leo's. We'd just about finished and were heading back from Leo's to Douglas' when it started raining. It was winter, 'dry' time, but it rained all night. We branded the next day in the rain. It kept raining, but I thought 'It's winter rain, it'll stop soon. Tomorrow it'll stop.' We didn't head for home. We waited for the rain to stop, for things to dry out a bit and be less slippery. But it kept raining, so we kept on waiting. It rained for ten days. The blacks camped under one tarpaulin and I camped under the other with all the gear, food, packs. Everything. Once it had stopped raining we still didn't head for the station because, by this time, all the creeks and rivers were 'up', plus we had a lot of black soil to cross. So we stayed and we were there for six weeks.

I was the only white man in the camp. The blacks went out during the day catching goannas. It was pretty miserable, for the horses too, standing about in the puddles and plagued by flies. During this time, with the boredom, I went to the tucker box one day and got a tin of tobacco, a packet of papers and a box of matches. I went for a walk and rolled my first cigarette. I wasn't very good at it, but after I'd smoked it I rolled myself another straight away. The green grass had started to grow by then, and after the two cigarettes I had on that walk I felt pretty good. They were the cigarettes I should never have had. After that I didn't stop smoking for thirty years. I smoked Log Cabin and over time I became a champion smoker, starting to roll my next smoke before I'd finished the last. I'd steer vehicles with my knee whilst I built my next rolly and when breaking in horses, would rattle a tobacco tin, rustle cigarette papers and strike matches, so it would be safe to roll smokes on horseback. I was a true addict.

Meanwhile, back at Douglas', the cattle we'd had in hand when the rain started were in a trap paddock, about a mile square. When this was eaten out, we began tailing them. Once the rain stopped falling and we'd waited a few days till it was less slippery, we began mustering the area again. We thought fresh cattle would have moved in, because of the rain and green feed. We did quite a few small musters and each muster we got fresh cattle, which we branded. We kept working while we waited for the creeks, rivers and country to dry out enough for us to cross the blacksoil and head for home. We ended up branding heaps and heaps of cattle while we were out there.

Eventually the owners and the manager drove out to where we were.

"Jeez, you've done a good job out here. We haven't seen a cleanskin the whole way." They observed. You didn't get too much praise on cattle stations, so I've always remembered that. Soon after we finally headed back home across the blacksoil, with the bulls and bullocks. We'd been at Douglas' for six weeks. From then on, whenever there has been winter rain, I've never assumed it will only last a day or two. Once back at the station we mustered up another plant of horses and went out mustering again.

## Pneumonia

In those days Napier was run from Kimberley Downs. I was running the camp. We'd been out for several weeks and had mustered around Kongrow Pool on Napier Downs. I had got sick and didn't know what was wrong with me. I kept running out of wind and felt really crook. The boys kept mustering and I'd try to work, but I couldn't really do anything. I had a terrible pain in my chest and I'd have to go and lie down again. I didn't feel real good at all. This day we were shifting camp from

Kongrow to Hans Hole. I caught and saddled Cheeky, my good mule, and felt a bit better. When we set off a beast broke out. I chased it on Cheeky and we put it back in the mob. After that I was absolutely buggered and I didn't seem to be able to get any oxygen. I rode back to the camp and unsaddled the mule. I put the saddle on the old truck, an ex army Blitz, and got a lift to Hans Hole on that. Whilst we were camped there I kept going downhill. Robin Campbell came out several times to check on us, to see that we were all right and still alive. I asked him to take me in to the station.

"You'll be right. You stay on here and we'll see how you are next time I'm out this way." He fobbed me off. The next time I would be no better, but same thing, till I got worse and worse.

Tommy Hedley was the only other white man in the camp at the time. One day I told him to fuel up the Blitz, check the oil and drive me back to Kimberley Downs. It was a fair sort of a drive and when we got to 'Old Napier' we pulled up for a spell. While we were there Graeme Hutton drove up. He was a geologist, out prospecting. We had been at Scotch together as kids. He asked what we were doing and when we told him he said he'd drive me in to the station instead. When we got there he dropped me at the main house, but there didn't seem to be too much co-operation in getting me into hospital. Eventually the teacher at the station, Kerry Lamb, offered to take me in to Derby.

I had a girlfriend in town, Dawn, who had my car, so we rang and arranged for her to drive out to meet us. We met along the way and she then drove me straight to the hospital, where I was admitted immediately. I was an inpatient there for two weeks with pneumonia. Once I was discharged I went back to Kimberley Downs and was sent straight back out to the stockcamp, to continue mustering.

## Arthur Smith and a threat of war

Old Arthur Smith was a boundary rider on Kimberley Downs and he looked after a bore called Mac's Pool. In those days blokes used to camp at certain bores to pump water for the cattle, towards the end of the year when the water holes had dried up. They were mainly older fellows, past their prime, usually white, although occasionally a native couple might do the job. It was a pretty lonely existence, but it suited some old fellas, who didn't seem to mind their own company.

Arthur Smith had fought in two World Wars and was a really top bloke. He had a mule called Barramundi and a horse called Victory. Victory was an old stockhorse, but he ended up being a race horse for one of the managers, and did all right in his time. So the mule and the horse and old Arthur Smith were all about the same age, that is in horse years, mule years and man years. About seventy. Old Arthur Smith was practically blind and people used to say he was 'that blind he'd have to catch his mule, to get his binoculars, to see where his mule was.' Barramundi was half blind too, but a good old mule, and reliable.

Arthur used to check the bullock paddock fence, which was about ten miles square. He'd take his old mule with a pack, have his swag, hobbles, halter, a bit of tucker and that kind of thing and he'd ride Victory. One day he'd gone out after the 'wet'. It had been a very light wet season that year and things had begun to dry up a bit. He was riding along and it was getting late and pretty hot. He was getting thirsty, so he rode into a billabong and lent down to get a pannikin of water, but he couldn't reach. He rode in a bit more and lent down and still couldn't reach it, and rode in a bit more and then realised it wasn't going to get any deeper. So he stretched right down to get a drink of water and the next thing, plop! off he fell into the water. He said, 'Old Victory jumped away a bit, went out onto the bank where the mule was waiting, looked back at him and said 'Jeez Arthur, you're a silly old bastard'. I really like blokes who can laugh at themselves and Arthur was one them.

Arthur must have been tough in his younger days. He was working for the Roads Board once, building a section of road, abandoned now, at the back of where Birdwood Downs is today. It was a very sandy stretch of track, through thick wattle scrub, on what used to be the old main road to Kimberley Downs. He had one other bloke helping him, and they had a horse and tip cart, shovel and crowbar each. They had to dig the gravel, shovel it onto the cart, tip it onto the sandy section they were working on, then spread it out. When they had finished they carted ironstone boulders, which they put along the edges of the track, to hold the gravel in place. It would have been as hot as hell, with the heat off the sand, and the thick wattle scrub blocking any breeze.

## The threat of war, JFK and the Cuban crisis

There was a time, while I was running the stockcamp, when it looked like a war was going to start. This was when Kennedy told Castro to get the missile out of Cuba and to turn the one that was coming, around, or it would 'be on'. I had been at boarding school when the Suez crisis blew up and I remember the teachers telling us 'If this goes wrong most of you boys will be off to war before it stops.' It had frightened the living daylights out of me and I'd never forgotten it. I wasn't a schoolboy anymore, but this latest 'blue' scared me just as much. We had a white fellow in the camp with us who was pretty excited about it all. He kept saying, "I hope they do have a war. I'll be able to go and I'll join the airforce. Prr Prr Prr," and all this sort of talk. I kept thinking to myself, 'Jeez I don't want to have to go to war' and 'I don't want to have to kill somebody.' Anyway this bloke was going on about it so much I thought 'I mustn't be normal.' So when no-one was around I went to Arthur Smith, the old war veteran, and said, "I've got a bit of a problem Arthur"

"What's that?" He asked.

"Well, this Cuban missile crisis. I'm a bit worried about it. Scotty's talking about how he hopes there's a war, and he wants to go, and all this. But I'm dead scared. I don't want to have to go to war."

"Don't worry John. How you are feeling is quite normal." Arthur told me."Scotty is the one that's not quite right." Then he recalled the first time he went to war. "You don't want to kill anybody at first, but as soon as a couple of your mates go, then you start to become a soldier." Talking to Arthur helped a fair bit. I was still very worried, but at least I knew my fear was natural.

Once Arthur asked me to go with him way out in the back country around Oobagooma, where he reckoned he'd found a seam of gold in a really dry year. He was very vague about where it was and we never ended up going, though I would have liked to. He was a good old fella Arthur Smith and I always had a lot of respect for him.

Years later, when I was managing Myroodah, I went into Derby one day and my mother told me that Arthur was very sick in hospital. He was very old by then and not too many people knew him. I asked her if she would wire me, if things didn't go well for him, that I'd like to go to his funeral. The next day I received a telegram to say that Arthur's funeral had been held the day before, whilst I'd been in the town. I was pretty upset about that. Being a veteran of two world wars, he had led a tough life, and received little recognition. Now no-one even knows, with any certainty, which grave site is his in the Derby cemetery. This makes me deeply regret that I never got around to putting a headstone up for him.

## Bullocks in Six Mile Paddock and an assassination

We had mustered down from Police Camp to Mac's Pool. We had dinner camp at Horse Pool and then we went on to Lukins. We put the cattle in the horse paddock there for the night. The next day we went on to Six Mile. We put all the cattle, including the bullocks, in the yard that night. The following day we cut out the sale bullocks from the rest of the mob. Robin Campbell said to put the bullocks in the Six Mile Paddock for the rest of that day and overnight. Then the following day we could 'sheep muster' them down the paddock, then feed them along towards the homestead. 'Sheep mustering' is when you go in a line, make a bit of noise and keep the cattle running in front of you. No-one is in the lead. You haven't got control of them.

"Putting them into Six Mile Paddock for one night isn't worth it. Why don't we yard them here at Six Mile, then feed them down to Homestead Yard tomorrow and yard them up there tomorrow night?" I asked Robin.

"No. They'll be right in Six Mile Paddock." The manager told me. "I've got the fence checked. It's all O.K." So that is what we did. The next day we 'sheep mustered' these bullocks, the result of six weeks mustering, running them down into one of the corners of Six Mile Paddock. No one was in the lead. When we got to the corner I could see all these bullocks streaming out of the paddock, out into the river, and away bush. The gate had been left wide open. I was riding Cheeky, the mule. I came out of the paddock, me and another boy, whilst somebody else blocked the gate to keep the rest of the cattle from getting out. The two of us took off. The bullocks had crossed the creek and were over the other side. Down in that country there are big holes, a metre or so wide. Some of them four metres wide. You can't gallop in that country because you have to keep dodging these holes, and it's fairly dangerous. A lot of grass grows around them, so at least you know they are there, even though you can't actually see a hole there. But the grass warns you. Anyway, me and this other fella went through this stuff. We blocked up a fair few bullocks, but a lot of them had too big a spring on us and they just siphoned off into the bush. We'd got a fair mob of them and other stockmen came and they held them there for dinner. I went out to Douglas' Bore to tell Robin Campbell what had happened. On the way out I heard on the radio that John F. Kennedy had just been shot. Robin told me not to worry about the bullocks. He said we had enough, but it wasn't a very good day.

## Phil musters the boundary in the 'wet'

One time, early in the year, Robin Campbell sent us out to Munjaweela to muster. There was a place called Marowan Springs and a lot of cattle used to live there. Phil Le Lievre was working on Fairfield at the time and, because we were close to their boundary, we had Fairfield blokes attending. While we were out there I noticed cattle tracks in the mud and after a while I picked up some horse tracks also. I rode around to this good black fella, Paddy, a Fairfield man.

"You bin mustering here Paddy?" I asked. He denied it. "Well there's been cattle and horses here, in the 'wet', so I'll be finding out Paddy. I'll get onto the police about it." I added. This was to frighten him a bit and it worked.

"Well, I bin 'ere. But 'dat Pilip Le Beer, he bin de boss." he admitted. So the next time I saw Phil I had a go at him.

"Don't ever do that again, or the 'shit will hit the fan'." We were mates and he took it all right.

On another occasion Phil sent his men over attending, and he tried to lure my men away from me. After a few days I noticed several of my blokes were sporting new shirts. Each day another native stockman would front up in flash new gear. Eventually I asked where it came from, because I knew we didn't have shirts like them in our station store. It turned out that one of Phil's men, Roland Thompson, had been handing the shirts out to my blokes. Phil had apparently sent them over with him, to try and draw my men over to Fairfield, to work for him. Again I fronted Phil about it and told him it wasn't the right thing to do. Phil Le Lievre was one of my very good friends although he wasn't above a bit of skulduggery if he thought he could get away with it.

## Elsie

There was an old girl at Kimberley Downs, called Elsie, who had been a kid on Brooking Springs when Dad was growing up there. She was Frank Hunter's mother and she used to look after me when I had falls. I think it was because she grew up with Dad that she looked after me especially.

Once I had a 'good' fall. We were camped at Douglas' on K.D. and I was running the camp. It really knocked me about a bit and I have no clear recollection of the circumstances, or even what horse I was riding, which is unusual for me. It happened straight after dinner and the horse tailer was still around. You didn't let loose horses go in front of where you were going to muster, but as we had already mustered there, the horse tailer was going back to feed and hobble the horses. When he got back to camp he must have told Elsie 'Dat 'guddia 'im had good fall an' bit chick'.

After we had yarded up, when I got into camp, I dismounted and said to one of the young fellas, "You can unsaddle this horse, wash him, feed him and hobble him for me." Something I would normally do myself, but I was feeling too crook. When I went to get my swag to lie down, I found it was already opened out, shaken out and re-made. Grass had been cut and put underneath it for a mattress. There was a pannikin of water and bottle of Aspros put ready beside it. That was as much as anybody could do for you in the stockcamp in those days. There was no outside communication. If you were badly hurt someone had to ride to the station to get somebody to come out and fetch you. That's just how it was. Anyway I took a couple of Aspros and I lay down and went to sleep. I didn't have tea that evening, but in the night Elsie came over and shook me.

"Shohn, you bin al'right?" She asked me.

"Yeah, I reckon I'm right" I told her, so she went back to bed. She was a really good old girl. She didn't have to do that for me, but she did. I wasn't too bad in the morning, so I was lucky.

## Trying to hold bullocks in the rocks, on foot at night

At Limestone Springs there was a yard, which was really just a pocket amongst the rocks. Previous stockcamps had stacked up rocks in the gaps, or put trees and branches across them. They'd put a fence, about thirty yards wide, across the entrance. It was there that we camped. I reckon it was one of the best death traps I've ever been in. It was really very dangerous, because if the cattle 'rushed' that was where they'd come out. We would have night horses tied up and we always lit about four fires across the entrance, just in case the cattle 'rushed' and trampled us in the night. The whole set-up was bloody ridiculous, stupid and dangerous. I hated it. I used to camp right up against the wall amongst the rocks, so if anything did go wrong I was, hopefully, out of harm's way. Most of the blokes did the same, though some of them, even some of the natives, would roll their swags out on the flat. But pretty much everyone would have a fire alongside them, and they'd get up and keep stoking it during the night.

On one occasion, we'd finished mustering down at Mundooma and were on our way back, heading towards the station. For some reason, I don't know how, we picked up a big mob of big bullocks. I thought this was a real fluke and 'how good was that?' So we had these bullocks and we put them in this yard, this 'pocket amongst the rocks' for the night. We had our night horses tied up, the fires lit across the entrance, where the fence and cockies gate was, and I rolled my swag out of harm's way, tight against the rock wall. I woke in the middle of the night and could hear cattle rattling around up on top of the hills, and dislodged rocks and boulders rolling about. It was all our big, fresh bullocks getting out! I realised that instead of coming out where we were camped, they'd gone up the back and out over the range. I jumped up and climbed up the rocks, but I had no hope of turning anything back. All the fresh big bullocks I'd been so pleased to get, had gone. I felt pretty cheesed off. I thought we'd had a big win, then all of a sudden, nothing. We did a lap around in the morning but we didn't pick up too many of them.

That set-up was sheer stupidity. We would work hard to get cattle and sometimes we'd win a good mob of bullocks, like on that day, just to lose them through not having the proper facilities. We risked our lives, did all this work mustering, but didn't have the amenities to hold the money cattle. However, on this occasion we still had all our quiet cattle. They had been educated and just lay down and went to sleep, waiting till we opened the gate in the morning. We headed on towards home, with just them and a feeling of disappointment and frustration.

Some time afterwards, when we had a couple of weeks spare, we returned to Limestone Springs and built a tailing yard, with a bronco panel in it. We built it well away from the range and it made things a lot easier, from then on. We must have cut eighty posts. Drilled them and got wire and built the wire yard and bronco panel and made it all better. It probably took us two weeks to build and it was much safer. After that, if the cattle rushed and smashed the yard, at least we were out on more open ground and had some chance of re-gaining control of them.

## Mustering at Mundooma

We were out mustering around Mundooma, way down the back of Napier, in pretty wild country near the Oobagooma boundary. Michael Bear was riding a ginny mule called 'Blackie', when a bull broke out of the mob. Michael jumped off for it and this bloody mule took off. I went after her, but when I got close to her she would prop and go behind my horse. She did this over and over and I was getting pretty 'hot'. Then she propped and put the boots into me. One hoof in the arm and one in the guts. Eventually she 'stood up' and I jumped off and caught her. Other blokes rode over and I was wild. I could just about have killed her that day for her goings on.

Really Blackie was a very good cattle mule, and she won a few mule races in Derby, but she had a chronic sore back which is probably what made her such a bitch. When I first went to Kimberley Downs she was ridden by 'Razor Arse Charlie', but was later allocated to Michael Bear, after Charlie left to follow Paddy Le Lievre. Another of Blackie's dirty little tricks was to go and stand out in the middle of a billabong, sometimes with just her head out of the water, so that you had to ride in on a horse to try and hunt her out. Then she'd keep turning her bum towards you. She'd do the same thing out on the flat, when you tried to catch her, and it wasted a lot of time. I s'pose you couldn't really blame her for not wanting to go to work, but all the messing about, and time wasted on her used to make me pretty cross. If she wasn't such a good cattle mule I'd have got rid of her.

One time when we were again mustering at Mundooma, the blacks told me how they used to muster. They said if we did it their way we'd get big bullocks, so we tried it. The blacks tee-ed up for the coachers to be held in the fork of two water courses, which were a good distance apart. Five or six of us went out, again the blacks organising where we were to go. This place was like a pocket, or a valley, and I'd never been there before. The natives said to me, "You bin keep pushin' these cattle from behind. We gotta go an' block 'em gaps an stoppem gettin' out 'dis place." So eventually, when we came out into the open, there were bullocks, maybe eight or ten under each tree, all blowing like hell and exhausted. The fresher bullocks were still running away. I'd never seen so many bullocks, in one mob, out of control. Our horses were knocked up, so we stood under trees till they seemed to have got their wind back. Then we took what bullocks we could, pushing them on to where the coachers were meant to be. But the coachers weren't there. We kept moving the cattle along and eventually we came upon the coachers. Then we took the mob back to Mundooma and yarded them. I was pretty pleased, although we'd only got a fraction of the bullocks we could have got that day.

At this time I was the camp cook as well as headstockman, so I was fairly tired, probably a bit short tempered too. I didn't get paid for doing both jobs of course. That kind of thing wasn't even thought of in those days. But I did get an unexpected break from being the 'babbler' for a bit, when late that same evening a 'hatter' wandered in to the camp. A man called Cecil Roderick.

*Kimberley Downs stockmen. L-R Benn Bibingnulli on 'Rothmans',Raymond on 'Rose',*
*Micheal Bear on 'Blackie the mule, Murray Scott on 'Rita', Gary Ah Chee on ?,*
*Me on 'Earldon', Brian Djigbar on 'Barry's Mare'. Kimberley Downs native camp*
*in the background.*

*The stockcamp team at Douglas'. L-R George Ngumburra, native boy Kim Rose.*
*me, Ringer Campton, Windbag, Big Don, Rastus, Bruce Wallaby, Razor Arse Charlie,*
*remainder unknown. circa 1963*

*Native stockman Windbag at Barnes' bore. The mare has a collar rope on as she was difficult to mount.*

*Drafting cattle in the trap yard at Windjana Gorge. 2nd from right is Michael Bear. circa 1966*

*Dust rises from the cattle in the trap yard at Windjana Gorge. circa 1966*

*I practice for the Derby rodeo steer ride on mickey bulls at Rarrigee.*

*My good friend Phil Le Lievre beats me to the finish on 'Charlie' in the Stockman's Race at Derby. I am riding 'Boab' August 1963.*

# CHAPTER SIX

# CECIL RODERICK

*And so the day had ended and darkness veiled the yard,*
*Though the stockmen and the horses had found the mustering hard,*
*And over by the campfire, on their swags beneath a tree,*
*He sat and watched, contented, as the tired boys ate their tea.*

Cecil was called 'The Mystery Man'. Nobody knew much about him, but he was a pretty intelligent fella and well read. He had worked for a pastoral family down in the Gascoyne in his younger years. When the owner died from a shooting accident, leaving a widow with several young children, Cecil stayed on and ended up running the station for them. There was no money and the property wasn't making any money. Eventually it was sold and when it came time to leave, the family gave Cecil the pick of the horses and he ended up owning a mob of about twenty-five. He headed north with his horses, riding and droving them, up into the Kimberley. He worked for my Dad, on Meda, for a while, when I was still a boy. Nobody really seemed to know much about him, hence his name 'The Mystery Man'. It wasn't until many years later that I learned a bit more.

Once the sale of the property had been finalised, the money owing to Cecil was invested for him. The family took out a life insurance policy, or something equivalent, as payment for the years he'd helped them. Cecil was to eventually become a wealthy man in his own right, although you would never have known it. He remained in the Kimberley, working here and there on stations and eventually ended up working as a 'dogger' for the government during the time I was on Kimberley Downs.

Cecil lived on the edge of Napier and Mount Hart, up in the ranges country. He used to 'dog' on about three stations, Kimberley Downs, Napier and Blina. He would also go up to Mt Hart. I don't think he was getting paid to go into that country, but there were a lot of dingoes in the ranges and he got paid per scalp, so it was worth his while to extend his territory a bit. He was a hatter. He ended up living on his own, right out in the bush and you never knew where he was, or where he'd turn up.

Sometimes we'd go mustering and there'd be no cattle around. We wouldn't be able to work out why there were no cattle. Then we'd come across Cecil having lunch in the shade, a boab nut and a billy of tea. That would be why there were no cattle about. They would have smelt him and all shot through, so it buggered the muster up for us.

When we were camped at Mundooma, we were out with packs. That is, eight or ten mules packed up with all our food, swags horse-shoes, salt and flour. Everything. We were right out the back blocks, miles from anywhere. Quite often, if it was packs no bloke would come with us to cook, so I'd be the headstockman and I'd be the camp cook as well. That meant I'd have to be up in the morning to get breakfast, go mustering all day, or branding or whatever. Sometimes, when mustering, we wouldn't get back till 9 o'clock at night. Then I'd have to feed the blokes. After that I had to cook for the next day. Something for tomorrow's breakfast, lunch and tomorrow's tea. I'd always be a lot of hours behind, but this is how it went all the time. Two men's job, but only one man's pay. If the powers that be employed a cook he'd be getting a wage and I'd be getting a wage. So the station was cutting out one blokes wage and I was the 'mug' doing two men's work. I've been like that all my life!

Anyway on this occasion it was on again. I was running the camp and I was the cook, so I was pretty tired. One night we were sitting around the fire thinking about going to bed, when the mules started snorting. When there are mules in a stockcamp, they will tell you if there's a stranger about. You can walk out half a mile to have a poo, or a wee and that's all right. The horses and mules don't make a sound, because they know you belong there. But if a stranger comes along they'll snort and blow and carry on. Mainly it's the mules that tell you when something is wrong, but then the horses start, and this snorting is going on everywhere. When this happens the hairs stand up on the back of your neck, because you know somebody who shouldn't be there, is there.

We'd got back to camp late this night. It was well after dark and everybody had been fed. It would have been about half past eight, or nine o'clock, when we heard snorting out amongst the horses and mules. The blacks were all shitting themselves. I wasn't feeling too good about it either. We were sitting by the camp-fire, easy to see by whatever, or whoever it was that was out there. It's not a very good feeling. You don't know what to do. You're miles from anywhere. You don't know where the odd thing is, or what it might be. A camel? Pigs? A person? Everyone is edgy. I began to feel very prickly, when all of a sudden a man walked in, out of the dark, into the firelight. It was Cecil! He was carrying a swag, very short and very thin, plus another bag, which had his belongings and his food in it. When he wandered out of the darkness into our camp, there was a great sense of relief amongst us. Cecil had a base up in the hills, in no-man's land. Although he did have an old Land Rover at one time, he travelled long distances on foot. He would walk for miles, in the bush, camp at different places and basically live off goannas, rice and bush tucker.

After Cecil rolled up that night he offered to do the cooking for us. I thought 'Ah, you beauty! That's good.' Although it took a fair bit of pressure off me, all the blacks in the camp were a bit toey. They knew he was a dogger. When we killed a killer Cecil would get bits of meat off it and he'd drag them two hundred yards this way, two hundred yards that way. He had a knife on his belt and he always had a bottle, or two, of strychnine. He'd use his knife to cut the meat, then sprinkle on the strychnine. When he went back to the camp, he'd be cutting up the meat and damper for us with the same knife. So everybody was trembling and shaking, wondering if there was any poison left on it. Cecil might be our camp cook, but he was still a dogger, baiting for dingoes. We were always a bit edgy while old Cec was doing the cooking. But nobody ever got poisoned, or even touched, which was lucky. Cecil stayed in the camp doing the cooking for a good while, but one day I came back from mustering and nothing had been done and Cecil was gone. That's just how he was. Not a word said. He'd just up and vanish.

Another time we went out with the stockcamp, sixty or seventy unshod horses, all the black fellas, and me, the only white man in the camp. The boss seemed to just want us out of the place, saying 'we could shoe the horses once we were bush'. Again Cecil rocked up unexpectedly in the camp. He was still there when my mate Phil Le Lievre came over from Fairfield, a neighbouring station. Phil asked me if I'd go to a gymkhana meeting with him up at Fitzroy Crossing. His nickname for me was Womba Wells.

"What about coming up with us, Womba? We'll make you a member and you can vote on the committee?" I didn't particularly want to go, but Phil said he'd spoken to my boss, Robin Campbell and squared it up with him.

"Yeah, yeah, it's all sorted and O.K." He assured me, when I tried to object.

In the end I couldn't really get out of it, so I went to Cecil, "I've got to go up to Fitzroy tonight. Can you keep an eye on the camp while I'm gone? These blokes have got to shoe all the horses in the camp. You just keep an eye on the tucker and on what's going on." Cecil agreed. That night Phil picked me up and took me to Fairfield Station where we camped the night. We left early next morning, went to Fitzroy Crossing for the meeting, left that afternoon to drive back and camped that night at his station again. He dropped me back at the stockcamp on Kimberley Downs next morning. When I got there Cecil was gone. He hadn't looked after anything for me. He'd just floated.

Sometimes Cecil would end up in Derby. At races time all the ringers and managers would be in there and grog was really heavy. We'd all be in the bar. There might be ten people in the school and Cecil would be there so you'd buy him a beer. There might be ten rounds, Cecil would still be there and he'd buy in his shout. Then, without a word Cecil would be gone. Each round people would keep buying for Cecil. Then after about three rounds there'd be three beers sitting there not drunk.

"Where's Cecil?" someone would ask. "We'll count him out for the next round."

After another six or eight rounds Cecil still wouldn't have reappeared. He'd never say, "I'm going now, so count me out." No warning, nothing. He'd just disappear.

One time when I was on Napier we all got the flu. Everyone was crook. Cecil had been to town and he'd brought this brew back with him. He reckoned this stuff really fixed the flu. I had a couple of nips of it. I don't know what he had in it. I thought it tasted strong, but it was pretty good gear. After that I went to bed. When I got up in the morning all my men were pissed, and old Cecil had gone.

I used to come across Cecil quite regularly in the bush, often in rivers, or somewhere where there was water. When you came across him, if he was near one of his camps, he'd always love you to have a cup of tea with him. He led such a solitary life, if he asked you, you sort of had to have a cup with him. He'd have this pair of shorts on, with a fly and the top bit and he'd say, "Are you going to have a cup of tea? I'll light a fire and we'll have a brew."

"Yeah, righto Cecil" I'd say. Then when he turned around to make a fire, there'd be no trousers in the back. These shorts of his were just like an apron. The top bit was there, holding his strides up, but his bum was as bare as the moon. And off he'd go.

Then when he was serving up a cup of tea, everything would be hanging out. It didn't worry him a bit. As long as there were no women there it was all OK. He'd give brown eyes and everything. It didn't shake a rivet with him. It was just as if everybody got around like that. It seems funny now, but we took no notice at the time. That was sort of how it was. For this cup of tea he'd find you an old jam tin and that was your pannikin. It wasn't all that hygienic but he'd say, "Don't worry about that mate!" Then when he'd boiled the billy and it was all over, he didn't dice the tea leaves. He'd get all the tea leaves and spread them on a stone, dry them all out, then scrape them up and put them back in the packet ready for next time. He was very well educated and it was always interesting talking to him. He would also give you information about cattle and where they were running, which was quite helpful.

When I was managing Napier Downs I was coming back from a hundred and eighty mile round trip looking about the station. I'd been into pretty rugged country and it was well after dark, maybe eight o'clock at night, when I crossed the Barker River. Out of the river walked a bloke. It was Cecil.

"G'day, how you goin?" I asked.

"I'm goin' good. When are you going to town next John?" I told him I was going in to Derby the next day.

"That's good. Can I get a ride home to the station with you tonight? Then I'll come to town with you tomorrow." Cecil asked. I noticed he was standing oddly, as if one side was spastic.

"No worries." I agreed. He hopped in the vehicle and we headed for the homestead. As we were driving along he was talking to me. He was talking a lot of rubbish. He told me he'd been having trouble with his Land Rover, that he'd jacked it up and it had fallen on him. He said it had taken him about a day and a half to get out from under it. We were about six kilometres from New Napier. I chatted with him as we drove along, but he was talking more and more nonsense. I started to think something wasn't quite right.

Although I had planned to go to Derby in the morning, having brought Cecil home and realising he wasn't his usual self, I decided I needed to take him into town that night. I told those at the homestead about the change of plan, and Cecil. It was all right with him, so soon after we took off. It was a hundred mile drive from Napier into Derby. We drove from Napier to Kimberley Downs, then on to Meda. When we got to Meda there was a bloody great bushfire burning.

"What's that?" Cecil asked.

"It's a bloody big bushfire Cecil." I told him.

"Oh?" He said, acting like he didn't know what it was. That really worried me. I knew something was very wrong with him. I got him into town and asked where he wanted to go.

"Drop me off at Prowsie's." I pulled up right outside the gate of Prowsie's place. Cecil was on the passenger's side, the gate right alongside him. He got out of the car. I stayed sitting in the driver's seat. He got his gear out of the motor car. Then I didn't see him again. I thought 'He's gone off somewhere to have a leak before he goes into his friend's place'. So I sat and waited and waited. Cecil didn't go in the gate. I thought 'Gee this is a bit odd'. After a fair while I went in and asked the people if Cecil was there. I thought he might have gone around the back and I'd missed him. They said they hadn't seen him, so I drove down the street and there was Cecil walking off down town. I asked him where he was going?

"Down to Prowsie's place."

"But I pulled up at the gate of Prowsie's, Cecil." I told him. "Come on jump in and I'll take you back there." I took him back again. This time I went in with him and saw the people and he camped there the night. By now it was the middle of the night. I went round to my parent's place, in Neville Street, and slept there. The following day Cecil went down to the hospital and made an appointment to see the doctor later in the afternoon. An appointment he didn't attend. Instead, unbeknown to any of us, he met a pilot he knew, who flew freighter planes. They had a talk and Cecil told him he'd got a doctor's appointment in the afternoon.

"Well I'm heading for Perth with this freighter plane. You be out at the airport and I'll take you to Perth with me to see the specialist." The pilot offered. So that's what Cecil did.

In the meantime I'd gone back out to Napier. The people Cecil was staying with in town were making enquiries as to where he'd got to. The police were notified. Cecil had missed his appointment with the doctor in Derby and his bed at Prowse's hadn't been slept in. The next day the police were on the pedal set to me. Cecil had gone missing!

It was late in the year and there was a big storm around. The cops wanted to know if Cecil had been past the station.

"Well, the house is right alongside the road, and no vehicles have been past here." I told them.

"He might have gone back up to his camp." they suggested. I asked all the blacks, but they didn't know anything.

"Then can you send a couple of men out with horses to check his camp and see if he's been back there?" The police asked.

Cecil was living on the edge of Napier, up in the ranges near Mount Hart country. There was big rain around, so we packed a mule and two black fellas rode out to Cecil's camp. One of them was Harry Martin. The pair left after the morning sked. (radio session) and came back the following night. The next day I got on the radio to the cops.

"There's no sign of him having been out there. My men have ridden out and there are no tracks, but there has been a lot of rain. The fire's dead. Nothing. No man has been there."

After that everything went pretty quiet for about two weeks, then one day Cecil ends up back at the station. He had been down to Perth, he told us.

"Went down on this freight plane with a bloke I know." He'd seen a specialist then flew back on a domestic flight to Derby, bought his groceries before leaving town and there he was, large as life, back at the station. He'd told nobody. He'd just gone. He had this idea that no-one worried about him. He was wrong. A lot of people liked him and were concerned for him. He was a good bloke.

At the end of one cattle season a mate of mine, Scotty, was going to drive across to Queensland. Cecil was still employed to be dogging, but despite this he asked my mate if he'd give him a lift to Queensland. Scotty said 'Yes'. As Cecil was still supposed to be working, he wrote out two letters before he left, one for October, one for November, to say what he'd been doing and where he'd been dogging during the two months. Of course it was all bullshit, because he wrote them in advance and just made it all up. He left them with someone in town to hand in, on his behalf, when the time came. The October 'worksheet' at the end of October and the second one at the end of November.

But the person didn't. Instead they handed the November one in first and Cecil got found out.

He and Scotty headed over to Queensland and Cecil was dropped off in Tully, or somewhere, for his holiday. When it was time to go home my mate went to the house where he'd dropped Cecil off, but the people said he wasn't staying there any more. They told Scotty that 'Cecil had bought a big house over at such and such and 'you'll have to go over and pick him up there.' So Scotty went round to the big house, found Cecil and told him he'd be heading back to the Kimberley in a couple of days, to be ready and he'd take him home.

"I hear you bought this place." Scotty probed the old man.

"No, I haven't bought it." Cecil said, but he had, he just wasn't admitting it. Scotty picked him up and brought him back to the Kimberley, but when Cecil got there he didn't have his job any more.

In latter years, after his dogging days were over, Cecil lived up on Oobagooma. He had a mob of pigs that lived with him and all of them had names, politicians names mostly! He'd say, "That's Gough Whitlam over there, this is Joe Bjielke Peterson and that one, rooting about at the edge of the billabong, is Charlie Court." There weren't too many female pollies in those days, so the sows might be Sonia McMahon, or Princess Margaret. They were his friends. He knew them all and shared his camp with them. It was a bit of a worry because if he'd got badly hurt, or been taken seriously ill, these pigs could easily have ended up eating him. But Cecil wasn't one to worry about that kind of thing and he lived up there for a long time. Well into old age.

People used to visit Cecil if they were up Oobagooma way. They would take up a few supplies and any old magazines and newspapers they might have. Cecil was an avid reader. He'd read the magazines from cover to cover, even old racing journals, and remember everything he read. He could talk about anything, world affairs, sport, you name it, he had an opinion on it. Usually a well informed opinion, though perhaps some of his facts were a bit out of date. It was said that he'd had a good education as a boy, at an Eastern States school, but no-one really knew for sure.

One day, out of the blue, I received a telephone call from a bloke who lived down at Dandaragen. He had come up to Derby to see Cecil and had been told I would be the best person to ring. I was managing Meda Station at the time. Oobagooma was on our northern boundary and the only access, other than by sea, was to drive through Meda country, a distance of some eighty miles. It turned out this bloke was the son off the sheep property in the Gascoyne, where Cecil had worked in his youth. Apparently he had power of attorney for Cecil and needed to speak to him about a life insurance policy that was maturing. He'd been told this wouldn't be that easy and unless he went out to Oobagooma with somebody who was well known, and trusted, by Cecil it was unlikely he would even set eyes on the old fellow. This was true. When strangers were about Cecil was like a frill necked lizard. He'd circle a tree, watching them from a distance. If he knew them, and liked them, he'd show himself, if not he'd keep hidden until the visitor left. Anyway, this bloke who rang up, seemed ridgy-didge, so I told him to come out and sleep at the Meda homestead that night and I'd take him to Oobagooma the following day. He said he would and asked if there was anything he could get in town to take up for Cecil.

"Yeah. A couple of loaves of bread, a cabbage, a few spuds and onions, a packet of tea and a bit of sugar. Maybe a bottle of rum. That should do him."

My wife made up a batch of sandwiches for us to take, because I knew we wouldn't want to eat anything Cecil had to offer. It would likely kill us, certainly the fella from down south. So we set off early next day, myself, our young son George and this bloke, John Cusack, who turned out to be a really nice fellow. We crossed the May River and drove out past Number Four, Daley's and Euringa, crossed the Meda River and continued on beyond Rarriwell, and up towards Oobagooma. When we got there we found Cecil and had a cup of tea with him. After awhile young George and I left the two men to talk privately. When they had finished their discussion old Cec invited us to share lunch with him.

"I knocked a heifer the other day and you're just lucky I've still got the fillet left. We'll go up to the homestead and cook it." The homestead on Oobagooma was not flash. It was pretty much derelict at this time, no windows, just posts where the louvres used to be and pretty much cactus. While Cecil was gathering up his billy cans, tea leaves and sugar I said to John Cusack.

"Now, whatever happens, you *do not* eat this meat Cecil is cooking for us. He's got no refrigeration. It will be 'off' and if you eat it you will be violently ill. I could probably eat it and, maybe vomit it up, but if you eat any, it will likely kill you. Your stomach won't handle it."

At the homestead Cecil lit the two gas burners on the stove. He got the piece of meat. It had already gone green on him, and was covered in tea leaves. He cut the fillet in half, lengthways, opened it out, then placed it directly on the gas stove. No dish, no pan, nothing. The juices started running out of it all over the stove top. While the meat was being cooked we opened our pack of sandwiches and hopped into them. We offered one to Cecil. He didn't have any decent tucker, so he couldn't get the sandwiches into himself quick enough. By the time we'd finished our packed lunch Cecil had rolled the fillet over a couple of times and was satisfied it was done.

"I think she's about ready now. Do you want a bit?" He offered.

"No thanks. We're all full."

"Ah, that's good" said Cecil. "Now I've got my tea cooked and ready for tonight."

He must have had a cast iron constitution, or he'd have died of food poisoning years ago.

A good while later, after I'd left Meda and was managing a fuel depot in Derby, we used to deliver fuel to Kimbolton, out beyond where Cecil lived. I asked Aubrey, the truck driver, if he'd check up on Cecil while he was up that way and I'd buy a few stores to send out for him. This happened a couple of times. On one of the trips Aubrey found Cecil crook, so he brought him back into Derby to the hospital. When Cecil had recovered and returned to Oobagooma he found people had been out there and shot all his pigs. This really upset him. He went off the rails a bit after that, and used to let a few shots off now and then. You couldn't really blame him. Those pigs were his family. The only family he had. They took his firearm off him and eventually he ended up at Numbla Nunga Nursing Home in Derby. After a time he picked up a stray dog. He wasn't allowed it in the old people's home, so he made a camp in the grounds for himself, sleeping in his swag, with the dog for company. It was quite good for him really. He died at Numbla Nunga a few years later, but had made arrangements to ensure that the stray dog was cared for after he'd gone. Poor old Cecil. He died intestate and his executor had a bit of a job sorting everything out. In the end fourteen long lost, or perhaps 'never before heard of" relations came out of the woodwork for a cut of his estate.

*The 'mystery man' Cecil Roderick.*

*Cecil 'boating' on the billabong at Oobagooma.*

*Me and Cecil. An intelligent man, with a cast iron stomach and a hide like leather.*

*circa mid to late 1980's*

# CHAPTER SEVEN

# TRUCK DRIVING

*Your love of the horse is the star on your course,*
*And there's nothing can take up it's place,*
*And with bridle and rein, and a pat on the mane*
*There are many that won a good race.*

## Big FreddySambo

I had a pretty good bunch of native stockmen with me when I was running the camp on Kimberley Downs. Good smart men who knew what they were about. They included men such as Michael Bear, Ringer Campton, Brian Djigbar, Ben Bibingnulli, Eddie Bear, George Numburra, Windbag, Rastus, Harry Martin, Big Don. They were all good men. But there was one fellow who gave me a bit of strife. His name was Freddy. Big Freddy Sambo. He was always agitating, headstrong and difficult. Often he was the horse tailer, but he would dawdle about, or sit around and not get on with the job. I'd say to him 'Are you going to get the horses Freddy?' and he'd say 'Yeah, yeah.' but he'd still stay there and not go and bring the horses up. He had this style about him that he'd only do the job when he was good and ready. This sort of thing was on all the time with him and it really used to try me. I couldn't get along with him at all and Robin Campbell knew it. Sometimes Big Freddy would be sent out into another stockcamp, to work for someone else, but he always seemed to end up back in mine. I don't know why this was. Perhaps he was the same with everybody.

One time we were at Womberella and I noticed all these sores on Big Freddy. He was standing very close to the campfire, so close you'd reckon it would have burnt him, but he didn't seem to notice. I thought 'This fella has got leprosy', so I told Robin Campbell. After that Freddy Sambo was taken away and treated. He can't have been put in the Leprosarium because after a while he was back on Kimberley Downs. Needless to say, his attitude towards me hadn't improved.

One day towards the end of the season Frank Bridge, once the manager of Mornington, now retired and working as a pumpman on Kimberley Downs, came and had a talk to me. He said his wife, a native woman, had told him that Freddy Sambo was going to fix me up. Frank Bridge told me to be very careful. Often, I was the only white fella in the stockcamp, so I was quite worried about this.

It was close to the end of the year and I was in Derby one day, when I ran into Donny Archer and we got talking. Donny had a cartage business and he offered me a job. He told me what he would pay me if I went to work for him and it was three times what I was earning on the station. I couldn't believe it. It sounded marvellous and the hours would be a lot less. I returned to Kimberley Downs and thought about it for a while. After a bit I told Campbell I was leaving. He was fine and seemed OK about it. He didn't try to persuade me to stay on, or offer me more money, or anything, so I left. That was at the end of 1966.

## A union ticket

I started working for Donny Archer after Christmas, or early in the New Year of 1967. Although I really loved my job on Kimberley Downs, and I was in love with a lot of the horses, I went into Derby to work for Donny chasing the money. He had offered me such good pay I couldn't refuse it. I didn't have a truck driver's license, so Donny arranged for me to get a truck license. I just had to pass a verbal test, then once I'd got that I delivered gear around the town for him.

Some station blokes, laid off during the 'wet' season, would go down to the wharf, when the ships came in, and wait at the 'pick up point' hoping to be taken on at the wharf to help unload cargo. I'd done this too from time to time. It was a bugger of a job, but well paid. At least I thought it was, and they fed you. A union ticket was needed and you had to stick to the wharfie's rules, otherwise you wouldn't be 'picked up' next time. Depending on the cargo it could be hard yakka. I remember unloading salt one time. I was fit and energetic in those days and to start with the work didn't seem hard. But after a while my hands began to get very sore, from hefting the heavy hessian bags, and the salt made it worse. It was like when I'd worked as a brickies labourer. There were no gloves.

Depending on the tides, State Ships could come in by day, or night. Night time was easier for the wharfies, being cooler, although it was still very hot in the ship's hold. If the ship was in at night, Donny, who I found to be a very fair man, would pay me overtime. Having come off stations, this was a new experience for me and I thought it was pretty good.

Some of the wharfies were bastards. The union boss was a bloke called Fitzgerald, who sported a walrus moustache and thought he was really something. He reckoned I couldn't step out of the truck onto the ramp, or into the goods shed, without buying a union ticket. 'Fritz' used to come and front me about it and often it would develop into an argument. I didn't consider myself a wharfie when I was truck driving for Donny Archer, so I didn't see why I had to buy a union ticket. We had a few blues about it, me and the union man. But I was lucky. I had a good dog at the time, who backed me up whenever voices were raised. His name was Yogi. He was a bull terrier, labrador, boxer cross. Black and tan. A big heavy dog. If things got a bit heated Yogi would get off the truck, the hair would all stand up along his spine and his tail would go straight up. He'd come around the truck and start growling. There would be no more talk of a union ticket that day. But the problem didn't go away completely and in the end Donny Archer paid for a union ticket for me and things were easier after that.

When the ships came in I'd have to go down to the wharf to pick up cargo and deliver it around the town. I had to deliver to places like the hospital, the hotel, Mrs. Preest's tuck shop, which was where the Raintree Craft Cottage was in later years, and to the swimming pool kiosk. Rusty's had their own truck, so I didn't deliver to the grocery shop. Amongst other things I had to deliver freezer goods. The goods would be unloaded from the freezer unit on the ship, into the goods shed, then onto the back of Donny's truck. It was a hell of a job to get it delivered around the place, and unloaded at each destination as quickly as possible, before it deteriorated, or melted in the heat.

Sometimes I carted stores out to Meda Station, flour, spuds, onions, groceries, or I might have to cart sand in from Meda for someone in town. The sand came from the May River and was shovelled onto the truck by hand. I would take out four or five natives from Derby to give a hand with the shovelling. They didn't mind. They seemed to like coming out for the run and they got paid.

Another job I did for Donny was cart gravel and rock, to fix up Langi Crossing which had been washed away during the 'wet'. We were carting out of a gravel pit on the Fitzroy road, about ten kilometres up from the Broome, Derby, Fitzroy turnoff. We would be out there, ready to start carting, early in the morning. There was a bloke with a loader and as each truck came in he'd load it. You might have to wait for one to be loaded in front of you, then it would be your turn. We'd drive back and forth, from there to Langi Crossing, all day long. I used to get very tired doing this job. I'd sit in the truck while it was loaded, then once I got going I'd begin to feel drowsy. The sound of the engine, and the heat off it, really sends you. It makes you very sleepy. There was no radio or CD player, or anything like that, to help keep you awake and the only air conditioning was an open window! One day I was driving along, when suddenly I woke up and found myself off the road. The truck was fully loaded. I was cutting across over big rocks and everything, near where the Fitzroy turnoff is now. I went over the top of the rocks and somehow, I've no idea how, managed to bring it back onto the road. It was just a fluke. I never said anything about it to Donny, but Jeez I was lucky.

It was during this period, about Easter time, that I met Rae, a good looking, vivacious, party loving, young teacher who could really dance. I mean, really dance. My life would never be the same again.

Donny Archer was paying me $80 a week wages, with an additional $10 a night to get up and serve fuel if need be, so I was earning good money. But Donny's work, to me, was boring and the hours seemed to drag. On the station I had earned $18 a week. That was for seven days, work all hours and ride anything! Mostly on a diet of salt beef and damper. But on the station the days went by pretty quickly. I loved the cattle work. Really I lived for it and, although it may not have been much, they even paid me.

One day Robin Campbell saw me in town. He told me he was leaving Kimberley Downs and that if I wanted the job of manager I should apply. I told him I didn't think I was ready and was too young for it, but Campbell didn't seem to think so. I mulled it over for a few days, then decided to give it a go. I went to see Rowell, but he told me he already had a bloke lined up. His name was Fred Wright. I continued to work for Donny in Derby, I continued to date Rae and I continued to enjoy earning decent money. The time would come, however, when I was to get to know Fred Wright and how he operated, better than I ever could have guessed.

## Horses in town

I had several horses in town whilst I worked for Donny. Four of these were kept at Sunnyside, just outside Derby, and included Earldon and Graymond. They were used specifically for taking bullocks from Myall's Bore Yards down to the wharf. Droving days were coming to an end and bullocks were starting to be trucked in from the stations, rather than being walked in. Robert Rowell, the shipping agent, had the use of my four horses at Sunnyside and would pay me each time they were ridden. I had another two horses, which I kept on a block across the road from my parents place in Neville Street. Jubilee, who I bought off Robin Campbell and Hong Kong, my camp horse. I fed these two night and morning. Mum and Dad owned three vacant blocks there at one time, so it was pretty good for me. If I wasn't doing a job for Donny Archer, or later Bob Skuthorpe, and there were shipping bullocks at Myall's Bore, I would help take them down to the wharf. I used to really enjoy that. It relieved the tedium of my town job.

On one occasion there was a mob of GoGo bullocks at Myall's Bore Yards. Harry Scrivener was there with them. He was Emanuel's 'eyes'. Also camped nearby was Maurice McKarron, known to most as the 'Mad Scotchman'. During the night the cattle rushed. Harry Scrivener always maintained the Mad Scotchman's dogs had caused it. Whether this was right or not, I don't know, but whatever the cause the bullocks must have got a big fright. Myall's Bore Yard was built of 6"x4" jarrah timbers. The posts were railway iron, set in concrete. When the cattle 'jumped' they smashed their way out of four internal yards, post and rails, exiting the yard by breaking through one external section, from which they got out. Some of the railway irons were bent over to within a foot of the ground, such was the force of the rush. Harry Scrivener didn't raise the alarm till morning. He didn't want to wake anybody up! Early that morning Robert Rowell rang my parents, to see if I was there, which I was. He told me what had happened and asked if I could help. I saddled one of my horses from over the road, Jubilee, and rode out to the yards. I got four good blacks from the town reserve, one of whom was Tommy May, to ride the horses from Sunnyside.

Initially we didn't think it would be a big job to get the mob of GoGo bullocks back in hand, but it was. We managed to gather a good number of them quite quickly, but a fair few others were still away. A couple of the native boys followed them up, tracking them for a considerable distance before eventually picking them up near Millards Soak, on Meda, some fifteen miles away. They walked them back in to Myall's Bore, but the cattle were too stressed to go on the ship with the others. They were sent to the local abattoir instead.

The ship was not only taking live cattle on board, but also frozen meat from Demco, the abattoir in town. I ended up earning a lot of money that weekend. Rowell paid me for helping get the cattle back and also for the use of my horses. Then I earned overtime rates from Donny, for carting the frozen meat from Demco down to the ship.

Apart from the stock horses I had in town, I also owned a thoroughbred racehorse, called Capuire, as well as a couple of local bred horses, in training with Brian Moore. I wasn't paying Brian to train my horses. Instead I would get up early and head out to the racecourse, getting there just on daylight, and ride track work for him. I paid Brian for the feed for my horses and I worked any of his horses that needed riding. This was before I began my working day with Donny and I used to enjoy the hour or so out there on the race track. It was a very good feeling riding racehorses, with the wind and speed and feeling of freedom.

When it was races time it was decided to take four or five of the horses down for the Broome race meeting. Capuire was amongst them. He was a black gelding, sired by Copper Blend out of Huatrix. Brian organised for us to use Donny's truck. A crate was put on, the horses were loaded and away we went. When we got to Broome we camped near the racecourse. There were stalls for visiting racehorses, situated along the edge of the sandhills, on the beach side of the road. Southerners would come up and camp there for a fair while before races time, and train their horses from there. It was a good set up.

Capuire was nominated for the maiden. The odds on him were good and I put money on him to win. He was leading the field coming round the turn and looked really promising, until the 'monkey' on his back looked over his shoulder. This caused Capuire to drift to the outside rail and he came home in sand about a foot deep. He ran second, but we'd shown him to everyone and the odds on him were never as good again. On the second day of racing a mare from Carnarvon, called Banana Girl, was nominated to run. She had a good reputation so I decided not to race Capuire against her. A day or so before the race her owner came to me and asked if I'd be running my gelding. I said, "No".

He told me I should. He said, "I'm not starting my mare in that race." I thought 'That's good' and on the strength of what he'd told me I decided I would run Capuire after all. When the day came Banana Girl's owner hadn't scratched her at all. It was too late for me to withdraw Capuire, so they raced against each other. Banana Girl won and Capuire ran second. I wasn't too happy, but dirty little tricks like that are common in the racing game. Afterwards Kevin Kent's jockey, Dennis Gates, came to me.

"I'll ride that horse for you John, if I'm free and not committed to ride for Kevin." He told me, so that is what happened. At the next race meeting, which was in Derby, Dennis rode Capuire to a win, though the odds on him weren't good. After that he was put in a higher grade but didn't come a place. At the end of the three day meeting I sold him to a bloke called Don Laidlaw, who had approached me some time earlier asking to buy him.

When Brian Moore and I returned to Derby from the Broome races we were a day later than expected. Elsia Archer, Donny's wife, had a fair bit to say about it. Elsia was sort of the boss and when we got back she slipped a cog.

"You've been away from work for a day. You're using the truck and we needed the truck." She told me. She was pretty snakey. I said, "Look, it's nothing to do with me Elsia. I'm just doing what I'm told to do. The truck deal is between you, Donny and Brian Moore. It's nothing to do with me. Brian has my horse and he's in charge of it, but that doesn't come into me working here. I don't know what arrangement Brian made with Donny. It's none of my business." But after that things weren't very good. The ill feeling sort of triggered things and I pulled the pin.

Bob Skuthorpe said he would give me a job. I had met Rae by then and I was liking the money I earned in town. I wanted to stay in Derby, so I accepted Bob's offer and began driving for Fitzroy Valley Transport.

## Fitzroy Valley Transport

When I was working for Bob Skuthorpe, who owned Fitzroy Valley Transport, the truck I was driving had the engine in the middle of the cab, right alongside the driver's seat. A fair bit of heat came off it and I found it hard to stay awake. I found daytime the worst for wanting to doze off. I used to have to pull up every couple of hours and go to sleep, then wake up and drive on again. I really hated long distance driving, but I saw places I'd never been to before.

I was carting gear up to Fitzroy Crossing, maybe perishables for The Crossing Inn, or perhaps gear for Jubilee Downs, or casing for Fossil Downs Station. We would load the truck up during the day, then in the evening I'd take off. I was burning the candle at both ends, because I was going out with Rae then, but I was young and thought I could handle it. One night I was driving along when all of a sudden I saw a bloody grader parked in the middle of the road, on a cattle grid. I hit the brakes and carried on as if it was a real emergency. When I pulled up I found there was nothing there at all. I'd been seeing things. Another time the same thing happened. Suddenly out of the dark I saw a man and a boy walking down the road. For a moment or two I was frantic. I did my utmost to miss them. But there was no man and boy. It's a terrible feeling. You hit the brakes and go to swerve, then in a flash it's all gone. There's nothing there. I don't know where these things appear from, but it's bloody frightening.

One time I took Rae with me for the run. It was a Friday and we had the truck all loaded and ready to go. The last item to go on was ice-cream for The Crossing Inn. There was no refrigeration, but the heavy steel cylinders were placed in large insulated containers. I had forgotten to fuel up before leaving Derby and we ran out of fuel fourteen miles out from Fitzroy Crossing. We were there on the side of the road all night. Fortunately Bob Skuthorpe was coming along with another truckload of gear the following morning, including forty-four gallon drums of fuel. We siphoned some from one of the drums into the truck and got going again. The ice-cream was still all right when we eventually got there.

Except for the long straight drives back and forth between Derby and Fitzroy Crossing it was a good job, although it did have its moments. One in particular that comes to mind was the day I delivered a load of casing to Fossil Downs. Twenty foot lengths of six inch, or eight inch casing, I don't remember which. It doesn't matter, either way it was bloody heavy. Me and one other bloke unloaded it. He was a Fossil man. We had almost finished when this little 'Suzie', who also worked there, told us to straighten them all up, so that the ends were even. I was good friends with John and Annette Henwood and knew they were fastidious, but these weren't bamboo garden stakes we were hefting about, and I wasn't Don Athaldo.

I continued to work for Bob Skuthorpe for the remainder of the year, then I went to Perth for Christmas. Soon after New Year Rae and I were married. I was twenty-four.

## Married life

We began our married life in Perth, living in my parents' house in Clifton Street, Nedlands. This house had belonged to my paternal grandmother and had been left to Dad, because he'd helped maintain mortgage payments on the property after the death of my grandfather. Mum and Dad were still living in Derby, only coming to Perth during the wet season, so the house was vacant. Mum was nursing at Derby Regional Hospital and Dad was reading brands and earmarks at Demco.

Rae got a job teaching in Perth and I worked at the Midland Abattoir. I was just a worker on the chain and I didn't enjoy it much. I used to get home from work at about six in the evening, often to an empty house. Sometimes Rae wouldn't get in until nine, or later. After several months of this I decided I couldn't hack city life any longer. I told Rae I wanted to go back north. I rang Robert Rowell and asked if he had a job for me. He said he did. I handed in my notice at Midland and made preparations to drive back to the Kimberley.

I headed up the coast road from Perth to Geraldton, Geraldton to Carnarvon and on up through Roebourne and Whim Creek towards Port Hedland. The road was unsealed from Carnarvon onwards and roadhouses were few and far between. I carried my own fuel, in forty four gallon drums, on the back of the Holden ute. I had plenty of water, some tucker, spare wheels, belts, filters, all that sort of thing with me, in case of breakdowns. There was no 'Roadside Assistance' in those days. One had to be self reliant, but I was used to that. I rang Rae several times along the way, to let her know where I was, and to see how things were in Perth. I did this, as usual, when I reached Roebourne. Rae told me she had managed to get a transfer, with the Education Department, to Derby and would be flying up the next day. She said she would see me in Port Hedland. When the plane landed in Hedland we met briefly at the airport, before she flew on up to Derby to take up her teaching post. I continued driving north, crossing the De Grey river, then on up a long corrugated stretch of the Great Northern Highway, with it's bulldust holes and treacherous potholes at every cattle grid, any one of which could cause untold damage to the unwary. I stopped at Sandfire Roadhouse where Eddie and Kath Norton provided an invaluable service to travellers. Fuel, food and a few yarns over an ale. Sandfire was pretty much the half way point along that stretch of road to Broome, and always a welcome break in the journey. When I reached Derby the following day Rae was already settled in a spacious school house, which she shared with other teachers. After a brief catch up with her, I headed out to Kimberley Downs.

## Back to Kimberley Downs

When I rang Rowell from Perth asking for a job, I had requested that all my old riding horses and mule come back to me. He had agreed. Robin Campbell had left K.D. so when I returned to the station I was working under a new manager, Fred Wright, who had previously been managing Anna Plains, just north of Sandfire. I was to run one of two stockcamps on Kimberley Downs that season. The other was being run by a native stockman, Billy Munroe, who had worked for Dad on Meda, when I was a boy.

When I arrived I was taken straight out to my stockcamp, which was then at Police Camp. I found that despite Rowell having given me an assurance that I would have my previous string of horses back, when I returned it didn't happen. Instead I had one wall eyed mare, but no others from my previous string, and none of the night horses either. I took over the camp immediately and we began mustering. We mustered to Munjaweela, around Barnes', across to Windjana Gorge and back to Police Camp, spending about a week at each camp, depending on what cattle were around. Police Camp, in those days, had no yard, just wire and star pickets. From there we went on down to Rarrigee. Fred Wright came out to Rarrigee to see us. He told us to take the cattle to The Six Mile, then do a lap around the bullock paddock.

The moon was right, so I told the blokes we would get up in the middle of the night and take the bullocks half way between Rarrigee and Six Mile in the moonlight. So that's what we did. I left four blokes to tail the bullocks and feed them on to The Six Mile, while the rest of us cut across to Telephone Dam Paddock. We mustered in the bullock paddock, back to The Six Mile, getting there about lunch time. As we approached we could see people working cattle, so we pulled our mob up outside the fence. I rode over to see what was going on. When I got there I found Billy Munroe and his crew, cutting out, and I saw that they were using all the night horses on the face of the camp.

When I came upon him using night horses, my night horses from when I was ringing there previously, on the face of the camp, I was annoyed. I rode over to him.

"What's going on here?" I asked.

"Why what's wrong?" he challenged.

"You know what's wrong. You don't use night horses working in the face of the camp. Their job is to get the horses, if they have to, night and morning, maybe do a late yard up, and be night horses. That's their job. They're special horses. Night horses is their job. Not on the face of the camp. You know that as well as I do." I was very annoyed about it. Billy Munroe knew perfectly well, that what he was doing was wrong. Very wrong. I was one of the blokes who usually ended up on a night horse, if there was a rush. To see the poor things being used to open camp draft made me see red.

"You not der boss here boy!" Billy Munroe told me.

When Fred Wright came out to Six Mile he never said anything about the night horses being used. I don't really think Fred knew a lot, or had a lot of cattle ability, despite having been on Anna Plains.

Billy Munroe was a smart, capable man, but there was a sly streak in him and I think this incident was the beginning of the end, for me, on Kimberley Downs.

One morning, soon after this, we were drafting horses off in preparation to go out on a second mustering round. Last year's breakers were amongst them. I'd been away the previous season, so I didn't know the good from the bad. Earlier a black fella had said to me, "I got 'im one good colt longa station. You can hab 'im Shohn. He's a prop'ly good horse, jad'un."

"I s'pose the bastard bucks like hell" I told him. "But I'll take him anyway."

So when we drafted the colts off I took this horse. Richender was his name. Once we'd finished drafting Fred Wright turned up. He asked me to go with him to help peg out a drafting yard at Police Camp. He'd asked me several times before, but I'd said it wasn't my job to peg yards, it was his. But on this occasion I couldn't very well refuse. I told the boys to let the working horses out of the yard, then take each of the colts for a ride. I said, "Leave Richender in the yard for me to ride when I get back." Fred and I went and pegged the new drafting yard. Goodness knows whether the native boys rode all the colts or not. I wasn't there to see and I was the only white man in the camp, so there was no-one who could tell me. When I got back I saddled up my colt and ran him around the round yard for a bit. He seemed pretty good, so I told the boys to grab some old horses and go and muster the rest of the workers.

"Don't muster them on the young horses." I told them "And we'll leave after lunch."

Big Freddy Sambo was there. He seemed to be dawdling about, still on his colt. "Haven't you gone to get the horses in yet, what have you been doing?"

"I'll go and get them now" He told me.

"Not on that horse you're not." I said. He was a surly, troublesome bastard. A big bloke. You had to stand over him a bit, or he'd please himself. Anyway he took no notice. By this time I'd got on my colt, Richender, and I'd ridden him out of the yard. He was good. Freddy Sambo rode back to me, still on his colt, and said, "I'm going to get those horses."

"I wouldn't if I were you." I warned him. Big Freddy turned his colt around and rode off.

"Right, if you're going to be like that I don't need you. You're finished. You can unsaddle your horse." I told him. With that he rode back to me and dropped his whip on the arse of my horse, so next thing Richender was 'into it'. He couldn't buck out of sight on a dark night, or maybe I was lucky my blood was fairly up, after having the blue. Anyway I rode him. Then he stopped bucking, so I went to get off and he started again. I gave him a good larraping and he pulled up. I jumped off, pulled the saddle off him, saddle cloth and bridle and walked up to see Fred Wright. I told him what had happened.

"I've sacked Freddy Sambo." I told him.

"Well he's not going. You are." Fred Wright said.

I'd only completed one round of mustering, been back less than two months and it was over already. I'd been sacked for the first time in my life. It seemed to me Fred Wright was working for the black fellas, not the other way round. Under the circumstances, me running a stockcamp for him was never going to work. I packed up my gear and away I went.

I called in at Meda on my way through to Derby, to see Dave Ledger. His wife Margaret told me he was mustering in the Bullock Paddock, so I drove down there and saw him. He asked if I had a job and I told him I didn't anymore.

"Well you've got one here. Start tomorrow morning." Dave said.

"I'd better go into town first and let Rowell know that I've pulled the pin, or rather, that I've got the arse." I told him. When I got into Derby, Rowell wasn't there. Norm Longdon, his right hand man, was in the office.

"Rowell's in Perth, but he'll be back in a few days." Norm told me. "Don't take the Meda job yet."

"I'd better take the job. I need the work."

"No. You wait till I get onto Rowell." So I rang Meda and told them I wouldn't be there next day after all. When I went back to see Norm Longdon the following day, he told me Rowell would be back in Derby in a week.

"Rowell says he'll keep you on full pay until he gets back." Norm told me. Anyway he never got back for a month, so I got a months free pay. I stayed with Rae in the school house during this time. When Rowell eventually got back I was called to the office.

"I don't want you to go anywhere else. We're going to start Napier up, and you can go over there and manage it," Rowell told me. "I'll build a homestead for you." In time they did, but a lot happened before then.

# PART TWO

# CHAPTER EIGHT

# OLD NAPIER

*Tall and lean he stood between*
*The concrete slab where the house had been,*
*Looking back at the chimney stack,*
*To the ranges beyond the river.*

Napier seemed to be the unwanted child. It was always put down and to the back, but Napier was where a lot of the good bullocks came from, so I was happy to go there. A million acres in size, it was the home of cattle.

The homestead at Napier was in a state of disrepair. It was situated on the banks of the Barker River and Womberella Creek, in a fork of highly fertile country, enriched over the years by river silt, where we later grew a wonderful vegetable garden. It was to become known, in future years, as 'Old Napier', so as not to be confused with a modern homestead yet to be built and 'Old Old Napier' which was the very first homestead site, a further fifteen kilometres down the range. There once was a well at the old original homestead site, which later dried up. A bore was then put down and the water from this sustained the inhabitants for a while longer. Eventually that too went dry and the homestead was shifted to its present location, on the banks of the Barker River. At the time the blacks said not to build there. 'Dat place no good. It plood water place, ja'dun.' But the whites knew better, so here it was, my new home from where I would manage Napier for the next two years.

There were two main buildings at the homestead, the larger of which was the men's quarters, the other a kitchen, with storeroom attached. The kitchen had a cement floor, a verandah on three sides, and damaged flyscreen and asbestos walls. In the kitchen area there was a large wood stove, a seven or eight foot long table, with bench seats either side, and a couple of kitchen dressers and work tables. There was also an enclosed room for the cook to sleep in. This became my room. I used an outside tap behind the kitchen for my ablutions. In the men's quarters the louvres were broken and flywire almost non existent. There was a wide breezeway running the length of the building, where some of the men slept. There was a shower room, with donkey for hot water, and a toilet. There were three or four small rooms. One of the small corner rooms was used by us as a saddle room, where we kept the horse feed. There was a workshop, with curved corrugated iron roof, cement floor, but no equipment. All repairs were done by Jim Douglas, the windmill man/mechanic at Kimberley Downs. Beyond this were the horse stables and the black's camp.

Napier had been abandoned for a number of years, used only as a base for a stockcamp sent across from Kimberley Downs. When the mustering season ended it would be deserted, unless someone chose to stay on, to mind the place during the 'wet'. We started there with basically nothing, apart from the cattle, the occasional buffalo and a lot of wild donkeys. I didn't mind the wild donkeys. I thought they helped us. They'd dig soaks for themselves, where the cattle could also water in dry times.

There were three timber drafting yards on the property when I went there. Tullochs, Billyarra and the Homestead yards. We had wire bronco yards at Mount Josef, Mt. Eliza, Womberella, Dromedaries, Butter Bore, Kongrow, Hans Hole, Billy More's and Mundooma, as well as a cock-rag set-up at Limestone Springs. There were bores at Tulloch's, Butter Bore, Red Bull and Homestead and a dam, windmill and trough at Womberella. The only paddocks were a small horse paddock and a bullock paddock. The bullock paddock was too small for our spell horses and sale cattle, and used to be eaten out.

## Cranking up

When Napier started up all the stockmen were given the choice of coming with me or staying at Kimberley Downs. This arrangement worked pretty well, with half choosing to stay and half coming with me. Needless to say Billy Munroe and Big Freddy Sambo opted to stay on Kimberley Downs, together with Rastus, Jack Bear and Jackie Dann. The latter suited me, as Jackie Dann's wife, Rita LeLe, was a headstrong woman. In a fit of temper she had thrown a fire-stick onto the roof of the large bough shed at Kimberley Downs, burning it to the ground. I wasn't seeking to take that kind of aggravation with me. I was more than happy with those who did choose to come. These included Michael, Eddie and Vincent Bear. Victor Joy, Gordon LeLievre, Ringer Campton, and 'Fat' Brian Djigbar. Reggie Woods came along too, bringing Flash Ada with him. Willie Lennard, who had been out pearling, also came. I'd known him all my life and was delighted to have him in my crew. Along with the stockmen came their riding horses and mules. The remaining working horses, were run through the yard one for one.

As we were starting from scratch, we had to take everything with us. Initially we were given leftover stores, including a box of thongs, sandshoes, various odds and ends and an assortment of tucker. We took spare hobbles, chains, leather gear and a few tools, but we also needed brooms, rakes, axes, wheelbarrows and so on, which were ordered in and came later. We had an old ex army Blitz truck, four wheel drive, later replaced by a tractor and trailer, and a Ford ute, which was pretty much useless to us. It was only two wheel drive and couldn't get over the rocky outcrops, nor the many sandy creeks. In time it was replaced by a blue Toyota, previously used by the Demco cattle buyer, which was much more suitable.

I was given three worn out chainsaws, two Stihls and a McCulloch. When we got them to Napier they didn't work. I took them into Derby to get fixed up, but was told that they weren't worth repairing. It seemed as if Napier was given all the rubbish. Everything which was undersize that came through the K.D. store, and they couldn't sell, came to me. When I found I had three useless chainsaws into the bargain I complained to one of the owners. Bob Maxted said he'd send the chainsaws to Perth, which he did. Eventually he too was told they weren't worth repairing, that they were worn out. Next thing, Maxted comes out to Napier bringing with him two brand new Stihl chainsaws. I was delighted and they were soon put to good use.

No maintenance had been done on the property for a long, long time. Everywhere I looked there was work to be done. This included the airstrip, which had to be cleared, graded and marker drums painted. The grader was sent across from Kimberley Downs, to grade the strip. As with most things, we were dependent on the 'parent' station and the co-operation of it's manager. What Fred Wright must have thought of my going to manage Napier, after he'd fired me, I don't know, but I don't suppose he was thrilled.

Apart from getting the airstrip in order, one of our first jobs when starting up Napier was to check the horse paddock and bullock paddock fences. Then we were away, off mustering. It was still early in the year, the horses a bit fat, so we did a few short musters first, down to Butter Bore and back to the homestead, to harden them up. Then later we went further out. A typical round might be to go up from the Homestead to Womberella mustering, then up to The Dromedaries, down to Hans Hole and on to Kongrow, then to Red Bull. From there we would take the meatworkers back home and put them in the bullock paddock, leaving our plant horses at Red Bull. Then depending on how the horses were holding up, we would return to Red Bull this time going on to Billy More's. We usually spent quite a while mustering the area around Billy More's before moving on to Limestone Springs. From there the stockcamp would move on to Mundooma, then back to Limestone Springs, to Tullochs, to Butter Bore and back to the homestead. Depending on what cattle were about, each mustering round would take about six weeks to complete.

As I was running the stockcamp and managing Napier, it was my responsibility to check the bores. Early in the year the waters were not too much of a concern for me, but as the season progressed the more frequent the bore runs became. Usually I would do this on the days when we were branding, leaving the men to do any earmarking, castrating or other cattlework that was required. In my absence they would mark the branders with a notch, made with a pocket knife, on a stick. Later that day, when I returned from the bore run I would count up the notches to write in my branding book.

## Napier men

I was fortunate the best of the native stockmen chose to come with me. Really, I couldn't have picked a better crew. Most of my men were as keen to get cattle as I was. Catching cattle, on horseback, was what they lived for. Like me, it was what they'd grown up with. The noise, the smell, the thrill of Kimberley cattle camps. For me, work was deadly serious. We were working with wild cattle and when I wanted something done, I wanted it done 'now' and 'quickly'. That included opening and closing gates. It meant 'run'. Cattlework wasn't a sleepy job, it wasn't a joke. It was serious and risky and you had to be awake. The class of cattle we were working with meant we always had to be alert. Watching. Looking for cattle that were looking 'for out'. If I saw a beast wanting to leave the mob I'd yell out 'move and block that beast' which meant 'do it now and do it fast.' Having mustered them, I wanted to keep them, not let them get away from us. When I see someone dawdling, slow to respond to a situation, I class him as 'useless'. I don't need him if he hasn't got an accelerator. Likewise when working in the yard, running cattle through, castrating, branding, tipping horns and earmarking, speed and efficiency is important. The yards are hot and they're dusty. Neither cattle, nor men need be there longer than necessary, and I like things to flow smoothly. People may think I'm harsh on my blokes, but I reckon I make smart men and they are all pretty lively in the yard.

There were a lot of good native stockmen before the advent of award wages for aboriginal pastoral workers and I learnt a lot of what I know from those good old fellows.

It was about this time that award wages came in and within a few years there was a sharp decline in the number of capable, experienced aboriginal stockmen on stations. I was lucky to have some of the best and, as it turned out, some of the last working on Napier with me.

## The three Bears

Michael, Eddie and Vincent Bear, were all half brothers and fine stockmen. They'd grown up living and breathing stockwork. When I first went to Kimberley Downs as a ringer the boys were still going to school on the station. When we were working at the homestead yards, if it was a weekend, after school hours, or holiday time, the kids would come down to the yards to watch us. We might be drafting, branding, or horse breaking. Whatever stockwork was going on, they'd be there. Sometimes, if horses had to be taken back out to a paddock, these kids would be chucked on a quiet old horse, bareback. We'd put bridles on and send an older fellow with them, and they'd take the spell horses out to where they had to go, then ride back in again to the yard. The three Bears and another youngster, Philip Duckhole, were always keen to lend a hand in this way. They seriously belonged to the ringing game, watching and learning from a very young age.

Michael Bear came into the stockcamp a year or so after I first went to work on Kimberley Downs, joined soon after by Eddie and eventually Vincent. Old Jack Bear was still working in the stockcamp when Vincent joined us. Jack was a big man. He had had a bad fall in previous years and broken his pelvis, but later returned to the ringing game. His boys were all competent riders by the time they joined the camp and were put on wages. One day we were mustering when I noticed Vincent hanging back. I told him 'to 'get up' that beast and let your horse go.' He did as I said, but when he came back his father gave him a lecture.

"Don't gallop too fast you'll hit a hole." He told him.

"That's what he's paid to do." I said. Jack and I had a few words over this. Ironically, years later I was chipping Vincent for the opposite reason, for being too reckless, but that is another story and circumstances had changed.

## Michael

Michael, the eldest Bear boy, was by far the best cattle and horseman of the three. He was a tall man, who throughout his life held his long, lean physique. Though his parentage was not commonly known, the likeness he bore to his father, an aboriginal stockman called Jimmy Maline, was remarkable. His mother, Maisie, worked in the kitchen on Kimberley Downs and was a fine and well respected woman. Michael worked for me for many years and his ability not only saved the day, but his hide as well, on quite a few occasions.

Once we were out mustering and we had a useless black fella with us, riding a horse called Kangaroo. Kangaroo was a long, limousine type horse, with not much body weight. Michael Bear was with us this day. His horse was knocked up, so I said to Michael, "You grab that horse, Kangaroo, off that other bloke. Sweat him for a bit and give your horse a spell." which he did. Presently a bull broke out of the mob. He was a big strong bull, he hadn't been thrown before and he was heading towards the creek. We had fresh bulls, and yesterday's thrown bulls in the mob. Michael didn't want him to cross the creek. Sometimes you can get into a bit of trouble crossing creeks, because the fresh bulls try to sneak off along the bank. Anyway Michael jumped off for this bull, but the bull whipped round on him. It was really quick. There was a big white gum tree and the bull was nearly onto Michael. The stockman put his arm onto the tree and ran around it, but the bull met him on the other side. I thought my man was a goner, but somehow or other he got out of it. We decked the bull and got him. I've often thought, if it had been anyone but Michael Bear we'd have had a dead man on our hands out of that.

Later that day, on the same watercourse, another bull wanted to cross the creek. Michael was still riding 'Kangaroo'. He was trying to shoulder the bull, but the horse was too light. It didn't have the strength to do it. The bull shoved man and horse over the edge of an eight foot high creek bank. As the pair were falling, Michael was off the horse and as they hit the creek bed he landed on both feet, in front of the horse, still holding the reins. He was an extraordinarily capable and agile man.

I was well aware of Michael's ability, despite him suffering from epilepsy, brought on after a bad fall during my time on Kimberley Downs. We were mustering at Mundooma, on the Oobagooma end of Napier. Michael was in the camp. On this particular day we had mustered in the morning and had a fair mob of cattle and quite a lot of bullocks. Before cutting out the bullocks and meatworks cattle from the cows and calves we had dinner. After dinner we changed our horses. Michael was riding a young horse called Thunder, who had not long been broken in, maybe two or three weeks. While we were camp drafting a bullock broke out of the mob. Michael took off after it, 'opening out' this young horse. There was a thin, young bauhinia tree, about a foot or eighteen inches high, the horse's hoof went right to the base of it, hindering his next stride and down he and Michael went. The horse ploughed into a large dead tree on the ground, which split his forehead open like a big 'Y'. Michael was between Thunder's legs, which were thrashing around. I galloped over, jumped off and pulled Michael out. He was unconscious. The young horse, Thunder, was shot there and then.

When Michael regained consciousness he was taken back to camp, a boy walking along with him, leading the other horse. We had no means of communication and were miles from anywhere. Although Michael wasn't too good for a few days he never went to hospital, had a check up or anything. That's just how it was. He stayed in the camp for a couple of days recuperating, then went back mustering again. It was after that, Michael started having fits and ended up an epileptic.

One time we were back at Napier homestead when someone came and said 'Come quick. Michael is fitting in the quarters.' I raced over there and grabbed something out of the drawer to put in his mouth. I had been told by then, that when he had a fit I was to put something in his mouth, but to make sure I didn't put my fingers in, or he'd bite them off. Then I was to roll him onto his side and make sure his tongue was forward so he didn't swallow it. So this is what I did. Michael would black out while this was going on, and froth at the mouth. He would writhe around a bit, and you'd have to get a bloke or two to hold him. This was about all we could do for him. He'd have these fits anywhere, but it never seemed to happen when he was on a horse. If we were out bush I used to get my pocket knife to put in his mouth to bite on. Later he was put on tablets, but not at first. He suffered from epilepsy all his life after that. He should have got compensation, but it was unheard of in those days, not that his disability stopped him from ringing. Despite his trouble he remained a much valued member of my crew, not only on Kimberley Downs and Napier, but later on Meda as well.

## Eddie Bear and Vincent Bear

The second eldest of the Bear boys was born to Maisie, but fathered by Jack Bear. Eddie was a good all round man. Lightly built as a young fellow, he later grew to become a big man, closely resembling his father.

The youngest of the boys was Vincent, who's mother was a gin from Mt. Josef, on the eastern end of Napier. She died giving birth. Vincent's father was Jack Bear and he was raised by Maisie from infancy. Vincent was the most intelligent of the three boys, but prone to do as he felt, rather than what he was told, as became evident later on. Vincent could have done anything, if he put his mind to it. He had a good brain and at one time commenced a pilot's training course, but he didn't stick to it. He was always a bit prone to please himself, but he and his older brothers became competent stockmen whilst on Kimberley Downs, and I was pleased to have the three of them come across to Napier with me.

## Victor Joy

Another very smart fellow was Victor Joy. He had been brought across from Queensland by Jack Camp, with whom he'd worked prior to coming to Kimberley Downs. Victor was a clean-cut kind of fellow, lightweight, but very, very handy. You could chuck him on any horse and he'd ride it, and although he was only of light build, he was good at catching and throwing bulls. He earned himself a reputation for being a highly competent stockman. Unfortunately he died prematurely, some time later, of cancer, although the inevitable rumour amongst the blacks was that 'he had been sung.

## Ben Bibingnulli

Ben Bibingnulli had something wrong with him. I don't know what it was, but he was sent down to hospital, in Perth, for a while, and came back when I first went to Kimberley Downs. When he first returned he was very quiet and subdued. He would ride in the back of the vehicle, with his head down and say nothing. After a time he began to come good. He got better and better and eventually was able to ride colts mustering, and work as well as any man. I really liked him. He was a good decent fellow. He never bludged, and if there were cattle to be had, he was as dinkum about getting them as I was. If I went after a beast, Ben would be there behind me, to back me up. If you wanted cattle, he wanted cattle, and you couldn't ask more from a ringer than that. A good man, he later broke his leg whilst working on Blina and died of a blood clot in hospital.

## 'Fat' Brian Djigbar

Another loyal man to have in my crew was 'Fat Brian', a Looma man. When we had cattle in hand he, and a couple of other men, would tail my bullocks for me. A couple of times the cattle 'jumped' while on 'dinner camp'. Brian would ride out to meet me, as we were returning from mustering to tell me.

"Bullock 'bin rush."

"Did you lose any?" I'd ask him.

"No, no. We gott'em whole lot, Shohn." So then I'd count them, to see if he was telling me the truth. He was always cheerful and had a good sense of humour. He held a lot of power amongst the blacks. Things didn't always go smoothly amongst the men. Sometimes blokes would get cross, or simply become cheesed off with the situation for some reason. Then they might tell me they were 'pulling out'. With the camp unsettled, they'd often take another couple of blokes with them, and I'd be left short of men. When this happened I'd get 'Fat Brian' and take him with me to town, ahead of the fellows pulling out. Brian would help me 'pick up' fresh men. We'd go down to the town reserve and he'd say, "You want 'im shob with ja'dun Shohn Well, longa Napier?" and I'd end up replacing my blokes quite easily. If I waited until the disgruntled men got into town they might talk and spread 'poison' around the place, and make it hard finding blokes willing to come out to Napier. Brian Djigbar was a big help to me in this way. After doing this he would say, "You gotta 'ho me chumting now."

I'd say, "Yeah? What do I owe you?"

"You bin ho' me two chicks tobacco." A lot of the older blacks would chew stick tobacco, or 'nicky, nicky, as it was known. Brian would tell funny stories and laugh like hell, whether they were funny or not. But if you ever lent him money you always got it back, which is more than you can say for some people.

One time Brian found a bloke, not much more than a kid, who like himself was from Looma. His name was Stephen Midmee and he had been working for George Lanigan.

"You got'im shob por 'im?" Brian asked me. I asked the youngster where he'd been working and why he wasn't still there. He said George Lanigan told him he was a horse killer.

"Can you 'hang up'?" I asked. He said he could, so I gave him a job. He turned out a damned good young fellow. When allocating horses and a horse came through the yard I might say, "This horse can buck a bit. Who wants him?"

Stephen would say, "I'll take him." Then, later, another might come through and I'd say the same thing. "Which can buck the best, this one or that other one?" the young bloke would ask.

"You can have them both." I'd say. He would ride anything. He wasn't frightened to gallop, he understood cattle, was lively and always ready to go. He was everything you wanted in a young bloke.

## Reggie Woods and Flash Ada

A coloured bloke, Reggie Woods, came to Napier with me as well, bringing his gin, Flash Ada, with him. Reggie did yard repairs for me, would check the bullock paddock fence and do any other maintenance jobs around the place. In the early days Flash Ada did a bit of cooking.

Flash Ada brought a dog with her, which was very protective of her. I still had old Yogi, but he had no teeth left, mainly from hooking onto bulls in his younger days. One day Flash Ada's dog and Yogi had a fight in the kitchen. Yogi got hold of the other dog, but being toothless, couldn't get a good grip on him. He ended up polishing the floor with it. In Yogi's youth the outcome of this tussle wouldn't have been so amusing.

Later on, when I'd been at Napier for a while I picked up a couple of other blokes to give us a hand. Jack Spratt, from Beagle Bay, was one of them. He came to Napier at about the same time as we got the old Austin Champ, which we later used for knocking down bulls. He was mechanically minded, could drive and was a useful man to have. A coloured fellow, he was a handy stockman, he could cook and was very good natured.

One day the police came to me and said there was a bloke in town who had been in a bit of trouble. He had been involved in a bad accident, while drunk, and had 'done time' for it. They told me he was not a bad bloke, but an alcoholic who needed to get out of town. Did I have a job for him? I agreed to give the poor bugger a try and over the years he came and went, working for me on several different stations. He was a white man and a very strange bloke, but he was handy around cattle and could be depended upon to mind a mob diligently. He had a propensity for telling tall stories and claimed to have a son who was a commercial pilot, though whether this was true or not I don't know. Bill Hymas would often tell me about letters he received from his son, but none ever came through the Napier mailbag. He had once worked on Roy Hill and managed Mt Vernon, or so he said, but this was well before the 'catastrophe' that, I think, drove him to drink and ruined his life.

## Terry Hillman and Mickey Michael

Terry Hillman and Mickey Michael were half caste fellas, originally from Queensland, who also came and worked for me. They were both able men and hardworking. Later I nearly lost the pair of them, in one of the biggest floods seen on Napier.

At the end of each year, because of it's location, the 'Old Napier' homestead would be closed down.

The horses were taken back to Kimberley Downs for the wet season and everything taken off the place in case of flooding. When I had been working for Robin Campbell a few years earlier, he had a bloke camped there, called Joe Rodgers. With him was his wife, Tilly, a good woman, and their two blue heeler dogs. While they were there, there was a flood and the couple ended up marooned on the roof of the kitchen. With them were their dogs, which at the time had a litter of pups. Once the waters receded they walked up the Barker to Mount Hart Station. Floodwater would flow six foot deep through the homestead regularly during the monsoon, evident from watermarks left on the walls.

During the course of the dry season talk inevitably turned to the annual exodus from Napier. Who would go where, what holidays were planned, which of the blokes would sit out the wet at Kimberley Downs, in Derby or travel south to Perth, or east to Queensland. During one such conversation Terry Hillman and Mickey Michael told me they didn't want to go to town or to K.D. for the wet. Or anywhere else for that matter. They wanted to stay at Napier. I told them I needed the homestead yard repaired and extended and said 'What about you do that over the wet?' They agreed, on wages of course. They cut posts and rails needed to do the job, well in advance, carted them in, and barked them. Then at the end of the year, when the rest of us dispersed, these two blokes stayed behind. We left them with a fair bit of tucker. Their only transport was the tractor and left there alone, they set to work on the yard.

While the rest of us were away big rains came. Terry Hillman and Mickey Michael woke one morning to find the river had risen rapidly overnight. During that day the spreading water was coming quickly onto the homestead. The two men decided to start walking out. By now it was late in the day, and with the weather about, darkness fell early. They had walked out beyond the cattle yards when they came upon more floodwater. Realising that the Barker River and Womberella Creek had joined up, they returned to the stockyard, climbed onto the yard rails and spent the night perched up there. They stayed there until the water dropped down a bit, then decided to try and swim the Barker, then walk and wade to Rarrigee, a distance of some twelve miles. From Rarrigee they'd walk on to Kimberley Downs homestead, a further eighteen miles away.

Having swum across the river they set off, through water waist deep. It was difficult going and they frequently dropped into deep holes, concealed under the floodwater. The current was getting stronger from the Lennard River, which had also broken its banks. The two men were getting knocked up. They knew they couldn't make it. They decided to slosh their way back to Napier and re-cross the Barker River. With remarkable tenacity they somehow accomplished it. Having got back to where they'd started from, they then set out along the Napier Range. They walked to Yamara Gap. From there they made their way down the unsealed road towards the Lennard River crossing. The two knew there was no chance of anyone coming upon them, because the road was impassable. With the Lennard River in flood, the Barker banked up and unable to flow into it, likewise Womberella Creek, floodwater had spread across the low lying country for as far as the eye could see. Faced with no other option the two struggled on doggedly towards Kimberley Downs.

I was down in Perth with Rae, staying at her parent's place, when the big rains came to the West Kimberley. The first I knew of my workers plight was when I received a phone call from Bob Maxted, telling me the two men were missing. I was told to get on an aeroplane and come home immediately, which I did. When I got back to Derby, Maxted chartered a plane and I went out to search for them. The flood waters had dropped down by this time, though the rivers were still running fiercely. I hoped, if either of the men were out there, that they'd light a fire and make a smoke that we could pick up from the air, but there was none. No sign of life. Nothing. Just vast expanses of sodden ground, swollen watercourses seeping over the land, but no sign of my men. Seeing the conditions out there and realising there was little chance of there being anything dry enough to enable them to put up a smoke, we returned to Derby. I remained in town, camping at Mum and Dad's place, anxiously awaiting news of the missing pair. I didn't feel too good during this time. I was extremely worried and I feared we had lost them. As the days passed I thought 'They are gone for sure. I should never have left them in that flood prone place.

Thankfully, after a few days Bob Maxted rang me.

"They've turned up!" He told me. "They walked into Kimberley Downs. They're OK." The relief was really something. I flew down to Perth to resume my holiday, later driving back up to the Kimberley in my ute to start preparing for the next season. When I returned to Napier the ferocity of the flood was starkly evident, with the remains of a bullock, stuck fast by its horns, forty feet up a tree. At a similar height, wedged between the branches of a gum tree, a table that had been swept away by the swirling water. Tangled debris hung in great clumps, like giant stork's nests, metres above the ground, and swathes of twisted timber was lying about in the wake of the floodwaters. Evidence of the deluge was everywhere. Not since then has there been a flood like it on Napier, and the endurance and determination of those two men is still talked about today.

## Slim Wells

Apart from the team of blokes I had on Napier on a full time basis, there were others who came and went as work required. These included yard builders, the grader driver, mechanic and a horse breaker. The brood mares all stayed on Kimberley Downs, so each year we would get our youngsters from there, take them back to Napier and the horse breaker would come across to break them in.

The horse breaker at that time was a fellow called Slim Wells. No relation of mine. He had worked on Kimberley Downs for quite some time, so I knew him and his antics of old. He was a big, wedge shaped man, with broad shoulders and narrow hips. Slim Wells, sober, was a top bloke. He was a very good horse breaker, but alcohol had control of him. When he was breaking in, Slim wouldn't knock off until well after dark. He had Tilley lights placed on every post of the round yard, and he would be breaking in horses till nine or ten o'clock at night, before letting them go. He would be up again early and have them in the yard by four in the morning, using the Tilley lights, or hurricane lamps, till daylight came. He would work them until about ten o'clock, then, before the day got too hot, he'd let them go. He wouldn't bring them in again till three or four o'clock in the afternoon, then do the same thing. It was really very good, because he was only breaking in when it was cool. He wasn't lazy. He was a good worker, but once he got to drinking the fuel for lighting his lamps, well, it all went downhill from there.

I had first come across Slim on Kimberley Downs and when he ran amok it was a bit of a worry. Unbeknown to us he would horde the metho, needed to light the lamps, then one day he'd decide to drink it and he'd get rotten drunk. When this happened he'd say, "I've got to go down to where a bloke earns his crust and blow myself away." Off he'd go and next thing you'd hear 'Boom' and you'd think 'Oh Jeez.' Everybody would be in a big panic, too frightened to get the rifle off him. Blokes would be hopping in motor cars and you'd go down near the yard and there he'd be, lying on the ground, the gun nearby, but there wouldn't be a leak in him. So eventually, when he'd say this, nobody took any notice of him. If he ever had done it, we wouldn't have worried till the next day when the crows would have shown us.

I never had any trouble with Slim Wells when he was horse breaking for me on Napier and the horses he broke were all good. No skin off them, no hair off them. There never seemed to be a bad one amongst his colts. They had good mouths, were civil, could be shod easily and were free movers. He knew his job and he did it well. It was not until later on, when I left him alone on Napier for a week that I had any strife with him.

## Kanso nearly drowns

We had been aerial mustering, with a jackeroo chopper pilot and were crossing the Barker River, at a yard called Hans Hole. We put the cattle into the river. There was shallow water at the crossing. A big bull and a bullock went down into the water and began to walk, then swim, downstream. The river had steep banks. I was riding Kanso, a good strong horse from Mardathuna, named after Kanzo Makame the diver, (Banjo Paterson's poem 'The Pearl Diver'). I was up in the lead on the same side of the river and saw the two beasts trying to sneak away. I thought they'll come back in a minute, but they kept going further downstream. I cantered over the sand in the river, got in front of them, then tried to turn them back. But they wouldn't turn. I urged my horse into the water. Kanso was a bought horse and I'd never swum with him before. We were walking in, when all of a sudden, we stepped into a deep hole and down we went. Kanso's head went under and he started panicking. He was rearing and climbing, then he went under again. I realised, then, that this horse couldn't swim. While he was floundering in the water I managed to pull him round to one side. He touched some ground and came out of there as hard and as fast as he could. He kept losing his footing, the sand moving as he climbed up onto it in the water. He was very pleased when he came out of it. My ticker was going like hell. He was basically a very gutsy horse. (He had been known as Father Reilly on Mardathuna, and he was by England's Dust, or by an England's Dust colt.)

## I lose Vincent Bear to Kimberley Downs

One day we were out mustering at Womberella. I was in the camp as usual, but my back was crook and I wasn't feeling too well. I had a horse in my string called Zenith, a Liveringa horse, who was sometimes inclined to buck. After dinner that day it was Zenith's turn to be ridden, so I saddled him up and led him around for a bit. I noticed Vincent Bear had grabbed a horse called Alcabeer, who he had already used. I asked him what he was doing.

"I'm riding Alcabeer."

"No you're not. You know every horse gets ridden in turn. You've just ridden that horse. It's not his turn. You get your right horse, because if you ride that Alcabeer you haven't got a job." When I said this Vincent got the sulks. I didn't know what he was going to do, so I got Michael Bear and said, "You ride this Zenith for me for a bit. I'll catch you up with your horse when I see what Vincent is up to." I hung around the camp for a while watching Vincent. He wasn't doing anything, so I caught up with the mob and Michael and I swapped horses. When we got back to the stockcamp later that day, there was no Vincent and no Alcabeer. The next I hear, Vincent is working for the Ghan on Kimberley Downs and I never got Alcabeer back.

## Hallilee gets horned

We were working up in the ranges, near Billyarra, and had a mob of cattle out of wild country. I was riding a horse called Boab. A good old quiet horse that we had raced in Derby. A smart native stockman, Snowy Thompson, was with us this day, riding a little black mare called Hallilee. There was a pass through the hills and we went over with six beasts at a time. I was on the tail with three or four other blokes. All the cattle had gone over the pass when a bull suddenly whipped around and went for the mare Hallilee. It gored her from her udder to the back of her tail, then turned around and trotted over the hill. I saw it all and I thought 'Jeez you're not getting away with that.' I spun my horse around and went after the bull. We got half way down the hill, which was covered in smooth round boulders. I hopped off Boab and hunted him away. The bull was standing a few metres from me. I was hoping he'd charge and I'd be able to step around him and grab his tail, but he wouldn't come. He kept shaking his head and standing his ground. I was getting closer and closer. When I was about two metres from him he did come. I went to step to one side of him, but I trod on a round rock and down I went. The next moment he was on top of me, trying to gore me.

I knew I was in a lot of trouble. I was dead scared that he'd put his horn under my belt or into the stitching of my jeans and toss me up into the air. I didn't want that to happen because that's where he wanted me. Then he could just keep tossing me. So I thought for a while. If I hadn't had a bit of experience I'd probably have got frightened and been in some trouble. But I thought, 'Well, if these blokes don't come back to help me, the only way out of this is to get a hand on each horn, then let him stand me up.' I'd have hold of one horn, but I'd miss the other. So I'd lie down again while he had another go at me. Sometimes I'd get hold of both horns, but not with a good enough grip. Not enough horn in each hand, so I'd have to lie down again. I noticed each time my hand touched his horn he'd go towards it. He seemed to reckon he was goring me. So I thought 'everything is OK' and really it was. Eventually I did manage to get both my hands on his horns and had a good grip on them. He stood me straight up and I was gone. I had plenty of adrenalin flowing and was far smarter and quicker than when he'd first got me on the ground.

Once I knew I was free, the bull decided he didn't want to know me anymore and he trotted off. I'd probably frightened the daylights out of him too. So everything was all right and when I looked up there were three or four blokes coming back over the hill to look for me. They raced over to me and asked if I was OK. I said, "Yeah I'm fine, but just get that 'lovely little fella', knock him down and cut his throat." Which they did. I got on my horse and caught up with the cattle, who by this time were about a mile away. I was riding slowly behind the mob, because I didn't feel real good. Then the shakes started. My hands, my feet in the stirrup irons, my whole body started vibrating. I couldn't believe what was wrong with me. I didn't really know what it was, but after a fair while it passed. Then I became very thirsty and I could hardly keep awake. Then I made a big mistake. I told the blokes I'd mind the cattle while they had their dinner. Really I should have gone and had a sleep. I was in shock, but I didn't know it. My ticker was going like hell. I didn't like blokes who got off their horses while they were watching cattle, so I stayed there, sitting on my horse waiting for dinner watch to end, though I could hardly sit upright in the saddle. I felt like it was the middle of the night, and it seemed like it went on for a fortnight. I woke up falling off the horse, so I grabbed Boab and pulled myself back on. That gave me a fright. I thought I'd be alright after that, but ten minutes later the same thing happened. It was terrible. Just trying to stay awake was a real ordeal. After several hours I came good. The mare, Hallilee, was led back to camp where kerosene was put on the wound. She died a few days later.[2]

## A horse fall at Old Napier

I recall one occasion when we were working cattle at the Homestead Yard. We had finished branding the day before and were letting the cattle out of the yard next

---

2   Some may feel that killing the bull that gored Hallilee that day was unnecessary and perhaps an explanation is warranted.

If we had let him go, the next time somebody came to throw that bull he had already been half taught. When you come to throw a bull that a bloke has previously 'played' with, then let go, he is a much more dangerous bull to deal with. He has learnt a lesson already and someone may end up being killed by him. After it's encounter with me, the only safe thing to do was destroy it.

One other comment I'd like to make is the absurdity of a remark I read in a book recently. It was written by someone reputed to have been up amongst the best in the game. The fellow, finding himself in a similar situation to the one I faced that day in the hills, wrote 'I froze and shut my eyes.' How crazy is that? It seems to me it's the best way to end up dead.

morning. We needed meat, so I told the blokes to get a killer. There was a good fat heifer that had kept breaking out while we were yarding up, so I told the blokes to get her for a killer.

Once we'd let the cattle out of the yard this same heifer took off. A black fellow chased her. He was on a horse called Minty, a pretty little thing with a blaze and two hind white. I was watching from the motor car, waiting for telegrams to come through over the radio. I saw the stockman fall. He landed on his head. I called Willie Lennard over and said, "You'd better go up and have a look at that bloke." Willie came back looking concerned.

"He's bleeding from the nose, the mouth and his ears. He's out to it." So I butted in on the portable radio.

"We've just had a horse fall here and a bloke is bleeding from his nose, mouth and ears. I need a flying doctor plane sent out pretty quickly please."

"But have you got an airstrip there John?" Mrs Keasey asked. Although they were good people running the RFDS base at the time I thought to myself 'I'm not that bloody stupid, to be calling for a plane if I didn't have anywhere for it to land.' I told her we did have a landing strip, so they said they'd send a plane out. In the meantime the stockman had started writhing around, and the blokes were having to hold him down. When the plane eventually got there they couldn't control him, so they gave him a needle and put him under before they took him away.

I went in to the hospital to visit the poor wretch a couple of times. The nursing staff had him where they could watch him all the time. He was in his bed on his knees, his head on the pillow and his arms up over his head. He was from Balgo, or Billiluna way, and pretty much Myall. He didn't seem to be getting any better and I never went in again. I don't know whatever happened to him.

Really the bloke was quite fortunate to have sustained his injuries so near the Napier homestead, with an airstrip close-by and a radio set at hand. Sadly, despite this, I don't think the outcome for him was very good. If that incident had happened down at Mount Eliza, Mundooma, or Limestone Springs, there would have been no help to be had at all. Quite often we only had pack mules with us. No vehicle. No radio. There were no helicopters. Somebody would have had to ride in to get help, then hope to God they could get a vehicle out to us. What roads we had were very rough to get him out on. If he was still with us by then. When you think about it, it was really very dangerous. But we didn't think about it. We never really considered the risks we took. All we thought about was getting the cattle, holding the bullocks. All for the sake of the owner's bank balance and our own adrenalin rush.

## The man in a coongleberry bush

The owner, or agent, would give me shipping dates, in advance. It was my responsibility to ensure we had the required number of bullocks in hand, when it came time to send them off the place. Droving had come to an end by this time and bullocks were taken in to Myall's Bore on roadtrains. We would truck our horses in, then use them to walk the bullocks, from Myall's Bore, down to the wharf, in much the same way as during the droving days. As it depended on the ship and the tides when they were loaded, sometimes we might have to hold the bullocks at Myall's Bore for a few days before they were shipped.

One time we were at Myall's Bore for two or three days waiting to load. A lot of our bullocks weren't used to drinking out of troughs and were frightened of the long trough. There was an artesian bore there, with an overflow which went out into a bit of a swamp. So we used to shepherd those toey bullocks, with a few others, out into the swamp, or sometimes they'd smell water and go straight to it themselves. On this occasion, on the first day we were camped there, we were going to give these trough shy bullocks a drink at the swamp. It was around lunch time, so we'd put them into some shade. One of my men, Ringer Campton, rode around to see me.

"'Der's guddia fella sleepin' longa 'dat coongleberry bush ober 'der" he said. I thought he was pulling my leg.

"Yeah?" I humoured him.

"No, no. He bin der all right Shohn. Might be 'im shcarem' dem bullicks, make'em rush." He seemed pretty dinkum.

"Righto', I'll go around and see him." So I rode over and a white man was there all right.

"G'day mate. What are you doing here?" I asked.

"I've got nowhere else to go." He looked pretty worn out and buggered.

"Well you can't stop here, because if you give these bullocks a fright we'll have a hell of a job holding them. They'll rush." I told him "You can go over to our camp. Tell the cook that John Wells sent you over. That's my name. If you want a feed tell him John Wells said to give you a feed."

"Thanks very much mate." He grabbed his bit of a swag and a few odds and ends and went over to our camp and the cook gave him a feed. He was in serious trouble this fellow. We watered the bullocks, yarded them and eventually came in to camp and had a yarn to the stranger.

"What are you doing out here on your own?" I asked.

"I've got a few problems." He told me.

"Well, you can hang around here and we'll feed you, if you like. But when we go back to the station you'll be on your own again." So that's what he did. Later, when the time came for us to leave I asked him what his plans were.

"Have you got anywhere to go to? Have you got any relations, or anyone you know?"

"No, no-one." I felt sorry for him.

"Look, you can come with us and try and sort yourself out. Then, you can leave whenever you like. We'll feed you and see if we can't get you on track again." So we took him out to the station with us. He was dirty and we had to get him cleaned up, gave him a bit of gear and washed his clothes.

"I'll work for you." He told me. "I'll make a big vegetable garden for you." I didn't have anybody to mind things at the homestead then, so I agreed.

"You can stay here when we go bush and look after the place." He did and I discovered this bloke could work like bloody hell. He'd be out there in the sun, while everybody was knocked off, digging up vegie gardens. Old Napier, being on the banks of the Barker River and the Wombarella Creek, had very good, fertile soil. He grew good vegetables, looked after the place and cooked for us. He stayed a long time.

After a while all the blacks began to get very toey of this bloke. He was telling them that there was going to be a war, and that there were detonator lizards living in the kitchen and the quarters. We had a few rasp tail lizards in the quarters, that's all, but he was frightening the natives, because black fellas and coloureds are very prone to believe stories. I told them that it was all bullshit. Don't take any notice of him. But it was getting that bad I was going to lose some of my men over it, so I went and had a chat to him.

"Look, can you cut all this talk out about these invaders coming, and these detonator lizards that let off explosives. I need my crew to get the jobs done here and without them I can't do it."

"Yeah, all right." he agreed. But the blacks were toey of him from then on and eventually I had to tell him he'd have to go.

He went into town and apparently he came good. He later married some girl from the hospital. I never saw or heard anything of him after that. I don't know what had gone wrong with him. Whether he'd lost a wife, or what had happened to him. Where he'd come from or where he'd worked. But something was really, really wrong. Nowadays I wouldn't be game to take him home. I'd be too frightened of him. But in those days you didn't see that sort of thing. You saw it amongst the blacks. They'd go off their heads sometimes. But people out of their minds on drugs was still a thing of the future, in the Kimberley, at that time. Alcohol was the only demon around in those days.

## Some hardened drinkers drop in

I would go into Derby from time to time, to pick up fuel, gear or fresh men if need be. On one such trip to town I ran into Phyllis Bin Haji Hali, a coloured woman who wanted a job, so she came out to Napier and did the cooking. Things got a lot better after that. Phyllis stayed at the homestead and looked after things while we were out mustering, keeping the place clean and tidy. She cooked good meals and cakes for us, when we were home from the stockcamp, as well as doing our washing. She was utterly reliable and was entrusted with a store room key, which I had no qualms about leaving in her possession. On one occasion this responsibility caused her a fair bit of trouble.

The new yard, which I had helped Fred Wright peg out, was being built at Police Camp. Two white blokes, Kevin Green and Kevin Brady were amongst those building it. Although these men were wonderful workers, they were notorious alcoholics. They would drink anything they could get their hands on, that might give them a kick. Although Police Camp was on Kimberley Downs it was nearer to the Napier homestead. Sometimes these blokes would come over and they caused me a fair bit of trouble. If they were drunk, that didn't much concern me. But if they got my men drunk, that was different. One day these blokes came down to Napier and they were drinking. I was away in the stockcamp at the time. When they had finished all their grog they told Phyllis Bin Haji Ali to open up the store-room. She refused and the men became aggressive. They threatened to kill her if she didn't unlock the door for them. Eventually she had to do as they asked. Having run out of their own supply of alcohol they were looking for methylated spirits, vanilla essence, or any other essence there might be. Anything they could get drunk on. In their search these fellows would splash a bit of likely gear on the storeroom floor, hit it with a match and if it burnt they'd take it and drink it. They weren't fussy.

Another time these same two men had been repairing the yard at Traveller's for Robin Campbell. At the same time Gerry Ash, Keith Bolger and Ray Jorgenson were building the new yard at Douglas'. It was around Christmas time, during the wet and Gerry Ash and his mob decided to walk across to Traveller's to visit Kevin Green and Kevin Brady. Then, because the rain had set in and they couldn't drive out, they all walked in to Kimberley Downs together, to get some stores. They collected a heap of provisions. Salt, tea, sugar, tobacco, metho, flour, a bucket and broom, no doubt several other grocery items and it being Christmas, they were also given some apples and oranges. Carrying all of it they then walked back to their camp. Once there they mixed themselves a brew. They put in a bit of metho and other things they had there, cut up the apples and oranges and put them in too, then poured all this gear into the bucket. In a day or so they stirred it with the broom and all the paint came off the broom handle. The galvanize was floating off the bucket. Then they proceeded to drink it. I don't know how it didn't kill them. When they started drinking this stuff, one of the blokes, Keith Bolger, had enough brains to fill up a couple of beer bottles, which he planted. There was no-one there to help them if something went wrong, but at least they had that to assist them a little when they were coming out of the rats. This incident had occurred long before they came across to Napier and accosted Phyllis Bin Haji Ali, so I was well aware of what these blokes were like with grog in them. I told the cook not to worry about letting them into the station store. It was the only thing she could possibly have done in that situation.

One year I returned from Perth, where I had been on holidays with Rae, and I couldn't get back to Napier because the river was too high. The manager of Kimberley Downs at the time was Bill Barrett. He was away on holidays, so the station was being looked after by young Robert Rowell, the son of one of the owners. When I got there he said I could take over and he left. I don't think he liked it much because he couldn't get off the place quick enough. So I found myself caretaking Kimberley Downs.

Kevin Green, Kevin Brady and others were there building trap yards. The posts and rails had all been cut and carted in the dry time. They had been to town and come back with cartons and cartons of whiskey, rum and beer. You wouldn't have been able to fit any more in the station wagon they had. When they came back they were rotten drunk. They couldn't stand up, scratch themselves or anything. They were camped up on a ridge near the gate at the main entrance to the homestead. If they had been further out bush I wouldn't have been able to get there, so wouldn't have had the worry of it. I wanted to keep away, but had to go up every day or two to see that they were still alive. I'd go up there and the camp would stink. The flies were horrific. These blokes didn't go to the toilet. They'd stagger out a few metres, go to the toilet and crash right there. Later they'd wake up and crawl back to their camp. There were bottles of scotch tipped over, so they'd open another one and have a big swig from that. I'd go there to see them and they'd just stare at me. No expression on their face, just look at me as if to say 'what the bloody hell's this bastard doing here?' They didn't know where they'd put anything. It was pitiful. I don't know how they stayed alive. There was grog spilled and wasted, half empty bottles lying around everywhere. I used to think, 'God, they'll be dead in the morning.' But you know man has got a great tolerance and these blokes, when they'd finished it all, give them two days and they'd be back at work. When I've written myself off I've felt like I should be dead. Yet here these blokes would be, out in the sun, the heat and the humidity, building yards. No post hole diggers. Heavy timber posts and rails and all the holes dug by hand. I don't know how their heads didn't explode. The sad part about it is that these men were damn good workers. Basically good men taken over by grog. And they weren't alone. There were many like them on stations around the Kimberley at that time and a lot of them made a huge contribution, in terms of physical labour, to the development of pastoral properties of that time. I really don't think their worth was ever properly valued, or their sheer physical toughness fully appreciated.

## A modern style of catching bulls

One day when I was heading into Derby, from Old Napier, I met Dave Ledger near the Meda turn off. Known as the 'Galloping Pom' he waved me down, offered me a beer and we sat on the roadside and had a yarn. He told me they were going out bull catching at Big Springs the next day, using a bull buggy. This was a new style of getting bulls which I hadn't seen. It involved the use of a cut down Land Rover, or Toyota, to pursue the bull, knock it down and pin it to the ground while it's legs were tied. To avoid injury to the animal tyres, attached to the bull bar of the modified vehicle, cushion the beast when it's knocked over. Once the hind legs are tied the vehicle backs off. The animal is then dealt with, horns tipped, earmarked and later picked up by a truck.

While we drank a bottle of beer each, the Galloping Pom invited me to come over the next day to see how it was done. I wasn't keen. I still had gear to pick up from town, which I had to get back to Napier with that night.

"Well do whatever it is you've got to do in town, go home, then come back here ready for an early start tomorrow." Ledger persuaded. Eventually, I agreed.

"All right then. If I'm at Meda in the morning, OK. If I'm not, just go without me." We left it at that.

I went on into town, picked up what was needed, drove the hundred miles back home to Old Napier, did what I had to do there, then turned around and drove all the way back to Meda. By the time I got there, having driven almost three hundred miles that day, it was late at night. The station was in darkness, everyone long asleep. I rolled my swag out on the flat between the men's quarters and the meathouse and went out like a light. Next thing, I was being woken by Ledger. It was still pitch dark, the early hours of the morning. I felt as if I'd not long gone to sleep.

"Come on Wellsy, we're ready to go." I dragged myself from my swag saying

"Righto'. But I'll drive my vehicle out to Big Springs, so I can leave when I need to." but when I went to leave I discovered I had a flat tyre.

"Don't worry about the puncture now." Ledger told me. "Just jump in here. I'll get someone to fix it for you while we're gone." Obviously eager to get going I hopped in his vehicle and away we went.

I liked Ledger. He was an amusing man who always seemed in a hurry. He was excitable, sometimes impetuous, occasionally moody, but generally very likeable. Born in England he had once been a drover in Central Australia, was a highly regarded horse-breaker and had come to the Kimberley from the Northern Territory with his delightful, loyal and intelligent English wife, Margaret. I knew, as I tried to shake off the effects of too little sleep that I was in for a lively and entertaining day in his company.

We took off in the dark. On the back of the Land Rover was a 44 gallon drum of water. It was not tied on and the drum had no bung. Also on the back was a bag with a few loaves of bread in it, another with fresh meat. The track was rough and on the way out to Big Springs we hit a few bumps. The drum moved, hit the back window, broke it and water splashed in on us for the rest of the way. When we got near Rarriwell, after hitting a bigger bump in one of the creeks, Ledger pulled up to check things. The bread was all squishy and the meat soaking wet.

The stockcamp was at Gum Hole and the men were still asleep when we arrived. It was daylight by now and the Galloping Pom was, understandably, not impressed. He gave them all a rev got the fire going and boiled the billy. The meat was put on some bushes under a trailer. The stockmen caught their horses, ate their breakfast, then rode off to flush out bulls. The days work had begun.

The horsemen were running bulls, or bullocks, out of the scrub onto the marsh. Once out in the open, on good ground, they would be bowled over with one of the bull buggies. There were two or three bull buggies working that day. We were knocking down bulls and bullocks, tying them up by the hind legs, as well as barren cows. In areas where there are too many bulls you end up with barren cows. Phil Lukin and Bob Skuthorpe each had a truck there, picking up the cattle we had got. They were taken to a small set of timber yards at Big Springs. After lunch the men saddled fresh horses and we went over to Gordon Smith Island.

On Gordon Smith Island there was grass two metres high. The class of cattle that lived there would run and sit down amongst it, their heads out straight, totally concealed. You had to really watch for any movement in the grass that might alert you to a bull hidden in it. Sometimes one could ride onto a bull and not know he was there until your horse practically ran onto him. Then he might stand up and charge you straight out. If your horse didn't respond quickly you'd be gone. This country was considered so dangerous that when I was a big kid in the stockcamp I wasn't allowed to go mustering there. I would always be left tailing the bullocks, with a couple of very old black fellas.

This day the horsemen were running bulls out of the long grass and scrub. We were knocking them down, tying them up, earmarking them and tipping their horns. Then loading them on a truck. For the whole day I would have tied up close to fifty head of cattle. Bulls and bullocks. After that was finished we went back to camp, had tea and waited until just on dark. Then went out again, picking up more bulls that were coming in for water in the dark. During the night we came across a Kimberley Downs bullock which I pointed out to Ledger.

"That's a K.D. bullock there, let's get him."

"I'm not here to catch bullocks for you," he said. Never mind that I'd put in a whole day and half a night getting bulls for him. I thought that was pretty funny. Ignoring the 'stranger' bullock we kept going. We came upon one big bull a fair way out on the marsh. When he saw us he took off, but Ledger was onto him. At the last minute the bull veered off. It was a moonlit night.

"Swing off this way, Dave. That's all wet mud there." I warned, just in time. We swung off, clipping the edge and sending wet mud out in a great shower. The bull turned out of the treacherous area, we got him on drier ground, rolled him and tied him up.

After everything had been picked up and unloaded, Ledger finally called it a day. It had been a long one, action filled and I was pretty buggered. But the day wasn't quite over yet. Ledger drove. It was about a two hour drive back to the homestead and by the time we got to the Meda River Ledger was falling asleep at the wheel. I had to wake him up every now and then and didn't dare nod off myself. As we got near Daley's Bore there were a lot of cattle about. We nearly ran into them a couple of times.

"You'd better let me drive" I suggested.

"No, no, I'm all right" Ledger insisted. He kept driving but it was a big worry.

"Look Ledger, shove over. You can't keep awake. I'll drive." I finally persuaded him. He was asleep in an instant. I drove home to Meda, slept there the night, then went home to Napier in the morning. I'd certainly seen first hand how to get cattle with a bull buggy, but it had been a fairly gruelling day and one I have always remembered.[3]

## Red Bull Yard is built

One day I was in Derby picking up gear when I met a bloke who had worked for Dad, on Meda, years ago. He was some sort of foreigner and he wanted to know if I could give him a job. His name was Charlie Jessock. We were going to build a timber drafting yard at Red Bull, so I asked if he was interested in doing that. He said he was, so I gave him a job. At the time the only yards on Napier were Homestead yard, a small timber yard at Billyarra and one at Tullocks. Napier had two brand new chainsaws, one I had given to Reggie Woods, for yard repairs. The other I gave to Willie Lennard and Charlie Jessock, to build the new drafting yard. It was the only mechanical aid they had on the job. Willie and Charlie dug every post hole for Red Bull yard with crowbar and shovel, through limestone, which was pretty hard digging, and they cut all the timber posts and rails. Basically it was built by just those two men. Every now and then I might pick up a bloke in town, if he looked as if he could work, and

---

3    Dave and Margaret Ledger became close friends over coming years and were very good to me and my family, in many ways. Although I did not know it then they were to feature prominently in one of the most important days of my life. There are several tales I could tell of times spent with the Galloping Pom, who sadly died prematurely some years ago, but in deference to the kindness shown me I have chosen not to share them here.

take him out there to give them a hand for a while, but most of the work was done by these two. Red Bull was built on hard ground, really hard ground, but eventually it was finished and became one of the major improvements on the property.

Unfortunately, despite being a significant asset for Napier, the yards later burned down. This happened some years after I'd left when, through poor management, a bushfire was allowed to burn unchecked. Without firebreaks around it's perimeter Red Bull yard was lost to the flames; as was another yard, at Police Camp, on Kimberley Downs, which I had pegged out with Fred Wright, some years earlier. I have always viewed the loss of both these yards as something of a tragedy, knowing the toil it took to construct them in harsh conditions. I suppose men have different values of what is important and what isn't, but for me the workmanship alone made Red Bull a structure worth preserving.

Much later, when Peter Leutenegger, a top operator, owned Napier, a replacement yard was erected at Red Bull. It was a steel yard, built with all the benefits of modern equipment, including a post hole digger. The contractors still found that the ground was too hard for them where the old yard had been, so the site was shifted onto easier ground. To me this is testament to the stamina of those two fine men, Willie Lennard and Charlie Jessock, who I was privileged to have working for me. They did a damn good job. It's a crying shame the result of their hard yakka was allowed to go up in smoke.

## Billy Bunter

Fred Wright left Kimberley Downs soon after I went over to Napier. He was replaced by a bloke who knew nothing about managing cattle stations. His name was Bill Barrett, though he was known to all as 'Billy Bunter'.

We had mustered the horses on Kimberley Downs, finished breaking in and had taken our own horses and colts back to Napier, before Billy Bunter arrived to take over at K.D. Once back home we got everything ready for the start of the season, then went out mustering. I knew we had missed some horses when we'd mustered the herd and that there were about twenty still away, running in Geoff's Paddock, on Kimberley Downs, near the Meda, Blina boundary. I wasn't particularly worried. We had enough to begin the season and I knew they could be got later, once the new man took over.

We were branding cattle at Womberella when I first met Billy Bunter. Bob Maxted brought him out to meet me. Formerly a psychiatric nurse, it was clear, early on, that he was way out of his depth. I don't think he'd done much more than ride in his local pony club. He was hopeless. His blacks used to tell me stories about him and some of the things he did.

In the stockcamp he would have seven horses in his string, when most blokes had three, or maybe four at the most. Billy Bunter's would all be reliable horses. None that would duck out from underneath him as he tried to get on, or be inclined to buck. He would ask the blacks what was what, then allocate himself the best. He didn't have a bloody clue about anything. The natives told me when they went out 'moonlighting' this idiot would be making a bloody racket, yakkiing and carrying on, frightening all the cattle. He had no concept that the idea of 'moonlighting' was one of stealth. How he was ever given the job of running a cattle station I've no idea, and this was the man I had to liaise with for many of Napier's needs.

After we had been out mustering for a while my working horses were getting knocked up, so when I was over at Kimberley Downs one day I said to this fella, "There are still some horses away. They're running in Geoff's Paddock, about twenty of them. Half of them are yours and half are ours. Our plant horses are getting tired and I need some fresh ones. Do you reckon you could get them mustered up for us?" Billy Bunter didn't seem to understand. He was very casual, saying he supposed he would get around to it sometime. I waited about two weeks, then I mentioned the horses to him again.

"I need those horses. Ours are getting tired. Do you reckon you can get those others in, so I can give some of mine a spell?" Again the manager was pretty off-hand and again nothing happened. I waited another couple of weeks, but Billy Bunter didn't seem interested in doing anything about getting those horses in for me. I was becoming impatient. 'He must have too many horses on K.D.' I thought. 'Otherwise he'd be needing the fresh ones too.' I asked a third time, but still nothing was done. I gave him a bit longer, then I got sick of waiting and decided to do something about it myself. I got four of my blokes and told them to get a couple of packs and their gear ready. Swags, tucker, tea, sugar, billycans, and whatever else they needed. I told them they were going over to Kimberley Downs to muster Geoff's Paddock.

"I want you blokes to ride over to Sisters Dam, but don't go along any roads. Go cross country. I don't want anybody to see you, or your tracks. Take a couple of spare horses with you. I'll drive over with your swags and gear and I'll bring two or three other fellas to give you a hand. I'll meet you at Sisters." So off they went.

We loaded up the ute with gear and spare saddles. I left late, after dinner, taking three more men with me and their quartpots and swags. I didn't drive directly to Sisters Dam, but took a circuitous route, to confuse anyone who might see the tyre tracks. On the way we hit a bulldust hole, with a star picket in it. The star picket nearly came through the back tray of the ute, where one of the men was sitting. It made a big dent and we had a hell of a job getting it out. When we got to Sisters Dam the riders were already there. We unloaded the gear, tucker, saddles and all that. Before I left I gave them further instructions.

"Now when you've mustered these horses, I want you to head for home with them, but don't go on any tracks or roads. Bring them cross country and don't let anybody see you." I left the three extra fellas there with them and I headed back to Napier, again taking a roundabout route. Three days later my men arrived back home on Napier with all the horses. I was able to give my stockmen two fresh horses each and we went back out mustering cattle again.

A couple of weeks later I was at Kimberley Downs homestead and Billy Bunter offered me tea. I accepted. We had a bit of a yarn before the meal and he brought up the subject of the horses.

"We went out to Geoffrey's Paddock to get those nags you mentioned, but they've gone. What do you think I should do? Tell the police?"

"Yeah." I agreed.

We ate the meal and afterwards Billy Bunter brought up the subject of the horses again. "I'll ring the police in the morning and report them missing." I was unsure what to do. I held my tongue for a moment or two while I thought about it, then I said, "Actually I wouldn't bother. I've already got them all." The man looked at me in surprise. He rocked back on his chair and it broke. As he went down I was off out the door like a shot.

Billy Bunter left Kimberley Downs not long after that, though I did see him again once or twice before he left. Nothing was ever said about what I'd done and I kept all twenty of those working horses, for our Napier plant. I don't know what ever happened to Billy Bunter, but hopefully he returned to nursing in some psychiatric ward, where I am sure he was better suited.

## The Ghan

The next manager to take over at Kimberley Downs was 'The Ghan'. The Ghan was a bastard of a bloke, but he did belong to cattle stations and, unlike his poor ill equipped predecessor, he had the experience necessary to do the job. His wife, Dot, was a top woman, kind hearted and gentle. I went to school with their son, in Derby, when I was a little boy. He ended up a bit simple, poor kid. I think this had a bit to do with how he was treated by his father. The Ghan, if he drank too much, got very aggressive, especially towards those he could stand over. There was a daughter also, some years younger than me, who grew up tough as any man. She was fully switched on and had the ability and stamina of a bloke, especially where horses were concerned. There was no mollycoddling in her upbringing and she later became one of the first female jockeys in Perth.

Napier was still heavily reliant on Kimberley Downs, so I had a fair bit to do with the Ghan. If any of my bores or windmills broke down Jim Douglas, or whoever the windmillman/mechanic was at the time, would come over and fix them for me. Any other mechanical work would be done in the Kimberley Downs workshop. One day the Austin Champ was being fixed up. The man fixing it was Charlie Jessock, who had originally come to work for me at Napier, yard building. He was now employed as mechanic on Kimberley Downs and had been working on the Austin Champ most of the day. He wasn't going to be finished until after tea. As I was waiting to drive the Napier vehicle home, Dot said to me, "You'd better stay here John, and have something to eat with the rest of the blokes."

"No. I'll just wait and go home as soon as this job is finished." I told her, but she wouldn't have it.

"Look, you're on your own over there. You may as well have a decent feed here, while you're waiting." In the end I agreed. I was sitting down at the table eating my meal with the blokes when the Ghan walked in.

"What are you doing in here?" he asked.

"Dot said I'm to have some tea, while I wait for the vehicle to be finished."

"Get out!" he said. I was a bit nonplussed.

"What, when I've finished my tea?" I asked.

"No, now!" There wasn't too much I could do, so I got up, in front of all the men and walked out. Then I waited for Charlie Jessock to finish his tea, so that he could finish work on the vehicle, then I could drive back to Napier, where I could have something to eat.

Another day I was over at K.D. again. Time was getting on and while I waited for some gear to be fixed Dot came down and talked to me. As the Ghan wasn't about Dot said, "Before you leave, I'll put some tea for you in a plastic bag on the cool room compressor. Go up after dark and grab it to take with you." I didn't need the tucker, but Dot, who was friends with my mother, was trying to look after me. Because she 'd gone to the trouble of hiding the tucker for me I had to sneak up and get it, or The Ghan might find it later. Dot was a really good, kind hearted woman, but I think her husband used to give her hell.

One year Dot had reared three poddy calves at the homestead. They were standing out on the flat, as usual, when The Ghan came home one afternoon. He got the .303 and went, bang, bang, bang and blew the three of them away. He must have had the shits on, but there was no need for that. If he didn't want the poddies around the homestead anymore they could have been taken out bush, been dropped off at a bore and they would have been fine. They were fair lumps of calves, because Dot had put in all the hard work on them by then. But that was the type of man he was. He had Afghan blood in him and he was a standover merchant. I say this because it was a characteristic I saw in him on numerous occasions.

We were at Billyarra, on the south eastern end of Napier. We had been mustering around Mt. Eliza and had come back from there to Billyarra, where we had the trap yard set. We yarded up our cattle, drafted and sorted them. We had had our lunch and were starting on the trap cattle when a willie willie came through. It picked up the campfire and carried it into the trap paddock, which caught alight. The paddock was fairly well eaten out and we hoped the fire wouldn't take hold. We tried to contain it but couldn't. I drove to Kimberley Downs straight away to see about getting a lend of the grader, but The Ghan refused to let me have it. I asked if I could use the telephone. I rang Rowell and told him what had happened.

"We've got cattle in the trap paddock at Billyarra. This is an emergency. I need the grader over there now, to put in some cut lines to burn back from." Rowell asked to speak to The Ghan and he told him he was to let me have the grader. When I got back the fire had already reached the Gibb River road. When we went back to the trap paddock, after the fire had been through, there were cattle that we had to destroy. In almost half a century living on stations, that is the only time I recall a campfire getting away on us.

## Race week and the Hong Kong flu epidemic

It was Boab Week. The 'dry' time, when traditionally stations pulled up for a spell, both for men and horses. I'd given the men their wages, with time off to go into Derby for the festivities. Although I knew Slim Wells was a fully fledged alcoholic I left him in charge, to look after things at Napier while we were away. I thought he would be all right. Because the homestead was a long way off the road, no-one would be calling in to supply him with grog.

This particular year I didn't have a race horse in training, but I had sent Mamlette and Wren into town a couple of weeks before races. They were with Brian Moore and only had about two weeks training with him before the race round began. When race day came I needed a jockey and I asked an ex Queenslander, Harry Furman, or Hotspur Harry as he was better known, if he would ride Mamlette for me. Before the race I gave him his instructions.

"This mare hasn't had a lot of training, so I don't want you to jump her out and take her to the lead. I just want you to bowl along. She has never raced in her life. She's a good little cattle mare, fairly quick, but I don't know for how long. I just want you to bowl along. Don't push her." After this Hotspur Harry rode out to the start where he completely ignored everything I'd said. When the starter let them go, the bloody idiot jumped Mamlette out and took her to the lead. She was in the lead until a quarter way up the straight, then she dropped back to finish last. At the end of the race I took her to the unsaddling enclosure and her backside had turned inside out. The vet came and put it back in. He told me to never race the horse again. I didn't and I never did any cattle work with her either. Nor was Harry Hotspur put on any of my horses again.

Whilst at the races I ran into a bloke called Vic Russell. He had a lead mine at Napier, in the ranges and they were looking for minerals out there.

"We've been out to Napier homestead and we've put all our gear in the quarters." He told me. I wasn't too happy about this.

"Well you can take it out of there. That's for my men to use." Then he said they were going to burn the Napier Range and that they would be getting themselves a killer. I felt pretty annoyed. I told him he was not burning the range and they would not be getting a killer for themselves.

"You will do what I tell you you can do, and if you're not careful I will see the police. If you want meat, you come and ask me. I'll get it for you. You don't just help yourself." After this, when I returned to Napier, we removed all their gear from the men's quarters, which they had basically taken over. I don't know what they thought they were doing. Napier may have been abandoned for some years, but by then it was an up and running concern and I took my job of managing it very seriously.

During the course of Boab Week, if it wasn't a race day, I would take a run back out to Napier to check up on things. This particular day I took a friend of ours, Jocelyn Cooke, with me for the run. When we got to Napier I found a four gallon tin of methylated spirits out on the kitchen table. In those days I often used to have a carton of orange juice and tomato juice on the place. Slim Wells had been into my personal supply of fruit juice and had been mixing it with metho, or 'The White Lady' as it was often known. Slim must have been on it for most of the week, because there wasn't much of anything left. I was fairly cross about it and told him so.

"I left you here to mind the place and instead of that you've been into my gear and got yourself pissed."

When we left Napier to head back to Derby Jocelyn said to me, "That fellow wanted to ask you something. I think he was hoping for a lift back into town with us, but he wasn't game enough to ask."

"I wouldn't have given him one even if he had." I told her. "He is there to look after the place and being paid to do it."

When we arrived back in Derby, Rae, Jocelyn and I went down to the Spinifex Hotel for a drink. We hadn't been there very long when who should walk in, but Slim Wells. I was angry.

"What the f----- hell are you doing here? You're meant to be minding the station." Slim wanted me to give him some money. He kept pestering me for it. "No. There's no bloody way I'm giving you money." I knew he would just spend it on grog. "You just get yourself back out to Napier and do what you're meant to be doing. How did you get in here, anyway?" I asked.

"Vic Russell, who has the lead mine, gave me a lift." Slim told me. As I was already feeling peeved with Vic this information irritated me further, although I heard later that it wasn't quite that straight forward. Apparently when Slim had asked Vic to run him into Derby, Vic told him he was only going as far as Meda. Slim Wells said that was fine, but when they got to Meda and Vic stopped to let him out of the vehicle, Slim had grabbed him by the throat.

"No way mate! You're taking me all the way in to Derby," and Vic did.

Meanwhile, in the Spinifex Hotel, Slim was getting annoyed when I wouldn't give him any money. He told me I had no right to withhold his money. It was his wages. He grabbed me by the shirt and I thought 'Oh shit!' but I couldn't back off. He was a fair bit taller than me, so I grabbed him by his shirt and gave it a good reef, to pull his head down. The whole of the front of his shirt came off and there I was with it in my hands. I told him to step outside but he wouldn't. The arse fell clean out of him. I told him again he was getting nothing and to go home, but he persisted. In the end I ran out of patience.

"Look, you get bloody nothing, or, you get the bloody lot, but you won't have a job to go back to." The end of it was, I paid him and told him he was finished.

It was 1969 and the Hong Kong flu epidemic was on. During Race week, with all the visitors in town, people were dropping like flies. In Derby seven people died of it in one week, several of them tourists. People were lying down ill all over the place. The poor public health nurse had a hell of a job on her hands. I caught it and I was too crook to go to the last days races. I couldn't do anything and I felt ratshit. I went and saw Rowell and told him I was too crook to go back out to the station. He arranged for someone to run the blacks out to Kimberley Downs. This was so that no other station would pinch our blokes off us, while they were hanging around town waiting for me to get better. Eventually, after about a week, I felt well enough to go home. I got a lift out to K.D. where I was to pick up the native boys and take them on to Napier. While I was there I saw the old Napier vehicle coming down over the hill, and who should be driving it but Slim Wells. I was ropeable. I asked him what the hell he thought he was doing. He told me he'd headed back out to Napier the same night we'd had the blue at the Spinifex Hotel, when I'd paid him off. He started telling me what jobs he'd been doing since then, but I told him not to bother.

"You had no right to be there, no right to be doing those jobs and no right to be driving round the country in the station ute." I told him. "You're fired. I told you that before."

Just at that moment Vic Russell rolled up. It was great timing. I said to Slim

"Righto', you leave that vehicle with me, and Vic can drive you to Derby, right now" which he did.

With the race round behind us life settled back into it's usual routine. A fresh plant of horses was put together, the tucker box replenished, swags freshened, rolled and tossed on the trailer as we prepared to head out for the next round of mustering. We were well into the 'dry'. A strong easterly blew across the blacksoil plains and buffeted the kurrajongs growing along the range. Chilly mornings found us hugging our campfires and cold nights saw us seeking the warmth of our spartan swags. Before dawn, with the morning star still bright in the east I'd call out 'Horses', stir up the campfire, fill the billycans and prepare for another day.

## A sudden change of plan

It was getting late in the year. The season was finishing, and I decided we would go up to the Dromedaries, do a late muster and get some bulls. We had about fifty horses in the horse paddock at Old Napier, so I left two young blokes at home, to feed some of the horses night and morning, and take a few of them for a ride each day. Reggie Woods was left in charge.

I took with me some very good men, who really knew their job and could work. Nearly all were Aboriginal stockmen, who had been with me for a long time. They were men you could trust to back you up and be there, when needed. The likes of Victor Joy, Michael Bear, Brumby Jack and others. These fellas had a good sense of humour, they enjoyed the work, and we'd have a lot of laughs together. With this loyal band of blokes we rode up to our eastern boundary to see what we could get. We were out for ten days, up around the Dromedaries, and in that time we threw, and held, a hundred and ten bulls. We headed for home with the mob, well pleased with the result of our efforts.

When we got to Bull Hole yard, inside the Napier bullock paddock, I received a telegram from Rowell. It read, 'Request muster. If no Avgas come in and pick up immediately.' This instruction came out of the blue. I'd had no prior warning of an impending late muster and it threw a bit of a spanner in the works. We had a few cleanskins with us in the mob, so I said to my blokes, "Brand these cleanskins, then bush them. Get a killer, salt some and take some fresh meat to the homestead." The bulls were to be left in the paddock, where they would stay until the following season, then be sent to the meatworks. I left my men to do as I'd instructed and drove into Derby to pick up the Avgas. By the time I got back to Napier that night I was totally exhausted. I fell asleep in the truck near the New Napier homestead site. In the morning I drove on towards Old Napier. When I got to the bullock paddock fence I came across the bulls we had just brought home. They had rushed and broken the bronco yard at Bull Hole, then followed the fence down to the Napier range. No-one seemed to have followed them up. I drove on to Old Napier, where I was met by Reggie Woods. When I arrived I could see that the canopy on the Land Rover had been burnt. Also some 44 gallon drums.

"What's been going on here?" I asked.

Reggie told me what had happened. The young blokes were filling the vehicle with petrol, after dark. They had a hurricane lamp. The fumes went from the Land Rover to the lamp, ignited and jumped back to the vehicle, burning the canopy, the seats, and the drums. Then Reggie went on to tell me that the same two fellas went to get a killer, using the tractor. They were driving through long grass, hit a stump and broke the front end. I was not very happy. They'd burnt the Land Rover and broken the tractor, we were now two vehicles down. I drove out to drop off the Avgas so Sean Murphy could muster, ruefully reflecting on the trouble the sudden change of plan had caused me. We later went out and retrieved most of the bulls, which were now educated and pliable, having been in hand since we'd caught them. They were returned to the bullock paddock. The problem of the burnt vehicle and the broken tractor took longer to fix.

*L-R Horse breaker Slim Wells, me, Murray Scott and Michael Bear.*

*The long trough at Myall's Bore, Derby.*

# CHAPTER NINE

# NEW NAPIER

*The stock routes are now covered with stands of waving grass,*
*Gone are the dusty cattle pads where the stock once used to pass.*

As the season drew to a close we again made preparations to shut down the homestead for the 'wet' season. The difference this time was that we knew the exodus was to be permanent. The site on the banks of the Barker was being abandoned forever. This was when it became known as 'Old Napier'. When we returned from holidays, at the start of the next season, the station would be run from 'New Napier', where a new homestead was to be built, in a new location. I had been running the station from 'Old Napier' for about two years.

Originally it was intended that the new homestead be built at Dingo Gap, in the Napier Range. A bore was put down there, but they only drilled to a certain depth and there wasn't enough water. In those days owners were frightened of spending the money and never seemed willing to go deep enough. A bore was put down at Yamara Gap after that, or Queen Victoria's Head as it is now known, and 'New Napier' was built nearby.

The first building to go up was a store-room and for a long while this was all there was. On the end of the store we erected a bough shed for ourselves, where we lived and cooked. Our saddles and tucker were kept in the store-room, out of the weather. The buildings from the black's camp at Old Napier were dismantled and re-erected at the new site, where septics were put in. I lived under the bough shed for most of that year, along with anyone else who might be there working.

Over time the homestead began to take shape. Carpenters came out from Derby to work on the main house, which was a transportable. Bud Crockett was amongst them. The same Bud Crockett who became a well known identity in rodeo circles, for calf roping, still competing in his eighties. Later came the men's quarters, also a transportable building. Frank Rodriguez put up the new tank for us, and he too slept in the bough shed with us. Terry Hillman and Mickey Michael made a flash new horse paddock, complete with stables and horse yard. In the meantime life for the rest of us continued much as usual, out in the stockcamp most of the time, under the bough shed if we were at the station.

At this time Napier was owned by a syndicate, comprising Robert Rowell, his brother Harold, Bob Maxted and Geoff Rose. For some reason Napier was never thought much of. It had always been considered the poor relation. Really it was one of the better cattle stations in the West Kimberley. I really loved Napier. I used to lie in bed at night trying to work out how I could own it. I thought it was a great place and I thought it had great potential. The trouble was I had no money, and on my wages I was never likely to have any. Not the kind of money needed to buy a cattle station anyway, even by the standards of those days. I was still only in my twenties then, but I was realistic enough to know that blokes like me could never own their own joint. Without thieving, finding a rich relative, or marrying the owner's daughter, it was impossible. None of them were options I'd even consider. Wells' can't steal, however tempting. The owner's daughter was unthinkable and none of my relations were even moderately well off. Even though I didn't own it and knew I never could, I worked it as if it were mine. I didn't spare one ounce of effort in all the time I was there, from a ringer in the stockcamp, managing from Old Napier, to running it from New Napier. Everything was for the station. I gave it my best, always.

## Jack Camp, contract musterer

One morning I got a telegram from Maxted and Rowell saying 'Will be at Napier at such and such a time, on such and such a day, to collect you.' That was all. I didn't know what was going on, but at the appointed time they landed in a plane, got out and told me I was to go with them over to Oobagooma to look at some horses.

"We're going to buy them, and Jack Camp will be coming to contract muster for us." They informed me. This news surprised me.

Newly introduced award wages for aborigines meant many owners were re-thinking how best to deal with the changes. If only they had realised then, what they learned, the hard way, years later. That despite having to pay award wages, their aboriginal stockmen were the backbone of the industry. They knew their job, they knew the country. They were well adapted to the conditions, both climatic and the tough living standards. They never complained about the things white stockmen were to whinge about in coming years. Most importantly, they were a reliable perennial labour force. Happy to be laid off over the 'wet', they were able to go 'walkabout' and were ready to return to work at the beginning of the 'dry', in time for a new mustering season. It was ideal. Station owners at the time, in my view, did not fully appreciate the value of the aboriginal stockmen. Many were laid off and owners began employing white men instead, presumably thinking they would get better value for the wage they had to pay. The trouble was many white ringers did not like being out of work each 'wet' season. Some would find alternative employment and it was by no means a sure thing that employees would come back the following season. This meant new blokes would be brought in, who didn't know the country, the system, anything. They had to be taught from scratch and the same problem arose, year after year. Within a decade owners were lamenting the loss of their old indigenous workforce. By then it was too late, the mistake unfixable.

I presumed Rowell and Maxted's decision to engage Jack Camp as contract musterer had something to do with the recent changes, award wages for the blacks. Who knows? I just did what I was told and off we went over to Oobagooma. We landed and went to look at the horses. We were all there together, Rob Rowell, Bob Maxted, me and Jack Camp.

"Well what d'ya reckon?" Jack asked.

I was still having a look around them, but I said, "I don't think any of them are any good. These horses are burnt out. Most of them are going to die during the next wet season. There are four or five which look all right, but I'd say they're unbroken."

Maxted beckoned me over, and took me aside.

"Jack Camp is coming to muster for us, with these horses. He'll be riding the horses, so you'd better tell him we're taking them."

"Righto, it's your money, but I wouldn't buy them." I said. "They're all rubbish. They're burnt out."

Anyway, we bought them. I don't really know why I had to go along that day, because the decision to take them had already been made. Shortly afterwards Jack Camp came mustering for us.

The deal was, Kimberley Downs had to contribute two or three men. Vincent Bear was amongst them. I had to send two or three men also and Jack Camp had four or five men himself. His two sons, Peter and George, a white bloke with a broken arm who was the horse tailer, Big Don, Victor Joy and a couple of others. His wife was the camp cook. We had to provide horses for our own men. I sent mature working horses, but The Ghan sent some colts along with his stockmen. The contract mustering plant was made up of a combination of men and horses from three places. This probably wasn't such a bad idea, having eyes and ears in the camp to keep the contractor honest. Jack wouldn't have been the first to try and feather his own nest and he certainly wasn't the last.

## Vincent has an accident

Jack Camp's contract mustering team were mustering from Leo's to Douglas' on Kimberley Downs.

Vincent Bear was riding a colt on this particular day. He was a competent rider, not frightened of young horses that hadn't long been broken in. They were out on a black soil plain, where there was one tree. As man and rider approached the tree, Vincent reckoned they were going to one side of it, but at the last minute the young horse changed it's mind. It hit the tree, at pace, and wiped Vincent off. Men came to his aid. They got Vincent and sat him up. Then they picked him up and carried him to the shade of the tree. They were shifting camp that day, so when the truck came along, they picked Vincent up again, and carried him across the blacksoil plain onto the road. They put him on the back of the truck. It was a wonder it didn't kill him.

Vincent had a broken neck. They drove on to Douglas' Bore where they unloaded the injured man. He was lapsing in and out of consciousness. Screaming with pain whenever they moved him. Realising something was seriously wrong, a message was sent to the homestead and an ambulance was called out from Derby. From there it went out to Douglas' to pick up the injured stockman. Sand bags were placed either side of him and he was strapped down. The ambulance made a long, slow trip back to town.

Vincent was later transferred to Perth and ended up in hospital in Fremantle. I went and visited him there when I was next down south. He had plaster over his head, shoulders, around his abdomen and down to his hips. He was encased in it, like a suit of armour, but eventually he made a full recovery.

## Trucking off our breeders

The contract mustering team had been out in the back country, down around Mundooma. They had a camp at Mundooma and a camp at Limestone Springs. Jack Camp knew how to get cattle. He really had a knack. The black fellas did what he said. If he told them to jump off for a beast, they did. They had got some big bullocks and bulls. Two of my blokes came to me after they'd been out with Jack for a while.

"You take us back longa our stockcamp Shohn? We don't wanna stay longa dis man."

"Why's that?" I asked. "This bloke needs you."

"Dat fella gottim dem unbroken horses der. We bin gotta shuck 'im rope longa dem horse. Knock'em down, put'em hobble on. Let 'im up again." They showed me their hands. Both of their hands were covered in big blisters, balls of them. No wonder they weren't too happy about it, but they stayed.

I was taking horse feed down to Jack. It was late in the season, just before the meatworks was due to close for the 'wet'. Jack was getting a lot of big bullocks and a lot of bulls. Some bullocks had their horns sawn off at the butt. They were to go to the abattoirs. It was sheer stupidity, because those bullocks would go straight down the chute as 'condemns'. You might get away with it with bulls, but not bullocks.

No-one was going to get paid for them. But it was no good me saying anything to Jack. I wasn't controlling him.

They had mustered from Mundooma up to Tullochs. Jack was telling me how many roadtrains we'd need at each yard. The first was Tullochs. He said he'd need five roadtrains. By the look of the mob I thought that was pretty right. They were single deck in those days. Then they went on to Hawkstone yards, and he asked me to book a couple of roadtrains for there, which I did. From Hawkstone they were going over to Douglas', Leo's, and onto Traveller's. Jack told me to order four roadtrains for Travellers. I was a bit concerned. I thought four was too many.

"Look Jack, you're getting into quieter country now. I think you need to back off. There aren't the bullocks and bulls that you think there are. You'll find you run out of them on the inside country and you won't get what you think you're going to get."

"You just order what I ask for. I'll get them." He told me tersely.

"All right." I agreed. "I'll order the roadtrains for you, but I'm not happy about this."

The day the musterers got to Travellers, I went to see them. I took some horse feed down with me. I was working hard to supply Jack with horse feed, trying to keep some condition on the horses in his plant. Several of them were in poor nick before they'd even started. I got to Travellers early, but I could hear them coming in with the cattle, so I drove out and waited on the flat. I watched while they brought the mob in. Jack had his two sons there and when a young mickey broke out of the mob he told them to get off and throw it. The younger fellow was frightened. You can teach young fellows to throw, but if a bloke says 'no' you don't force him. If he hasn't got the confidence, or the gameness you mustn't make him do it, because that's when you get into trouble. But Jack Camp did things differently to me. He rode around to the lad and when the youngster wasn't suspecting it, pushed him clean off his horse. It was his son, but I decided I didn't need to see any more.

Once they'd yarded the cattle I went over and sat up on the yard rail to have a good look at the mob. I thought, 'Jeez, there's nowhere near four roadtrains here.' At first I decided I wouldn't say anything. I ummed and erred about it for a while, then I went over to the camp. I said to Jack "You'll need to knock your roadtrains back. You haven't got the cattle for four roadtrains."

"Oh yes I have." He assured me.

"All right." I wasn't happy about it but I had a pannikin of tea with them, then changed the subject. "I've got a load of horse feed here for you."

"I've still got all the other horse feed you gave me. I don't need any more." Jack replied.

"Well, you're borrowing these horses. The idea is that you feed the bloody things and try to keep them alive." Jack got wild then. He called out to the black fellas.

"Oi you boys. Get this horse feed off the motor car. Take it down to that dry billabong, open the bags up and tip it all out." So that's what they did. Just chucked all the feed out, loose, on the dry mud. I was appalled. All the horses came in there kicking, squealing and fighting over it. If my life had been on the back of those horses, I would have been pumping the feed into them as fast as I was able. I couldn't believe it. Here was a man with a reputation as a 'gun cattleman', yet this was how he did things. Jack Camp knew how to get cattle, there's no doubt about it, but he didn't know how to look after stock and he didn't seem to care much about them. Before I left the camp I said, "I'll be back in the morning Jack."

"Oh? So you'll be back to draft these cattle off for us for the meatworks?"

"No. I haven't drafted any cattle since you've been doing this contract Jack, and I'm not starting tomorrow. I've ordered the roadtrains for you, but you'll be doing the drafting. I'll just be here to see what's going on."

The next day I got there just on daylight. The roadtrains were already there waiting. I watched as Jack began drafting. Any big cow that came through was 'meatworks.' Five wet cows, 'meatworks'. Straight onto the truck as they were drafting them. More good red cows, in milk, 'meatworks'. Two skinny cows, 'bush'. One good cow in calf, 'meatworks'. I watched for a while, then interrupted him.

"Jack, these aren't meatworks cattle. These are our breeders."

"They're good fat meatworks cattle," he replied.

"All right, as you will." I got in the vehicle and drove straight to Kimberley Downs, where I rang Bob Maxted.

"You need to get out here in a hurry, because the best cows you've got on the place are being sent to the meatworks. One roadtrain will be on it's way pretty shortly. You need to come and have a look at what's going on." After I had made the phone call I didn't stick around. I went back to Napier, to get the hell out of it. Maxted did come out and he met one roadtrain on his way. He had a look at the cattle and spoke to the driver.

"Take them on to the meatworks," he instructed. He met another roadtrain near Kimberley Downs. He stopped it and looked at the cattle being transported.

"You can turn around, take this truck back to where you came from and unload it." He told the driver. Bob Maxted put a stop to the whole deal and that was the end of Jack Camp on Napier. If Maxted hadn't backed me up that day I would have had to pull out. Needless to say my rating with Jack Camp, after that, wasn't very good.

## Good gear for catching bulls

We were up at a place known as The Dromaderies, in the King Leopold Range, when Bob Rowell rocked up one day.

"I've been looking into getting some sort of tranquilliser for getting these bulls." He told me. "I've got onto something you blokes can use." He proceeded to explain how it worked. "You can get a firearm with a syringe mechanism. Ampoules of a nicotine based tranquilliser can be inserted in the device and fired at the bull. The ampoules come in different sizes. You just need to calculate the size and weight of the bull, to determine what sized ampoule you need to use."

"So we carry this gear with us in our saddle bag while we're mustering?" I asked.

"Yes."

"Right. So while we're chasing a bull on horseback, we decide it's weight, pick the correct sized ampoule from the saddle bag, load it up and fire it?" Rowell nodded.

"Yes, that's it. You should be able to get a lot of bulls with this stuff." I was a bit sceptical. It sounded like a helluva palaver to me.

"What happens if you accidentally needle yourself doing this? Is there an antidote for this stuff."

"No. There's no antidote." Rowell informed me.

"Then I don't want anything to do with it." I told him.

Later on I was talking to a vet. He told me about a tranquilliser you could inject into a bull, that would knock him out for a while. I asked if he would get me some and I'd try it. It proved most effective. We still had to throw the bull in order to needle it, but because he was sedated we were able to hold him much more easily once he was let up. We didn't lose nearly as many bulls. It was great gear. There was still a certain amount of trial and error involved. The quantity used depended on how hot the bull was when we needled him, the heat of the day and the distance the animal had run before being thrown. The hotter he was the less tranquilliser was administered, the cooler it was the more we had to use. On average I reckoned there were ten bulls to a bottle. Once I'd discovered its value I asked the local chemist, Kevin Bogue, to get some in for me. I bought ten bottles, for a total cost of a hundred dollars. When Rowell got the bill he slipped a cog.

"There's ten bulls in each bottle." I told him. "That's a dollar a bull. Not a bad deal." I wasn't very impressed with him for giving me a rev. We still risked life and limb to throw the bulls for him, but at least we held them once we'd got them.

## Help from Main Roads Department

Over the years quite a lot of blokes left the ringing game chasing better money. A lot of them swapped their love of riding horses for a love of driving trucks, whilst others, Old Blue Gum Watson, Sammy Lovell and blokes like that, worked with the Main Roads Department. There was a Main Roads camp up at the Dromedaries, known as 110 Mile Camp and sometimes they would come and get meat off me. I didn't charge them. I'd tell them to come out to the stock-camp at a certain time, and place, and we'd knock one for them. Then they'd butcher it themselves. It was a good deal for the station, because if I had a bushfire and they saw the smoke, I didn't even need to go and get them. They'd be right onto it. If I did go up to see them I'd usually meet the grader already on it's way. Quite often they'd be on the fire before I even got there.

If I had a vehicle broken down and didn't have a mechanic, then they'd come and fix it for me.

When I was at New Napier they'd drop in at the homestead twice a week, on the way into town, to see if we had any mail to go in, or parts needing to be picked up. They were always very good and helpful to me. I couldn't fault them. I never understood why some blokes on stations were so stingy about letting them have a bit of decent beef, because they more than re-paid the favour. That was how things worked in those days. You tried to help each other out the best way you could.

## Attending with Mt Hart

Napier shared a boundary with Mt Hart, a rugged property to the north east of us, where we would attend musters from time to time. Mt Hart and Silent Grove stations were owned by Thiess and managed by a man called Peter Murray. One year, while our stockcamp mustered around Mt Josef and Mt Eliza, I attended with Michael Bear and another bloke.

The Mt Hart camp had mustered down as far as The Dromedaries, on the Gibb River Road, where there was a yard. They had a load of bulls there, ready to be trucked out. They didn't have a ramp, but just dug a hole, then drove the truck into the hole. The bulls were to be pushed up into the forcing pens, to the race and onto the truck. This was the first day that Michael and I were there.

In some situations, when there are too many blokes trying to do the same job, you can get in each others way. Because of this, once we'd pushed the bulls up, I decided to hang back a bit.

"You're frightened of these bulls are you Wellsy?" The Mt Hart fellows taunted.

"Yeah. There's too many blokes. Somebody will knock somebody over, then a bull will have a go at them." These bulls belonged to Mt Hart and their men were trying to push them up into the yard to load them. They got them in the yard, but none of them would run up to shut the gate. I raced in to shut it, but it was too late. The bulls came back. Now they'd had a win the job would be harder. We pushed them up again and I ran in once more to shut the gate. I went to hook the gate but I missed it. The bulls were coming back, I could see them. They'd had one win and learnt from it. I thought 'I'd better get out of here.' As I jumped back the gate hit me. It caught me right on my hip bone and knocked me down. It hurt like bloody hell. The bulls hit the gate and went over the top of me, but not one of them put a foot on me. So then everyone had a big laugh about it. That's normal amongst blokes when someone has a near miss. I was in a lot of pain. Later I said to the Mt Hart fellas,

"You know I'm not game, but somehow you blokes all get further away when it's time to close the gate." Eventually they got the bulls back up and went to shut the gate, but they hit it once more and back they came yet again. Bob O'Sullivan, the headstockman for Mt Hart, had jumped on the gate. When the bulls hit it, they shot him clean over the fence. He landed on his head and he was in a fair bit of pain. Eventually we got the bulls up and loaded onto the truck, and away they went to the meatworks. After they'd gone someone said we'd better take Bob into town to get his neck looked at. I went to the hospital with them and got my hip checked out at the same time. Bob O'Sullivan had a fractured bone in his neck and they kept him in. I had a chipped pelvis, but there was nothing they could do for me, so I was taken back out to the stockcamp again.

We spent the next four days mustering along the boundary, with the Mt Hart crew. The deal we had with Mt Hart was that whoever threw a cleanskin, could put their earmark on it. The beast would then belong to that station. On our last day attending we mustered over towards Mount Eliza. There was a gap in the ranges, that Michael knew of, which would bring us back to where our stockcamp was. Michael and I were mustering, while the third fella was bringing our spare horses and the pack mule along. The Mt Hart crew were still with us, and we came across some cattle. I was riding a good, strong Wallal horse, called Officer, a grey gelding. (He was later used as clerk of the course horse at the Derby Races.) A big roan bull appeared, but he decided he wasn't going to run into the mob. He took off and I took off after him. He was running towards the river and creeks. We were on red ground and coming onto breakaway country. I jumped off my horse. I was just about to grab the tail of this bull to throw him, when I noticed a grey horse alongside me, which at first I took to be Officer. Next thing I was being shouldered off, with this horse, into the breakaways. I had to jump and somehow managed to come out of it all right. In the meantime, Michael Bear had jumped off his horse, decked the bull and was holding him down. So we put a Napier earmark on it. It wasn't till then that Michael told me what had happened. It wasn't Officer who had shouldered me, but a Mt Hart man, on another grey, hoping to stop me from throwing the cleanskin, so he could claim it instead. Despite their best efforts, and thanks to Michael Bear, the bull was ours. We couldn't take him along with us. We had too few cattle to be able to hold him. Instead we had to leave him with the Mt Hart mob and, although he was now legally ours, I reckon it would have lost his ear soon after that, or the dogs would have eaten it off.

## 'Hey Boy'

I was still living in the bough shed at New Napier, when I first met Carey Crutcher. He was a yank and used to smoke a big cigar. He owned oil wells in America and was a very rich man and he appeared to have a significant financial interest in Napier, which was in the throes of changing hands. Whenever he addressed me, instead of calling me John, it was always 'Hey Boy' which I didn't like much. He came to Napier and was asking me a lot of questions about this and that, which I answered as best I could. I told him we had some cattle going to the meatworks in a day or two, would he like to see them?

"Yeah, boy. I reckon I would." We hopped in the vehicle and I took him down to where the cattle were being tailed, on the ranges side of Womberella Creek, on a bit of good grass near the old homestead. When we got there the yank spotted some old pikers amongst the mob. "Hey Boy! What are those ones there?" I told him they were old piker bullocks we had managed to fluke. "And what are ya goin' to do with 'em Boy?"

"They'll be going to the meatworks with the rest of the mob."

"Aw, no. Don't send them there. We'll truck 'em over to Camballin, put them in the Inkata feedlot and put a bit of beef on 'em first."

These were shelly old pikers, about fifteen of them. Probably the only reason we had got them in hand was that they were too old and buggered to get away from us.

"Look, the quicker you get these fellas into the meatworks and get their heads lopped off, the better. You'll be in front. If you take them and lock them up in a feedlot they'll lie down on you and die. It's a wonder they haven't got the sulks and died as it is. That's what old bullocks do when they're finally caught. You'll never 'put any beef' on these fellas. They're too old. They're finished." That was when I realised how little this yank knew about wild Kimberley cattle. He might have a big cigar and a lot of money to throw around, but 'Hey Boy!' didn't have a bloody clue. After a fair bit of persuasion, eventually common sense prevailed and they all went to the meatworks as intended.

## Bantum Bob and Moulting Maud

When I worked for Rowell and Maxted I was allowed to choose my own 'wet season' caretakers. When ALCO took over it was the opposite. They told me who would be caretaking while I was away. One year they decided a bloke called Dana could do the job.

This particular year, before I went on holiday, we had done some bull catching. As in previous years, we'd brought the bulls home and put them in the bullock paddock ready to sell next season. As the bulls still had shiny shins and swollen legs, from being thrown and tied, we didn't castrate them, but they were still civilised enough to be handled with a horse. We cut their horns off at the butt and earmarked them. Soon after I left to go down south for my annual break.

When I returned from Perth I was crossing the road in Derby one day, when a fellow hailed me. He had his wife with him. "Are you John Wells?" he asked.

"Yeah. Why?"

"We thought you were. We knew you by that blue Toyota."

"How's that?" I asked.

"Well, while you were away on holidays we went out to Napier Downs with Dana. He had some rogue bulls there, so we went out and shot them." I pricked up my ears at this.

"Oh? What did these rogue bulls look like?"

"They had earmarks and they'd had their horns cut off." He told me. He was a pommy bloke. A chicken farmer. He was known as Bantum Bob and his wife, Moulting Maud. I couldn't believe what I was hearing.

"Well we risked our lives throwing those bulls, shouldering them back into the mob.

We walked them home, earmarked them, got them behind wire and you go out there and bloody shoot them!" Surprised that I was cross, Bantum Bob tried to explain.

"Well we didn't know all that. Dana said they were rogue bulls." This did little to mollify me. I felt really peeved. Dana was supposed to have a ranking, in the Kimberley, as a bit of a cattleman, but it seemed he couldn't work out that a bull with his horns taken off, and an earmark, wasn't a rogue bull. Or perhaps he could, but had decided to have some sport with them anyway. Either way the pommy pair reckoned they'd had a real station experience, while I wasn't there to keep an eye on things. It just went to show you really had to know who you'd got looking after the station over the 'wet'. The caretaker was put there to make sure nobody else came onto the place and did that kind of thing, not go and shoot the bloody stock himself. I couldn't believe Dana was so damned stupid.

## Horses missing after the 'wet'

That same 'wet' season a lot of our horses went missing. I didn't discover this until later on, when we mustered the horse paddock at New Napier. I thought there must be a hole in the fence and they'd got out, so we rode around the fence to check. No hole. Quite a few of the missing horses were the ones I rode. There wasn't much I could do about it, but I thought 'one day they'll turn up'. They never did, but a couple of years later some light was finally shed on the mystery. I was in conversation with a couple of Napier black fellas. They told me they had been returning from a man-making ceremony at Mount House, were walking back to Derby, during the 'wet' and had stopped off at Napier for a day or two to rest.

"You bin 'way longa 'oliday one time an 'dat black fella belong'en Jack Camp bin cum 'ere." They told me.

"Yeah? What did he want?"

"He bin chay he bin lost'em way, go back 'longa Oobagooma." This was the first I'd heard of it and, because of the missing horses, I was very interested. He wasn't bloody lost. I reckon he'd been sent in to see who was at Napier at the time. How much time they had to do the job and who was going to follow them. It wasn't all I learnt from the conversation. These two native boys went on to tell me, "We bin chit down longa dat Kimm'ly Down one time, longa 'wet'. We go walkabout longa dat paddick der, an' bin chee dat Shack, an' his men. 'im bin muster dem horses belongen Kimberley Down." The blacks used to tell me lots of things. Sometimes it took a while, but bye'n'bye I found out what was going on in the country. There were times when I didn't need to be told, because it was so obvious, I could work it out for myself. Like when I'd come across cattle and horse tracks where they shouldn't be, or found bullock carcasses in the yard at Mundooma, after the 'wet', that hadn't been left there by us. There was no doubt that thievery went on and managers and caretakers alike had to be a wake-up to it.

## Vincent gives me a fright

I met Vincent Bear in Derby one day, after he got back from Perth. He had made a good recovery from his horse fall and he wanted a job back on Napier with me. I said I'd give him one. I knew he was prone to please himself, I hadn't forgotten that he had ridden off Napier taking the horse Alcabeer with him, but I have always given blokes a second chance. I gave Vincent his.

When he came into the camp we were already out mustering, so I lent him my horse Kanso. When you set Kanso after a beast he was very hard to hold, but if you knew him you just let him go and he did all the work. You didn't have to steer him. I reckoned he was a crackerjack horse and I lent him to Vincent. We were cutting out some cattle at Billyarra, at the other end of Windjana Gorge. A mickey bull took off out of the mob. Kanso just grabbed the bit and went. Vincent was right onto the beast, but there was a big coolibah tree coming up. I saw what was happening. As I watched I thought 'Christ, he's going to hit this.' It looked inevitable. At the last moment the horse went one way, the beast the other and when they were round the tree Kanso was straight back onto the mickey, with Vincent still in the saddle. When Vincent had brought the young bull back to the mob I said to him, in not the politest of words, "Jesus Christ, you ----- idiot. You could bloody well break your neck again doing that and you mightn't be so lucky the next time."

"Don't worry John. You could probably hit a tree and break your neck, and it be the last time you do it. We're the same you an' me." Which was true, but gee, I was shaking. It had scared the daylights out of me. I reckoned he was gone.

## Leah is born

Rae was expecting a baby and had remained in Perth for a while, after I returned to the Kimberley, later flying back to Derby where she stayed until the birth. It was early 1970. The stockcamp had been down at Mundooma. We had finished mustering the area and were heading towards home. When we got to Limestone Springs it started to rain. We left there and headed for Tullochs. I was riding a black filly, called Tennesee. She was only young, not long broken in, but already a smart little horse. It was quite boggy and I felt very sorry for her, but there was nothing I could do to help her. It rained all that day and conditions were miserable for both man and horse.

We spent a day at Tullochs, where we tipped horns and earmarked the cattle, but it was too wet for us to brand. We left the bullocks in the trap paddock at Tullochs and I instructed Vincent Bear and three other ringers, to head home with the horses. I drove the vehicle, via Kimberley Downs, back to New Napier. The rivers were all up and running, and I was lucky to get across the Lennard River. The tractor and trailer, loaded up with all the gear, including the cook, Lucy Ward, and the rest of the stockcamp, headed for Kimberley Downs, where they waited for it to dry out. In the meantime, when Vincent and the men bringing the horses home reached the Barker River, they found it running full width and flowing swiftly. They were unable to cross. They sat it out for a day or two, with next to no tucker, until the river dropped sufficiently for them to swim the horses over. Once across they let the horses go in the horse paddock at Old Napier, then rode on home to New Napier.

I had been home at New Napier for a day or two when a telegram came through, telling me that Rae had given birth to a baby girl. Because the rivers were up and still impassable it was several days before I was able to drive into Derby to see her. There was no bridge at the Lennard River in those days. Once the water level dropped, enabling me to drive over the Lennard River Crossing, I made my way into town to see Leah for the first time. After visiting the hospital I called on my parents, before going down to the Spinifex Hotel. Lenny Roser and his band were there playing. Lenny asked after Rae and when I told him our news he sang a song for us, called Leah.

## Working for ALCO

Napier and Kimberley Downs had been sold, although Robert Rowell, I learned years later, still retained a financial interest. The Ghan and I were now employed by ALCO. The Australian Land and Cattle Company. My pay went up from $65 dollars a week to $100 a week. The new homestead was finished. Days under the bough shed were over. Rae and Leah were with me in the new homestead. Things were changing on Napier. I still lay in bed and dreamt of owning the place myself.

The Australian Land and Cattle Company had big plans for the Kimberley and I was beginning to learn something about the people I was now working for. They had an office in Pier Street, Perth. In the waiting room there was a picture of an American cowboy roping a beast, which had tits on it like a milk bar. Beneath it was a small plaque which read *'Cowboy roping wild steer.'* This used to amuse me a lot whenever I went in there.

The driving force, the 'ideas' man, the name synonymous with ALCO was, still is, 'Texas Jack'. A man with big dreams, a loud voice, plenty of front and a white 'cowboy' hat, he made his presence felt wherever he went. There was no ignoring Texas Jack. The world was going to hear what his plans for the West Kimberley were. In a way Jack Fletcher did have the right idea, but he made a big mistake. He brought a lot of his men over from America. Men who didn't know how to work wild cattle. It all boiled down to not having the right men in the key places. 'Hey Boy' had the wealth, but he was ignorant to the class of cattle we had on Napier at that time. We had very little fencing, few paddocks and plenty of open country. Napier was not Texas. What ALCO needed were West Australian ringers and managers. Men who knew wild cattle and who knew the conditions.

We threw cleanskin bulls all the time when we were mustering. If we decked a bull, his horns came off at the butt. Once you've held a bull for three days you've got him for life. I would have thrown bulls in my bullock mob. Jack Fletcher and his men would come along and have a look at them while I had them yarded up, often way out bush.

"How many have you got here for the meatworks?" They'd ask.

"Might be ninety head. A hundred and twenty, perhaps. I don't really know yet."

"Oh no. You've got more than that." They'd tell me.

"I don't think so." Eventually I'd realise they were including the thrown bulls in their count. I'd have to explain.

"Those bulls with their horns knocked off, they're not in the market cattle. They're going into the paddock. We'll walk them home, draft them at home, put them into the bullock paddock and then at the end of the season we'll bush the lot of them. Next year we'll muster them up and they'll be good solid clean bulls. You'll get good money for them next year. Not this year."

Sometimes, if we were trucking and had some of these bulls in the yard, even though I had told them, the ALCO blokes would want them put on the truck, then and there. So off they'd go to Broome abattoir, where they'd be condemned and sent down the chute for by products. I couldn't see the sense in it. They'd paid the freight, but they got no money for them. If only they had kept them till the following season, when they would have been good heavy, healthy bulls and earnt them and the station a good dollar.

I was always hearing how stations didn't make much money, but in a lot of cases the bosses did silly things. Something else that used to annoy me was when 'the powers that be' wanted young steers sent off Napier to go to the Inkata feedlot. Later I'd go down to the abattoir and there would be young bullocks in the meatworks yard, that weren't heavy enough yet to be making any money. Crazy. They were spending money to get nothing. I was told 'It's just a figure on the books John.' To me that didn't make sense. ALCO weren't the only ones doing this kind of thing. I came across it later in my career, and found it no less annoying.

After I'd been working for ALCO for about six months they offered me an American saddle.

"If you ride in it for six months we'll give it to you." I thought this was pretty good. Flash. Like being in the Parmelia when you're down south. So I rode in it for a week, or a fortnight and I thought 'Bugger it. I don't want this saddle, even if I do stick in it for the six months.' I went back to my old Carpentaria, which I'd had for years. I didn't like the Yankee saddle, and I was frightened of the horn. If you had a gutser and that landed on the back of your head, you'd be dead.

Texas Jack had a couple of sons. He gave his boys too much authority. They didn't know very much, but they were headstrong and thought they knew the lot. It made things pretty difficult. They built a rodeo arena for themselves, at Inkata. I don't know why we needed that expense. It could have come twenty years later. Everything was for show. ALCO was a big noise. As part of their self promotion they decided to make a movie. It was called 'ALCO Down Under' and some of it was shot on Napier.

## The movie 'ALCO Down Under'

We were working at Tullochs. The film crew got to the yard late. By the time they arrived we had finished branding, we'd let the bronco horses go, and everything was done. We were sitting down in the camp, having a cup of tea when they got there and they joined us for smoko. After a while they said, "Well are we going to do some filming?"

"We're all finished. You're too late. The job's been done." I told them.

"Oh. Well can't you just do a bit again, and pretend?" I said I supposed we could. So we re-lit the branding fires, caught the bronco horses and roped a white heifer. We pulled her up to the bronco panel, re-branded her, with a nice black brand on her nice white hide, and then pretended to ear-mark her. They got all of this on film.

"We hear you throw a few bulls. Can you organise that for us?" they asked hopefully.

"We've got some bulls in this paddock here, but it's very rough ground." I was a bit reluctant.

"That doesn't matter" They said enthusiastically, and it didn't to them. I had a lot of smart men who could deck bulls, so I picked a couple out and told them what I wanted them to do.

"Eddie, grab a horse and Brumby you grab a horse and go out into that paddock. These blokes want you to get a bull, cut him out and throw him. They're going to take a photo of it." I went on to say "Now don't go and pick the biggest, flashest, strongest bull. Go and get some dying old bastard that's easy. It'll look all right on the camera and no-one will know that it's not as firey as these other ones." So they go in, first up they pick the biggest, prettiest, fittest, bull of the lot. Well he was too quick. These bulls were only in a small paddock. We had a bull buggy there, which

I was driving and we're out there, with the cameraman. Barry Cobb was there also, with his arm around this fellow, holding him onto the roll bar of the buggy, because it was bumping about over the rough ground. After the first effort I called the boys over and said to them again, "Don't go for that sort of bull. Get a 'not so strong' one." They brought the mob of cattle round past the motor car. Then they hooked onto this bull. Eddie Bear was in front and just about ready to jump off, when he hit a hole and down he went. He was riding a really flash black mare, with a blaze and two hind legs white. Reverse, we called her. Brumby had jumped off and he was with this bull. So he's on the ground, rough ground, with a bull. Eddie has had a fall and he is hurt. I'm in the bull buggy. I left the motor car and ran in to help. We got the bull, threw him and tied him up. When we'd finished the film crew said, "Ah, that was real good. Can you do it again?"

"No," I said curtly. "That's enough." Eddie Bear had to be taken into hospital, so out of this I'd lost one of my best men.

I heard later, once the movie was released, that people said the whole thing was a stunt. It was no stunt. We did this sort of thing every day, though we tried to be a little bit sensible. We wouldn't normally pull on bull throwing on such holey ground. Nearly four decades later Texas Jack was good enough to send me a DVD of 'ALCO Down Under'. Watching it from my three score years and ten, I can't believe how lean and agile I was back in those days.

## Computer mustering

One of Texas Jack's top men was a yank called Wes Roddy. He was a nice bloke, but he was way out of his depth. Gordon Napier was Texas Jack's 'stock' man, and a West Australian. I got into a bit of strife with these two men. At the start of one season they came to see me. We were all sitting around a table talking about this and that. Paperwork and computers were spread about and notes being made.

"So how many calves do you reckon you'll brand next year John?" they asked. There were a lot of cattle down the Oobagooma end that were hard to get, but I had just built a couple of traps on Napier, one at Limestone Springs and the other at Mundooma. Taking them into consideration I said, "I reckon we'll probably brand four and a half, to five thousand calves."

"Oh no. You'll brand more than that. More like six to six and a half thousand."

"Yeah? How do you work that out?" I asked.

"The computer says so."

"Oh! All right then." But I'm thinking 'Jeez. Smart machine.' There was a bit more discussion, then,

"We'd like to know what numbers you'll send off this year. How many bullocks do you reckon you'll have for the abattoirs?"

"Might be two and half, or maybe three thousand, with a bit of luck." Again I was counting on the two new traps at Limestone Springs and Mundooma.

"No, no. You'll get more than that." I was getting a bit sick of this and I started to heckle up.

"How many will I get then?" I enquired.

"Probably three and half to four thousand head." I asked how they came up with that figure.

"The computer can tell us how many you'll get John." They explained. By this time the blood was really up.

"Well you get the computer here to muster the bastards for you." I told them.

Although I was the manager, these blokes were always interfering. There seemed to be a lot of 'heads' and not too many who knew much about Kimberley cattle stations. Not as they were then. There wasn't much organisation either, or so it seemed to me. On one occasion The Ghan, on Kimberley Downs, was supposed to supply a mob of bullocks by a certain date. About four days before they were due to go, I was sent a telegram. 'Short of two hundred bullocks. Can you supply?' I replied back 'Yes. Have two hundred bullocks in hand now.' Another telegram came. 'OK roadtrains will be there on such and such a day, at such and such a time.' I made sure I had the bullocks in the yard ready to go and they were trucked off the place. A week later I was supposed to supply four or five hundred Napier bullocks. A telegram came over the session, 'Are you OK for your quota of bullocks?' I sent one back. 'No. I've already given you two hundred of them.' In fact I did have them, because I always had a few in the bullock paddock, so we scraped them together to get the numbers. But it was always gimme, gimme. All the time, it was 'you just keep running and running to get what you can and we'll take it off you.' At one stage I was told to sell eight hundred aged cows. I wasn't happy about this.

"I'll send off the cows that are barren, have a buggered udder, or are mental, but I'm not selling eight hundred aged cows."

"Why can't you send off these other cows?" they asked.

"Because the quiet cows here are my coachers. I need the older quiet cattle to handle the rest. The other thing is, we haven't got enough bores here for the number of cattle running on the place. The older cows know where the main waters are. There are a lot of wild cattle on Napier, in the ranges, in the scrub, and along the creeks. In a crook year, a drought year, you'll need these older cows to show the wilder stuff where the water is. They are the ones that will take the cattle off the perishing areas, back to the waters." But Texas Jack and his men couldn't see that, or understand it. After a few months Wes Roddy said to me.

"John Wells you haven't put a dent in these cows that you were meant to send off."

"I told you before, I'm not sending them. I'm paid to look after this property, and that is what I'll do."

"Well if you don't get these cows off by August, you won't have a job here." he warned.

"That's up to you." I replied.

## Prelude to getting the arse

The Ghan had pulled the pin from Kimberley Downs. ALCO sent the Liveringa crew over to muster K.D. and the headstockman was going to take over as manager. By this time the money had run out for ALCO and they wanted to take the station cheque book off me. I wouldn't give it to them. There was a good reason why I wouldn't give it to them. I would go into Derby with the cheque book and get gear from Elders, such as flour, salt, tea and sugar. Basic things the station had to have. We weren't 'living flash' on Napier. Other ALCO blokes were building aeroplanes for themselves, and a rodeo arena at Camballin. Wasting money doing stupid things that weren't needed. I saw a lot of things, heard a lot of stories, and the blacks used to tell me a lot of what was going on. The whole show had to go down hill. It was inevitable.

The Liveringa crew were working in the bullock paddock on Kimberley Downs. There's a fair bit of scrub, but you can get bullocks out of it, if you keep hammering at them. It takes a bit of time and effort, but eventually they'll move out of that area and you do get them. The Liveringa boys had bull buggies, which are all right if you know how to use them. But these blokes didn't. They were knocking bullocks down, killing them and driving around with 'antlers' on the back of the bull buggy. Crazy. Killing good big money bullocks for their horns and leaving the rest to rot. Nothing wrong with them. But what really annoyed me was, they've got ten or fifteen perfectly good bullocks lying out there in the paddock, yet they were buying meat from town. Tinned sausages, tinned dog, spam, everything. The other thing was that they had tins of fruit, something we didn't have on Napier. They were so well fed, they'd get a tin of fruit, puncture both sides of it, drink the juice and chuck the can out. Oh golly! The waste. Whilst on Napier, we were knocking a killer salting a lot of it and eating all that before getting the next. And we never saw a tin of fruit, except when Maxted had occasionally brought us out a carton toward the end of the season, when he needed a bit more petrol out of us. Here I was trying to look after the show and keep it going for ALCO, when their top men, from the Liveringa camp were riding in yankee saddles, driving bull buggies festooned with trophy horns, living off fancy tucker and killing money bullocks for no good reason. It got my blood up a bit. I was trying to run a tight ship, while other blokes were throwing money away. I didn't see why I should hand in the cheque book when we only bought what was really needed.

## Cutting edges and cutting costs

The roadtrain era had arrived and cattle were being trucked instead of walked, as they had been in the past. Napier did not have many roads and what station tracks we did have were rough and unsuitable. A fair amount of work needed to be done to improve them, so our cattle could be transported safely. We didn't have any machinery to do it with, but ALCO had a couple of graders over at Camballin. Everything was for Camballin at that time. It was ALCO's big venture. A vast area of flat Liveringa country, where they grew endless acres of sorghum. The crops were irrigated from the Fitzroy River and Texas Jack and his cohorts planned to transform the region into a food bowl for Southeast Asian. Large amounts of money were being sunk into the enterprise, which was the talk of the district.

In time a grader was sent over to Napier to do up our roads, but no spare blades came with it. Napier is hard country, with a lot of limestone. Within ten days the cutting edges were worn down. Camballin said they didn't have any spare cutting edges. I needed the grader to keep working, so I borrowed a set off Mt Hart. Then I ordered three sets to come up from Perth. One set was to go on the grader, to finish the job at Napier, one was for Mt Hart to replace those loaned to me, and the third set would go back with the grader, to Camballin, when we'd finished with it. I told the supplier I needed them as soon as possible, and to send them on the first available truck. I asked them to wire me the arrival day in Derby, because the grader was now sitting down, having also worn out the borrowed Mt Hart cutting edges. One morning I got a telegram on the session, 'Grader blades arriving Derby eleven o'clock today.' I told Rae I had to go to town to pick up these cutting edges. She was coming with me, so we jumped in the car, with baby Leah, and away we went to town. A hundred mile trip on mostly unsealed road. It was about ten to twelve by the time we got there. In those days it was still 'shut up shop from twelve noon till two', so first stop was Rowell's office, then called Australian Land & Cattle Co. office. I went in. Norm Longdon was there and he greeted me.

"G'day John how are you going? What can we do for you?"

"I got a wire this morning that said the cutting edges have come for the grader. I need them urgently, so I'll grab them and get going."

"Ah. They're already gone."

"Yeah? How did that happen?"

"Wes Roddy's done that."

"So where is Wes Roddy?" I asked and the blood went straight up.

"He's on the phone."

"Well you tell him, when he gets off, that I'm waiting."

I did wait, for quite a while, but he didn't get off the phone. Eventually I said to Rae, "We'd better go and have something to eat and we'll come back here after lunch." So we went down to the pub and had a meal and returned to the office afterwards. This time Wes Roddy was in.

"G'day John. I hear you've come in for those cutting edges for the grader."

"Yeah, I have."

"I've already sold them." He told me.

"What?"

"I've already sold them."

"What did you do that for?" I asked.

"I was cutting the expenses down on Napier."

"Well how am I supposed to get roadtrains in and out of the country, to get your cattle off if I can't do the roads up?" I asked. "If you're that broke you can cut my wages out too." I was fuming. I went back out to the car, where Rae was waiting with Leah. I was that livid I wrote my resignation out twice, on the one piece of paper, or so Rae told me later. I don't know what it said. I didn't even read it. I just scribbled it down and took it in.

"Here!" I said, handing it over. I couldn't believe they were interfering with the running of the show to that extent. Wes Roddy took the letter and looked at it.

"Think about this for a while John. I'll come out to Napier in a few days and see if you've changed your mind."

"I won't have." I told him and left.

A week or two later they did come out. Gordon Napier, Wes Roddy and another bloke. We had a bit of a meal and things were amicable enough.

"So you'll stay on here, John?" They eventually asked. I thought this was a bit amusing, since they'd threatened to give me the arse if I didn't sell the breeders by August, which I hadn't. It was the perfect opportunity for them to get rid of me, but it seemed they weren't taking it.

"No, I'm not staying." I told them "But, I'll set three traps before I leave, so everything will still be running when the new man takes over." I had several horses of my own on Napier, but there was a very good mule, Cheeky, which I also wanted. I asked Wes Roddy if I could buy him. He agreed.

"How much for?" I asked.

"A hundred bucks."

Later when I got the receipt it stated 'One red mule, known as Cheeky, sold to John Wells for $1 and other considerations'. The other considerations turned out to be holiday pay.

## Three traps set before I leave Napier

When it came time for me to leave Napier I said to the bosses, "I've set those three traps I told you about. There's one trap set up on a dam at 110 mile, with a forcing pen and loading ramp there. Another trap is set at Black Rocks yard, and Wombarella trap is also set. There will be a big mob of cattle in there. I reckon there'll be a thousand head or more, in that Wombarella trap, but I bet you a thousand bucks your new man can't take them away from there up to Billyarra yard."

"We're not in the business of making bets." They told me, which was wise of them, because later the black fellas told me the story of what happened.

The tale, told to me by the native stock boys, was that they did trap a big mob of cattle at Wombarella, but the new man didn't know how to handle them. He should have worked the cattle around the trap paddock for a couple of days, placing a few men outside, for the rogue bulls and bullocks who reckoned they were going over the fence. I'd had a graded track put in, which should have made it easier. When it came time to let the cattle out, if I'd been doing it, I would have walked them around in the heat of the day, then taken off the tail, the quiet ones and put them four or five hundred yards outside the gate. This would help to steady the rest of the mob as they were let out. Instead, the new bloke only walked the trap cattle around for one morning, then before dinner he took the whole lot out in one hit. Of course all the bullocks and bulls were in the lead and as soon as they got out of the gate they were away. Gone. The blacks were all killing themselves, while they were telling me. They reckoned it was a hell of a joke. So poor fellow, by the time he got to Billyarra, out of a mob a thousand strong, he ended up with only twenty-five or thirty head.

Not so funny was the fate of the cattle trapped at 110 mile and Black Rocks. They perished. The water dried up and no-one checked on them. When I heard this I wished I hadn't ever set those traps. He should have gone and opened the gates and just let them go, rather than let that happen to them. The story saddened me, but I have no reason to disbelieve it.

## Leaving Napier

When I pulled the pin from Napier, The Ghan changed his mind about leaving Kimberley Downs. He ended up staying on for another couple of seasons. I had my personal horses to take with me, from Napier, including my newly acquired mule. I was going to walk them as far as Meda, where Dave Ledger said I could leave them for the time being. I had to notify The Ghan that I would be travelling through with horses and asked if I could camp the night on Kimberley Downs, at their yards. He told me I could.

I had a couple of boys with me bringing the horses along, whilst I drove my ute, loaded with swags, tucker and my gear. When we got to K.D. we watered and fed the horses and put them in the yard. I went in search of The Ghan to tell him we were there. I couldn't find him anywhere. Eventually I went up to the top of the hill and found old Wally Jenky, the dogger, up there. The Ghan was with him and both men were rotten drunk. I said to The Ghan, "I've just come to tell you I've got the horses down at the yard." then I left them to it. Half an hour later The Ghan came along. To check on me I suppose.

"That mule you've got there has a Kimberley Downs brand on it." He pointed out.

"Yes."

"Well you'd better leave him here." He told me.

"He's not staying with you. I'm buying this mule."

"Well I don't know anything about it. I'll ring up the office and see what's going on." So The Ghan rang up the office in town. While he did so I went and spoke to my blokes.

"Grab a couple of fresh horses and saddle them. Pull the nose bags off the others and get these horses ready to go."

The Ghan came down from the kitchen yelling out to me, so I went up to meet him.

"I've got Wes Roddy on the phone. He wants to have a talk to you. You come up and get on the phone in our house, I'll get on the phone in the kitchen." He instructed me. I walked up to the house and was about to walk in when I thought, 'Bugger this. I could get in there and The Ghan come in, welt me with a stick or something, then say that I'd attacked him. I'd be in trouble. I'm in his house and he can claim something that never happened.' Perhaps I was over suspicious, but I knew the man of old. He was very drunk and I simply didn't trust him.

Instead of going indoors I said, "Look, I don't have to do what you tell me. If you want to keep talking to them you keep talking. I'm leaving." With that I walked back down to the yard and spoke to my blokes.

"Quick, get going with these horses. Don't go down the old Derby road." In those days that road wasn't used much and it had quite a few fallen trees over it. But The Ghan was full of grog and I thought if he was determined enough he'd drive straight through them. So I got them to go straight into the scrub. I waited up at the top of the hill for a good while, to see what the Ghan did. I thought he might follow, possibly with a firearm. I didn't know what the Ghan might do, but I knew he was unpredictable, he was pissed and he didn't like me. At the main access gate I bent the fastener over so it couldn't easily be unhooked, hoping this would give us a bit more time if he decided to follow us up. To my knowledge he didn't. We went on to Poulton's yard that night, where we left the horses. Two or three days later I took them on to Meda.

*New Napier, homestead, bough shed and store. Circa 1970*

*The bough shed where I lived while New Napier was being built.*

*Yamera Gap in the Napier Range. Now known as Queen Victoria's Head*

*The loading ramp is all that is left of the yard we built at Limestone Springs.*
*Photo taken 2014*

# CHAPTER TEN

# MYROODAH

*The sun shines on a drooping brim,*
*Which casts it's shade beneath,*
*Upon the stockman's head within,*
*And shadows of his grief.*

## A perishing on Napier

After I left Napier Rae and I lived in Derby for a while, where our second child was born. A son, Benn. I worked as a 'jam stacker' at Rusty's grocery shop. I earned this 'title' after a rodeo invitation arrived for me one day, from Mount House Station addressed to 'The 'jam stacker' c/o Rusty's Store. It stuck and that is what I was known as for sometime. I was working for Ken Birch, Rusty's son, who I'd known for years. Ken was very good to me. I got paid well working for him. I had a lot of laughs and we drank a lot of grog. He is still my very good friend.

One day some blokes approached me. They said they'd heard I knew Napier country pretty well. They wanted me to go out and peg a claim for them. They told me the location, gave me the paperwork and said they'd pay me to do it. I hired a four wheel drive vehicle and one Saturday Ken and I set out to do the job. We took a small amount of tucker with us and a carton of beer. Although it was January there hadn't been any rain. The country was still very dry and there was a bushfire burning. We went out through Kimberley Downs, down to the river crossing, over that and on out to Hawkstone. We then drove on to Limestone Springs. From there we crossed to a yard known as Billy More's, then headed up to Red Bull. We were a long way out when we came to a creek we had to cross. I knew I couldn't drive straight across this particular crossing. Instead you had to drive into the creek at a certain spot, follow the creek bed downstream a short distance, then drive out on the other side. We did this, but there was a bit of sand. We weren't able to engage the 4WD and couldn't get out of the creek bed. We got bogged.

We tried, for a long time, to get the vehicle out. It was about midday. We dug and tried again. And again. But we couldn't get out. As we had come in through Kimberley Downs onto Napier, no-one really knew where we were. We kept trying, but we were getting nowhere, so after a good while we had a beer. Then we had another beer, until we had drunk half a carton each. I said to Ken, "We'll wait here till night time, then we'll walk to Napier in the cool." But Ken couldn't lie down and wouldn't go to sleep. He kept saying, "Come on, why don't we go now?"

"No. It's too hot and we've drunk too much piss. Just lie down and go to sleep. We'll walk in the night." But on and on this went. Ken wanting to get going, me wanting to wait. In the end I agreed. By then it was about three o'clock in the afternoon. Some of the country was on fire, from lightning strikes. We had two litre bottles of water, one each. Because we had drunk the beer Ken wanted a drink all the time. He was drinking his water pretty quickly.

"You don't want to be drinking that water too fast, or you'll be finishing it and we've got a fair way to go. If the bore isn't working we'll be in trouble. It's a long way on to Old Napier homestead." I warned him. Although Old Napier was abandoned at this time I knew we could get a drink from the trough there. We walked on and night fell. We had no torch with us. A bushfire was burning nearby, though where we walked was, as yet, unburnt country. Ken had finished his water. I had a drink out of mine, then shared it with Ken, till eventually the whole lot had gone.

"I know where there's a soak up here. Hopefully the donkeys have dug it out." I told Ken, but when we got to the soak it was all filled in. There didn't seem to be many cattle or donkeys around. This worried me. It told me there was a shortage of water and that they had moved out of the area. In conditions like that you can be walking along, come across a bull that's perishing, and he'll 'go you'. It was a concern I carried silently, in the back of my mind.

When we reached the soak we found it caved in.

"We'll have to dig for water here." I told Ken. We dug, with our hands, in the dark, but the water was a lot further down than I thought it would be. Instead of digging a big hole we dug a long narrow hole, on an angle, through the sand. Eventually, about a metre down, we got through to water. The water was coming in OK. Good clean water. We tried to get the water out of the hole using the lid of the bottle, then pouring it into the container. It was pretty slow and difficult. In the end I said,

"You hold onto my feet. I'm going to go down into this hole to suck up as much as I can." The hole was so tight I couldn't breathe and I needed Ken to hang onto me in case it caved in on me. We did this and I got a bit of a drink. Then it was Ken's turn, but he was too frightened. He was bigger than me and it was even tighter for him. So in the end we dug the hole out bigger. We filled the bottles up and both had a drink. We sat there for a good while, before setting off to walk through the darkness towards Red Bull. As we walked along in the dark, there were bush turkeys flying down the road. There was scrub on either side of us and we could hear them coming, but we couldn't see where they were. We were frightened they'd hit us in the face. Every now and then there'd be cattle rustling in the bush, or a donkey. As we got nearer to Red Bull bore there were more cattle, but I knew something was wrong.

When we got there the tank was empty. There were cattle 'down' around the trough, which had no water in it. I knew the bore must have been broken down for a long time, for cattle to be dead and dying around the trough. There were delirious cattle standing about nearby, hoping for water, but all the stronger cattle had long gone. Ken and I were perishing again by the time we got to Red Bull and we needed another drink. The windmillman had obviously been at the bore during the day, because there were tools there. It looked as if they had been working on it all day. They had pulled the bore, fixed it up, then left, probably on dark. The bore would only pump when the wind blew, there wasn't enough water in the tank for us to get any from there, and not enough wind to pump any water into the tank. But we were very lucky. We were able to fill the bottle up with what little trickled through the delivery pipe and things were pretty good for us. Even if no-one came back next day, at least we had a drink and some tools. After we'd both quenched our thirst we lay down and slept for the remainder of the night.

When we woke up in the morning we found we'd been sleeping on a bed of donkey dung. Donkeys are very clean animals and defecate in one spot. We had been woken by the sound of a vehicle. The windmill crew had rolled up with a tractor. They got a fair sort of a fright when they saw us two blokes sit up out of the dirt. I knew the windmillman and Terry Hillman was with him. We told them what had happened to us the previous day. They took us back to where our vehicle was bogged and pulled it out of the creek with the tractor and away we went back to Derby. We never did get the pegging job done.

In the meantime Ken's father, Rusty Birch, had been notified that we hadn't returned. Because of the bushfire burning on Napier at the time he was very concerned. The MMA passenger plane going through to Darwin had been asked to keep a look out for us and one passenger said she'd seen a rolled vehicle on fire. That caused a fair bit of panic. I think she must have imagined it, unless it was an old wreck long abandoned in the bush. Rusty also had a plane out looking for us. When we rocked up in Derby late that afternoon, and we hadn't rolled over, or burnt, there was a fair bit of relief all round.[4]

## How I got the job at Myroodah

Rae and I weren't travelling very well. I was in the pub one day and Rae came down and found me.

"Duncan Ord is looking for you. He's got a job for you, managing stations. I told him I didn't know where you were." Later I went to see Duncan Ord, out at Demco. He told me there was a job going as general manager for the Northern Cattle Company, which was owned by AMP and Kaiser Steel.

---

4 Although we had got ourselves in a spot of bother I wasn't too worried. Even if we hadn't managed to get water at Red Bull I reckon I still would have been OK. I had the choice of walking on from Red Bull to Kongrow Pool, which isn't that far across country, or have gone on from Red Bull to Old Napier. We would have been all right. But Ken was very worried, especially when I said to him
"We might have to skin one of these dying beasts here at the trough to have a feed." He wasn't too impressed with that. But it taught us a valuable lesson. Never to drink grog when you're in a situation like that.

"Scott McColl was in Derby recently. He's looking for a manager for Myroodah, Luluigui and Kalyeeda." Duncan Ord told me. "George Lanigan is being retired. I recommended you. Are you interested?"

"Yeah, I'm interested. I haven't got any other job. I'm only working at Rusty's filling in time, stacking shelves."

Eventually I got a letter from Scott McColl saying he'd like to meet with me. He had once worked as headstockman and later as manager on Brunette and Victoria River Downs in the Northern Territory. He was now the managing director of the Northern Cattle Company. I had met him before when the company had considered buying Napier Downs. For some reason they ended up buying Myroodah, Luluigui and Kalyeeda instead. They also owned Moola Bulla, in the east Kimberly and Mt. Amhurst.

When McColl came to Derby I went out to Demco to meet with him. We had a yarn and he asked me how many cattle we branded on Napier, how many horses we had. All that sort of stuff. I didn't have any bookwork or anything to refer to. I just rattled it all off. Because those kinds of things interest me, they seem to stick in my head no worries. McColl seemed satisfied.

"I'll write you a letter to confirm it, but I'd like you to run these places for us." He told me afterwards, and in due course a letter came to ask if I'd accept the job, saying he'd like me to start mid January. I said I would.

I'd been out to Myroodah with Rowell once before, to see about helicopter mustering, while I was on Napier. I thought then 'what a bloody crap place this is'. In hindsight I should never have accepted the job Scott McColl offered. I already knew in my own head that I didn't belong to that place, but I needed a job. Circumstances had brought me to a point where I just wanted to get back working with cattle, horses and the station life. This seemed to be a way to do it.

## Myroodah homestead

There were no trees around the house at Myroodah. Just a few tamarisks. The homestead was like a desert. The chook's pen was out on the flat. It had a tin roof, but no other shade. It was the same for the black fellas, tin roof, no shade. It was generally just a hot place, built on a scalded flat. Water was very scarce and pumped. Scott McColl got a dam built, down in one of the outer water courses of a creek. From the dam water was pumped up to a turkey's nest. A windmill put it up into an overhead tank and that watered the whole homestead. I was pretty cheesed off with this set-up. The water ran from the men's quarters, houses, goats yard, chook yard, and the open drainage blacks camp, where there was only a shower, no toilet, straight down into the dam. Then it was pumped up for our drinking water. I didn't think it was very smart, or hygienic.

When I went to run Myroodah, the previous manager, George Lanigan, stayed there for two weeks showing me this and that. After the handover period he went down to manage Luluigui, pronounced Loolaguy. He was a bit of an old woman and the blacks were putting it over him and pleasing themselves, although Mrs Lanigan really got stuck into the kitchen blacks. She fairly flew at them. With old George, they just drifted about and did as they pleased. Most of the Myroodah blacks were spoilt. They came to work at about 8.30 in the morning, or didn't turn up for work at all and they expected the store to be opened for them twenty-four hours a day. You couldn't run a station like that. The natives didn't like me, because they had to come to work at a certain time. Work started at seven o'clock and we knocked off at five o'clock, or whenever we finished what we were doing. Having George about the place didn't help, because the natives still looked upon him as the boss. It was a bloody headache. Later, a young fellow was brought in to manage Luluigui under me. He was a nice bloke, but he was put there before he was ready. He didn't have any experience with that class of cattle, or scrub, which made it very hard for him.

Kalyeeda just had a caretaker, to make sure nothing was hooked. Not that there was much to hook down there. There were two caretakers during my time. The first was Bill Hymas, who I had had at Napier. He had a bit of a past and was looking for a job. To help him out I got him to go down to care-take at Kalyeeda. He had his own motor bike, which he used to do bore runs on, or check fences. He wasn't a bad old bloke and there was always a feed there if you needed one.

Unfortunately, when a reconciliation was done of the RFDS medical chest at Kalyeeda it was discovered that Bill had been helping himself to the morphine. After that I had to get rid of him.

The next bloke to come there was a much younger fellow and a whole different story.

## Kangaroos

When I went to Myroodah I took four dogs with me. Yogi, who by then was pretty old, Gutter, Lady and another little Australian terrier. There were hundreds of kangaroos at Myroodah and they would come in onto the lawn to feed. In the middle of the night there'd be a hell of a racket, dogs, kangaroos, and big boomers hitting the fences. In the morning I'd go around with a vehicle and pick up all the dead 'roos the dogs had killed, chuck them on the back and take them out bush and dispose of them. The next night would be the same. But in the end there would be forty, or more, kangaroos grazing on the lawn, in the middle of the night and the dogs slept. They took no notice. Nor did anyone else.

I had race horses at that time and before I went to bed I'd go and give them a feed and I'd put any leftover feed over the fence in a drum. The station working horses would come up and eat the scraps. Sometimes I'd go over and there'd be roos in the drum. As they jumped out of the feed bin I'd get them and whack them on the head. There were so many living on the joint, when you drove in at night you had to go very slowly, because they just ran out from the shed and under the vehicle. They were everywhere, thick, like a plague of rats, but bigger. We had some donkey shooters working on the property and when they saw the kangaroos they asked if they could shoot them.

"There's not much meat on them." I told them.

"No, but there are enough of them here to make a dollar out of it." So they went around shooting them, left, right and centre. They were a husband and wife team. Colin and Sylvia Haskett. Very good shots. One shot, one roo, straight through the head, or ribs. They'd discard the forequarters and bottom part of the hind leg. The remaining hind quarters they'd hang in the fridge. About once a week a truck would come up to collect the kangaroo meat. Once the Hasketts got onto them the kangaroos were thinned out a lot.

## Bought horses off Anna Plains

Myroodah was a very sad place for horses. Horses didn't live very long there. This was because a lot of poison, 'crotalaria crispata', grew there and many horses died of 'walkabout'. It was basically break a horse in, work him and work him, then try and get hold of some more. It was a very sad show. While I was there I bought some mules, from GoGo and we broke them in. Not being susceptible to 'walkabout' they had a much better chance of survival.

Early on, before we got the GoGo mules, we bought horses from Anna Plains. A station on the coast, south of Broome, which was being managed by Bruce Grey at the time. In the mob there were both broken in and unbroken horses, with some quite good lookers amongst them. It was early in the year and the Fitzroy River was still running, so we were unable to get to Myroodah with the truck. It was decided, beforehand, to unload the horses at Liveringa. We took about twenty coachers over from Myroodah, and six or seven blokes, including Henry Skinner, a very smart stockman who I was privileged to have working for me.

We let the horses out of the Liveringa yards and began to walk them towards the Fitzroy River, intending to take them over at Myroodah Crossing. Some of the bought horses were hard to handle. We managed to get them out through two gates on Liveringa, then we were in open country. Several kept trying to break out of the mob and we had to keep blocking them. We headed for the river, trying to keep to the road, but the troublesome horses kept breaking out, forcing us further up the river. It was all open country. Eventually I saw half a dozen, or more, getting further away from the saddle horses. Two or three blokes went after them but the horses were going. I was in an F100. It was good ground, so I followed them up with the vehicle. The breakaway mob consisted of six or seven horses. As I got nearer, four at the tail wheeled away from the vehicle. The mounted riders were able to pick them up and took them back to the road and into the main mob. The remaining three horses kept going. They weren't going to be stopped, so I continued after them. I tried to get on the side of them, to hunt them down towards the river crossing, where we planned to take the horses over. As I neared the river I came into timbered country and had to abandon the vehicle.

I went on foot from there. When I reached the Fitzroy I found they'd run straight to the river and down into the water.

These horses had come from Anna Plains, on the coast. They didn't know what water was. I think they got the shock of their lives. When I got there they were on the far side of the river, in the water, swimming up and down. The bank was too steep for them to get out. They were going first one way, then the other. Swimming back and forth along the river bank. When I saw this I took my clothes and boots off and swam across. First I tried to turn them in the water, but I was knocking up. I had trouble getting out of the river as well, but eventually I managed to climb onto an overhanging tree, then out onto the bank. I ran up and down the far side bank trying to turn the three animals downstream, where they would meet the other horses at the crossing. I'd get them going in the right direction for a bit, but then they'd turn and swim upstream again. All this time, me barefoot, with no clothes on.

After trying for a fair while I could see I was losing the battle. I gave up, hoping they'd eventually swim back down the river to the crossing, or go back over to the side where they'd gone in. I swam across the river, got my clothes and walked back to the vehicle. I drove down to Myroodah crossing, saw Skinner and told him what had happened. He and the blokes held the other horses up for quite a while, waiting for the other three to join them. They didn't come. I thought 'There's not much else we can do here. We'll just have to leave them and hope they'll pick up the scent of the main mob and follow them on to Myroodah, or end up at Luluigui, Yeeda or back at Liveringa.

We left Myroodah Crossing and took the other horses on home. They seemed to travel better without the wayward ones amongst them and we had no further problems the rest of the way.

Next day I went back to see if I could find the missing horses. I found them all right. When I got to the river, the three of them were up against the low level crossing, drowned.[5]

---

5    In hindsight, had I realised they were that bad, I would have put shin tappers on them. Shin tappers, or a dragging chain. Shin tappers are a hobble chain with a hobble strap around one foot, and a piece of wood on the other end. When the horse gallops it keeps hitting their shin, eventually slowing them down. I've had experience with other Anna Plains horses, one in particular, a well known mare called Milky Way. She wouldn't go into water, or across water courses, whether there was water in them or not.

## Storm in a teacup. Jack Fletcher's letter to Scott McColl

It was 1972. I had men attending over at Liveringa, where the bloke who had replaced me at Napier was now headstockman. Liveringa was owned by ALCO and I would go down about twice a week, to see my blokes. There was a shorthorn Myroodah cow there, with a half bred weanable Brahman calf on it. Because the Liveringa men were holding our cattle as well as theirs, I watched for it every time I went, to see that it was still there. Eventually, when our cattle came back to us, the calf wasn't amongst them. I said to ALCO's man, "There was a half bred Brahman weanable calf on a Myroodah shorthorn cow. The calf isn't there, but the cow is."

"You didn't have a calf on her. It wasn't your calf." The headstockman told me.

"It is our calf. It was on a Myroodah cow. That makes it ours." I told him. That was the end of it. I wasn't going to fight about one calf. I could get ten of them if I wanted. I was just letting him know that I knew. I was perfectly within my rights to visit my attenders, but the headstockman wasn't happy that I'd seen something he would rather I hadn't.

Next thing, out of the blue, a letter arrived for me, from Scott McColl. It was dated 9th May 1972 and marked 'Personal'. Enclosed with it was a copy of a letter from Jack M. Fletcher, my old boss. Jack 's letter stated *'John Wells is proving to be a poor neighbour and a nuisance in general.'* It then went on to say what a good relationship they had had with my predecessor, George Lanigan. In the final paragraphs he bluntly attacked my honesty, making reference to something about which he knew absolutely nothing.

> *... In closing, when John was relieved of duties as Manager of Napier Downs Station we found 37 Leopold/Fairfield bullocks in our bullock paddock. These were immediately shipped to the Broome works. We have a firm company policy that all stranger cattle are to be shipped when picked up by our muster teams. I, for one, feel that cattle represent too valuable an asset in this day and time for Station Managers to play the game of eating the other fella's beef. I think that someone has to make a move in this direction. And you can rest assured that should any of your brand be found at Liveringa Station that you will be so advised. We want to get along with Mr Wells and will get along if he*

*acts in a proper manner. However, if he continues pursuit of his present conduct then I am afraid there could be unfortunate consequences on both sides. I felt that you would want this matter brought to your attention.*
*Sincerely, Jack M. Fletcher Managing Director.*

So this was the result of my noticing the disappearance of one half bred Brahman calf off a Myroodah cow. Scott McColl ordered me to explain. I did.

## The explanation

Whilst I was managing Napier, my good friend Phil Le Lievre was at Fairfield. There was no boundary fence between Fairfield and Napier Downs. Phil was a bit prone to do musters on Kimberley Downs and Napier country, while he was there. I didn't go mustering on Fairfield, but I did let Phil know that I knew when his men had been on our country, and I told him if I found out he'd done it again I would report him. But that was just water off a duck's back. A mate warning a mate. Nothing more to it.

Towards the end of my time with ALCO, although I didn't know it then, we did a muster on the Fairfield boundary. Phil's men were attending and we picked up a fair few Leopold/Fairfield, cattle. We had a lot of our own branding to do, so we drafted off all the Fairfield cattle and I said to Phil's men, who were going to leave the next day to go back to Fairfield.

"Don't go tomorrow. We'll be finished with all our cattle by then. They'll be tidied up and the bullocks and meatworks cattle will be trucked. There's a mob of your cattle in the bullock paddock and we'll get them in then." But Race Week was coming up and all the blokes were toey that they'd miss out on the races. We were going to go to the races as well. The Fairfield boys had time to get their cattle home. I wasn't about to say, 'you wait here and take your cattle home. The races are on, but you can miss out.' I had everything worked out. I knew we could be finished, they could be finished and we would all be in time to go in for Race Week. But No. They wouldn't have it.

"No, no. We're leaving tomorrow morning. We gotta get home for races." Roland Thompson was the headstockman. I tried to reason with him.

"Look, you'll have time to get your cattle and brand them and still get home in time for races." but it was 'No, we're going.' So they went, their bullocks, thirty seven of them, still in our bullock paddock.

There was no hiding these bullocks. The Fairfield boys simply left without taking them home. It wasn't a matter of me keeping them. I didn't want the bloody things in our bullock paddock eating my bullock's feed. Really, I should have bushed them. Our bullocks and horses had to live in that paddock and at the end of the year it was just bare ground. We could have done without three dozen head of the neighbour's bullocks grazing there as well. It definitely wasn't to my advantage to keep the Fairfield cattle there. It was a bit silly of Phil's blokes, because we would have helped them to muster and draft them. Cows and calves would have been drafted out on the flat and their cows and cleanskin calves would have gone home. Everything would have been finished and fine, and everyone of us would have got to the races on time.

So there it is. That is what happened. Once races were over the Fairfield fellas didn't come back and get them. I suppose we could have trucked them back to Fairfield, but we didn't need to muster the paddock for their cattle and then truck them for them. It was an expense Napier didn't need. That year I left ALCO. It wasn't planned. I just went in to get my grader cutting edges, which I'd ordered up urgently and 'boom' that was it. The shit hit the fan and that's when I pulled the pin. So Jack Fletcher didn't know what he was talking about when he wrote that letter to Scott McColl. He'd gone off half cocked with his accusations, without knowing the smallest part of what had happened. I'll give McColl his due, he did back me up once he knew the facts, but this incident always left a bad taste.

## Jim O'Neil

I had a fellow, a young bloke, who came looking for a job. Bill Hymas had gone and it was fairly hard to find someone to caretake Kalyeeda and be on their own all the time. This bloke, Jim O'Neill, was his name, didn't seem to mind. He reckoned he was a builder, so as well as checking bores and fences, he was supposed to be re-building part of the homestead, which was basically only one little cottage. I'd go up to Kalyeeda quite often to check on him and he'd be nowhere to be seen. Other times I'd get there and he'd look as if he hadn't been to bed for three or four days.

No building was ever done. This bloke never had much to say. You had to ask him everything.

I went up one day with a 44 gallon drum of drinking water for him. I had a dog with me, called Little Yogi, by Yogi out of Lady. On the way over we hit a bump. The dog got the ball of his foot under the bottom of the drum and it cut the ball clean out. Because of this I left the dog up at Kalyeeda with the young fellow and told him I'd be back in a day or two to pick it up. When I got back, the dog was gone.

"What happened to the dog?" I asked.

"My dogs killed it." He told me.

This same fella, Jim O'Neill, would go into Fitzroy Crossing. I don't know how long he'd be away. Sometimes he'd say he'd just got back that morning, or yesterday, but he looked a wreck. I don't know that he drank a lot. I never saw any signs of cartons, or beer bottles or cans. No evidence that he was a drinker. He had worked at Fossil and cooked in a camp for Ross Fraser, when he was contract mustering. He also worked for the Ag Dept at Laurel Downs and goodness knows what else he'd done. Later on he was jailed in Tasmania for murdering a child or two.

Many years afterwards, someone got in touch with me about this bloke. They were making some enquiries into a child who had gone missing in Derby, soon after this fella was on Kalyeeda. I didn't know the missing boy, but I knew his mother. It was thought O'Neill might have been implicated and they wanted to know what I knew about him, not that I could tell them much. They thought he may also have been implicated in the murder of the Beaumont children. A friend of mine had told me that these people might get onto me, because they'd been and spoken to him about the boy's disappearance. They interviewed me and there has been a documentary on television about him called 'The Fisherman', which was quite chilling. So it turned out, decades later, that this bloke wasn't a very nice bloke and they don't really know how many crimes he may have committed over the years.

## Goose Hole Yard, all for a good snap

Before I went to manage Myroodah, Luluigui and Kalyeeda I'd heard stories about Goose Hole and what a bastard of a place it was for yarding up cattle. Years before, when I'd visited Myroodah with Rowell, and saw the country for the first time, I thought 'there's no chance I'll ever be working here', so the stories I heard about Goose Hole never worried me. But I did end up working there and the day that I thought would never come, did come. I ended up at Goose Hole Yard, with a mob of cattle, and they weren't joking.

The yard was on Kalyeeda, at the homestead, and the first problem with it was it yarded up from the wrong side. Outside the yard it was like a space landscape. Circular mounds, like upside down plum puddings, were dotted all over the place. These mounds were near the gateway, so when you came to yard up, if any cattle broke away, you couldn't really chase them. To make things worse, coming into the yard was heavy sand. Cattle learned not to go into the yards. It was very dusty and they knew they'd get a fair bit of punishment. Even for man it wasn't a good place to work. Because of this it would usually take a fair while to yard cattle up at Goose Hole. It was always a big worry and a bit risky, with the potential for a bad accident.

I had been on Myroodah for a while and we had yarded up at Goose Hole a couple of times, so I knew the pitfalls. I had always thought I'd get the set up changed, to make it better, but it was a case of, one day, one day and the day still hadn't come.

We had a fixed wing plane working, the pilot living with Rae and me at Myroodah homestead. We had been getting a mob of cattle together for Scott McColl. Bullocks to be trucked to the meatworks, and steers to go down to Yathroo, Yere Yere and Mungedar. These southern properties were also owned by the Northern Cattle Company, and comprised 82,000 acres near Moora, well over a thousand miles further south.

After each muster, the cattle were drafted through the yard. The cows were let go, the calves branded and also let go. The steers, drafted through the yards with the cows and calves, were taken off and put with the bullocks. Both the bullocks and steers were let out into one big paddock, 'river frontage paddock' which was about eight miles long and three or four miles wide. Over time we had put together a big mob of steers and bullocks ready to be trucked off. All had been drafted once, before being let out into 'river frontage paddock'. The trucks were all booked ready to come.

Scott McColl didn't like bullocks being drafted in the yard. He wanted them drafted out on the flat, which meant having to yard them up a second time. Because cattle were so hard to yard at Goose Hole, I decided to build a little holding yard, in the corner of the horse paddock. It was made of barbed wire and star pickets, about two hundred yards square. This was to put the cattle in, so we didn't have to yard them twice. I thought if we yarded them into the holding yard we'd built, for the first night, the next day we could draft the cattle out on the open flat, which was what McColl wanted. Then we could put the meatworks bullocks back in the holding yard the following night, and watch them again. We went down a few days earlier and put wood at each corner of this barbed wire enclosure, so we could light fires at night to help hold the bullocks in there.

We were working there one afternoon when Scott McColl rocked up. He saw the new tailing yard we'd put up. We were having a cup of tea and he said, "What's the yard that's been put up in the corner of the horse paddock?"

"That's to put the cattle into the first afternoon, when we've got them out of 'river frontage paddock'. We'll tail them around, then put them in there for the night. Next day we will draft the bullocks off out on the flat. Then we'll yard the steers." I explained.

"I want you to go and pull all that down." McColl told me. I felt like pulling the pin then and there, but I didn't. Instead we went and pulled it all down again, and McColl left.

The following day, with the help of the fixed wing, we got the paddocked cattle together and were bringing them up along the fence near the back of the yard. There was a big sandhill there with a lot of wattle on it. We pulled the cattle up for a while. The pilot had left earlier to return to the homestead. Next thing, the plane returned. It came flying low, straight up the fence line towards the mob of cattle. I thought this was very strange and wondered what was going on? The plane buzzed around on the wrong side of the fence. I thought 'Shit, something has happened.' I couldn't see anything from where I was, so I galloped back in the direction we'd come from, around the back of the mob. Then I saw that the plane, flying front on at the cattle, had scattered them and put them through the fence. There were horsemen on the wrong side of the fence and cattle were going all over the place. Eventually, with the help of the plane, we got control of them. When we got them back in hand we took them out onto the flat and fed them there for the afternoon. Scott McColl came and saw me. He said he had asked the pilot to take him up so that he could take a photograph. I couldn't believe it. Five thousand head of steers and bullocks, all in the one mob, might look impressive, but causing that much trouble for the sake of a snap?

The boss had left. We started to yard up at about three o'clock. The cattle were giving us heaps of trouble. They wouldn't go in and we were galloping horses everywhere and knocking up bullocks, so I told everybody to stop. I got them to take the cattle further out and let them feed. Then I sent some blokes back to the homestead to get a vehicle and told them to bring an axe, pliers and some eight gauge wire. When they came back we went round to the back of the yard. We took down four panels of rails. I sent somebody else to get the working horses. We pushed the horses back and forth through the gap where the rails had been. This was to flatten the grass growing there, which formed a bit of a line, which I knew would baulk the bullocks. After all this was done we brought the mob, some five thousand head, around the back of the yard, lined them up and they went into the yard like water running down a plughole. No messing about, straight in, good as gold. I thought, 'By gee, why hasn't somebody thought of this before.' But I had made one big mistake. I didn't mark each rail to a certain joggle, so later when we went to put all the rails into their right place we were there for a couple of hours. Anyway we got it done eventually and I wouldn't make that mistake twice.

In the morning we had to let them out again, because McColl wanted them drafted out on the flat. Next day we fed them round for a couple of hours and were about to start drafting when my boss rolled up. I was riding my black mare, Tennessee. He sat and watched us draft from his motor car. After we'd been drafting for a while one of the black fellas said to me, "Dat boss wanta chee you." I stopped what I was doing and rode over to the vehicle. We had a bit of a yarn, then McColl told me he had to be back at the homestead at one o'clock.

"A plane is coming to pick me up and I'm catching an MMA flight down to Perth today, so I've got to get going now."

When McColl had gone we stopped drafting and sat down for an hour. When I thought he'd gone too far to turn around and come back, we took the rails out of the back of the yard again and yarded the bullocks up and drafted them through the yard. Scott McColl was none the wiser. This was the first time cattle were taken down to AMP and Kaiser Steel's three southern properties, and there was a write-up about it in Queensland Country Life, October 12th 1972. I did this for them for two years while I was employed by the Northern Cattle Company.[6]

## Reggie Woods runs amok at Myroodah Crossing

I was depressed when I was on Myroodah. I thought it was a bugger of a place. I shouldn't even have been running a cattle station at that time in my life. I was very unhappy and my marriage wasn't going very well. Rae had gone back to Perth with no warning, taking the two children with her. After she left I was an emotional wreck. I went to town every weekend I could get away, and would go to the hotel and drink. Usually the cook, or housekeeper, would go in with me and she would drive me home, but not always. This particular weekend I went in on my own.

I had been in town since Friday night. On Sunday afternoon I was about to head home when I got a message, through the RFDS. It said I was not to come back out, because Reggie Woods was down at the river shooting everything up with his.303. I was told it would be very dangerous for me to go home, but if I did decide to, I should go around through Luluigui, not over Myroodah Crossing.

I knew Reggie Woods used to slip a cog every now and then, but he was all right. He was a good worker and had a good sense of humour. He'd followed me over from Napier to work at Myroodah. Reggie Woods did a lot of good work for me at Napier and that's where I first really got to know him. I worked with Reggie for a lot

---

6    Drafting bullocks out on the flat was the old way, when bullocks were never put in a yard until they were taken in for shipping. But by 1972 those days had long gone. These cattle had been worked at Luluigui as youngsters, brought to Myroodah and dipped, then been put in with other cattle and walked for a day and a bit up to Kalyeeda. There they'd been tailed for a few days before being let go. They were educated cattle. Even so they were still difficult to yard at Goose Hole Yard, because of the heat, dust and heavy sand. Before I left Myroodah I got two, twelve foot gates ready to be put in at Goose Hole Yard, where we had been taking the rails out, but I left before the job was done. Later I asked the blacks about them and whether it had made things easier.
"No, dey neber bin put in Shohn. Dey bin pall down and bin buried in dat sand longa dere."

of years and he'd been drunk a lot of times. But he'd never shown any aggression or nastiness towards me. When he got drunk, Reggie used to imagine things and fully believed they were real. That was when he got to be a bit of a worry.

The trouble had all started when Reggie had got on the grog. He was in the 'rats' and he was imagining things. Apparently he had Flash Ada sitting down in the river and he was dropping .303 bullets around her. I had another bloke working for me at the time, Jimmy Gunn. He had a car parked down at the Myroodah Crossing, because he couldn't get over the river. As he couldn't drive back the other way either, he'd left his vehicle down there and Reggie had put bullet holes through it for him.

After I had received the message that Sunday, I thought about it for a while. I decided I wasn't going to drive home through the back way. It was a lot longer and meant crossing the Fitzroy at Willare, then over Geegully Creek and on out through Luluigui. Despite what had been said, I would go back to Myroodah the normal way, but I thought I had better go and tell the cops first, then I'd get going. So after a while I went and told the cops what was happening, and I let them know I was heading off, back to the station.

"Oh no you're not. You'll wait for us." They told me.

"Well when are you going?"

"We're booked in to have tea at the Boab Inn first."

"That's a long time. I could be home by then." But they more or less ordered me to wait in town.

So I went back to the pub. Presently they came down to the hotel, into the bar and had a drink. They seemed to be taking their time and were dawdling around. I was still drinking while I waited. I had been drinking since Friday evening. Eventually I went and saw them again.

"Look this is crazy, me waiting for you." I said. "Time is getting on. I know this bloke. He's worked for me for years. On Kimberley Downs, on Napier and now he's followed me to Myroodah. I've been around this fella for a long time. I know him. He's not a bad man." But 'No', the police insisted it was too dangerous for me to go. They continued to take their time and in the end I got fed up waiting for them. I went and saw Gerry Ash, a friend of mine.

"What about coming out to Myroodah with me and we'll leave now?" I said. He agreed, so I went and told the cops.

"I don't care what you blokes are doing, but I'm heading off now. You're taking too long." After that Gerry and I left.

We were driving out between Liveringa and Myroodah Crossing when we got bogged. We were still trying to get the vehicle out when the cops rolled up. There were about four of them and they had rifles and revolvers with them. They gave me a bit of a rev for leaving town when I'd been ordered not to. Then, seeing as we were bogged they asked, "Are you coming with us?"

"No. You blokes are here now. You can handle the lot." They asked me to go along with them, but I wouldn't. I stayed in the vehicle. They let me, but they left one cop behind with me. The other police went on to the river, taking Gerry with them.

When the police had gone on, I was left sitting with this one cop. The policeman and I sat there for a good while. I began to wonder what was going on with Reggie. I didn't know how stirred up they'd get him. I thought 'I wouldn't have just rolled straight into the river.' Anyway, after a fair while I thought 'Bugger this waiting. I'm going on.' So the cop walked along with me, in the dark. Then I started to run. He ran also, for a while. Then he dropped off, so I kept going. I kept running and I caught up with the other police. I could hear them talking and I heard them loading their rifles. There was a big pool of swampy water, just off the road, and I went straight into it and lay there doggo. I was battling not to make a noise with my breathing. I could hear the cops talking. They were a bit worried. I stayed there in the water for a long, long time. Eventually the police headed off again. I never went back on to the road again. Instead I crossed country, in the dark and I kept going until I came to the river. When I reached the Fitzroy I couldn't hear the cops and I couldn't hear anything down at the river crossing either. No voices, no disturbance, nothing. I decided against going up to where the police might be. I didn't want to give them a fright and them maybe shoot me. Instead I took all my clothes off, left them on the bank and swam across the Fitzroy. Saltwater crocs live in the river there. When I got to the other side the bank was too steep for me to get out. It was the same story as what happened with the Anna Plains horses that time. I tried and tried but I couldn't climb out. I swam up and down the bank a bit, looking for a good place, but I couldn't find any way out. Eventually I found a tree hanging over the water, I climbed up a branch into the tree and then down onto the bank.

Once I was out I headed across country again, towards Myroodah. It was black soil and soon I was pretty tired of the rough holey ground and was feeling absolutely exhausted. I curled up in a hole, in the black soil and went to sleep. I had no clothes on, just undies. Bare foot. No Hat. By Jeez I was cold, but I did sleep. I woke up just on daylight and walked on in to the homestead and went to bed.

The police had taken Reggie and Flash Ada into the cop shop. Reggie Woods was yarded after that incident and I didn't go to town for three or four months. Eventually of course I did go back into Derby. The policeman in charge there then was Bob Moore. He saw me in the street one day and chatted me.

"If you ever do that again we'll really hit you." He warned me.

"Well I don't think you blokes were very co-operative either."I replied and that was the end of that.

Reggie did time in jail for this little episode. I always regretted having gone to the police. I'm quite sure I could have talked Reggie round and everything would have been all right for him. After that he went up to Fitzroy Crossing and lived at one of the reserves with Flash Ada. If he just had a few beers he was OK. He was not a bad man, but the grog had got him. Years later both Reggie and Flash Ada drowned in the Fitzroy River, when their vehicle was washed off the low level crossing. It went under the water and they couldn't get out. Today it would be said 'alcohol was a factor', but in the parlance of the day people simply said 'They were both pissed.'

## I get a bashing from the blacks

While I was at Myroodah there was a bad incident with the blacks.

The young white fellow sent down from Moola Bulla, to look after Luluigui after George Lanigan left, was hospitalised for a few days. While he was away I had words with the Luluigui blacks. We had a mob of newly broken in La Grange horses, which the Luluigui men were supposed to be riding each day. They hadn't been doing what they were supposed to. They put the colts in a yard to put hobbles on them, but there was one they couldn't catch. They threw a rope on him and with the rope on, they let it go. The colt went over the top of the bronco yard and away bush. When I went out to Luluigui to check on things, a couple of days later, they told me about this.

"Well is the horse back now?" I asked.

"No"

"Well did anybody follow him and get the rope off?"

"No"

"Has anybody followed him at all?"

"No" This was not very good and I was cross with them.

"We had to buy that horse and break him in and we need him. With that rope on he could be tangled up around a tree, so somebody had better get off their bleeping arse and find him." With this, I'd upset them. The black fellas there didn't like me, and I didn't like them.

A short time later we were trucking a mob of bullocks from Kalyeeda. The white bloke from Moola Bulla was back in charge of his camp again, but he'd only been out of hospital for a day or two. His wife was at Luluigui, with a baby. No other whites there, just her. Both our stockcamps were at Goose Hole Yard. The Luluigui Camp was there to walk the steer mob back to Myroodah, where they'd be dipped at Garden Bore, after overnighting on the Nerrima/Kalyeeda Boundary. The Myroodah camp, being run by Henry Skinner, was also there and they would stay back and truck the bullocks the following afternoon.

I was still in the camp and we had an afternoon spare, so we decided we'd do a bit of a lap onto some country we shouldn't have been on. Only a small lap, on the corner of Kalyeeda, Liveringa and Noonkenbah. The fences were all down, so we just went in and took a sweep. We still had another truck load of meatworks cattle to go, so we hoped to pick up a few extra. We did a lap around and picked up a few more bullocks and some other cattle. The following morning we drafted them. There were some steers and a big mickey to be cut out into the steer mob. I was riding a little creamy mare called Butterfly. The mickey was the last to be cut out, but after I'd cut him out he took off bush. None of the Luluigui black fellas went to chase him, because they still had the shits on with me. I thought 'We're not letting this fella go.' You shouldn't go chasing cattle on your camp horse, but as no-one else moved I had no choice. I chased him, on Butterfly and jumped off to throw him. Then I heard a horse coming up behind me. I thought 'That's good, help is coming,' because this mickey had already started the business of turning around, wanting to charge. We were on a bit of fairly open ground. The mickey ran away from me a bit, then he whipped around to charge me. The next thing I got an almighty push in the back, onto this half grown bull. Somehow I missed it and was able to dodge him. I don't really know how I didn't end up on his horns, but I suppose you do things instinctively when you've been around wild cattle long enough.

The fellow who'd pushed me was called Hector, one of the Luluigui blacks. He'd ridden up behind me, dismounted, and instead of giving me a hand with the mickey, he'd put both hands into my back and given me a good shove towards it. Hector knew full well what he was doing, but he had drawn the beast's attention, so I was able to grab it. I threw it and we tied it up, cut his horns off, earmarked and nutted him. Then other blokes brought the mob up and we put him in with the mob. After this incident I left to return to the station. I don't know what ended up happening to the mickey, but I was pretty wild with Hector.

After I had gone back to Myroodah the young bloke, and his Luluigui stockcamp, took the steer mob and walked them to a yard on the boundary of Nerrima and Kalyeeda where they were to stay the night. When they got there two blokes were left minding the cattle, while the rest had a pannikin of tea in the camp. When it was time to yard up the young fellow called his men back to work.

"Come on, we'll go and yard up these steers now" but the black fellas didn't move.

"We're not yarding them. We're pulling out." they told him. This left the white bloke in a bit of a predicament. Luckily they had a Luluigui vehicle in the camp, so he told them to hang on a bit. Leaving the two blokes still out minding the mob, the remaining Luluigui blacks sitting on their arses in camp, he drove down to Kalyeeda to see Henry Skinner and get help. He picked up three or four of Skinner's men. There was a vehicle in the Myroodah stockcamp as well, so Skinner drove that up to the Nerrima boundary, where the steers were. They yarded the cattle up for the night, then Henry drove back to Goose Hole ready to truck the bullocks next day.

I was at home sitting down about to have tea, when the young Luluigui manager walked in to the Myroodah homestead.

"Sorry to disturb you John, but we've got a bit of trouble."

"Oh? What's that?" I went outside with him.

"These blokes jacked up on yarding the cattle. I went and got Henry and four of his men and we've yarded them now. I've left two blokes at the yard with the cattle, but I've got all these other Luluigui black fellas with me that reckon they're pulling out."

"Oh are they now? We'll sort this out." I told him and we went out to see them.

"What's going on?" I asked.

"We're pulling out."

"Why's that?"

"Ah, well you bin talk'im rough to us dat udder day, 'bout dat horse."

"Yeah." I agreed. "You're bloody useless. All of you know that you don't let a horse run away with a rope around his neck. Even if he's got no rope, you still follow him, pick him up with some other horses, and you bring him back to camp. You don't just let him run wild. And" I said "Bloody Hector here, this morning he tried to get me killed and I didn't say a bloody word about it. But now that this has happened I'm telling you that he tried to shove me onto the head of a young bull. As far as I'm concerned, Hector, you think that because you went down south with McLarty's that you are a bloody McLarty yourself. But you're not." With that it was 'on'. The white fella chucked his glasses into a nearby tamarisk tree, outside the homestead. The blacks were all wanting me. Ten of them. I was copping it left, right and centre. In the end I thought, 'I'm going to get done here' so I grabbed one bloke to pull him into me. I grabbed him by the hair and I went down. I still had his hair in my hand, but no body on the end of it. Then the boots went into me. My ribs were broken.

The young white bloke was there trying to help, but he couldn't do much with ten of them on to us. We had a bookkeeper there also, but he was bloody useless. He was more or less shitting himself the whole time. While all this was happening, the housekeeper was watching. I yelled out to her, "Bring a rifle and two bullets." When the blacks saw the gun they all got back.

"Now throw me the gun," she threw it and I caught it.

"Now throw me the bullets, one at a time." I caught the bullets and put one in the breech. It was a .410 shotgun.

"Now you bastards, fuck off, or you'll get this" and I pulled the trigger. The white bloke was just bending down to pick up his glasses and I blew his glasses to bits. The blacks all took off and I said, "Don't f----- come back, because the next one will be going through one of you."

They went down to another house, near the workshop and they stopped there.

I had a Falcon station wagon and I jumped in and drove down to them. I said, "Don't you bastards stop for anything, or you will get a bullet." With that I put the other one up the breech, put the gun out of the passenger window and pulled the trigger. Kevin Brady was standing at the kitchen and apparently I showered the corrugated iron next to him. The blacks kept walking.

"Any of your gear, I'll bring down and dump at Looma. When I feel like it." I added. I returned to the house. I told the housekeeper I needed to go back out to the stockcamp. I asked her if she would come with me, because I wasn't feeling too good. We drove down to the Nerrima/Kalyeeda boundary, where the steer mob was being held and stayed there overnight, without incident. Next morning, with the assistance of a couple of blokes from Skinner's camp, the steers were taken on to Kalyeeda. We drove back to the homestead and later, on into Derby hospital. I had broken ribs. I could hardly breathe, or move, or cough. They took X-rays. They said, "There's not much we can do for you. Just take a few Aspros and go and lie down for a fortnight."

I couldn't take a good breath and if I sneezed it nearly killed me. I used to get a towel and have it pinned tight around my chest. It knocked the shitter out me that did, but it wasn't the worst I got, although, thankfully I didn't know it then.

## Steers to go south and a roadtrain roll-over

At Garden Bore, on Myroodah, they put in a brand new drafting yard, spray dip, new bore, and new twenty, or twenty-five, thousand gallon tank. The only snag was that it wasn't a very good place for feeding cattle out, because there was basically only spinifex and wind grass for them to eat. We used to get steers off Luluigui, put Myroodah steers with them and take them all down to Kalyeeda, where we'd tail them for a few days. Then we'd go back home and carry on mustering. By the end of the year we would have another lot of steers to go down there. Kalyeeda was a very good cattle station. A lot better country than either Myroodah or Luluigui. It was only small, but it produced very good bullocks. It could grow rubbish into diamonds!

When we mustered bullocks off Kalyeeda we'd bring back all the steers, now in such good nick we'd hardly recognise them as those we took down. We would bring them back to Myroodah where they would be dipped twice at Garden Bore. The first dipping, a week or two before they were to be trucked South, the second dip on the day the trucks came. The steers were then loaded on six roadtrains, six decks on each and away they'd go, down to the southern properties near Moora.

I decided to check the bores on Kalyeeda, and the waters on that end of Myroodah. I didn't get home till about nine o'clock in the evening. As I pulled up at the homestead Patricia came running out. She was the cook/housekeeper at the time. Coloured and a very good girl. She said, "After you left this morning we got a message on the radio asking you to contact Derby police?' There's been a bad accident. One of Buntine's roadtrains has rolled over near Yeeda and the cattle have been tipped out. A lot of cattle were killed and a lot have had to be destroyed. About 130 head altogether. We couldn't get in touch with you to tell you." It sounded like a hell of a mess, but there was nothing I could do at that time of night, so I went to bed. In the morning I went down to the scene of the accident. By then the whole mess had been bulldozed and graded, the cattle buried, and the crates pushed up to one side. It was lucky the driver didn't get killed, but a lot of very nice steers were lost and a fair bit of money went down the drain. I think Buntines covered the insurance, which was good of them. I don't know what the hell happened that night. I suppose the driver lost control, or maybe fell asleep, or swerved for something. I always found the Buntine drivers to be really good decent blokes. They looked after the cattle while loading them and always did a good job.

## A false emergency

I came back to the homestead late one night to learn that one of the native stockman had had a horse fall. As I got out of the car, the housekeeper came out to tell me.

"He's been badly hurt. They think he's injured his back and his neck very seriously. The Flying Doctor's coming out to get him. We're putting out markers at the airstrip for the plane to land." It was well after dark.

"Where is the bloke now?"

"He's down in the camp, lying on his bed."

"Righto' I'll go and see him. You get on the wireless to the RFDS base. Tell them to hang on a bit with this plane." I went down to the camp, with a torch and found the black fella. He didn't look too bad.

"What's the matter with you?" I asked.

"Ah, prop'ly no good Shohn."

"Righto'. Stand up and let's have a look at you." He made out he was crook, getting off his stretcher bed slowly, but he was able to stand up all right.

"There's nothing wrong with you. The plane won't be coming." I told him. I went back to the house "Cancel the plane, there's no need for it." I instructed the women. The next day the fellow was fine. Nothing wrong with him. He was just acting and had wanted to get into town. Of course situations like that were a big risk, because if something was wrong I was in deep trouble. As manager it was my job to make the decision, whether they were bunging on, or was the injury for real? Sometimes it was a fine line, but on this occasion I had felt fairly confident.

## Kevin Green gets bogged

Kevin Green and Kevin Brady were a couple of smart men. Greeny had been to war and got shrapnel in his foot. He had been around for a long time and I knew him very well. The pair had been out on a job and were coming into the station. The wet was starting and they got bogged between Nerrima and Myroodah. Somebody called into the homestead and told me, so I went out to help them. I tried to pull the truck out, but it was hopeless.

"I can't get you out, you're too badly bogged." I told them.

"Ah well, we'll come home with you." Greeny said. So home we went. Then they told me they wanted to go into town. 'Their hides were cracking.'

"Righto." I agreed. I ordered them a taxi and while it was on it's way out from Derby I organised their pay cheque. Because they'd been yard building and fencing for three or four months, they were owed a lot of money. Greeny said to me,

"Don't give us all our money John. Just give us some of it. If we come back for the rest, don't you give it to us." Several times he said the same thing. "Make sure you don't give it to us, even if we ask you to."

"No worries." I told him.

"That's good. We'll be town for a few days, then we'll come home and go back to work."

I gave them a cheque, but only part of what they were owed and when the taxi arrived off they went to town. About a week later they rocked up at the station, drunk, demanding the rest of their money.

"No I'm not giving it to you. You told me to hang onto it for you, even if you asked for it." I reminded Greeny. They'd come out in a taxi, which was waiting for them and they began to give me a hard time. "Look, you're giving me the shits. Stop hassling me for money. You asked me not to give it to you. I'm not giving it to you. Now piss off."

"It's our money and you owe us." They kept on and on, no let-up. In the end I gave in.

"Right, that's enough. I'm sick of this. I'll write out a cheque and you can have the lot, then get going off the place." So that's what I did and away they went with their big mob of money.

The pair had been in town for a few weeks, when one day a plane arrived at the station. It was right on dinner-time when it landed. We weren't expecting anyone and I didn't know who it was, so I thought I'd better go up and see what was going on. When I got to the airstrip I found it was Brady and Green and the pair of them were absolutely rotten drunk. The pilot was a young 'God Botherer'. By the time I got up there, he was out of the plane, unloading all their gear, because his two passengers could barely stand. The aeroplane was loaded with grog. You couldn't have fitted another carton of spirits or beer on board. Greeny was trying to get out of the plane, but he couldn't work the door handle.

"Hang on Kevin, I'll get you out of there." Brady told him. In his hurry to get around to open the door for his mate, he walked into the thin edge of the wing and cut his forehead wide open. There was blood everywhere. Before Brady could get around to let him out, Greeny eventually found the catch. With all his weight on the door it burst open and flop, out he fell onto the ground, like a great big green frog. The 'God Botherer' must have wondered what the bloody hell he had there on that plane. I suspect he'd have been having heart failure, because I heard later, on the way out his passengers had been asking if he'd be a kamikaze pilot and fly into Mt. Anderson, or the Green Range. Once I arrived at the airstrip the poor fellow couldn't get into the plane and fly out of there quick enough. Once the plane had gone Brady and Greeny told me they wanted some food and they wanted me to run them out to the truck.

"First I'm going home to have my dinner." I told them.

"Ah, well have you got a smoke on you?" They asked.

"Yeah"

"Well, can you roll us a big mob before you go?" So I rolled about twenty cigarettes for them. Then they asked,

"Can you open up half a dozen bottles of beer for us?" because they didn't have the strength to take the tops off themselves. These were big bottles, 'king browns'. So I did that for them too, then I went and had dinner.

There was a spinifex bough shed at the airstrip on Myroodah – a pretty flash airport! I left the two of them there sitting on the ground, in the shade, intoxicated, and one bloke with his forehead half cut open, while I went and had dinner. I got some stores and meat for them, then went and picked them up and took them out to their truck. I dropped them off with all their gear, and all their grog and left them to it. A few days later somebody came past the station and said, "Do you know your men are out there in a dry bog hole, drinking piss and the grog they're drinking is that hot, they're passing it from one hand to the other?" I nodded.

"They'll be 'right." And they were. Once they'd finished all their grog and had 'dried out' they went back to work as hard as ever.

## Out of the rats with little tots of whisky

There are lots of blokes I've helped out of the 'rats' over the years. The worst case was at Christmas Creek and also at Meda. I don't drink spirits because it sends me to being a fully fledged idiot, but I always used to keep a bottle or two of rum or whisky, just to help wean these poor devils off it. While they were in the 'rats' they'd follow you around like a dog, pestering you and it would go on for several days.

"Can you give me one bottle of beer. Come on Wellsy. Look you know me I'm your friend and I work for you. Look just give me one bottle of beer." It was pitiful. They would follow me round and round, everywhere I went. I'd tell them to get going, but no, they'd be right there. If I went back to the house they'd be sitting outside, waiting, hoping they could get me to give them a drink.

I always found the best way was to go to them, and give them a nip. I didn't take the bottle. I just took a pannikin or something, because if they saw that I had a bottle they were worse. I'd just give them a little bit. I might give them two or three nips a day, then gradually reduce it to, maybe two a day, then one a day, then after that they'd be alright. They were very, very good men, a lot of them. They were tough men. Jeez those blokes could work. They toiled bloody hard and asked for nothing, while they were working, but when they got grog in them they were unbelievable. They could have been millionaires, some of them, but they just drank all their money, or gave it away. There were a lot of blow flies around when these blokes had grog in them. It was 'here, give us twenty bucks' then never pay it back, and the alcoholics wouldn't even know who they gave it to.

There were some amongst them, who borrowed money off me, when they were rotten drunk and I never thought I'd see it again. Then months and months later they'd come to me and say, "Here Wellsy, I owe you this." I'd have clean forgotten about it. A lot of them were good men. Many of them were characters and had a good sense of humour, while they were sober. Blokes liked them. They were highly thought of, but their lives were blighted by grog.

Whenever I went into Derby, to the pub, the same blokes would be sitting at the bar, in the same spot, on the same stool, drinking the same drinks, day in, day out. If it was races time, or I'd brought my blokes in from the stockcamp for a few days off, these same fella's would say to me, "I see you've got your mad ringers in town again, drinking, cutting up rough and making fools of themselves." They probably were too, but it used to amuse me a bit. If these same blokes at the bar, making the remarks, had had their grog cut off, been out bush, or in the stockcamp, for weeks on end, then let loose in town, it would have been interesting to see how they would conduct themselves. Really those regular pub goers, some of them good friends of mine too, weren't in a position to be passing judgement on my young fellows. They'd worked bloody hard, for little reward, in harsh conditions and in my opinion, were entitled to run a bit wild for a day or two. I didn't think it was unreasonable.

## Looking down the barrel of a gun

I had a mechanic on Myroodah, who seemed to be all right. He did his job and although he had a penchant for native women, he didn't cause me any undue worry. Sometimes he would have a few beers, his own grog, which he'd drink at his house between the store and the workshop.

We had a mob of cattle put together, steers, to go down south. The roadtrains had rocked up a bit later than expected, so we were loading them in the dark. While we were doing this a vehicle rolled up. I could hear the blokes saying it was Pete De Long, who owned nearby Dampier Downs and I recognised his Yankee voice. My men told him I was down the back of the yard, pushing cattle up and De Long came around and found me. He seemed to be wearing a peculiar looking shirt, with a loud pattern on it. Not his usual style at all.

"What have you been to, a bloody party? You've got a fancy dress shirt on." I observed.

"Shshh." Pete whispered "I've come to see you 'cos there's been a bit of trouble at the homestead."

"Righto, I'll be with you in a minute." When work slackened off a bit I went aside to where he waited.

"Your mechanic has been causing a bit of trouble in there. He's had a gin over at his house and she has come over to where the contractors are. She came over to get refuge, she's naked and the mechanic has belted her up." He went on to explain how the mechanic had then gone over to their quarters and he had a gun.

At the contractors cottage there was Pete De Long, Reggie Woods, Kevin Brady and Kevin Green. De Long had got into his motor car, to come and fetch me, but the mechanic had tried to pull him out of the vehicle. There had been a scuffle, hence the blood spattered over Pete's shirt. I could see now that it wasn't a pattern at all, but dark blood stains. Pete apparently gave the mechanic a few good welts, which had sorted him out. Then he drove to the trucking yards to get me.

"I'll be home in a while. I won't be much longer here. We've almost finished, then I'll come in." I told him.

We finished loading the steers. When I got back to the homestead, a short while later, the whole station was in darkness. It was as if no-one lived there. Dark and silent. I had the dogs with me. I went over to see Reggie and Pete and they told me a bit more of what had happened. Pete said the gin belonged to a black fella, who was in the camp at Garden Bore trucking yard. Two horses had got away and a couple of kids had been sent to find them. These kids had found the two horses and were bringing them back to the camp. They went via the homestead and had seen all the goings on. These kids heading back with the horses, would tell the bucks about all the happenings when they got there. We knew there could well be a bit more trouble coming later. After I heard this I went over to the house. Patricia was there, but she wouldn't answer for a good while, until she knew it was me and that everything was all right.

"We haven't seen the mechanic. I don't know where he is." She told me fearfully.

There was a bookkeeper there at the time, but he was planted. He was shitting himself. Then I went down to the blacks camp, but nobody would answer any doors, so I opened one door. Jeez! You'd reckon I'd thrown a fox into a box full of squirrels and rabbits. They were that frightened, they were all squealing at the same time, absolutely petrified.

"Eh eh, it's OK. It's only me. I just want to know where this mechanic fellow is and if he's got a gun." They settled down and everything got sorted out around the homestead. Then I went down to the mechanic's house and knocked on the door. There was no answer. I tried to open it. Locked. I knocked on the door again.

"It's John. Can you open this door, I want to talk to you." I could hear the key turn in the lock. The door opened and there was a rifle pointed right at me, about a yard away from me. I said to him, "Can you put that down?"

"No"

"Well, it doesn't matter what happens. Everybody knows what's been going on around here this afternoon. All the blacks down the camp are shitting themselves. The bookkeeper is shitting himself. Patricia is shitting herself. There's a mob of blokes camped over at the shearing shed. There's a buck going to be in here in a couple of hours, or in the morning, when those two kids tell him what's been going on round here. I want you off the place tonight. I don't want any more trouble here." He put the rifle down.

"I'm too drunk to go anywhere now." He told me.

"Right. I've got a cheque here. I'll be over at daylight in the morning. I want you packed up and ready and I'll give you the cheque and you f----- off."

"All right" he agreed.

I went home, had a couple of beers and a bit to eat. My ticker was going like hell.

It turned out that the mechanic had been down to Broome where he had left his regular gin. He then came back to the station and got onto the young buck's girl while her stud was in the stockcamp. Then the shit had hit the fan. There were two gates into the Myroodah homestead. Early next morning the buck was rolling in through one gate, as the mechanic was heading out of the other. It was a near thing, but further trouble had been averted.

## Not in a good place

Rae was on Myroodah with me for about a year before she took off back to Perth with the kids. We'd bought a house in Herdsman Parade, Wembley. At least I thought we had. It was meant to be in joint names and I fully believed it was. I was sending most of my wages down to Rae, to help pay the mortgage, but later I found out I didn't own anything. The stupid part of it was, I didn't have much money anyway, and I drank a lot of it too. I'd drink two king browns at midday and another four bottles at night. I was very unhappy at this time. I wasn't really in this world. I didn't like Myroodah as a place and I shouldn't even have been running a cattle station.

When I could, I'd go to town on a Friday night and not come home till Sunday arvo. When I was home at the station I was drinking fairly heavily, but I still did my work. I reckoned I was running Myroodah all right, but that was only in my head. Scott McColl can't have thought too badly of me, because he said if I needed any help they would help me, which was very good of him. I'd been on Myroodah for almost two years. Basically I had no money. My family was gone. I had nothing.

It was getting towards the end of the year and I had given notice. I didn't really care any more about anything. I'd had enough. A plane used to come out to the station to do a clinic run. One day it came out and there was a sister and a doctor on it. I drove out to see them.

"I think I'm suicidal. I don't know how far I can go before I tip right over the edge." I explained. They listened politely and said, "When you're next in town we'll get you to see a doctor." They took off and continued on their clinic run.

By the time I left Myroodah I was pretty much at rock bottom. I went up to the hospital and saw a doctor. The next thing I found myself on a plane to Perth, the doctor escorting me. I didn't need an escort. My mother, who worked at the hospital at the time, reckoned the doctor just wanted a free trip to Perth and that's how come I was sent down there. I was sent to this place where I should never have been sent. It was terrible. Anyway, after two days, I discharged myself. I rang Rae and she came and fetched me.[7]

---

7   In hindsight I should never have gone to Myroodah to work in the first place. If I had been my normal self and Scott McColl had offered me a job there, I'd have said 'No, I'm not interested.' As it was, I took it. It turned out to be a big mistake. I didn't like the country. I didn't like the loss of young horses every year from walkabout. I didn't like the pastoral inspector and the blacks didn't like me. The other thing about Myroodah was that while I was out in the stock camp the pilot was 'acting studmaster' at home. Ironically, years later, he received an Order of Australia Medal 'for services to the pastoral industry'. I was at the same ceremony, with my future brother in law, and by then I was a much happier man. I found the citation highly amusing.

*Me as a young father with my baby son Benn and daughter Leah. Late 1971*

*Myroodah Crossing. Photo taken in 2006*

*The workshop at Myroodah. Photo taken in 2006.*

# CHAPTER ELEVEN

# PERTH TO OOBAGOOMA

*Take me to where I long to be, where the wedge-tailed eagles soar,*
*In the hot wet north, to the Kimberley, where the flooding rivers roar.*

## Tabradden

After Rae collected me from the horrific situation I found myself in, I remained in Perth living with her and the children, in the house on Herdsman Parade, which I still believed was jointly owned. After a while I got a job working for Kevin Moore, at Tabradden Stables, in Belmont, riding racehorses. Kevin was Brian Moore's younger brother, for whom I rode track work in Derby when I was still single. A friend, Tommy Hedley, who'd been ringing in the stockcamp with me on Napier, was also at Tabradden. They had a horse there that was giving a bit of trouble. I was asked to ride him. He was called Pan Muir. Tommy came to me and told me to watch out for this horse. He said, "He'll let you get on him all right, but when you go to move him off he rears straight up in the air." Tommy had had first hand experience of this. I got on him and when I went to move him off he did exactly as Tommy had said. He reared straight up and I thought he was going over backwards. I started to slip off sideways, but he came back down again. I thought this was what he'd been doing the whole time, that he'd been making blokes think he would go over backwards with them. But I took him too cheap. The next time I went to move him off he went straight up in the air and over backwards. He definitely wasn't stopping. I'd stayed on board and he landed on top of me. I got up, grabbed hold of him and remounted. I treated him a bit roughly and then asked him to go and he went. Out onto the track at the racing establishment, good as gold. I took him round twice, then brought him back. I handed him over to the stable hand, got in the car and went home.

I went up to the doctor's surgery. He sent me to a nearby physio, or chiropractor, I'm not sure which, who manipulated my neck. I reckon he nearly broke it. It hurt like hell and was very sore. The following day I went back to Tabradden and rode the horse again. He was good as gold. I did this several more times without problem, then he was handed over to someone else to ride. I wasn't feeling too good. My back was giving me a fair bit of gyp. I stopped working and eventually went to see a bloke in West Perth, called Cecil Walkley. I could hardly drive myself, or get out of the car, but after he'd worked on me I'd walk out of there as if I was walking on clouds. It was magic. But by the time I'd driven myself home again I was back to square one. I ended up being off work for several months.

In time I began to pick up a bit of casual work with Bell Group, loading and unloading trucks. The hours were uncertain, but it was good money. A mate from Derby, Spud Willis, was also working for Bell Group at the time. He proved to be a true friend to me during this difficult period. By then I was learning who my real friends were and there weren't many of them. I also worked for Booth Bros. on a casual basis, truck driving and loading, or unloading, sheep at Fremantle, when there was a ship in.

After I had been in Perth for almost a year, although I was living in the family home, I knew my marriage was over. When station owner John Montague got in touch with me and asked if I would be interested in going to manage Oobagooma I agreed.

The McLarty family had owned Oobagooma at one time and my great uncle, Ned Wells, was there years ago. He later returned to Queensland to 'Early Storms', a station he owned near Carnarvon Gorge. Dr Lawson Holman also owned Oobagooma at one time. Over the years it had changed hands several times. Napier ran down onto Oobagooma and I knew there were pockets of good country. Mundooma, the last camp on Napier, was down that end. We used to muster down as far as a billabong called George's Yard, on the Meda, Napier, Oobagooma boundary and there were a lot of good big bullocks down there. I thought a job on Oobagooma would be all right.

## Oobagooma where tough times continue

Oobagooma shared a boundary with Napier, Meda, and Kimbolton. Geographically I was back in home territory, but oh golly! What a show that was.

I was thirty-one and supposed to be managing the place, but the reality was I was nothing more than a caretaker. The homestead was in a hell of a state. No flyscreens. Nothing. The bloody mosquitos just about ate you alive. There was no tucker to speak of. Maybe a bag of flour. We didn't have a fridge, freezer, or electric light. Just Tilley lights, or hurricane lamps. There was next to no equipment and what there was seemed to be worn out or rubbish. There were no staff either.

I got Terry Hillman to work with me on Oobagooma. He was a very good man who'd worked for me on Napier, later Frazier as well. Montague wanted yards repaired, so we'd go out to work on them, but it was like when I went to Old Napier. The bloody chain saws were worn out and useless. It was the same with everything on the place, including the vehicle.

We were a bit lucky to have had a light wet that year. It meant we were able to get in to town a couple of times, or we'd meet somebody who'd come out from town, and pick something up. If it had been a normal 'wet' season we would have been isolated with our nothingness and I don't know how we'd have got on.

One time Terry and I drove in from Oobagooma and left the unregistered, unroadworthy, Land Rover at Meda Station. Dad drove out from Derby, picked us up, and took us on in to town from there. When it was time to go home, a day or so later, we got a lift back out to Meda to pick up the Land Rover. The Land Rover used to boil, so we had brought a 20 litre tin of water with us in the back of the vehicle. We hadn't had to use any on the way in, because we'd filled the radiator when we'd got to the bores on Meda. We filled it again, at Meda homestead, before heading off home. We didn't check the water in the tin. I just thought 'we've got 20 litres of water with us, so that's OK' and away we went.

We had already driven past the bores and were well beyond Rarriwell, heading up through the scrub towards Oobagooma, when the engine cut out. Knowing we still had the tin in the back, we weren't worried. It wasn't until we went to put water in the radiator that we discovered the tin had leaked. It was completely empty. We hadn't realised this earlier, because the water from the leak must have dried up while we were in town, otherwise it would have alerted us. Because of the light 'wet' we knew the waterholes were going to be dry. That was why we 'd brought the 20 litres of water with us in the first place, but now we needed it we didn't have it. That year the Meda and May Rivers were dry. None of the creeks had any water in them.

We tried to start the vehicle. Nothing. We waited, tried again, waited some more. Again and again we tried starting the Land Rover. No joy. This went on for a good while, but we couldn't get it started. We knew we were in a bit of trouble. We could have followed the creeks up a bit, in the hope of finding water, but if there wasn't any we'd have to walk back again. It was too risky. There was nobody on Oobagooma to raise the alarm. We were on our own. Eventually Terry got fed up with trying to get the Land Rover going.

"Bugger this, I'm going to walk." he announced. He had no water with him. While Terry started to walk, I tried to get the Land Rover to start, but I couldn't. I waited another half an hour and tried again. Still nothing. I put some beer in the radiator but that wouldn't make it start. After about an hour and a half I thought 'Bugger this. I'm just getting thirstier and thirstier here. I might as well start walking too.'

I had my two dogs with me. Yogi and a little Australian Terrier called Lady. I started walking with the two dogs and after a couple of hours I passed Terry. He was crashed under a tree. Unlike Terry, I wasn't hung over. He'd been on the grog the whole weekend. He'd had it. Yogi had been trying to follow me, but he kept pulling up. When we caught up with Terry, the bigger dog pulled up and stayed there with him, but Lady wanted to keep coming with me. She was whimpering and crying, so I ended up picking her up and carrying her. It was getting very steamy and hot. By now it was well into the afternoon. Lady was getting heavier and heavier and I was getting thirstier. But there was nothing I could do but keep on walking. I was beginning to think this could be the death of us. I thought about writing a note.

At about three o'clock a big mob of clouds came up and it absolutely pelted. I was catching the rain in my hat and drinking it. It was absolutely marvellous. It gave us new life to keep going. I was just getting to the gate at Oobagooma when I heard a motor car. It was Gronya Poole, from Kimbolton. She had a bloke with her and they were coming to look for us. She gave us a drink of water. We left Lady at the homestead and drove back to where Terry was. We gave him a drink of water and left him in the shade, then drove on to the broken down Land Rover. We put water in the radiator and it started straight away. They told me to get going. I jumped in and was tearing along the road when the track rod fell off, so then there was no steering. There were big trees, woolly butt, and off the road we went, into the bush. The Land Rover had no brakes either. So off it went, through the trees. No brakes, no steering. Jeez! Eventually it pulled up and Gronya caught up to me. She drove over to where I was, we wired the track rod on and I drove, very steadily, homewards. I picked up Terry and Yogi and we continued on to Oobagooma. The Land Rover was the most roadworthy vehicle on the station. Actually, it was the only vehicle!

I was only on Oobagooma for one 'wet' season, but it was one of the longest 'wets' of my life. We used to catch a lot of barramundi and basically lived on fish. If we caught too many, we'd take them over to Kimbolton, where Gronya would put them in the fridge for us. Then, when we didn't catch anything, we had them to fall back on. One day I was driving down to where I used to go fishing. I was driving along the track and there was a gap, a big rut, about ten inches wide. I hit the rut and the whole Land Rover broke clean in half. It just collapsed. So that was another walk home. And did Montague go off his head over that. He reckoned I was driving too fast. You'd think I'd broken some flash new motorcar, the way he went on. In fact it had been broken for a long time, but nobody knew it. The chassis was rusted away, pretty well right through, and was only holding by a little bit. When I hit the bump it just broke in half. After that we had no vehicle at all.

I was still having a fair bit of trouble with my back and from time to time I could hardly do anything. One day it was giving me hell. I was lying on my bed. It was about ten o'clock in the morning, when in walked a dingo. Broad daylight, through the broken louvres. It had a sniff around the room and I thought 'I'll be able to grab this thing by the tail shortly'. It went under my bed, then back out through the louvres again. I couldn't believe it. But that's how good the homestead was.

In April that year the defence forces came to Oobagooma for a big military exercise. The RAAF were based in Derby, accommodated at the Boab Inn, but the army were camped on a big billabong on the station. With their arrival things got a lot better. Before they came it was pretty lonely out there and once the Land Rover broke in half, we were stuck and couldn't go anywhere. Also the army gave us a bit of tucker, which helped us out. Although it had been a very light 'wet' that year, the billabong still had a fair bit of water in it, helped by some late rain. It was quite good and there were lilies growing in it. Despite this the army had a purifying plant going, pumping water out of the billabong, purifying it and using it for their camp drinking water. I couldn't see the sense in it. They were there for training in outback conditions, yet here they were with an engine running, purifying water that was basically clean in the first place. Well, if the enemy was around you wouldn't be able to have an engine running, or you'd let the foe know where you were. It would have been more sensible to get the troops used to the bacteria, drink the water as it was and harden up to that sort of stuff. It wasn't as if it was crook water. I've drunk a lot worse and I've seen that billabong a lot filthier, when it's been nearly empty and pigs have been wallowing in the mud. The army had generators as well as the purifying plant, so they could keep their tucker cold. There were a couple of barra pigs running out there and one day the defence force fellows shot one and dressed it. That annoyed me a bit, because I thought of that as our tucker, for emergencies. In the 'wet', with no vehicle, where were we going to go to get anything? We couldn't go anywhere. But really the army were pretty good to me. I had no way of storing meat anyway, because most of the time I was on Oobagooma I had no power. Although I thought the army bosses should have been hardening their blokes up while they played 'war-games', instead of molly-coddling them, one thing was for sure, I wasn't being molly-coddled. Apart from no lighting plant, no tucker to speak of and no vehicle, Monty wasn't paying me either. He was supposed to be, but no wages came, so things weren't very good.

Towards the end of April my back got that crook the army flew me in to Derby and I was in hospital for a while. When I was discharged I went and saw a couple of the fuel agents in town. There were about two hundred empty Avgas drums on

Oobagooma, because Montague used helicopters a lot, for mustering. I told the fuel agents that I had these drums out there. That Montague had never paid me and I had no money. I asked them if they would take the drums, give me the money and 'I don't know where the drums went?' Both agreed. I went and saw Bob Skuthorpe and told him what I'd done. I'd driven trucks for Bob before my marriage. He was already aware that Montague hadn't ever sent me any wages, because I'd told him earlier. On that occasion Bob hadn't commented, but he had apparently done something on my behalf,

"I've rung Montague and had a talk to him. I told him, if your money doesn't come, there'll be some trouble and that he'd better send some. So you hang onto the drums, John. Don't let them go yet." Bob told me. After that I got a cheque from Montague, so I teed up for someone to collect the drums off Oobagooma and Monty got a credit for them.

One evening, after being discharged from hospital I met up with Colin and Sylvia Haskett, who had been donkey and roo shooting on Myroodah. They asked me to join them at the Boab Hotel for a drink. I did, although I was on the wagon at the time and only drinking coke. While I was in the 'Waterhole Bar' with them they introduced me to a 'Pommy Sheila' who was working there as a receptionist and had just come off duty. I thought it was pretty good being in town amongst friends again, after the loneliness of Oobagooma. Not long after that I pulled the pin. Terry Hillman was still out there then, but he left soon after.

While I was in Derby I saw old Bill Hymas and I asked him if he would go out and caretake at Oobagooma. My Australian terrier, Lady, was close to having pups at the time. I hadn't been able to bring her in with me on the plane, so I'd left her out at the station. Bill Hymas was supposed to look after the place and Lady as well. After a few days I went back out to the station to work out my notice.

Mervyn Norton was the manager of Meda then and he had a company plane. He flew out to see me once or twice and early in May he asked if I'd help draft the Meda horses. There were about three hundred, including fifteen of my own private horses, which I'd left there when I finished work at Myroodah a year or so earlier. About this time Mervyn offered me a job, as stud-master, on Meda. I said I'd take it.Once everything had been settled and sorted, Mervyn flew out to collect me. Bill was left at Oobagooma to caretake. I still wasn't able to take Lady with me, because she had had her pups by then. I left her with Hymas to look after and planned to drive up and collect her as soon as I got a chance. Not long after I received a letter from him. He told me the dingoes had come in and killed Lady, and all her pups. A sad end for a game little dog. It pretty much summed up the bleakness of life on Oobagooma at that time.

# CHAPTER TWELVE
# STUDMASTER ON MEDA 1975

*I thought you'd be wizened man,*
*An old prospector type,*
*With tattered hat and billy can,*
*Camp fire, smoking old clay pipe;*
*How deceiving minds can be,*
*To conjure up this view,*
*I never thought that I would see*
*A bloke as young as you.*

Things had changed a bit at Meda since my Dad was retired off the station in 1964. There had been a succession of managers since then, George Pollard, Frank Mugford, Dave Ledger and now Mervyn Norton. A new, transportable, homestead had been built to replace the old, verandah enclosed house in which I had grown up. Mervyn, his loyal wife Lyn and their two very young children, lived in the new house. My quarters were in the cottage where, years earlier, Stumpy Fraser and his family had been accommodated, before Stumpy's tragic accident. The old timber yards at the homestead were no longer in use, nor the old stables. Since my Dad's time a new drafting yard had been built, down at the Claypan, from where cattle were trucked. Droving cattle into Derby was a thing of the past. Everything was now sent on roadtrains.

Mervyn's brother Kevin, was the manager of Christmas Creek Station, another Emanuel property and Frank Mugford was on GoGo, the company's principal station. Jim Motter was on Cherrabun, the fourth station owned by Emanuel Brothers. Both Mervyn and Kevin Norton had a pilot's license and Merv had put in a second airstrip at Meda, on the homestead side of the billabong.

## A pub with no beer

It was mid May 1975 when I started my new job on Meda. By then I had formed a friendship with the English girl I'd met recently at the Boab Hotel. Her name was Janet, she seemed a good sort and she knew how to work. She had been having a hard time at the Boab Hotel over recent weeks when most of the staff had walked out, leaving only her and a couple of others trying to run the whole show. The trouble had started with the appointment of an unstable young hotel manager, who proved utterly incompetent. It didn't help that the hotel was fully booked at the time, with a delegation of 'top brass', including the Minister for Defence, visiting Derby for the final stage of the military exercises at Oobagooma. Janet was employed as hotel receptionist, but since the staff walkout her workload included, laundry, wine waitress, breakfast cook, cashier as well as her reception duties. The hotel was in such a state of turmoil that at one point it looked like running clean out of beer. With a full house of RAAF personnel and the military dignitaries, this was a bit of a crisis. To help carry them through until their next delivery, I offered to drive to Broome during the night, to collect ten kegs from The Roebuck Hotel. It was a round trip of seven or eight hours, the road then not as it is today, being unfenced and hazardous with straying stock, on Yeeda, which were hard to 'pick up' in the dark.

I left Derby early in the evening, and by the time I got to Broome it was almost closing time. As I entered The Roebuck Hotel a gin staggered past me on her way out. She was clutching two big bottles of beer. There were no other patrons left in the bar, but Martin Pearson Jones, the publican, was waiting for me. As I walked towards him, something whistled past my head and smashed against the wall behind the bar, closely missing both of us. I swung round to see what was going on and saw another 'king brown' on it's way. The native woman, now without either of her bottles of beer, lurched off into the night hurling abuse at no-one in particular. The publican and I loaded the ten kegs into the back of the vehicle and I headed back up the road to Derby, arriving in the early hours of the morning.

## A new job

Terry Hillman had left Oobagooma and Mervyn Norton said he'd give him a job as station cook, so on a Saturday afternoon I drove out to Meda taking Terry with me. He had been on the grog in town and was in a bad way. He was in the rats, delirium tremens. I knew it would be a while before he'd be up to cooking so I'd bought a bottle of whisky to help him, and would give him a nip three times a day, in an enamel pannikin, until he recovered. Janet, who seemed to enjoy escaping the chaos at the pub whenever she got a chance, came with us for the run. I had borrowed Dad's old Holden to shift my gear out to the station and Janet drove it back to town for me later that evening. Apart from weaning Terry off the grog, I spent the first weekend cleaning and settling into my quarters at the cottage.

Over the coming weeks, I was able to see a fair bit of Janet. Meda was only thirty miles from Derby, so trips to town were frequent. One of the station hands had crook feet at the time, which required regular dressings at the hospital. Mervyn would often ask me to run the fellow in. If the town visit coincided with Janet's off duty hours, she would sometimes come back with me out to the station. One day on our way back to Meda I did a detour, looking for a stud bull that had gone missing. I drove down from the Gibb River Road through the back of one of the paddocks, coming out near the Claypan. I found evidence of a fight on a fence, which explained why 'Cassius', as the Santa Gertrudis bull became known, was no longer in his correct paddock. As we drove back up towards the homestead we saw Mervyn, who had been doing an aerial search, flying overhead. He landed his plane on the bigger airstrip, on the far side of the billabong, so Janet and I drove over and picked him up and gave him a lift back to the homestead.

As we approached the station buildings we were met with a delegation of angry natives. Mervyn went to see what the problem was. It transpired that Terry, who was now working as the babbler, refused to cook meals for all the women and kids in the native camp. He would only cook for the working men. A dispute had erupted and the upshot was that Terry left. I felt pretty annoyed about him being 'let go'. I'd done the hard part of getting him out of the rats. I knew him to be a very able, all round station hand. He could cook, ride, fix windmills, do yard repairs, anything. Having been weaned off the grog he would have gone on to prove himself a good loyal worker on the station. It seemed a bloody shame to lose such a man, all for the want of a little diplomacy. Mervyn had no idea what a good bloke he'd just lost. I did, but I wasn't the manager and at that moment I was glad. The greatest pity was the likelihood that Terry would end up back on the grog in town, just when he'd been successfully 'dried out'.

After the disruption outside the station kitchen we finally headed up to the main house to drop Mervyn off. It was well after dark by this time. The manager's wife, Lyn, hurried out towards us, carrying her young baby, with a toddler at foot. She was frantic with worry. When she saw Mervyn was with us she gave full vent to her feelings. Having landed his plane on the far airstrip, she hadn't heard him come in to land. Likewise, I had approached the homestead from the direction of the Claypan, instead of down the usual access road, so she was unaware that her husband was with us. As night fell the young mother had feared the worst, thinking Mervyn's plane had come down somewhere out on the run. She unleashed her fury on him and although I thought she had every reason to be wild with him, Janet and I escaped to the cottage as soon as we could.

Over the coming weeks I realised a pattern was forming in the way Mervyn went about managing things on Meda. He was a frequent visitor at the cottage, dropping in each morning for two cups of coffee before work. Most evenings he would again walk over, on his short stocky legs, to visit. I'd offer him a coke and while he drank it he'd talk about station matters, asking my advice on what should be done and how best to do it.

"Wwww well, yes John," he'd say, "So tomorrow ww will you do that. Take Frank Skeen with you." Then the next evening it would be the same thing. I began to wonder who was actually running the show. On Tuesdays he went into Derby to collect the latest issue of Phantom. He was great mates with Lindsay LeLievre, younger brother of my good friend Phil. Lindsay had a clothing store in town, where all the ringers would buy their boots, hats, pocket knives and any other gear they needed, including country and western cassette tapes and comics. Mervyn was addicted to Phantom comics.

## To catch a croc

I'd been at Meda for a month. We were having trouble with a saltwater crocodile which had recently taken a full grown bullock. It was living in a stretch of the May River known locally as Mary's Well and Mervyn thought we should try and catch it. We decided to set a trap, made up of a twelve gallon drum, some steel cable with two large hooks on it and a big slab of beef, as bait. We drove as close as we could to the point where the croc had been seen, carrying the trap the last hundred metres. A slide mark at the water's edge, where the creature had come out of the river to sun itself, was easily visible. Skin pattern and jowl marks were imprinted in the soft wet mud. We made sure the drum was completely airtight, then attached the bait to the hook and wire line. This in turn was fastened to the drum which we left lying close to the slide marks at the river's edge. The idea was that if the crocodile swallowed the bait, hook, line and all, then took off into deep water, the drum would float and show us where the salty was lurking. We returned to the site some six hours later, only to find the drum had been moved a yard or two closer to the edge and the bait gone. We reset the trap, this time securing a much smaller piece of meat to the hooks. We knew the croc was unlikely to return for some time. It had already had a good feed that day.

The following morning we again made our way down to Mary's Well. This time success. The drum was floating near the far bank and we could see where it had been pulled into the river. I walked around until I was on the far side of the waterhole and could see better. The drum was afloat, the wire rope wrapped around a log and the crocodile clearly visible lying motionless a few inches beneath the surface. It looked as if it was dead, so I shot it to make sure. Other blokes arrived and we put a noose around it's neck. I got in the water and with a half hitch, tied it's top and bottom jaws shut. As I was doing this I looked down and saw the .303 bullet lying on the top of the salty's head. For a moment or two I was Jesus Christ. It wasn't a very good feeling. But the saltwater crocodile did appear to be well and truly dead. I think when it had taken the bait and crossed the river it must have rolled, gone over the log and the wire rope caught and locked onto the log. The croc had drowned. We untangled the cable and took the drum off, then we tried to float him around the edge of Millulla, the traditional name for Mary's Well. But it was too far and the water too shallow to float the huge reptile. We decided to walk shoulder deep, across the river. Once across we then had to tow the croc downstream for some distance until we were level with the Land Rover. I felt a bit toey doing this. There were two of us, pulling him along with the rope around his head, but sometimes the animal sank deeper and floated beneath us. When our feet and legs touched it the adrenalin fairly shot through us, making us yelp with the shock of it, whilst those on the bank laughed. Eventually we got it far enough downstream to pass the rope up the bank to be hitched onto the vehicle. It was then towed slowly up through the undergrowth away from the river. We took it back to the station and measured it. It was eleven and a half feet long.

## ... And is it still raining there in England?

It seemed I'd won a heart. Janet, who was supposed to have gone back to her home country by ship, had decided to fly instead. She finished work at the Boab Hotel and spent a couple of weeks extra in the Kimberley, to spend more time with me. She would still be back home with her family by the end of August, as she had promised them. She was visiting me at Meda and it was our last weekend together. We'd just come back into the station from checking bores when Mervyn sent me down onto a fire that had sprung up in the bullock paddock. It was about three o'clock in the afternoon.

"I'll organise for some other blokes to come down there later tonight." He told me. I presumed he would bring the stockcamp in to help. In the meantime there were just three of us. Simon, a young jackeroo from Perth, myself and old Jack Shaw, who couldn't do very much to help. We took two vehicles and drove down to the bullock paddock to try to put the fire out. We worked for several hours and night fell, but no other blokes came to give us a hand, so we kept doing the best we could.

During the night our two vehicles got widely separated. I was fighting the fire, going across country. I was trying to block all the grass from getting burnt, but in the end I couldn't keep awake any longer. It was about 2 o'clock in the morning by this time and I was dog tired. I didn't really know where the other vehicle was. I seemed to be on my own with one vehicle, but I hadn't seen the other blokes for a fair while. I lay down on a claypan and went to sleep. I woke up about an hour later and started working again on the fire. Eventually morning came and I heard a plane coming. Mervyn flew over and landed on a dry billabong. There were no men with him come to help, and no tucker either. We hadn't brought very much with us the previous afternoon, because we thought everybody else was coming to fire fight as well. All we had was a bit of water, a couple of tins of meat and a loaf of bread. That was it. We were left there alone, with hardly any tucker, from mid afternoon, all night and well into the next day, before another mob was finally sent to take over.

When we were dropped off at the cottage we'd fairly 'had it'. Janet cooked up a big feed for us and after we'd eaten I slept for several hours. That evening I took her into the airport and away she flew.

## 'Wet' season caretaker on Christmas Creek

Once Janet had gone back to England she wrote to me regularly, but I've never been one for letter writing, so she didn't get too many replies. I didn't expect to ever see her again. At the end of the season, during the 'wet', I was asked to go up to Christmas Creek to caretake, while Kevin Norton and his family went on holidays.

## Harry O'Bottomey

Harry O'Bottomey was on Christmas Creek station at the time. He was a very smart bush mechanic, but another victim of grog. His parent's had owned a hotel in Kalgoorlie. I'd known 'Bott since I was a kid, when he was working on Meda for my Dad. The first time I ever saw him he was fencing out at, what was to become, Charlie's Paddock. Timber fence posts, all drilled with brace and bit. He had some desert natives working with him, silent myall black fella's. Their women would go out hunting while the men worked. They'd dig for frogs, leaving big holes, which I found treacherous in later years when mustering out there. They'd get big mobs of frogs, break their legs and put them in a billy-can or cooliman, and carry them back to camp.

Later O'Bottomey was on Kimberley Downs when I was ringing there. He'd gone into town and got on the grog. I was sent in to fetch him, but he wouldn't come. Instead he asked me for money. He was rotten drunk. I gave him twenty dollars, a whole weeks wages for me in those days and then returned to Kimberley Downs without him. I never thought I'd see that money again. A long time later he brought the subject up, while we were working together one day.

"Ahhh. I think I owe you some money. Do I owe you?" I said he did and he asked me how much.

"Twenty dollars" I told him.

"Right. I'll give it to you when we get back to the station." and he did. Another time he said to me, "Wellsy, you need a tucker box and a tool box. If I tell you what materials to order, you pay for them and I'll make them for you." I've still got the tucker box to this day, but the tool box got hooked long ago. O'Bottomey was a thoroughly decent, honest bloke. I had great respect for him. He had the most beautiful copperplate handwriting, the best I have ever seen. I've heard tell he was a very good dancer also, not that I ever saw him dancing.

Although I was pleased to find him on Christmas Creek that 'wet' season, he was in a bad way. He'd been on the bottle, so again it was a case of administering nips to help him out of the 'Rats'. At night he'd nearly drive me mad. 'Roll us some smokes' he'd say, because he had the tremors so badly he couldn't do it himself.

## Roland Thompson and the gun incident

Roland Thompson was also on Christmas Creek during the 'wet' of 1975/1976 while I was caretaking. I had known him for a long time. He had worked for Phil Le Lievre on Fairfield and had been a very good man in his youth. Roland now had a plate in his head, the result of an accident, and he used to be a bit odd from time to time. His wife, Rosie, was a crackerjack woman and in latter years they both came to work for me on Meda.

I had been on Christmas Creek for a few weeks when I was woken in the middle of the night by a half caste kid yelling outside the homestead. It was David Lawford, then aged about nine years old.

"Shohn Well, you dere? You come quick. Roland, 'im got.303. He bin reckon he bin goin' shoot eberybody. You come." Taking the kid with me I drove down to the camp. There was a hut down at the camp and when I pulled up Roland's wife, Rosie, and all the family came out, pleased to see me. I got out of the motorcar and went in search of Roland. I found him easily enough, standing in a doorway holding the rifle. I approached him, talking to him as I did so. When I got close I asked him to hand over the gun. He was a bit agitated, but he handed it over without incident. The next morning you wouldn't have known anything was wrong. Life on the station was back to normal.

I celebrated Christmas that year in Fitzroy Crossing, attending a nurse's party at the old hospital, where my mother first came to work in 1939. It was a wild affair, but fun. When Kevin Norton returned from annual leave a few weeks later I went down to Perth for my holidays. I stayed with Mum and Dad at their house in Nedlands. While I was in Perth I tried to see my children, then I went across to Adelaide, before returning to Derby.

Janet was still writing to me. She was talking about coming back to Australia. I didn't think my lifestyle was suitable for her and eventually I put pen to paper and told her not to come.

## Horse-breaking at the Claypan

When I got back from holidays Mervyn got me to do horse-breaking down at the Claypan.

Although the yard was only a couple of kilometres from the homestead, he said we had to camp down there while we did the job and not come home at night. It was the 'wet' season, February 1976. We were well into the age of 'the motorcar on stations' by then. The man was just asserting his authority, but I thought it was a real bastard act.

It's always a bit hard when you first get back from holidays. You look forward to getting out of the city and back north onto stations, but once you get there you wonder why the hell you came home. You're soft and often carrying a bit of extra weight. You're not acclimatised to the heat and humidity and the sweat just pours out of you. Your clothes are ringing wet most of the time, not from the rain, but the perspiration. My clothes would have white salty tidelines on them and I often used to take a spare shirt with me, so I could alternate the sopping wet, for a dry one. By the end of the day they'd both be stiff with salt. I used to drink a lot of Staminade, an electrolyte replacement. You had to in that climate. Chafe was always a problem too, not to mention prickly heat.

The country was lush, billabongs and waterholes full, green grass everywhere. Humid and hot as hell. And always the mosquitos. The mozzies at the Claypan that year were absolutely horrific. Thick, day and night. If you went for a squat in the bush, the mozzies would be biting you on your bum, ball bag, and any other soft exposed skin they could get to, so you got to dread going to the toilet. The toilet in the bush that is. No 'long drop', Eco toilet or Port-a-Loo for us. It was take a shovel and squat where you choose, but be quick about it or the mosquitos will feast on your privates. It was bloody terrible. Flies up your nose and in the corner of your eyes, mosquitos biting your arse.

At night, because it was still very hot, you couldn't get under blankets to get away from the insects and you couldn't buy a mozzie net in Derby at the time. They were all sold out I suppose. I got hold of some sheets, to try and get some relief, but they just bit through them. After that I rubbed kero on myself and on the sheets. When that didn't work I resorted to diesel and even petrol. It was really terrible down there that year, for both man and horses, and it made the job of breaking in far more of an ordeal than it need have been. Even though the insects were enough to send you mad, there was no going back up to the homestead for some relief and a good nights sleep. That's what you got when the wrong bloke had authority. It was a real 'rat act', so I was surprised when, years later, the same fella said Dave Ledger and I were the two best horse breakers he'd seen.

I was given ten colts to break and was getting towards the end of the job when one day Mervyn drove down to see me.

"I've got a phone message for you. It's from Janet. She's come back from pommie land and she's in Derby. She wants to see you." This news shook a few rivets with me. I didn't know what to think, whether to feel pleased or not. I kept on with the job at hand, one that required my full concentration.

It was well after dark when I drove the thirty miles into town. I hadn't had a shower, shave nor changed my clothes. I'd been living rough and I guess I looked like it. When I walked into the bar at the Boab Janet was there waiting. I knew then that I was pleased. We spent the evening together talking and somewhere close to midnight I drove back to Meda and down to the Claypan, ready to continue horse breaking the next day.

Amongst the last of the colts I broke in that year there was one called Desmond. The first day I rode him out of the yard one of the men galloped up behind me, frightening the horse. Desmond bucked and fell with me, but he wasn't a bad horse. He was later chosen by one of Mervyn's most experienced men, Frank Skeen. A few days later I was told to go with Skeen, a young jackeroo and three kids out to Daley's bore to muster. Simon, the jackeroo, and the kids took the horses out ahead of us. Next morning Skeen went to get Desmond, but he couldn't catch him, so I caught the colt for him. Then he couldn't saddle him, so I did that too. Then Desmond wouldn't let him get on, so I took him and galloped him down the flat and back. Still this horse wouldn't let Skeen get on. By this time we'd wasted a lot of time on this colt, so I ended up taking him instead.

We had a lot of trouble getting the cattle that day. There was basically only Skeen and myself with any experience, and I was on a green colt doing his first muster. Eventually we managed to get the cattle together. We took them to a corner of the paddock closest to the direction we had to go in. We opened the fence at a strainer post and headed off towards Number Four Bore. We were on blacksoil country and it was hard going. Desmond had already had enough. Just before we reached Number Four we met Merv, who had driven out with our lunch. I left three blokes minding the cattle. I rode in and got a billy-can of water to pour over Desmond. He was exhausted, standing with his head almost touching the ground. I said to Mervyn.

"This horse needs a couple of weeks spell. He's knocked up. He might even be dead by morning. He's done a damned good job for a colt on his first muster."

After lunch the manager told us to take the cattle, put them through a gate into Claypan Paddock and leave them there. With our fresh horses we did as he said, but it was a big mistake. We should have taken the cattle on another mile or two, to where there was water, given them a drink and then let them go. I knew what we were doing that afternoon was the wrong thing. That the next day, when we went to yard them up, they would give us trouble, because by then they'd be pressing for water. We left our horses in Claypan Paddock overnight and went back to the homestead.

Everyone was heading into Derby that evening. I didn't want to go, but Merv said I should, it was a Saturday night. So, somewhat reluctantly, I went to town also, staying there overnight.

The next morning I got a lift back out to Meda and went down to the Claypan. The others were already saddled up and leaving. I saddled my horse, Penny, and rode out to catch up with the other riders. We mustered up the cattle and took them into a corner. When I saw that they were planning to take them up a fence close to a big billabong I rode up to Skeen.

"We can't do it like this." I told him. "They'll all force onto water and we won't be able to hold them. We need to take them back a bit, well away from that billabong, to the other side fence."

"You're not the boss here anymore. I am." Skeen replied. I thought 'Righto. I've just been told.' So we did it his way.

What I predicted would happen, did happen. The cattle all forced onto water. There were cattle going hell, west and crooked and Skeen gave up. I didn't do too much galloping. I couldn't see the sense in knocking Penny up, when the situation was clearly hopeless. When Frank Skeen gave up he didn't say anything to me. He just got the other three blokes and rode off. I waited for a while, but they didn't return, so I left also. We rode back towards the station, me a bit behind the others. Presently a vehicle drove towards us. It was Mervyn. He stopped and talked to Skeen, then he drove on to me.

"You're finished." He told me. "When you get home come up to the house and grab your cheque."

"That's good. 'Cos I was going to pull the pin anyway." I replied, which was foolish because that retort proved costly. When I picked up my pay the manager had docked me one weeks wages 'In Lieu of Notice'. It was the second and last time I've been fired in my life.

# I gather up my horses

I spent the night in Derby with my parents and the following morning Dad drove me back out to Meda. I caught my mare, Penny, who I'd left in the station paddock the previous day, and mustered the aerodrome paddock. I got some of my horses together and took them down to Claypan Paddock, where I left them. Penny and I then mustered the next paddock, pushing my remaining horses up to join the others. I had a mob of sixteen or eighteen horses altogether, several of them unbroken. Once they were all settled I rode over to the Claypan Yard to see Mervyn. It was now mid afternoon.

"I've got my horses together. Do you want to come over and look at them before I go?" I asked, "No. You can wait till we've finished these cattle, then you can run them through the yard for me." Time was getting on. I wanted to get going, but 'No'. I waited for them to finish with the cattle. There was no 'hurry up'. They took their own good time. Eventually I was able to run my horses through the yard, one at a time, for Mervyn to check. By now it was close on dark.

"Now get going" he told me when we'd finished running them through. Dad had arrived by this time, to run me back to town for the night. I walked over to see him.

"I've been told to 'get going' now with these horses." I explained "So I'll see you sometime tomorrow."

In the gloaming, still riding Penny, I set off to walk my horses to Derby. With unbroken horses amongst the mob, on my own, in the dark, I couldn't control the lead, but I held them together as best I could and headed down to Number One. From there I took them on to Butler's Lake and put them in the bullock yard for the rest of the night. I unsaddled Penny, who'd done a very good day's work for me, and with a saddle and saddle cloth for my bed, I lay down and went to sleep.

I woke early and waited for daylight. When it was light enough to see I checked the horses. I had lost six or seven unbroken horses the previous evening, but there was nothing I could do about it. I caught my mule, Cheeky, which took a bit of doing in the big yard, but eventually he stood up for me. I saddled him up and let the mob out of the yard, then let them feed for awhile. I watered them at Butlers Lake, then we retraced our steps of the previous night, until we reached the old Derby road. Once on the old track, away we went through the pindan, eventually coming out onto the marsh. From there I took the mob across to Yabbergoody windmill, then through to Myall's Bore. I still had all the horses I'd left Butler's Lake with that morning.

When I got to Myall's Bore Dad rocked up. It was about one o'clock in the afternoon by then and he was absolutely livid. I've never seen him so 'on my side', but Jeez he was savage on Mervyn.

That evening Frank Skeen rang me at Mum and Dad's house. He told me that my unbroken horses had turned up back at the Claypan and that he'd locked them in the yard for me. I told him I'd get a truck in the morning and come out and pick them up. I arranged with the local butcher to borrow his truck next day and I drove out to Meda. When I got there, there were no horses, and I never saw any of them ever again.

# CHAPTER THIRTEEN

# FRAZIER DOWNS

*Beneath a clear and cloudless sky,*
*I picture you in years gone by;*
*Your owners proud and working hard,*
*The new house built and lovely yard;*
*With sweat and toil a perfect run,*
*Fences fixed and shearing done,*
*Sheep in order, waters good,*
*Station management understood.*

Soon after I left Meda, I got a job breaking in horses at Blina, for a bloke called Dick Smith, who was the manager then. I'd been on Blina about a week when, late one afternoon, a plane came in and landed. It was John Henwood, from Fossil Downs and he wanted to know if I'd go down with him next day to Frazier Downs. The manager at Frazier had shot through, taking with him the station vehicle, fuel, saddles and the station cheque book, as well as cutting the telephone wires for good measure. They badly needed someone to look after the place, until a replacement manager could be found. My back was giving me a fair bit of gyp at the time, horse breaking wasn't making it any better, so Dick agreed to let me go. The following afternoon John Henwood flew back to Blina to pick me up and we went on down to Frazier.

The property, situated on the coast about eight miles south of La Grange Mission, or Bidyadanga, as it is now known, was owned by Annette Henwood's sister, Merrillee, and her husband Rodney Wells. No relation of mine. It used to be a sheep station, and a good one under it's previous owner Charlie De Marchi, but was changing over to cattle under it's present owners.

When we got down to Frazier we went for a fly around the property before landing. It was smaller than other places I'd been on, which were all a million acres. Being coastal it was flat, largely plain country, running up into pindan and wattle scrub, on the inland side. Skirted with sandhills on it's western edge it was bounded by the Indian Ocean. From the air I could see pockets of dense paperbark trees growing in low lying areas, where I soon discovered cattle liked to hide. We flew over several bores, doing a cursory check on each, and found one, obviously broken down, with thirsty stock hanging about the trough. We returned to the station shortly before sundown, landing close to the house. That first night we cooked ourselves a feed in the big old style homestead and next morning went out to fix the broken down bore. The next day, a Monday, John flew down to Port Hedland, whilst I fixed a hole in the tank, then checked some fences. They weren't very good. John returned from Hedland on Tuesday, bringing a few stores back with him. He left some with me then took off and flew back to Fossil Downs. I was on my own.

Frazier was a really nice place and unlike any I'd been on before. The homestead was a show place, large and solid with wide verandahs and heavy shutters that could be closed against the elements during the cyclone season. It had a formal dining room, lounge and office and several bedrooms. The grounds were extensive and had clearly been magnificent in their day, with palms and mature tropical shrubbery. A huge mango tree shaded the house and a large, mature cashew overhung the store and shower room. White shell paths meandered through the grounds and there was a crescent of lawn skirted with palm trees at the front of the house. Now sadly neglected, this had clearly been an imposing entrance in the past. The upkeep of such a substantial garden must have required the help of several willing gins to rake and water daily, but it was evident those times had long gone.

There were several outbuildings, a workshop, some stables, the engine shed, where there was a 32 volt battery generator, and several smaller sheds. The black's camp was situated beyond the homestead and consisted of several small huts and not a lot else. At the main house there was an outdoor 'dunny' under a large white gum tree. A shower room across the lawn adjacent to the store, was built of corrugated iron with a cement floor. A short distance away through a grove of tall coconut palms was an extensive laundry, with large cement wash troughs and an old Simpson washing machine complete with ringer. There was a bough shed beneath the mango tree at the opposite end of the house, where outside stairs led up to a square timber construction which I discovered to be another bedroom. This was known as 'the bird's nest', with shutters all round it was cool and breezy in hot weather. It was an impressive place.

A day or two after being deposited at Frazier I drove over to La Grange. I saw Father McKelson, who I'd met previously, whilst on a horse buying visit from Myroodah and he arranged for a couple of La Grange boys to come to Frazier to give me a hand. We were having trouble with the lighting plant and the homestead bore. By the following day we had no water at the homestead. I went to the mission again, seeking help.

On Thursday morning I drove to Broome, in the most roadworthy vehicle available, which wasn't saying much, taking the generator with me. Whilst in Broome I picked up an old fellow, Herbert Wilkinson, who I found in the Roebuck Hotel. I didn't know him and he was a bit of a dero' but I thought he could do odd jobs about the place, in exchange for his keep. There didn't seem to be any money to pay wages. The natives were paid through the mission, so I had no authority over them at all. They came to work when they felt like it and went home when they wanted. It wasn't a very good situation. Rodney Wells said he'd reimburse La Grange, which I presume he did. Later I discovered Herbie to be a bit of an artist. He didn't cause me any trouble and it was good to have another white man on the place to give me a hand.

I decided one of the first things to do was find out where all the bores were and begin to learn my way around the joint. Although I had a map, of sorts, with me, it wasn't easy. I'd go out and get onto a track, then follow it. I'd come to a bore, refer to the map and think 'Righto, this must be such and such a bore.' There was no road into the bore, or out, because the stock had obliterated all signs of a track. I had to go in a great big circle, out from the bore, until I could pick up a road. I'd follow that, thinking 'well the next bore along here must be such and such a bore.' I'd continue along that road, check the next bore and by the time I got home I didn't really know where I'd been. I only thought I did. It wasn't until later on that I discovered there were about four different tracks going into each bore, so it took me a while to work out exactly which bore was which. After I'd been on Frazier a couple of weeks Errol De Marchi came out and spent a weekend with me. Errol and his father, had once owned Frazier, and he helped show me around, told me a lot of useful things and made it all much easier for me.

## The tractor needs fixing

Like everything else on the joint, the tractor didn't work. I couldn't get it to start and I needed it to pump the water for the station homestead. I had been on Frazier a week and the telephone line had been fixed by then. I'd heard that Bill Wootton, a reasonable bush mechanic who I'd known since my teens, was working on the neighbouring station. I rang Nita Downs and asked the owners if I could borrow him to come over and help me get the tractor going. Jack Elezovitch agreed.

The next morning a Nita vehicle pulled up beneath the poinciana tree outside the workshop, but it wasn't Bill Wootton who got out. Instead a wiry looking man, several decades younger than Wootton, dressed in riding boots and stockman's hat, walked across to greet me.

"How're ya going?" I asked, somewhat surprised to see the stranger.

"I'm-m go'in goo-od." He drawled. "I've come t'er fix y'er tra-actor." I heckled up immediately. I know I've got a drawl and I don't mind my friends slinging off at me. When a stranger mimics me I see red.

"Where's Wootton?" I asked.

"Out rou-ound the mi-lls. Ja-ack se-ent me o-ver inste-ad." His drawl was so exaggerated I felt I wanted to flatten him there and then, but I thought better of it. I badly needed the tractor fixed. With difficulty I curbed my annoyance.

"Well, I'm John Wells" I said, offering him my hand.

"Har-rry Ba-anks" He responded, shaking it firmly. Formalities out of the way I chucked my cigarette butt away savagely, ground it into the sand and led the way towards the useless tractor. As the stranger looked into the unfathomable depths of it's dilapidated engine I rolled another smoke. My hands were shaking, my blood was fairly up. I kept telling myself to keep my cool. 'I'm not going to let this bastard get the better of me.' I thought. 'There'll be opportunity enough to tell him what I think of him, once the tractor is fixed.'

All morning the stranger worked on the tractor. Bent over the engine, his slender hips and skinny bowed legs looked somewhat peculiar, as if he should be astride a horse rather than standing on his own two feet. Occasionally he asked me to pass him a tool, always emphasising the slur he'd detected in my speech. Or he would pass some remark or other about what the fault might be, but he never let up on the mimicry. 'You'll keep, you bastard' I kept thinking. Finally he got the heap of shit going. He rubbed his grimy hands on a rag, "The-ere. Tha-at shoo-uld do-o ya. I'd kee-ep it running fe-rr a bit tho-ough."

I thanked him, telling him I'd drop off some mutton at Nita one day, in exchange for the favour. He didn't look pleased. Instead he turned on his Cuban heel, strode over to his vehicle and drove off without a glance in my direction. 'Strange bastard.' I thought, not for the first time.

Later that day I went over to the mission to pick up the native boys, but they wouldn't come back to work. While I was there I asked the lay missionaries what they knew about Harry Banks. I told them what I thought of him mimicking me. They started laughing.

"Harry wasn't mimicking you. He's got a drawl, worse than yours." They told me.

"He used to be a top rodeo rider in his day. Harry is all right, don't you worry about that."

Later, when I had the opportunity to go over to Nita Downs the owners told me the other side of the story. Apparently when Harry got back there that day he was wild.

"For Chris-sake do-on't send me ov-er th-ere ag-ain. Tha-at ba-astard wouldn't sto-op mimicking my dra-awl. Ke-ept it u-up a-all morn-ning. I fe-elt like te-elling him he co-ould ke-ep his blo-oody tra-actor."

## Ossie Shelton and a.22

The following Saturday, I left Frazier early in the morning to drive into Broome. The town was a good hundred and twenty miles away, badly corrugated gravel road most of the way in. I'd had to get a police permit to drive the unregistered vehicle into town, but it was all I had, since the previous bloke had stolen the best of the vehicles when he shot through. It was barely light as I drove out along the eight mile sand track, that would take me onto the highway, when I was surprised to come across a bloke parked through a gateway. I pulled up and knocked on the door of his van. I could hear someone getting up.

"Who is it?" The fellow called out.

"It's John Wells." At that point I didn't know who the bloke was, but when he came outside I had a .22 rifle pointed at me. That gave me a bit of a shock.

"What do you want?" he asked.

"I was wondering who you were and what you were doing camped here." He wasn't too pleased about answering my questions, so I added, "Why I'm asking is, I've come to look after Frazier Downs until they get a new manager. The previous bloke shot through and stole a bit of gear. I'm on my way into Broome and I thought I'd just see who you were."

"Ah! Well I'm chasing the bastard too. I sold him my old ambulance. He's got the vehicle, but he's never paid me for it." So I felt quite relieved then. He put the gun down and we had a bit of a chat. The bloke's name was Ossie Shelton and I realised I had seen him before, when he was working at the Fitzroy Crossing Store years earlier. He had been married then, but had since lost his wife. It seemed life had taken a heavy toll on him. Ossie ended up living at Frazier for a while, doing odd jobs around the place, in exchange for his keep. That was the only way it operated, because there was no money for any wages. He was fairly handy and had once minded Nerrima, before he was widowed. Ossie was a bit of a worry for me. There was something strange about him and I always felt wary of him after our early morning meeting.

## Tanks, fences and gates

Once the phone was back on, the owner would ring me. Frazier shared a party line with six or seven other properties, who were all able to listen in if they wanted to. The line was tested every morning and each place had it's own ring. When Rodney rang he was always telling me to make sure the gates were kept closed, between the station homestead and the main road. They were good steel gates, with panels either side and they worked very well. There were two or three gates along the eight mile access track and to start with I did as I was told.

Everything was a bit of a mess on Frazier. Because the station was still set up for sheep, the troughs were broken and delivery pipes walked over by the cattle. The first job we did was fix up a bore, tank and trough. We cemented the inside of the trough, with some bags of cement that were kicking around. We put panels along the delivery pipe to the trough, with rails along that to stop the cattle jumping over the trough. We got the tank full and when we came back to check it, it was all looking good. A fortnight later the whole bloody tank had caved in, so that was a big waste of effort. Another of the tanks, down on the coast at the far end of Frazier had had it's moundring carted away by thousands of hermit crabs and the tank had collapsed.

I started fixing up fences on the plain, that weren't too good. Eventually I got up into the scrub, where I found that the fence hardly existed. I was fixing it up as I went, but it was getting worse the further through I went. After a while I thought 'Bugger this. I think I'd better drive along this fence and see what's up ahead.' So I did. The scrub was higher than the vehicle, so I was basically scrub bashing. Eventually I came to a gate on the access road. One of the gates I had been keeping closed, where I had found Ossie that morning. The fence didn't exist in the direction I'd come, so I drove along on the other side. I found that was the same. No fence. So much for being told to keep all the gates shut, when there was no bloody fence on either side of it.

## Wasted windmills

At Frazier everything seemed to be for show. All neat, clean and tidy at the homestead, but outside on the run it was a joke. Troughs leaking, without protection rails. Heaps of windmills, tanks and troughs, but only a certain number of them working. But Rodney did have a couple of big mills, big tanks and big troughs. One had trough protection, the other one didn't. The property was on the coast. I was frightened of cyclones down there. The country I'd come from didn't seem to have cyclones, but I was well out of my home country now. I thought 'Gee, if a cyclone comes through here you wouldn't be able to do much about these windmills.' These were good windmills, standing up there doing nothing. So I got a couple of blokes and we went around and laid the windmills down, took the heads, wheels and tails off them, numbered each component and put them in an empty aeroplane hanger at the station.

A few years later I called into Frazier Downs and there was no-one there. It was owned by the Bidyadanga community then. I had a look around the place. When I looked at the home bore I noticed, over in the grass, a big mob of boxes and ends of bits of steel. I walked across to have a look and there were a mob of brand new windmills. Three or four of them. Brand spanking new. The white ants had just about eaten the boxes off the gear, which was lying, hidden, in the spinifex. I wondered why they were there, when they'd had all those other spare mills I'd stored away in the hanger? I wasn't too impressed about that and I've often wondered who ended up getting them.

## Tight purse strings

When I got to Frazier the store was pretty well empty, apart from what John Henwood had left me. There was some chewing gum, carb. soda, citric acid, one jar of fish paste and a carton of sand shoes. That was it. Luckily the mission helped us out a lot, because Rodney seemed reluctant to part with any money. Jack Elezovitch, on Nita Downs, was also very good to me, as were Errol and Jenny De Marchi, who were then at the Bali Hai caravan park at Cable Beach in Broome. There are some very kind people in the world, and some bastards as well. Rodney was one of the latter. He would ring up from Perth now and then, or I had to ring him to order stores. I was forever getting letters from him telling me to keep expenses to the barest minimum.

He seemed to really resent my not being mechanically minded, although I'd told John Henwood this from the start. All my life, whenever I'm offered a job, one of the first things I tell my new employer is 'I only got 3% for arithmetic and I'm not mechanically minded' so they know right from the beginning. I don't like bullshit, so I've always been upfront with them and much prefer to downplay my ability than spruik. I find it a lot easier to tell people what I can't do, than what I can. In hindsight this character trait has probably worked against me. Combined with my drawl I reckon some blokes reckon I'm a fully fledged idiot.

I was slowly getting a few things done. I had a mechanic, of sorts, who I'd picked up in Broome. He was decidedly odd and had a plate in his head, but I appreciated his help. Later his elderly lady friend joined him and she did the cooking. She was a good woman, but I think Karl gave her hell at times. I've often wondered what became of Ina in the end.

I had to get aboriginal staff from La Grange and the mission paid them. I didn't think this was right, because then the natives reckoned that the mission was their boss and I was just the bloke who gave the orders, which they didn't like. Later on, when it got close to mustering time, Vincent Bear also came and worked for me, as did Terry Hillman. We had horses to break in and I needed some good, reliable men, but getting Rodney to pay blokes wages was nigh impossible and it was hard to keep anyone for long.

## An Oscar winning performance

When I'd been there a couple of months Janet came down and joined me. She had been working in Derby at the YWCA and once I'd been whisked off Blina down to Frazier we never saw each other. It wasn't what she'd come back from England for. She had only been on Frazier for a day or two when one of the native boys got pelted off a horse. We were riding along with colts when all of a sudden a few horses got a fright. Some started to buck and this fella, Peter, was thrown. He was in a bad way and he reckoned his back was broken.

Janet was at the homestead operating the phone, taking messages and keeping the mission informed of what was going on. We ended up getting the RFDS plane down from Derby. We had to measure the length of the airstrip. It was too short for a plane of that size, and it was all a big worry, but after circling once or twice it landed safely. We had taken the door off a wardrobe to move the patient, so we could keep him rigid. He was putting on a great act about the pain he was in, but eventually he was transferred successfully onto the aircraft. The pilot was worried the airstrip was too short for him to take off with the weight he had on board, so we watched anxiously as he started taking the plane the wrong way down the strip. Revving it up, he brought it back towards where Janet and I were standing, spun it round and really 'gave it' to it. He got off all right, which was a great relief. Once the RFDS plane had gone I went back to where the horses were being held, out on the plain. We rode on and, after the lengthy delay, did the intended muster.

The injured man got to Derby without incident and was admitted to the regional hospital, with suspected spinal injuries. At seven o'clock the same evening he discharged himself and walked out. When Father McKelson rang and told me I thought 'What a mighty man, doing that with a broken back.' I was fairly annoyed about it. It had cost RFDS a lot of money and risk evacuating him, caused us a huge amount of concern, wasted half a day and the bastard had been acting the whole time.

## Sammy Jack and Bali

Another unfortunate incident occurred soon after Janet arrived. I'd been out on the run and when I returned to the homestead for smoko I noticed a couple of natives sitting in the shade at the edge of the garden. The gin was clutching a baby to her chest. Janet came out to meet me, looking worried.

"That woman has a sick baby. She's asking me for Bex, but I don't think I should give it to her. Can you talk to her for me."

"She'll be wanting Vicks, not Bex, Janet. The blacks can't say 'V'." I explained as we walked over to the couple.

"What's going on?" I asked.

"'Dis 'un baby got cold chick, need'um Bix." I looked at the infant. It was sick all right. Very sick.

"Missus here will run you to the mission. This baby prop'ly sick. It needs to be seen by the sister." I told the mother. "You drive them over Janet. I'll send Mischa with you to open the gates. Go now. Use the marsh road and you'd best hurry. I'll ring the mission and let them know you're coming." After I'd seen them away I went in and rang La Grange. After that there was nothing more I could do. I went and asked a couple of the natives when Sammy and Bali had arrived on Frazier. I didn't even know they were on the place until they'd come up into the garden. It turned out they'd been down at Sandfire Roadhouse, drinking, for a couple of days and had driven in to Frazier during the night. Their baby was only three weeks old. It had developed pneumonia and was dead before Janet reached the mission.

It was a crook start for Janet on stations. Brought up in a soft English environment, she'd had no experience of this kind of life before. She found the incident upsetting and felt foolish for having misunderstood the request for Vicks. I'd lived with the blacks all my life. I knew there were some sounds they couldn't make. Just as 'Sit', 'Sam', and 'Sarlie' means 'Shit, 'Jam' and 'Charlie', Bix is Vicks. As Annie, the La Grange mission nurse, told Janet that morning, no amount of Vicks was going to help that baby, so she mustn't blame herself. We were later told the infant was badly dehydrated, as well as having pneumonia and that it would inevitably have died even if it had been presented at the mission hospital early that morning, instead of in the garden at Frazier Downs.

## For sale

Despite the shortfall in my mechanical ability, somewhere along the way it was decided I should be kept on at Frazier indefinitely, as manager.

Life there was not easy and I continued to battle along over the coming weeks, pulling bores, fixing fences, repairing yards and generally getting frustrated with the mess the place was in. I was pleased to have the help of old Bert, Ossie and Karl, who earned their keep giving me a hand. The native boys from the mission continued to please themselves, only coming to work when it suited them and refusing to work on weekends. Rodney wrote regularly stressing the importance of keeping costs to a minimum, so it was nearly impossible to get the gear needed to do improvements. It seemed his main concern was to have the homestead looking flash and bugger the rest of the joint. He wrote a list of his requirements in this regard.

1  Ensure garage, workshop and all buildings kept swept & tidy.
2  Put all tools not in use, & immediately after use, in correct place & cleaned.
3  Before use of any engine or vehicle, check water, oil, fuel.
4  Regularly check air filters for grass seeds.
5  Wipe down & clean engines, including lawn mower, after use.
6  If vehicles get muddy, wash off, including underneath.
7  Wash all vehicles weekly, including interior and engines.
8  If horses in use, keep saddle blankets washed & soft.
9  Access to saddle room not permitted to natives & should be kept locked.
10  Ensure saddles are well cared for, when in camp or vehicles ensure counter-lining won't tear or chafe.
11  If natives in camp ensure camp & buildings kept tidy & rubbish bins used. Empty bins weekly & burn paper.
12  Keep chook yard clean & change water daily.
13  All fridges to be de-frosted and cleaned out regularly.
14  Keep garden tidy & trim. Ensure plants & lawns get sufficient water.
15  Keep diary written up each day & record any rainfall.
16  Check lighting plant batteries regularly, topped up & clean.
17  No burning off before Dec. Natives not to light fires at any time, under any circumstances.

... and so on. Never mind that the home bore was frequently out of use, so washing vehicles, changing chook waters and keeping lawns and gardens green were impossible to do. But these were Rodney's priorities, whilst mine was keeping the stock alive and watered.

## Dreams of a dude ranch

After I had been on the coastal property for a while, my mother rang up one evening.

"Did you know Frazier Downs is on the market?" she asked. "It was on TV tonight and there were some very nice pictures of it." This was news to me. Not long after Mum's phone call I had a visit from a couple of doctors and a dentist from Derby. They were interested in buying Frazier and setting it up as a bit of a tourist resort, for fishing. Frazier was right on the coast and it had a famous fishing spot, Whistle Creek, where people from all over Australia would come when the salmon were running.

The medicos discussed their proposal with me and asked if I would be interested in joining them in the venture. They reckoned it would cost about $150,000 to buy. We could convert the shearing shed into a bar and games room and do up the shearer's quarters. We might build a bit of a caravan park down the beach, that could be abandoned through the monsoon season. Buy a bus and in the mustering season charge people to watch and see what mustering and branding was all about. It sounded like a good idea. Tourism was still an untapped industry, north of the twenty-sixth parallel, at that time, but I had to tell them I didn't have two bob to rub together. I didn't either, because what little I once had was now spent, on child maintenance and living costs not covered by Rodney. They said they'd see what they could do and even if I didn't have a financial interest would I run it for them? They'd still take me in as a partner. We thought we could all do very well out of it, if they could pull it off. They tried their best to raise the money. $165,000 all up, but even being doctors and dentists they couldn't, so we missed out on a good opportunity.

After the place was put on the market Rodney would come up from Perth, bringing prospective buyers with him. Before he came he'd tell us to make sure the gardens were raked and well watered, the house all in good order. Janet would do all that and she'd get all the guest rooms ready. Then when Rodney arrived, usually by plane, he'd start slinging orders around, deciding who would sleep where, what we would have for dinner and all this sort of thing. Janet was a good worker, but she wasn't on the books. It was all a love job. She would make sure she cooked a good feed for everyone, get vegetables from La Grange if they had any, or go into Broome and buy something, if we knew in advance they were coming. Our money of course, whilst Rodney couldn't even bring us a bloody cabbage or newspaper.

The difference between how I was treated by Rodney, on the one hand, and Merrilee on the other, was extraordinary. Where Rodney would ring, or write and chastise me for running up some expense he thought unnecessary, (he thought all expenses were unnecessary on Frazier) his wife, Merrilee, seemed grateful for what I was trying to do.

*... 'Gosh it's good to know that you are at Frazier, though I do feel for you with all the problems you have to face, with water and staffwise. I wish I could be of assistance to you, but with two small children I feel you would wish me away.'*

She wrote at length telling me about all the horses on the place, directing me to a well kept horse-book which was very helpful when we got them in, concluding with,

*... 'John, thank you for all you are doing at Frazier. I am desperately sorry that it's so tough. Just as well it's a man of your calibre trying to cope with all it's many problems. We can not do anything to assist really, for it's essential Rodney keeps making some money down here to keep the place going a little longer.*
*All the best John, hold on, please, if you can. God knows where we would be if you were not on Frazier. I worry so about it all there. You are not 'out of sight out of mind', but constantly in my thoughts and prayers. You have the advantage of being born in the country and people like you are hard to come by and don't give up easily. Fighters to the end. Above all you are honest and God haven't we learnt the value of that. Good luck and God bless.*

## Sold, or perhaps not

The station was sold in August 1976, to an English jeweller from Exeter in Janet's home county, Devon. Her brother had audited their books years earlier. She recognized the name instantly and could hardly believe such a person would wish to buy a place such as Frazier. What would they do with it? It transpired it was to be a wedding present for his daughter and future son-in-law.

As it happened the sale never eventuated, and for the next couple of months we were left in limbo, although the young couple did come to look over the station. She was a keen, blonde English girl, her fiance a young Dutchman who displayed the well known character trait of his nation. The new purchasers, having paid the deposit, were then unable to come up with the remaining funds required to complete the deal. In view of this they didn't consider themselves the owners. The vendors, on the other hand, decided Frazier was sold. Neither party wanted to know about running costs. My wages stopped coming.

Fortunately there were still plenty of sheep there, so we never ran short of meat. When the salmon were running we had fish as well. We had a roof over our heads and a huge lemon tree. Sometimes we would go over to La Grange, if we had to buy stuff from their store. I think Father McKelson felt sorry for us, because he always gave us a paper bag full of monkey nuts and a tin of crushed pineapple. We found this combination of gifts amusing, but well meant.

For a while I kept things going on Frazier out of my own pocket, still believing my pay would arrive from someone, but it didn't. When my personal funds dried up I began to get sour. I tried ringing the jeweller, day after day, without success. I rang Rodney and told him how I felt. Very clearly. I told him I was resigning and he could tell whoever it was that employed me. After that I received a long letter from him, informing me that a postage stamp cost eighteen cents, a phone call a lot more. I was to write in future. He refused to pass on my resignation.

Many times during that period Janet and I considered walking off the station, but one thing held me back. What would become of the stock. The horses, the sheep and the cattle. The watering points were unreliable. Several times Janet had helped me pull a bore on the weekend, when no-one else was there. Sometimes, if there was a wind drought, water would have to be pumped. There was no way I could just leave. Although I now felt some sympathy for my predecessor who had floated, taking what he wanted with him, it was not possible for me to leave the stock to simply perish. They were the innocent victims in this mess and without me to keep things running they would surely have a slow and wretched end. I simply couldn't do it, however sensible it seemed.

We hung in there and finally, in November 1976, after a meeting with The Aboriginal Land Funds Commission we came out of the tunnel. The property was purchased for the La Grange aboriginal community and Quimbeena Pastoral Company was formed. As part of the agreement, prior to completion, I was asked to guarantee my services for a minimum of twelve months, as both manager and adviser. I had great respect for the two senior elders at La Grange, John Dodo and Jack Mulardy and after a comprehensive agreement was drawn up I agreed.

Eventually, during the course of settlement, I was reimbursed for most of my out of pocket expenses, and the wages owing to me were paid in full. However, I had to fight long and hard for the wages of Donny Patrick, an employee whom Rodney had met, but who he insisted was a 'phantom rider' on the books. This annoyed me to such a degree I've never been able to shake off the low opinion I have of the man. He questioned my honesty and integrity, when I'd done my damnedest to do the right thing for his stock and station under pretty difficult circumstances.

## Jim Gunn

The Fitzroy Races and Rodeo were coming up and I wanted to go. So too did Donny Patrick, one of our workers, who was keen to ride in the rodeo. It was too rough a show to take Janet to, so we arranged for her to stay with friends, Peg and Brian Williamson, in Derby. Janet had worked with Peggy in the office at the Boab Inn when she first came up to the Kimberley, so I knew she would be all right with them while I was away.

Having dropped Janet off, Donny and I drove on out to Fitzroy Crossing arriving late on a Thursday afternoon. I had a few beers at The Crossing Inn during the evening and caught up with a lot of people I knew, before rolling my swag out down by the creek. Over the next couple of days the gymkhana, rodeo and races were on. It was a good weekend. There was a bar at the rodeo grounds and lots of blokes were having a good time and a fair bit of alcohol was consumed. At the end of proceedings on the Saturday night the bar was closed down and people drifted back to camp. None of us felt very well next day. That Sunday morning a bloke said to his little boy, "You'd better go over and wake that fella up. He's sleeping out in the full sun." The boy went over as he was told, but soon came back.

"Dad, that man has got ants coming out of his mouth and I can't wake him." They went over to the man. He was dead. There had been a fight the previous evening, some time after I'd turned in. Later during the night, or very early next morning, someone had loaded their horses and left, unaware that they'd run over an injured man. It was a sombre start to the day.

Everyone gathered at the Crossing Inn that Sunday morning, where barbeques were set up at the back of the pub. After breakfast people started drinking again. A lot of people congregated there and some of the 'schools' were a carton a 'shout'. More beer was bought during the Sunday morning session and once the bar closed we decided we'd go down to the river, taking a few cartons with us. I got a lift in Sean Murphy's vehicle, a short sighted helicopter pilot from Halls Creek. A small pommy bloke, Jim Gunn, came with us and a few others blokes. A fair few people ended up down at the river that afternoon, skinny dipping and having a good time. When we'd been there for an hour or two I noticed Jim Gunn sitting on a log in the water. I'd been having a swim and had just got out when I heard someone saying, "That bloke has fallen in the river." I looked across at the log and Gunny had gone. I waited for a bit, but no-one came up.

"That bloke hasn't surfaced yet." I said. "I'd better go in and see if he's OK." No-one seemed to take much notice, so I jumped in and dived down for a look near where he had disappeared. I was just about to come up for more wind when I saw a pale shape on the bottom. I swam underwater to where he was and picked him up. He was very heavy. Somehow I got him to the surface, but I was really knocked up and short of breath. I yelled out for someone to grab his arm and pull him up the bank. No-one moved at first, but then somebody did grab hold of him and they hauled him up out of the water. I had a bit of trouble getting out. The riverbank was steep and slippery. When I'd managed to clamber out I saw that Gunny was just left lying there on his stomach. Someone had spread a towel out but no-one was doing anything for him. He looked blue and lifeless. I knew I had to get some air into him. I gave him a good thumping on his back, then rolled him over and blew into his mouth. I blew again and again, so hard it's a wonder the air didn't come out of an orifice at the other end. I don't know how many times I blew. Eventually someone tapped me on the shoulder, "Do you know what you're doing?" a girl asked.

"No. Not really." I moved aside and she took over. After a moment or two the drowned man gave a couple of feeble coughs. In the meantime someone had run to the nearby police station to call for an ambulance. The girl looked after Gunny and presently the ambulance arrived and took him away. He was alive, but the incident killed the party and things went very quiet after that for a long time.

Later we all went back for the afternoon session at the pub and later still adjourned to Dave Gray's house for a barbeque. During the evening we went up to the hospital to visit Gunny, to see how he was going. As the nurse escorted us in she said, "It's lucky he didn't die, or he'd have been put on the hotplate. The cold slab is already taken." She was referring to the poor fellow who'd been run over earlier. Gunny didn't look too good.

"My chest is bloody sore." He told us. "I don't know why, but I feel like my ribs are broken." I had a fair idea why, but I didn't say so.

"I don't know what the hell you pulled me up for Wellsy. You should've let me go. I wouldn't have known a thing. Nothing hurt, I'd just have been gone. Next time will prob'ly be a lot harder, and I'll blame you." That's gratitude for you, I thought, but he was probably right.

By Monday morning the party was well and truly over and no-one was feeling too good. Big Judy, the cook from Fossil Downs, came to me and asked if I'd run her back to the station.

"Felicity and I were supposed to be home last night." she explained. "Would you be able to run us out to Fossil now?" I agreed to and when we got there Annette Henwood was already in the station kitchen getting things sorted out. Big Judy went in straightaway to help. The women offered me a feed, but I didn't accept. Instead I had a cup of tea, then left.

Back in Fitzroy Crossing Dusty Miller was looking for a lift to Derby. We took half a dozen beers with us which we shared on the three hour drive. It had been a heavy weekend and we needed a heart starter. It was mid afternoon by the time I pulled up at Peg and Brian Williamson's house. I don't think Janet was too impressed. I was definitely looking the worse for wear and feeling it. I rolled my swag out on the back lawn and turned in early. I had a bad night. I was in the 'horrors' and could hear people 'talking to me' all night long. Next morning we gathered up our things, picked up Donny Patrick, and drove down to Broome. I was feeling pretty rough and we decided to stop off at Bali Hai caravan park, to see our friends Jenny and Errol DeMarchi. They loaned us a caravan where we had a couple of hours siesta, until the heat went out of the afternoon, before continuing on down the coast back to Frazier.

## Quimbeena Pastoral Company

Although our financial situation eased, now that the natives owned Frazier Downs times got really difficult. They employed me to be their boss, which didn't work too well. The blacks were still supposed to be at Frazier on Sunday night, ready for work next day, but usually they'd get there around dinner time on Monday. Then they'd pack up on Friday morning and head home to La Grange for the weekend. Because they owned the property they had to check their bores and fix their fences, but we would go around and check up on them afterwards. Nothing would have been done, although we'd see where they'd been digging for bandicoots. If a bore broke down on a Thursday or Friday they'd buggerize around that much it wouldn't get fixed. Then they'd pack up and knock off for the weekend. It didn't matter to them that there was no water for the stock. They'd just get in their vehicle and off they'd go, home to La Grange. Janet and I would then go and fix windmills, or pull a bore and get them going again. Because Frazier had been a sheep joint they were mostly only little tanks and small troughs, which wasn't a great help either, there not being much water storage. At other times the blacks might come back on the weekend and want fuel, oil or the station motor car, because we didn't own it, they now owned it. They would come into the garden and be very stroppy, half full of piss, demanding this and that. It got harder and harder all the time. Fortunately we did have a couple of very good aborigines there. Woopi and his wife Bertha. If I was away mustering they'd say to Janet.

"We'll stop 'ere longa station, an' bin look after you." They were really good and they didn't get on the grog like a lot of them. Really, without Woopi and Bertha it would have been an impossible situation for us.

## May school holidays

Working for Quimbeena Pastoral Company meant I got paid properly and regularly. Janet was also paid, forty dollars a week, to do the books. Because of the situation we were in, where everything was owned by the natives, Janet decided to buy herself a Hilux. She had always kept a nest egg in case there was ever an urgent need to go home to family, but she now decided it should be put to some use. She needed a sense of security and some independence, so she could go to Broome or Derby if required. My back had gone bad on me during October, about a month before the Department for Aboriginal Affairs bought Frazier and I had been admitted to Derby Regional Hospital for three or four days. It made sense that we had a vehicle of our own in case such a need arose again.

## A trip to Perth

I had been divorced for quite some time. It was May school holidays and I decided to try for access to my two children, who I hadn't seen for a long while. Janet and I, together with Brian McGaffin, a friend from Derby, drove down the inland road to Perth. On the way we pulled into Marble Bar late one afternoon, where we needed to get a tyre fixed. A ute drove down the street with much hooting and shouting from the occupants. It was my old school friend from Scotch, the geologist Graeme Hutton. While our wheel was being mended we agreed to meet him in the Iron Clad Hotel, where we ended up staying for several hours, before continuing the journey. Janet drove and though it was a bit of a squeeze, with three of us in the front of the Hilux, we were able to swap drivers frequently and made good time, getting down to the city in a bit over two days, instead of the usual three.

Once in Perth I had to attend the Family Court to make my case for access to my young son, Benn, and daughter, Leah. It was a difficult, frustrating experience which I have no desire to recall, but I eventually managed to gain permission to take the children up to the station for a holiday. The court ruled that I was to fly up, as the road journey was deemed too long for them. I was also told I must have a suitable female on hand to meet them at the other end and help with their care. This meant Janet had to drive back north immediately, in order to be there by the time the children and I arrived on the plane. It was a journey of over two thousand, two hundred kilometres. Being from England she had never driven a fraction of the distance, on her own, before. There were few roadhouses and it would be necessary to carry a forty four gallon drum of fuel with her. Because it was school holidays the fourteen year old brother of one of Janet's friends was able to go with her, to help her with the fuel and any punctures, or other problems she may have. Meanwhile I remained in Perth for two more days, until it was time to catch our flight to Broome.

When I got to Perth airport, early that May morning neither of my children, for various reasons, were able to come with me. I flew to Broome alone, carrying two obsolete airline tickets with me. Janet met me, fairly exhausted from her long drive. She had reached Frazier at nine o'clock the previous evening, then left again at daylight to drive on to Broome in order to be there when the plane landed. When I disembarked without either of the children I think she must have felt as shat off as I was. It had been an expensive exercise for us, to no good end.

## Lady luck

A month or two later we were invited to go in for the Broome Races, staying with Dave and Margaret Ledger and their two children. Janet and Margaret had become friends and it seemed like a good idea to get off Frazier Downs for a few days.

On the eve of the Broome Cup a calcutta was held at the Continental Hotel. Dave and I had gone to the hotel early, where I bought about ten calcutta tickets at a dollar each. As there were only four horses in the feature race there was next to no chance of our drawing one. The Lugger Bar was packed with locals and it was a good evening. When Margaret and Janet arrived later I gave Janet the calcutta tickets to look after. They went outside into the beer garden to find a table. Dave and I stayed inside. The draw started without us, but it didn't matter. Janet checked the ticket numbers and couldn't believe her eyes. Out of four horses we had managed to draw the favourite. A grey, called Bold Halo, brought up from Perth. The girls were sharing a table with Rod and Edna Quilty. Janet asked both Margaret and Edna to check the number. She simply couldn't believe our luck. She came into the Lugger Bar to tell me what had happened and before the auction began I moved outside to watch.

We had no money to speak of, so bidding for the horse ourselves was out of the question, but because we held the ticket, we stood to gain half of whatever price it sold for. Bold Halo was the last horse to be auctioned, the first three going for not much at all. The dearest of them only went for a hundred and fifty dollars. To our surprise the first bid for Bold Halo was five hundred dollars, rising rapidly to nine hundred and fifty. Then bidding stalled for a bit, before picking up again in a final flourish, the hammer coming down at one thousand three hundred dollars. Janet and I had just made a whopping six hundred and fifty dollars from a ten dollar outlay.

It could not have come at a better time. Janet collected our winnings, paid in cash, all twenty dollar notes. She put them under her pillow and slept on them that night. It was a thrilling stroke of luck neither of us has ever forgotten.

## I go mustering at La Grange

Father McKelson had left La Grange and a much younger priest had taken his place. Father Chris became a very good friend to us. One way and another La Grange did a lot of work for Frazier and Father Chris, Brother Richard and the lay missionaries were always friendly and helpful. Really we were fortunate to have the mission as our nearest neighbour. It was 1977 and La Grange didn't have anybody to run their stockcamp that season. As they were in a bit of a corner I agreed to help out.

"You've always been good to us and looked after things for me at Frazier. Done welding and all that, so I'll come over and muster your cattle for you." I told them, adding, "But I really need another white man in the camp with me. I'm not too keen on working with 'stranger black fellas' on my own." Father Chris agreed. As we had finished mustering on Frazier by then, we took over most of the stockboys and some of our horses, including my personal horses. There would be La Grange stockboys in the camp as well. The rest of the blacks were to stay at Frazier while I was away, to keep an eye on the bores. I didn't have a lot of faith in them, so before I left I said to Janet, "After they've been round the bores, make sure you go round that afternoon, or the next day, just to check that everything is all right. Do a little bit this day and a little bit another day. I want you to do this because the black fellas will go round and they'll pull up at the trough. If the trough has water in it, to them that means 'everything's good'. They won't stop to have a look in the tank. It might only have six inches of water left in it, which shows something is wrong. That's why I want you to go round after them, just to double check everything." I'd seen it too many times with these fella's doing the rounds of the mills. You didn't know whether the tank was, full, empty or 'little bit close-up full-up'. Or if the plug was even in the trough. Sometimes if things weren't very good, or there wasn't much wind, the cattle would all be camped around the bore. As soon as the windmill started turning all the cattle got up to go to the trough. But the delivery wasn't that quick, so there was a risk of the trough getting damaged. But these blokes didn't seem to really care. Away they'd go chasing goannas and these bloody bandicoots. They were great on killing jabadas and blue tongue lizards too. They'd chuck them on a little bit of grass, set it alight, roll them over a couple of times and eat them. A lot of them were pretty much still tribal.

The blacks and fires were a bit of a worry on Frazier also. One time, early in the morning, there was a big smoke and I thought 'That's on Frazier country', so I jumped in the motor car and raced down to the highway to have a look. When I got there, here were all these blokes from La Grange and some from Frazier, camping. I spun the motor car around and pulled up on their side of the road.

"How did this fire get away?" I asked.

"Ahh. We bin broken down here, Shohn, so we bin light 'im dis fire. We bin know when you chee 'im shmoke you be prop'ely worried and you'll come and hab a look." It didn't matter that they'd just burnt half the country out.

We were at the mission preparing to go mustering. As well as the Frazier horses and mine, we took some La Grange horses in the plant too. They had a lot of good horses, mares and foals, running on the place. Well bred, with some good lookers amongst them. While we were getting organised this day I said to Father Chris, "Who's going to be the babbler?"

"I've got a bloke here to do the cooking for you. He's called Windy." So I thought, ' Righto. I don't know this bloke Windy, but that's OK, we've got a camp cook.' Later, when I went over to where the tucker was, there was Windy getting things ready. He had bloody big sores, the size of three fifty cent pieces spread out alongside each other. Some smaller, and none looking too healthy. 'And this gravy eyed old bloke is to be the cook.' I thought. I went to Chris Saunders with my concerns.

"I don't think I'd like that bloke cooking for me too much. Besides, like I said I need another white bloke in the camp."

"Don't worry about it John. You'll be right." Father Chris told me. "We'll come out there regularly and we'll bring your food out for you." I thought that sounded pretty good and I stopped worrying about it. Windy was poking around sorting out the cooking gear and I saw him filling a gallon cooking oil tin with fly spray.

"What are you pouring that in there for?" I asked. "You don't really want to be doing that. You'll get it muddled up and end up putting fly spray in the tucker." He gave me a toothless grin, assuring me

"No, no Shohn. I'll b'rember 'dis 'un." I wondered if he would.

We took our horses over to La Grange the day before we were to go out. They'd had a few weeks spell and there were a few horses that I'd broken in before we did our mustering on Frazier. We rode the horses the afternoon we got there and they were all good. We also rode a few of the La Grange horses. Brother Richard wanted me to take a half clumper gelding. He was a big horse and Brother Richard told me his mother had got lost in a cyclone. They had rescued him and brought him up around the mission. I thought 'This will be a lovely bit of work, this thing.' I thought he must have had a fair bit of work and I was getting a horse that had done a couple of seasons. Well, he'd been broken in and he might have done a couple of days work, but that was the extent of it. He had a head like lead and he didn't know what 'go' meant. It made things fairly difficult and we had a lot of scrub that we were mustering. By the end of it he came a bit better. He would have been a pretty handy horse if he'd had more work. Apart from him, all the other horses I rode while mustering were my own.

One night we came in late from mustering. It was pretty much dark. I grabbed my meal, because so far no-one had been out from the mission with meals for me. It seemed it had been an idle promise that never eventuated. I took a mouthful and spat it out. It smelt and tasted of flyspray. I told Windy, then I had a piece of bread instead. There was no reaction from the blacks, so I don't know if they ate it or not, or whether mine was a 'special' meal just for me. At the best of times Windy's meals were basic. Salt meat, boiled beef, damper and always the thought of Windy's sores as you ate it. They were nothing to look forward to and you wouldn't eat that kind of tucker at home. But you had to have food, so you just had to push it on down as best you could.

The La Grange muster took about a month. We did two rounds, taking roughly a fortnight each. We were out at a place called Engedine. We mustered around there and got a few cattle together. We went up past Port Smith and mustered up the coast. There's open country along the coast, and good grass. There were a lot of cattle in there, but we couldn't get them. It was all shorthorn cattle in those days.

There were big bullocks, some young, some up to sixteen year old pikers. They knew all the tricks of the trade. They used to come down to the mangroves and get a drink on low tide. There were springs out there that the bullocks knew of, so that's where they got their water. They didn't need to go to any bores. They were too cunning for us and we didn't do very well, so I teed up with Chris Saunders to see if we could get a plane or a helicopter in. Well what does he do? He gets the then Bishop of Broome, Bishop Jobst, to be our aerial musterer. He didn't have a clue. He was making sure he stayed closer to God than to Satan. He was far too high. It was just a bloody joke. Instead of looking after what was going on below, he was trying to get closer to Heaven. Most of the time he was flying that high he never even frightened the cockies out of the trees. He had no idea where he should be. He just thought he had to give the cattle a bit of a fright, once, and he did a very good job of that, because we didn't see them again. It was just a waste of bloody time. If only they had got a couple of choppers in, we would have got a lot of bullocks. But, no. We got the bishop. We stopped mustering and built a barbed wire entanglement up on one of the flats. Then later we went back and did a second round. We got a few bullocks, but what we really needed were yards further out towards the highway, so we could muster out of the scrub back onto the coast. But it wasn't to be and there wasn't that much time. We mustered up a couple of paddocks where we'd put all the bullocks we had got. There were quite a few. Generally the bullocks seemed fairly quiet and civil, once you had got them into the mob. They weren't bad bullocks to handle. We headed back home with the mob.

We had to cross a tidal creek and the blacks knew whether the tide would be in or out. When we should go, in the morning, or afternoon. Once we'd crossed over the tidal creek I sent some of the young blokes in to get fresh horses. Because it was the first time I'd ever yarded cattle at those yards, and there was a lot of scrub close by, I didn't know how it was going to go. I told them, while they were in there, to check that all the gates were shut, except for the ones where we were going to yard up. When they came back we yarded the cattle up. I was riding the clumper horse of Brother Richards. By then he'd learnt to jump out and do as he was told. It was a pity the muster was finished. He wasn't a headache to ride anymore and had smartened up his ideas. Once we'd yarded up I dismounted and, leading my horse, went and wired the gates up. I continued on around the yard, checking that all the external gates were secure. When I got to the other side I came upon one of the stockboys mistreating a horse. She was a really nice looking chestnut mare, broken in earlier that year by Alan Simpson and the black fella was giving her 'a doing'. He'd got her pulled tight up against the rails, her face almost touching them. Held there with a rope around her neck and secured to the rails with a couple of half hitches, he was belting her across the head with a stick. I yelled out.

"What the f----- hell is going on here? That's not how you treat a horse." He kept going, so I said, "In a minute I'll get a stick and have a go at you. Let that horse go." So he let the horse go all right. Next thing the stick was coming for me. He was throwing fists at me and carrying on. I told him to cut it out, but he kept on coming. I didn't want to take any action towards him because the branding irons were lying on the ground and I didn't want him to pick one up and have a crack at me. I knew, if he had and I put my arm up for protection it would have broken it. But he kept coming and coming at me. I told him to bleep bleep off. I grabbed both his hands.

"I'm too strong for you Geoffrey, so lay off." I warned. Next thing I wore an RM Williams boot fair in the balls. He must have known it was a good kick because he half ran away. I thought I was pretty badly hurt, but I thought 'It's just pain. It'll go away in a bit.' By this time my horse had shot through to the tank and trough, which was about two or three hundred yards away. I walked down there and caught the horse, unsaddled him and washed his back. Then I just let him go where he was.

I was walking back up to the camp when the black fellow came up behind me and started punching me on the back. This time he'd got two or three other blokes there with him. I was worried that this was going to be a bit of a gang job coming up. I'd had one of them before, at Myroodah, and one of the blacks in that deal was here in this mob. My assailant ran up and hit me again. He was smaller than me, but when he kept this up, I got more and more sick of it and my blood began to rise. I said, "Look, you'd better cut this out because I'm going to lose my block shortly." Anyway he ran up again, then ran away. Then he came up again, but I was listening for him and when he got close enough I turned and grabbed hold of him. I gave him a bit of a shaking, then picked him up and chucked him into some scrub nearby. He didn't come back for anymore after that.

Back at camp I got my swag, rolled it out and lay down. By now I didn't feel too good. My head was spinning and I felt I wanted to vomit. It wasn't long until it was five o'clock, when you could go up to the mission store and everyone could get two cans of beer. I walked up there and thought 'I'll get a couple of beers.' When I got there a bloke came to talk to me, but I found out that I couldn't really speak, because when you talk it affects your testes. It's the same if you cough or sneeze. Even if you take a deep breath. So when I tried to speak I found it very difficult because it made the pain worse. I didn't say much at all. I just walked off with a can of beer and stood away on my own. The bloke must have said something to Father Chris about it because he came over to me.

"Are you all right?"

"No I'm not all right. I think you'd better ring Janet up and tell her to come and get me."

"Why? What's wrong?"

"I've been kicked in the balls and I'm very, very sore." He asked me what happened so I told him.

Father Chris went and rang Janet up straight away. When she came over I didn't get my swag or anything. I just left everything and went home to Frazier. But it wasn't that easy going home because I could hardly sit in the car. The movement of the car was unbearable and I had to get a cushion or a towel and put under my testes. We drove across the marsh, which was a short cut between the mission and Frazier Downs. When we got home I had a shower and saw that my nuts were as big as a stallions. I wasn't feeling at all well, so Janet ended up ringing the sister at the mission hospital. She was called Annie D'Alterio and she drove across to Frazier that evening and gave me a couple of needles. Annie said the doctor was coming out to the mission for a clinic in the morning and to go over and see him. I did. By then my balls were huge, black and shiny. They hurt like hell. I dropped my strides and showed the doctor the damage.

"Ah, yes. I've seen plenty of this in footballers down south." He told me nonchalantly. "The swelling will go down in a while, or you may need to get it drained. Come back next time I'm out here for a clinic, in a week or two." So that was that and I went back home.

At the time we had a young electrician rewiring the Frazier homestead. He and his wife were travelling around Australia on their honeymoon and we became lifelong friends. It was obvious I wasn't at all well. They offered to keep an eye on things at Frazier, so Janet could drive me up to Derby and see a doctor there. My mother was still sister-in-charge of outpatients then. We rang and told her we were coming. Next morning just as we were about to leave, the electrician, who had been working in the roof cavity, fell through the office ceiling. We went in to investigate and found the 'sparkie' sitting astride the rafters, the floor littered with plasterboard. This delayed our departure for a bit, but he was unhurt and we were thankful he too didn't need a trip to the hospital.

It was a long drive up to Derby. We tried wedging an assortment of padding under 'my bits' to ease the discomfort of the corrugations. Even so the first hundred miles of dirt road was a nightmare, with every bump hurting like hell. I had to keep packing around the testes to stop the pain, but it was still a long hard journey. Once in Derby I went to outpatients, where I saw a good doctor, a surgeon called Charles Butcher. I showed him what I had between my legs.

"So where's your testis?" he asked.

"I haven't got a bloody clue where the testis is. It's too sore to squeeze it. It's just hard and black, the whole lot, so I can't feel anything."

"Well, I'll tell you what you can do. Either go home to Frazier Downs and come back in ten days time. Or you can come into hospital this evening and I'll drain it for you tomorrow morning."

I was thinking, 'Jeez, I don't really want anyone touching me, so perhaps I'll go home.'

By now, when I stood up, my head spun, although if I stood up for long enough I would come good. Then when I sat down my head would spin again and I'd think I was going to fall over. Any change of position made me feel dizzy. I didn't really know what to do. I went across the road to my parent's place and lay on a bed. Mum was working at the hospital that day, in outpatients. When she came home she asked what the doctor had said.

"Well you're not going home to Frazier Downs. You're going back to the hospital. You can ring Dr Butcher up now. Tell him you'll be over there in the morning, you'll be fasted and he can drain it for you tomorrow." My Mum was a 'no nonsense' kind of person. A nurse from the old school. She was quite firm and it was clear she'd brook no argument. With the decision taken out of my hands I rang up and did as Mum said.

In the morning I went over to the hospital. I had to wait around for a while, then I ended up in this kind of a nightdress, on the table in theatre and I was out like a light. I woke up in a bed on the ward and I couldn't believe the bloody pain. I tried to sing out but as I went to pull the air in, it made it worse, so I just belted the wall with my fist. Nurses came from everywhere. I said I needed a pain killer and by gee, they weren't too slow getting it. I was knocked out again for another couple of hours. When I came to I didn't move a muscle. I was too worried about it hurting. Later that evening a nurse came to give me a wash.

"You're not even touching me, let alone washing me." I told her and I meant it.

"I've got to. That's what I've been told to do."

"I don't care what you've been told. I don't want to be moved, or touched or anything." I repeated.

She said she would come back in a minute. After a while she returned with the good news that the doctor said I didn't need to have anything done. Thankfully I was left alone.

Later on I was told what they'd done to me. When they'd got me into theatre and had a look, they found the whole testis was smashed. Mum was called in and the situation explained to her. They asked her if she'd give permission for them to remove the whole lot. She did. So that left me a 'rig', where just a few hours earlier I had resembled a six year old black stallion. But the pain was really something. The worst pain I've had in my life. I was thirty-four.

I remained in hospital for a while and Janet used to come in and feed me. They'd bring me my meals and put them at the end of the bed, but I couldn't sit up to get them. If I tried my head spun and the pain started again, but slowly, over the coming days I began to feel better. Janet was staying with friends during this time. She wasn't able to stay at Mum and Dad's place because Mum had lent their spare room to a girl who had been on Myroodah helping keep house, when I was there. It was fairly awkward, because she would come across to visit me. I think the situation caused some amusement amongst the nursing staff. Janet would be there to feed me or visit, then after she left the other girl would arrive. I don't suppose anyone knew what to think, especially Janet. I had other visitors as well, blokes I knew and ringers I'd worked with. They had heard stories about me, but didn't really know what happened, so I started telling them I'd been kicked by a horse. Some of these fellows could be a bit hot headed and I didn't want any trouble, so I didn't tell them the whole truth. By now I'd been told that if I hadn't had the operation I would have lost my life. If I'd waited the ten days before coming back gangrene would have set in, and I was told there wouldn't have been too much they could have done about it. Eventually I was let out of hospital and Janet and I set off on the long drive back to Frazier. On the way, as we approached Willare Roadhouse, I asked Janet if she would marry me. She said 'Yes'.

A day or so after I'd got home from hospital the manager of Christmas Creek telephoned me. He said he was flying down and bringing a mob of blokes with him to sort the blacks out, over what they'd done to me. I knew he was crazy enough to do it. I was a bit worried it could start a racial conflict, so I spun him a bit of a yarn.

"No, no. You've got it all wrong. It wasn't the blacks. I got kicked by a horse. Everything is all right Kevin. Don't worry about it. It was my own fault." I managed to convince him and he cooled off a bit. If I hadn't lied to him it would have been on for young and old. I was still convalescing then and it was a worrying time for a while, but eventually all talk of retaliation died down.

It took six months or more for me to fully recover. If I lifted anything heavy my head would spin and I'd go off balance, or if I stood up too quickly I'd feel dizzy. I had to be careful not to strain myself, or I felt it, and when I bent over I was in danger of going face down. But eventually all that went away and apart from being left lopsided, I've been fine ever since.

Despite this, by any measure, I was the victim of an assault and had sustained grievous bodily harm. I wrote to The Pastoralists and Graziers Association asking for advice. They told me to record the incident in detail, while it was still fresh in my mind and gave me the name of a law firm. Not long after this Father Chris came over to Frazier to have dinner with us. He brought the Broome magistrate with him. Over the course of the evening the conversation turned to the assault. The magistrate told me that if I brought an assault charge against my assailant the native in question would come up before him. He told me that he'd have to let the fellow off because he had no previous record. He might put him on a good behaviour bond and fine him fifty dollars, he told us.

After being told that, it was clear laying charges would be futile. The Catholic Mission wasn't going to help, and the other natives, who'd witnessed the incident, wouldn't give evidence against one of their own. The magistrate had already decided what the outcome would be and to top it all off, I had been telling everyone that a horse had kicked me. I felt a bit annoyed because I had been trying to save the mission a lot of trouble. The other thing that annoyed me was that I had asked Father for another white man to be in the camp with me while we mustered La Grange, but it hadn't happened. If he'd fulfilled his promise at least there would have been one other person to back me up that day. All in all I felt rather let down.[8]

## Time to move on

After what had happened over the assault and the mission's reluctance to bring Geoffrey to justice, Janet and I decided it wouldn't be sensible to remain at Frazier for another season. We had no idea what we would do, or where we would start our married life. We just knew the time had come for us to leave.

In November 1977 I handed in my notice. I also wrote to the Minister for Lands listing the improvements done on the property during the previous twelve months.

---

8   In Geoffrey's case, white man's law had failed and that failure ultimately cost several people dearly. After he got away with assaulting me he went on to rack up a string of offences, most of them going unpunished. First he went down to Port Hedland where he pulled a rifle on a bloke. Then he went to Looma and wielded an axe. Another time he was coming out from Sandfire Roadhouse, drunk. He ran into a mob of his own tribe, breaking arms and legs and leaving one really good bloke, Woopi, crippled for life. Later he was 'on' with the daughter of one of the La Grange elders. She was sick in hospital in Broome. Geoffrey got her out of hospital and took her drinking. It was June or July, winter rain and very cold. They had a fight in the middle of the night. Geoffrey left her, bashed up, out in the rain. By the time she was found and taken back to hospital she was critically ill. She died on the operating table. Amazingly Geoffrey was still a free man. He drifted up around Fitzroy Crossing and started interfering with girls and that's where black fella law caught up with him. He was found floating down the Fitzroy river with both his hands tied behind a big log.

These included three, twenty thousand gallon concrete water tanks, and seven concrete troughs, erected on existing bores. One new bore, equipped with a twelve foot windmill, twenty thousand gallon concrete tank and two concrete troughs. Three tanks had been fibre-glassed. New paddock fencing and additions to cattle yards, as well as the purchase of two new station vehicles and other equipment. I recommended a follow-up pastoral inspection be carried out on the property, as had been done at the time of purchase twelve months earlier, and I expressed my concerns for the future management of the property if left solely in the hands of the Aboriginal owners, without strict supervision.

The condition of the three thousand head cattle herd was markedly improved since I first went to Frazier. I conveyed to the minister my fear that the quality and size of the present herd may diminish, through neglect and indiscriminate slaughter by the Aboriginal owners. For John Dodo and Jack Mulardy I wrote a list of suggested improvements for the coming year and a work plan for the season, including the expected number of meatworks cattle to be turned off, cows to be spayed and geldings to be broken. I didn't think there was much more I could do to help them, but I feared the task ahead would prove too much for these two fine dignified men to handle. After that Janet and I waited out the end of the year, satisfied with what had been accomplished, yet saddened at the prospect of what lay ahead for the property and it's livestock.

## Married again

Despite everything we remained good friends with Father Chris for many years. We even asked him to marry us, but he said the bishop wouldn't allow it. This was probably fair enough. Neither of us were Catholic and I had been divorced. Instead Janet and I were married in the Uniting Church at Broome, two days before Christmas in 1977. It was a small affair. None of Janet's family were present and of mine, only Mum and Dad attended. Janet was given away by our friend Dave Ledger, his wife Margaret as witness. Two dozen invited guests sat down to lunch at the Mangrove Hotel after we'd tied the knot and we spent the evening at Woodside's Bocal Club, where Tony Di Guiseppe, manager of the meatworks, sang for us. We stayed in Broome over Christmas, returning to Frazier to pack up ready to leave early in the

New Year. We had been there a little over eighteen months.

In the last week before we left the station we were plagued by the emergence of numerous centipedes, big scorpions, some inches long, and a large number of death adders. We had seen nothing like it during the time we had been living there. They just seemed to appear from nowhere in great numbers. In the days before we were due to leave it began to rain. Not just a heavy downpour, but continual soaking rains and we began to wonder if we would get out of the place.

We left around lunch time, planning to drive through to Derby, where we were to pick up a vehicle someone wanted us to take down to Perth. It was still raining heavily and the highway was fairly treacherous. By the time we got to the Broome turn-off it was late in the afternoon and we knew we wouldn't be able to reach Derby before dark. With so much water about we decided it would be best not to attempt it. We decided to stay in Broome overnight and complete the journey in daylight next day. It never happened. The highway we'd just driven along was closed behind us. The road from Broome to Derby was closed ahead of us. By morning we were going nowhere.

We waited in Broome for a week. Each day thinking the rain would ease, enabling us to leave. It didn't. Eventually we flew to Derby. The Great Northern Highway was cut in several places. After another week of waiting it out in Mum and Dad's little corrugated iron house in Derby, we finally decided to fly down the Perth. It was one of the wettest January's on record, but what amazed me the most was how the sand dwelling creatures at Frazier, the snakes, scorpions and centipedes, had known in advance that 'big rain' was coming. I'd never seen it before and I've never seen it since.

## New wife, new life

Janet and I stayed down in Perth for several weeks, living at the Clifton Street house in Nedlands. Janet was not very well at the time and underwent various tests, so the holiday was not all it might have been, but I was able to see my two young children, Leah and Benn, a few times which made it worthwhile. Towards the end of February, with no definite answers as to why Janet was unwell, we set off to drive back to Broome. While in Perth we had bought ourselves a second-hand Kingswood sedan and another, even older, vehicle. A very cheap Rover, with a tendency to overheat. With Janet driving the Rover and me the Holden we set off, in convoy, for the three day drive up the coast road, fingers crossed all would be well. We were still unsure what the future held for us, although I had been told there would be a job for me at the Broome meatworks when the season started. In the meantime I would go horse-breaking at Mandora for Joe De Pledge, while Janet planned to find employment in Broome. Hence the need for the two vehicles.

The trip North was reasonably uneventful, although Janet suffered a dizzy spell and pain a couple of hundred kilometres south of Carnarvon, which was a bit worrying. We pulled over for a while, then drove on slowly to the small coastal town, where we spent the afternoon. She was feeling better after an hour or two and we were able to press on without further incident. It was a long, slow, hot trip and I enjoyed a few cold tinnies along the way to help pass the time. As we approached Port Hedland, the effect of the refreshments purchased at the Whim Creek Hotel made driving difficult. Janet was unhappy with me and we pulled up on the side of the road. I got out of the car, lay down on the verge and went to sleep.

The following day, having left Port Hedland behind us, we tackled the long unsealed section of the Great Northern Highway to Broome. Both vehicles seemed to be running OK. We called into Mandora Station, then Sandfire Roadhouse, where I caught up with Eddie Norton. From there on past Frazier Downs to Broome, then still a small pearling town. In Broome we settled into a sixteen foot caravan we had bought from friends in Derby. It was parked at Dave and Margaret Ledger's house, overlooking the mangroves on the edge of Roebuck Bay. Janet still wasn't in the best of health and chose not to come with me back down to Mandora. Instead she remained in Broome, where she got casual work at the Mangrove Hotel, while I went away horse-breaking for a couple of weeks.

## Horse breaking at Mandora

I had known Joe and Jane De Pledge for many years and they had always been very good to me. Janet and I had spent a couple of Christmas' at Mandora and gone to some good parties there as well. They had two young children, Polly and Cobb and

I consider the family to be my very good friends. Joe had let me leave my horses at Mandora after we left Frazier, amongst them my good mare Penny, who I used as coacher horse whilst breaking in there. Young Cobby would come down to the yard each day to watch and began befriending the mare. He'd fetch green grass for her from up at the house and feed it to her. One day I asked if he'd like me to chuck him on her, but he said he didn't want me to. A few days later I was busy breaking in and when I looked up, there was Cobby sitting up on Penny's back. No saddle or anything. He'd just climbed up her front leg and clambered on. Penny was a beautiful natured mare and smart. At one time Joey wanted to get some of his horses registered as Australian Stockhorses and the assessors came to Mandora to inspect them. Because Penny was such a good mare Joe thought he'd try and get her registered as well. When it came time to inspect them, Penny was first up, but she was rejected as having a bit of a goose arse, or some such defect.

"But this is a really smart mare." Jo insisted. But no, they wouldn't accept her.

"Well if she's not good enough to register, don't bother looking at the rest of them." He told them and that was the end of that. The assessors went on their way. Some years later I was at a gymkhana in Derby. I took in a really good looking grey filly belonging to Meda. The Australian Stockhorse mob were there and they came and talked to me.

"That's a good looking filly you've got there. What about getting her registered?" they prompted.

"She's a good looker" I agreed, "But she's useless. There's no point registering her. Besides she doesn't belong to me."

"But she's a good looking filly. You could register her and there would be ways of getting round the ownership issue." They insisted. To my mind they had their priorities wrong. Ability ought to come into it, but it's all about looks, never mind there's no brains. I've always remembered that. Now when I see Australian Stockhorses I wonder 'Just how good are they?' What's the point of registering them, putting them into an elite class of their own and breeding from them, unless they have exceptional ability. I can't see the sense in it. There's plenty of good looking people, but some have no brains and it's the same with horses.

## An unlucky fluke

When I returned from breaking in at Mandora, Janet and I shifted our caravan a few kilometres out of town onto a block belonging to Gordon Bryce. Gordon had an abattoir there where he slaughtered cattle for his butcher's shop in Chinatown. He also had a dipping depot for Clover Meats cattle going south. It was a great set-up for him. A local lady, Jackie Knox, was also living in a caravan on the same block and we shared the same set-up for our ablutions. Jackie had planted a bit of a garden and a few paw paw trees, so we decided we would do the same. To make the digging easier I filed down the edge of a shovel and we filled half forty-four gallon drums with soil, then planted herbs and vinkers in them. We also planted paw paws, although as it turned out we weren't there long enough to reap any benefit from them. One evening, well after dark, Janet was taken ill. Rather than have her walk through the bush to the 'long drop' loo I took our sharpened shovel and went out to dig a hole for her convenience. It was pindan country, wattle scrub and pretty hard ground. I lifted the shovel and thrust it into the dirt. Instantly there was a gush of water and I realised, to my horror, that I'd hit the main pipeline to Brycie's slaughter yard. I couldn't believe it. The block was about a hundred acres in size. If I'd been trying I couldn't have done it, yet with one stab in the dark I'd created a ruddy fountain. There was nothing for it but to drive into Broome that night and let Gordon know what I'd done. He was not a happy man.

## Broome meatworks

Once the mustering season started and the meatworks reopened, we shifted our caravan back into town, parking it within metres of the Demco cattleyards. This became our home for the next six months. Janet's treadle sewing machine stood at the door of the van, a dusty pot plant perched on top. Half a dozen struggling tomato plants grew in the shade of the fence behind. Not that we needed to grow our own vegies anymore, because we ate in the canteen and the food was number one. Better than I'd had anywhere else, especially stockcamps. Janet had secured a clerical job in the office at the meatworks and between us we began earning real money.

I was employed as 'stockman' and I worked long hours, seven days a week, from season's start to season's finish. I'd start at five in the morning, or earlier, pushing cattle up for the primary industry inspectors to check. After breakfast there was no messing around. I'd head straight back to the yards, push the cattle up and the slaughtermen would start the days kill. As I pushed each beast up to the knocking box I'd read and write down the brands. Sometimes there would be a dispute over whose cattle were who's. After a few such disputes I took to cutting the ear off any stranger cattle in a mob, keeping the marked ears in a bag. At the end of that line of cattle I would tie the bag up, mark it with the name of the station that sent them in, the kill date and the number of strangers in the mob. The bag was then stored in the cool room. I did this for each line of cattle and it put an end to any uncertainty of ownership.

After the slaughtermen were done for the day my offsider would knock off. I'd get the next day's cattle pushed up undercover and off feed, then I'd feed any remaining cattle in the back yards. If a truck, or roadtrain came in I'd stop what I was doing, go and unload it and count them off. Cattle trucks would roll up at any time, day or night, seven days a week. Many came in late at night and I became adept at hearing them as they approached and would be dressed and ready by the time they reached the unloading ramp. Because my sleep was broken most nights, sometimes several times, I grew progressively more tired. I would go to bed pretty much straight after tea. Janet, who didn't start work until seven o'clock in the morning, would lie in bed, reading. She'd lie as still and quietly as she could on the narrow mattress opposite, so as not to disturb me. She'd learnt from experience that if she coughed or cleared her throat I would be up and out of bed in a flash, pulling on my jeans and calling out 'Righto' I'll be with you in a minute', all ready to unload another roadtrain that wasn't actually there. On weekends, if we weren't killing, I'd sweep and hose down the yards, feed up and on Sunday afternoon bring up cattle for Monday's kill.

Occasionally cattle would get out and I would have to fetch them back. One time the manager at Myroodah, Tony Laing, had a horse delivered to the meatworks. She was a good creamy mare, called Butterfly, which he reckoned he owned, though how he ever bought her off the station I don't know. Myroodah was always short of horses and I knew Butterfly to be a valuable working mare. When Tony came to collect her I gave him the key to the yard, so he could get her out to take to the Shinju Matsuri rodeo gymkhana. He got Butterfly all right, but failed to shut the gate properly and we lost a hundred and fifty head of meatworks cattle.

There was a stable down the back where I kept a couple of my own horses and with the help of two or three blokes we mustered up the cattle next day. They'd gone out onto open country and wandered all over the golf course, which didn't please the golfers much. We got all but one back and he came in for water a day or two later, got his horns stuck through the rails whilst trying to get a drink, so we got him as well. But the exertion ruined one of my horses and he was never the same after that. He was a young horse called Chips. A grey out of a good mare, Peppy, a Wallal horse I'd had on Napier. He had to do a fair bit of work that day and it de-arranged his head, which happens to a lot of horses if they're hit with too much work first up. After that, when you asked him to go he would grab the bit and go all right. He'd gallop and not want to pull up. He had done next to no work during that year and was really only there as a companion horse for Penny. My other horse, Penny, was being prepared for the rodeo gymkhana and on weekends, if I had any spare time, I'd put her round barrels and give her a work out. She was in tip top condition and looked the best she had in her life. I thought it was great having her there with me, while I was restricted from going anywhere because of my job.

## A letter comes

One day a letter arrived for me. The envelope, written in a hand I didn't recognise, was addressed to Mr John Wells, (stockman) c/o Broome Meat Works.

I opened it, feeling some curiosity and out fell a slip of newspaper. It was a job advertisement.

### CATTLE STATION MANAGER

*In October/November the position of Manager*

*at Meda Station, Derby will become vacant.*

*Experienced cattlemen are invited to contact*

*Mr T.S. Emanuel, G.P.O. Box A27, Perth*

*or telephone 322 6401 to discuss the position.*

There was no accompanying letter, or note of any kind. My only clue as to who might have sent it was the handwriting on the envelope. At the time an elderly employee of Emanuel Bros was at the meatworks watching and checking their kill. Harry Scrivener from GoGo station would stand at the scales and meticulously record the weight of every half beast owned by Emanuels that came through the meatworks. I took the envelope to him and asked if he recognised the writing. He did.

## I meet my mother-in-law

Despite the long hours I was working, life was pretty good for us. Janet had recovered from whatever ailed her during the first few months of our marriage. We were managing to accumulate a bit of money for ourselves and when the meatworks season ended I knew I had a good job to go to.

I had applied for the management of Meda twice before, without success. I would not have tried for it a third time, had I not received the encouragement I did. But the arrival of the job application, prompted me to contact Tim Emanuel. Janet and I later met Tim and his father S.F. Emanuel for dinner at the Continental Hotel and at the beginning of August my appointment as manager of Meda Station was confirmed. I thought this was pretty good. Life was looking a lot better than it had for several years.

Within weeks another letter arrived, this time for Janet. It was from her mother who was coming out from England and wanted to visit us in Broome. It was obvious she couldn't stay in our tiny caravan, or be expected to cope with the dust, bellowing cattle, heat or smell of by-products, which at times could be sickening. So Janet rented a small flat for two weeks, where she and her mother could stay. I guess, as the new and unknown son-in-law, I was being checked out, but it didn't bother me that much. I was working long hours, I had a good job in front of me on the station I'd grown up on, so things were looking pretty good for us.

As it turned out Meg was a good sport. She seemed to cope fine in Broome, loved the heat and was happy for Janet to drive her about showing her the area. One day they set off from Broome and drove to Derby where Meg met my parents, then on out to Meda, so she could see where we would be living once the meatworks closed at the end of the season. A rodeo gymkhana was held in Broome while she was there. Work stopped for a day or two at the meatworks and I was able to compete. I was preparing to ride Penny out to the rodeo grounds, now known as the Jack Knox Arena, and asked Meg to hold Penny while I fetched something from the caravan. Penny was looking really good, dappled and fit. She was frisky, dancing and eager to go. My mother in law handled her all right, though I think she was a bit surprised. It turned out a very successful gymkhana for me. We won the barrel race, bull dogging and with Alan Young top pick-up team. It was a good day.

With me working, Janet and her mother staying in the flat, the two weeks went by quickly enough and it seemed no time at all before Meg flew off again, down to Perth to stay with Janet's brother in Pinjarra. It was nice to have Janet back with me in the caravan, but a mere two days after Meg left we discovered a lump the size of a fifty cent coin in Janet's breast. This gave us a good fright and she went off to the hospital first thing next day. Dr T. O'Sullivan saw her.

"Is there any chance you could be pregnant" he asked. "Because I think this is hormonal, rather than sinister." He was right. Janet and I were expecting our first child.

*Cattle in the forcing pen at Frazier Downs yard. 1976*

*Branding at Frazier Downs. 1976*

*I see my parents off at the Frazier Downs airstrip.*

*Me with a throw net at Whistle Creek preparing to catch our dinner whilst at Frazier Downs.*

*Branding at Engerdine, La Grange. 1977*

*Janet and I on our wedding day. Broome 1977*

# PART THREE

# CHAPTER FOURTEEN

# MEDA

*Six years we have lived on this station,*
*A station we do not own,*
*But we love it with quiet adoration*
*And feel that this station is home.*
*No words can describe our great pleasure,*
*When we first came to manage this place,*
*Where the work was my husband's leisure,*
*And laughter lines wrinkled his face.*

## Taking up the reins on Meda

It was October 1978 when I went to manage Meda, taking over from Mervyn Norton who was sent up to GoGo. Emanuel Brothers were long time owners of four West Kimberley pastoral properties at the time, GoGo, Christmas Creek, Cherrabun and Meda. They were influential and well respected in the industry, with a reputation for being fair but lean. I was more than happy to be working for them and to be back on home ground. Having grown up there, I'd roamed Meda as a boy, worked there as a green young ringer, later as an experienced stockman and was now back as manager. I knew my way around the run and took up my new position with enthusiasm.

Enthusiasm aside, I soon learned what a mistake it is to take over the running of a joint at the end of the season, when there is little feed, natural waters have dried up and before the rains have come. Being back on home soil I may not have had the geographical difficulties experienced by most incoming managers, but I soon realised there were other serious problems to face.

Keeping water up to the cattle was the most immediate problem. There were three types of engine on Meda, but engine blocks and mountings were only made for a certain engine type, YB, EDC or EFE and although there were a lot of spare engines in the workshop, none had been maintained. Sometimes we had to shift engines from one bore to another in order to keep up. YB engines were the smallest and easiest to shift, but were not suited to all mountings. We'd pump all night, then take the engine to another bore, set it up, pump all day, then take it back again. It entailed a lot of extra work and wasted time. We also found several pump-jacks incorrectly set, the arms uneven and the pump-jack working in a lopsided manner, like a bloke with a shortened leg. In some areas it was impossible for us to keep up the water supply, no matter what we did and I had to go to town and pick up some men to help shift cattle from Geoff's onto Meda Well. Until the rains came the pressure was constant. Later I got all the spare engines in the workshop fixed up and with the co-operation of Frank Mugford, Emanuel's pastoral inspector, and Alex McFadzean, we got it so they could go onto any bore. This saved a lot of messing about and ensured we would never be in such a precarious position again. Almost a decade later, in WACCO times, Peter Murray saw all the spare engines we had in good working order and he told his other station managers, if they ever needed one, just to go and get it from Meda.

## The horse herd

Early in the new year, as the 'wet' season was coming to an end, I turned my attention to the horses. We mustered them, then drafted down at the Claypan yards. I was surprised to find the horse herd so out of control. It was only a couple of years since I'd last seen them, when I was there as studmaster. When we drafted we found there were a lot of stallions in the mob, very few working horses and breakers of all ages. We kept all the good lookers, selling the reject fillies and colts to Jackie Dann and Gibb River Station, who were pleased to get them. We shot half a dozen stallions and several old unbroken geldings. Six better looking stallions, too good to destroy, went up the Gibb River Road. Because of the variation in age I decided to begin brand numbers from the start, rather than carrying on from the horse book. We were branding horses from foals to five year old breakers and it made no sense to number them as if they were all of an age. We gelded a lot of colts, then began breaking in. Dickie Wilson broke in the first lot of horses for me, before going out to run the stockcamp. After that I got Roy Walker to break in. Roy had worked for me on Napier Downs years earlier and was a very good horse breaker, but he'd lost his nerve during the intervening years. When he came to Meda it took him two weeks to break in two colts. I had to tell him he was past it and to give the game away. He was very upset but I said not to worry, it happens to everyone eventually. It was pretty sad, but Meda couldn't afford to keep paying him to do a job that was proving beyond him.

Over time we got Meda's horses sorted out and heading in the right direction. Each year from then on, we broke in a good number of colts, increasing our plant of working horses significantly, improving the quality of our brood mares and ensuring no unwanted stallions were running with the mob. We ended up with a good mob of horses, enabling us to pension off workers and 'spell' horses as need be, without fear of running short. It was a far cry from the sad situation I'd experienced on Myroodah.

## An uncomfortable time

During January the station lighting plant began playing up and eventually 'shit' itself completely, leaving us with no power. Parts were ordered from Perth and we waited patiently for them to arrive. It was hot and humid, but I had lived in similar and worse conditions many times. Janet, who was in the latter half of her pregnancy, found the heat more difficult to cope with. With no fans to cool us, or blow the milling mosquitos from whining around us during the night, she would get up and take a cold shower numerous times. Throwing her towel into the shower recess she would then wrap the sodden cloth around her swollen body, lie back on the mattress and sleep until it was dry. She'd repeat the routine time and again in an effort to keep cool. It was six weeks before the lighting plant was eventually fixed. In early May it began to rain, Janet went into labour and seven hours later our daughter Adele was born.

## An assortment of blokes

Although I usually had a few loyal blokes I'd known for years follow me from station to station, you never really knew who you had working for you. You might pick them up in town if you were short of men, or they may approach you asking for a job. You'd take them on and think you knew their name and something about them, but the reality was, you could never be certain they were who they said they were. Some blokes were plain odd, some were criminals, others might be running from a broken marriage and maintenance orders. A lot were hooked on grog and just liked working out bush, away from temptation. Of course we did have blokes who were genuine, normal fellows who weren't running from anything. But the truth is, stations were a good place to hide if you wanted to escape your past. No one asked too many questions. You didn't have to prove who you were, or provide a police clearance, written reference or any of that paraphernalia. Nobody really cared if you were who you said you were, or what you might have done. The only criteria was to have the ability to work hard, live rough and eat whatever was going. It helped if you were smart enough to keep yourself alive, but fortunately that comes naturally to most people.

## Billy, Willie, Freddy and others

Since the introduction of award wages the Aboriginal population on stations had fallen dramatically and native camps were far smaller than when I was a kid. Many had moved into town onto Aboriginal Reserves and the old life and old ways were becoming a thing of the past. Few natives were living in the camp when I first went to manage Meda, although there were one or two I'd known for years, some who'd been there when I was a kid. Amongst these were Billy Munroe and his wife Weeda. For a time Billy had been a headstockman when I was on Kimberley Downs. He was always a bit of a smarty and thought himself pretty important. Billy and I didn't always see eye to eye, though he undoubtedly had a lot of ability. It was a pity he had such a cocky style about him. In latter years he claimed to have taught me how to ride, but the truth is Willie Lennard taught me most of what I know.

Willie was like a father to me and I can't speak highly enough of him. When Willie, heard I was managing Meda he asked me for a job there and I was only too pleased to give him one. His wife, Roslyn, had been my nursemaid, in my parent's day. I'd known them both all my life. Willie and Roslyn had numerous children, some old enough to work and now parents themselves, others still young and going to school. Others had been gripped by the demon alcohol and were of no value to anyone, least of all themselves. Willie and his wife gathered up any uncared for grandchildren and reared them as their own. They did a mighty job.

As well as Willie and his extensive family we had another good fellow, Freddie Marker, who stayed with me. His sister, Maudie, was married to Willie's brother Con Lennard. Despite being a smart man in his youth, Con turned almost blind and helpless with alcoholism and lived in Derby, where he died prematurely. Maudie and her brother Freddie, were both lean individuals with stick like limbs. Freddie was teetotal and a slow but methodical worker. He would mind the chooks, work in the garden, or give a hand with the mills if needed. He was unhurried in all things, but would dig a hole to China, if you asked him to.

Jack Shaw was the Meda windmillman when I first took over. He and his wife Sarah lived in a small cottage away from the native camp, with a prodigious family, expanding almost annually.

Apart from the natives, my good friend Phil LeLievre was also living on Meda, with his wife, Annette, and their two children, Craig and Kylie. They were housed in the old homestead in which I'd grown up, though was now in a sad state of disrepair. They didn't stay long, moving on during the first year to follow Mervyn Norton. Jim Gunn, who I'd rescued from the bottom of the Fitzroy River a couple of years earlier, came to work for us as a welder for a time, but he too left towards the end of the first season. For me work was very serious and I expected an honest day out of my men. Some blokes thrived on it, others fell by the wayside. Over time I built up a crew who knew what was expected of them and were well able to hack the pace.

## Tex Brown and his lady

Tex Brown was a white man and he wanted a job at Meda. I'd heard that he'd done a lot of horse tailing on other stations and was pretty useful in the camp, so I gave him a job. Before coming to Meda he'd been working for Brian Fielder on a nearby station, Yeeda. He was an older bloke, in his forties I'd say, and pretty useful. He knew what had to be done, how everything worked and you could chuck him on any horse. That was the good part about it. But he had a partner and she was a bit hard to put up with. She was a fairly volatile woman and there were a few domestic incidents. At first the couple lived up at the station, but later shifted to the hut at the Claypan, where Tex made his camp.

Tex had a weekend off and he had been to town. It was his birthday and we were invited down to his camp for a few drinks. Tex had 'had it' and was lying down in the hut. His 'lady', a big powerful woman, wanted him to get up, but he wouldn't. She got a piece of pipe, with a few spikes about two inches long welded on it, and clouted him across his thigh with it. One spike penetrated deep into his leg. It must have hurt like hell, but Tex said nothing. He came out and just sat there quietly with us. We had a few drinks with them, but after that incident we soon left.

The fourth Christmas we were on Meda we held a New Years Eve party at the homestead. We invited friends and people we knew who had helped me out with a lot of things, when life had been a bit hard. They came from Broome, Derby and neighbouring stations. It was a very good party and everyone seemed to enjoy it. Quite a few people stayed over and played cricket on New Years Day, but by the following evening most of our guests had left. Tex, who had crashed on the verandah on the night of the party, stayed there most of the next day. Late in the afternoon he asked for a lift down to the Claypan. He took a bit of meat from the cool room and some for his dogs. His partner had walked back down to their hut the previous night. We gave him a few beers to take down for them both and I got somebody to run him back to his camp.

It was New Years Day, 1982. Janet and I went to bed very early. One of the children was running a fever and we thought we might be up during the night with her. It had been a late night the evening before and a long day. We both went straight to sleep. It would have been before eight o'clock. Not long after the headstockman, Macaulay, came over to the main homestead and woke us. He told us that Tex's partner had walked up from the Claypan and said that Tex had shot himself. I jumped in the vehicle and we drove down to their camp. Tex was lying out on the flat, about a hundred metres from the hut. He was still alive, but he was shot all right. I sent

Macaulay back to the station. I told him to take the 'wife' to the homestead and to tell Janet to keep her there. I stayed down at the Claypan. We'd taken a torch with us, but it had gone out. I went to Tex's camp and got a flour drum to sit on and I sat there in the dark with him. I knew Tex was in a bad way. I could faintly make out a dark pool by his head and he was making noises which I didn't like. There was very little wind, but when there was a breeze the windmill would start to turn and I found this comforting. It drowned out the sounds Tex was making. It wasn't very good because there was nothing I could do to help him. I knew he was in serious trouble.

Back at the homestead, Janet had ordered an ambulance. When Tex's 'lady' was brought across to the house it became clear she was injured as well. She had a glancing bullet wound to her head, but although she was filthy and bedraggled she didn't seem to be in too bad a way. Janet cleaned the woman up a bit, cut her hair back from the wound and washed it. Then, with the help of the headstockman's wife, tried to keep her calm while we waited for the ambulance.

We had had some good rain. When the ambulance arrived at the homestead they couldn't drive down to the Claypan, because it was too wet. A doctor and a nurse had come out with it. The gear and everything necessary was moved onto a four wheel drive station vehicle. While all this was going on I stayed with Tex. After about and hour and a half medical help arrived, but they were short of oxygen. Janet went and woke the mechanic and he got a bottle of oxy from the workshop. He took it down to the Claypan and they put that on their patient. They drove back up to the homestead, transferred Tex to the ambulance, then went in to the hospital. The injured woman was sent in a separate vehicle.

In the morning we got word that Tex had passed away on the way into town. He was shot in the head, through the ear. The bullet was just under the skin on the other side.

We couldn't find any next of kin other than his partner. I had to go into Derby and identify him at the hospital, in the morgue. The police came out and the detective from Derby, to investigate the incident. Things didn't quite seem to add up, so ballistic experts were flown up from Perth. They looked around for several days. The whole business was a bit smelly. Time seemed to stand still, or at least go very slowly and, because of the investigations, the funeral wasn't held for quite a long time. It was all pretty terrible and it took a while for us to get over it.[9]

## The schizophrenic and a Puerto Rican

We had a bloke on Meda, for a short time, who was living with Barbara Lennard, one of Willie's daughters, in Jack Shaw's old house. He was a schizophrenic. At the time I'm talking about the illness was quite rare, but the fellow had had a few episodes of going off the rails. On this occasion I was out in the stockcamp, and as usual Janet was at home. Our mechanic, Dennis, came knocking on the homestead door in the middle of the night. The fellow had gone completely berserk with a knife. He had tied up Willie's daughter, Barbara, and was threatening to do away with her. Then he reckoned he was going to start blowing things up. There was a hollow boab tree at Meda, that lay on it's side, where a case of gelignite had been put a long time ago. Somehow or other this fellow had found out it was there. He reckoned he was going to go and get it and blow the homestead up. Then he'd vanished into the night and no-one knew where he was. It worried the living daylights out of us.

After I heard about this episode I got Willie to shift the dynamite. It had been there a long long time, since before we came to Meda. It was used for putting in post holes, when building yards and fences. They'd drill a hole through the ironstone, then blast it out with dynamite. Moving it was a risky business, dangerous because it was weeping and highly volatile. It could have gone off on us at any moment.

At about the same time there was a fellow known to us only as The Puerto Rican. He was a really strange character. He was also on with one of the Meda native women, but he went to town and he captured himself another one and brought her out to the station. He locked the original one in a shed. It was one of the black fella huts, all tin, with a tin roof and built on a coffee rock ridge. He kept the windows shut and it must have been as hot as hell in there. He brought her water and passed tucker through the door to her, but he kept her locked in there while he was on with the other woman. When I found out about it I sent him on his way.

---

9   Some years later we learned that Tex had two uncles who owned a property over east. Neither had married and when they died the executors were looking for Tex. They contacted the manager of Yeeda Station, who then got onto me. Their property had been left to Tex, but sadly, by then he was no longer with us.

One of the problems with living close to town was that these fellas, and there were some weird ones amongst them, could come out, or get lifts out to the station, and we'd be landed with all this sort of crap. It was on all the time, though thankfully none were so odd as these two.

## Before Mick Dundee

A year after we lost Tex Janet decided to go home to England with the children, for Christmas. We had a mining mob working on Meda, drilling for oil. One of the bosses was from Yorkshire and, although I had never intended accompanying Janet, he persuaded me to go too. He was a likeable amusing bloke and he said he wanted to show me around Yorkshire and would make sure I had a good time. It sounded all right so I agreed. It was a bit of a last minute decision, and I think it threw a spanner in the works. Janet had already booked her flights and planned to be with her family for eight weeks. Her parents had recently moved from the big house, where my wife was born, into a small cottage. When they heard I was coming they said they didn't have room for all of us to sleep there. Janet's twin brother had also moved and was living several miles away in another village, so I was to stay with him. I was lent a car, so I could drive back and forth between my in law's home, and her brother's place. In theory it sounded easy enough, but I soon found it wasn't. Janet's family lived in the heart of the Devon countryside, which people think is beautiful. I hated it. The roads, which they call lanes, were all about eight foot below ground level. They had great high hedges, so it was impossible to see any landmarks. With ditches either side and single lane, you had to reverse whenever you met an oncoming vehicle. It was like driving through a narrow tunnel. It was December, the sun hardly rose above the horizon, it didn't get light until smoko time and was dark by afternoon tea-time. The weather was mostly misty, cold and miserable and everybody seemed to have the flu. I was constantly cold but when I tried to run a hot bath, to get warm, I only managed to get about two inches of water in the bottom, then it ran out, because the dairy next door had used it all. I used to get about the place wrapped in so many jackets and jumpers my arms couldn't hang by my side. I felt like a yeti. I was given a thick woollen beanie to keep my head warm, but I'm allergic to wool and I soon had scabby sores across my forehead and eyebrows. I tried to grow a beard to protect my face from the icy wind, but it was that bloody cold my whiskers wouldn't grow. Jeez it was awful.

My brothers in law used to take me to the local pub where I met some nice blokes and I found the farmers friendly and hospitable. One day, just before Christmas Janet and I went to a nearby town, leaving the children with Janet's mother to look after. It was market day, late in the afternoon, and while Janet went to the bank I thought I'd go and look at the cattle and sheep. Janet told me where to go, but when I got there all the stalls were empty and the market had finished. I could hear a lot of noise coming from a nearby Inn so I wandered over and went inside. I had one of the best and most memorable evenings of the whole trip and I met some really nice people. Outside it was pitch black, though still only about five o'clock. Janet had finished what she had to do and was wondering what had become of me. Eventually she found me, though she'd never ventured inside that pub in her life before. One old farmer who befriended me, greeted her like a long lost daughter. She knew him well and he promised to look after me and deliver me home safely after we'd finished our conversation. He did, though I felt an icy blast of disapproval from my in-laws when I eventually got dropped off. I didn't understand how things worked over there, etiquette, decorum, the class system, it was all alien to me and even if I had understood it was unlikely I'd conform. It's not my style. If I like someone that's enough for me, I don't care what, or who, they are.

In January Janet took me to Switzerland to visit her sister. We caught a train to London and at Heathrow airport met my Swiss brother in law who had arranged to travel back to Geneva on the same flight as us. He was a big, generous hearted man with impeccable manners, but he travelled business class, whilst we were in economy. As we approached Geneva there was thick fog, and as the plane descended I looked out of the window and saw lights level with the aircraft. This worried me a lot and I waited for us to crash. Nothing happened and some while later we landed. In the customs lounge, still feeling relieved, I saw a good looking woman with a cockie on her shoulder. I walked over and started talking to her. She smiled a lot but didn't say much. After a few minutes of me chatting away about cockatoos back home, I realised she didn't speak any English. She put her hand in her pocket and offered me some Swiss chocolate. I felt embarrassed and rather stupid. The flight from London to Geneva was only short, so I kept forgetting we were now in another country.

After going through customs we followed my brother in law out of the terminal to where his car was parked. It was a smart Mercedes Benz. Janet and the children hopped in the back seat. I got in the front left hand side, where I found myself in front of the steering wheel. I felt more embarrassment, because it looked as if I thought I was going to drive Jean Pierre's car for him. I quickly got out and went to the right passenger side door and tried to relax as we drove through blinding fog to Tricia's home. It was a scary journey, for although Jean Pierre was a skilful driver it seemed to me he was turning the wrong way at all the intersections and I found myself gripping the edge of my seat expecting a collision at any moment.

I thoroughly enjoyed the two weeks we spent in Switzerland with Tricia, Jean Pierre and their four teenage girls. I saw snow for the first time, they took me to a Roman Amphitheatre, the state stallion stables, into the mountains and to Berne. They were hospitable, kind and generous, but they didn't seem to ever eat real meat. When it came time to leave I suggested to Janet that we buy them a couple of good big roasts. I was a heavy smoker at this time and as we walked through Migros an official came over to me and began saying something I didn't understand. I smiled politely, kept smoking and went to walk on through the shop. The official stopped me and began gesticulating and pointing to my smoke. Eventually the penny dropped and I butted out. I couldn't believe the price of meat, but we ended up buying a leg of lamb and a large chicken. The lamb cost forty dollars and the chicken thirty. I told the lady at the checkout that I could buy two whole sheep in Australia for that price, but as she spoke French I don't suppose she understood a word I said. Anyway, in those days it was a lot of money. No wonder the Swiss live on cheese and sausage.

Once back in England we returned to Devon for a few days before I caught a train up to Yorkshire to visit the bloke who'd persuaded me to come over. It was a long journey and eventually I went in search of a loo. While I was in there the train stopped briefly at a station with the name I'd been looking for. I'd missed my stop. At the next station I hopped off and went in search of a public phone. I rang the bloke and told him what had happened. He came and picked me up, but he seemed to be annoyed with me. He took me to his house. It was late in the evening by now and he said he was going to bed. He told me to help myself to something from the fridge if I wanted. I've never gone to someone else's fridge, and certainly not when I've only just arrived at their house and I'm in a foreign country. I felt pretty annoyed and upset about his behaviour. I didn't feel very welcome. I thought 'Bugger this. I'm not stopping here.' Although it was late I decided I'd leave. I had a big suitcase with me and it was heavy. I started to walk down the road, in the dark. It was cold and after a while the suitcase became harder to carry. I stopped walking, put the bag down at the side of the road and went to sleep. Sometime later a car pulled up alongside me. It was my host and he asked me what I was doing.

"I'm leaving." I told him.

"Well I'll give you a lift. Where do you want to go?" he asked.

"Take me back to the station." He did and I caught a train to London, arriving there the next day. I had no idea where I was, or what to do next. I found an information desk.

"Yes?" the attendant asked as I approached.

"I'm not really sure where I am. Can you help me?" I began.

"You're in London luv." The smart arse told me. I walked away and went in search of a phone box. I tried to ring a bloke I knew who'd once worked as a jackeroo on Mandora, for Joe De Pledge. His name was Rory and he was now a peer of the realm. I was lucky Rory answered, but the phone cut out before I could tell him anything. I tried a few times, but it kept cutting out.

Unbeknown to me at the time, Janet knew I was missing. The bloke in Yorkshire had rung and told her I'd gone off into the night and she was fairly concerned, it being mid winter and freezing. During lunch the telephone rang again at her parents house in Devon, and this time her father answered it.

"It's for you Janet. A friend of John's apparently. Says he's Lord something or other. He wants to speak to you." Janet recounted the incident to me later, telling me that as she left the room she overheard her father say ' Quite extraordinary Meg! How does John know a Lord I wonder?' Rory had rung Janet to ask if she knew my whereabouts. She didn't, but I later rang her myself and this time the phone worked.

"Rory says I'm to find out exactly where you are John. You are to wait there and he will come and pick you up, no matter where it is." She told me. "He says you can stay with him until he can get you onto a plane back to Australia. And don't worry about what has happened. Rory says the English can be absolutely bloody awful sometimes." So in the end that is what happened. Rory fetched me, looked after me, booked a flight back to Australia and took me to Heathrow a few days later, where he saw me safely onto the plane. It was very good of him. Apart from a madman, who tried to light a cigarette during re-fuelling at Muscat and was later met at Perth Airport and led away in handcuffs, I had an uneventful flight home. I vowed never to venture overseas again, not even to Rottnest Island, and I haven't.

## Trap paddock at Meda Well

Once safely back on home soil the challenges of managing a million acres seemed straight forward and I gladly got on with the job. The previous manager had built a trap paddock at a place called Meda Well, with a laneway through thick tea-tree, to take the trapped cattle across to Euringa yards. I knew it was all wrong, but I couldn't help thinking 'If they've been doing it this way, we can do it too', so my first season we tried. It was impossible. There was so much paperbark you couldn't move for the tea tree. The cattle out there were absolutely unbelievable. They'd get into all the paperbarks and when the stockmen rode around to try to get them out, the cattle would come out and 'into' the horse. We had six or seven hundred head of trap cattle that we were trying to take across to Euringa, using the laneway. I think we yarded twenty-five and we ended up with six horses gored. Six! Good stock horses were very valuable. I thought 'Bugger it. This set up is no good. We won't be doing this again.'

After this debacle, although it wasn't in the programme, I got Keith Bolger to put in two yards at Meda Well, one either side of the trough, with spears in. Two forcing pens up to the pound, a forcing pen and a race and ramp, all timber. Then, when we trapped, we put up portable yards. After this had been done, when we set the trap paddock we could get all the cattle in the trap yard, with no horses harmed. It worked very well and didn't cost Emanuels anything, apart from Bolger's wages. But I wasn't very popular, just the same.

The first time we trapped, using this set-up, we took eighty bulls out of there and I don't know how many bullocks. About a hundred and fifty full lumps of mickies, which we docked (tails docked), were sent up to GoGo. I don't recall how many steers and mickie bulls we got, but it paid for the trap first up, with spares.

We had a fellow working for us, Ronnie Palmer, who came to Meda when he was fifteen. One day we were out at Meda Well, drafting in the new set up, with the forcing pens and race up to the loading ramp. There was a bull amongst the mob. He kept breaking out and wouldn't go into the forcing pen. Eventually young Ronnie got game. He'd race up behind this bull and he'd give him a fright, but the bull still ended up going back into the yard. The numbers were getting less and less, until there were only about twenty head left and the bull was one of them. Ronnie raced up behind the bull and yelled at him, to try to frighten him into the gate. But he whipped around on him. Ronnie ran away and everybody was yelling out to him, "Look out, look out!" The bull was right behind him. Ronnie, who was a pretty athletic young fellow, just left the ground and jumped. His hands grabbed the top of the steel panels and his feet came over. Just as he let them go the bull hit the panels and shifted them a couple of metres. Ronnie landed on the other side still running. Our hearts were in our mouths. If he had just jumped up onto the rails, as was usual, he would have been squashed clean through them. I don't know why he decided to jump, rather than climb, over the rails, but by golly it was the right decision. Ronnie was a really smart man. He was a good hard worker, but by Jeez he played hard too. He was there with us quite a number of years.

## Willie Lennard has a close shave

It was the first week of June, 1982. Willie was giving us a hand in the yard at Poultons. He was hunting cattle up into the forcing pen, for me to draft. A beast went through and I yelled out, 'meatworks', 'bush' or whatever it was. Next thing I heard 'Look out old man!' I looked around and there was Willie, sitting a small distance away from me, at the bottom of the yard rails, his head back and a cow was ' into him'. I raced in and hunted the cow away. I grabbed Willie and tried to pass him over the rails, but all the blokes seemed stunned. They wouldn't move. I yelled at them, "Can all you 'nice' boys please help me." except I said it in good Australian. They'd gone useless. Dumb. Fright I suppose. Willie was too heavy for me to lift up, so I turned around and dragged him up to the gate. We were both still in the forcing pen with this cow.

"For Chris'sake open the gate and let this bitch out of here." I shouted. When I grabbed Willie his head was back. There was a gaping hole down into his throat and blood was coming from several places. He was unconscious.

What had happened was, when this cow had a go at him, Willie had jumped onto the rails, but she reared up and hooked the cuff of his trousers, pulling him back down into the forcing pen. As she did so, from five foot six high, he banged the back of his head as he went down and was knocked out. Then when he landed, unconscious, she'd got stuck into him. One horn went across his ribs and up under his arm. Another up into his throat. I said to Dennis, our Irish mechanic, "Go to the station and get Janet to ring an ambulance. Then come back and meet me, to see that my vehicle hasn't broken down." Dennis left and we got Willie out of the yard and into the front of the motor car. As I was driving off I saw that Willie's sons had jumped on the back. I knew I was going to be driving fairly fast so I stopped and told them to get off. At first they refused.

"No, we're coming. Dat's our father."

"You're not coming. You're not little boys and I'm going to be driving fairly fast. Now get off this motorcar 'please'." I told them. As they climbed off I checked Willie. There was blood running down and when his head was back I could see right in. I took my shirt off, folded it into a roll and wrapped it around his neck. Then I took my belt off and tied a couple of knots in it. By this time the injured man was coming round. Using my belt I put a tourniquet round his throat. I said to him, "I've gotta do this. You're hurt. You tell me when it's too tight and I'm stopping you breathing, but it has to be tight." I slowly tightened the belt until he indicated it was enough. Having done this we set off. I drove as fast as I dared until we ran up the tail of a bunch of Aborigines dawdling along in a station wagon. I was blowing the horn and putting the lights on and off, but do you think they'd get off the road and let us get past? No bloody way! Eventually we did pass them and soon after I met Dennis coming out of Meda. I pulled over.

"What do you want me to do now?" he asked.

"Stay behind us until we meet the ambulance. Then pull up." We met the ambulance the other side of Millards Soak. I got out of the motor car and went around to the far side of the ambulance. I was starting to get the shakes and I broke down. They came over to me and asked if I was all right.

"I'm OK. Just get Willie. He's been gored in the throat and I'm very worried about him." So they got him, put him in the ambulance and took him away.

"What do you want me to do?" Dennis asked again.

"You follow the ambulance to make sure it doesn't break down." I instructed, then I drove back home. I was in shock. Willie was like a father to me. He taught me to ride, taught me to drive, everything. He was really good to me for my whole life, from a little tiny thing. A few days later Janet was going into town for stores. I asked her to go to the hospital and ask for my shirt and belt back, which she did.

"John won't be wanting his shirt back." The hospital staff told her."We haven't got that any more, it's been incinerated, but here's the belt. Tell your husband, Willie is a very lucky man. If John hadn't done what he did that day Willie would have been dead before he reached us. The horn had nicked his jugular." I was pleased to hear that, especially as some of Willie's children had later accused me of trying to kill their father. I hadn't really known what to do, the tourniquet was all I could think of at the time. Willie went on to make a full recovery.

## A cleanskin bull gets an earmark at Fitzroy

I had given my blokes a few days off. Some of them wanted to go up to Fitzroy Crossing for the rodeo, gymkhana. I decided to go too, not to ride, only to spectate. It had been five or six years since I'd last been, when I'd pulled Gunny out of the river. As before, I left Janet at home, with the children and went on my own.

It was the second day, the gymkhana finished and the rodeo was on. I had had a few beers and my good mate Phil Le Lievre was there with me. He and I were sitting up on the rails watching the bull ride. A bull came out of the chute, decked his rider and trotted around the arena towards us.

"That's a cleanskin" I pointed out to Phil.

"Gee Wellsy, once upon a time you and I could've decked that bull and earmarked him, no trouble."

"What's with the 'once upon a time? I could still deck it."

"I bet you can't." Phil challenged me.

"If you come with me I'll deck him all right."

"OK then." Phil agreed. The bull was trotting back round the rails, in our direction. He came right up near me, so I jumped off the rails, grabbed hold of his tail and threw him. I held him down for a bit and he didn't resist, so I got out my pocket knife and put a Meda earmark on him. With that the bull decided to get up. I was about three feet from his head. Phil was still sitting on the rails. He hadn't come with me. I thought 'Jeez, I'm in a bit of trouble here.' As the bull was standing up I flicked a big mob of sand in his face and I was gone, out of there. There were spectators watching from around the arena, but I wasn't aware of them. A bloke rode over to me.

"If you do that again you'll be in serious trouble." He warned. I knew it was a silly thing to do and I shouldn't have risen to the bait. I felt a bit disappointed in myself. This was because many years earlier, while at a gymkhana in Broome, my name had been called out to compete in the open barrel race. I was just a spectator. I didn't have any horses there, so I don't know how they got my name in the programme. Just at that moment a kid rode past me on a horse I recognised. It was Alcabeer, the working horse Vincent Bear had taken off with at Napier. A good smart horse. I said to the kid, "Here, lend us that horse a minute." He did. I'd had an ale or two earlier in the afternoon. I lengthened the stirrup leathers, hopped on and away we went in the barrel race. As we went round the first barrel I fell straight in it. After that I promised myself never to do anything so silly again. Now, at Fitzroy I had and I wasn't very happy with myself. When I got back to Meda we wrote out a personal cheque for a hundred dollars, to pay for the bull I'd earmarked. It had been an expensive prank.

## Two go missing

We went out to Poultons to brand cattle at the old timber yards. We needed the calf cradle, which had last been used at a portable yard out at Rarriwell. Rarriwell was some distance from where we were working that day, so I sent two station hands off in a vehicle to fetch it. One of the blokes I sent was local and had a bit of age on him. The other was a young lad from Perth, working his first season on the station. He didn't seem to have much aptitude for the job, but he was brilliant at fixing transistor radios, which went down well in the men's quarters. I said to these two blokes, "Jump in the motorcar and go down the road back to the river. There is a cut line, (seismic line) which goes off on the right hand side. Follow that right the way through. It will eventually take you onto the Oobagooma Road, then you'll know where you are. Follow the Oobagooma road on up to Rarriwell, pick up the calf cradle, then come back here the same way. By the time you get back with it, we'll be ready to brand these calves." So off they went. After they had gone we began drafting the cattle.

There had been a lot of seismic work done on Meda at the time, and a grid of cut lines had been put in over much of the property. They were pretty handy for us, not only as firebreaks, but also as shortcuts to get from place to place, as was the case on this occasion, the one in question being Line Seventeen. We finished the drafting and as the two hadn't yet returned we had smoko. As there was still no sign of them, rather than continue waiting, we decided to scruff the calves and brand them, without the use of a calf cradle. Eventually we got the job done and finished. The pair still weren't back. We let the cattle out. There was nothing more to do, but they still hadn't returned. I thought they might have misunderstood me and taken the calf cradle straight to the homestead, so I went home. They weren't there. I said to Willie, "Can you go out and look for these fellas? They were sent from Poultons to Rarriwell on Line Seventeen, early this morning and we haven't seen them since." By this time it was late in the day.

Willie came back from his search at about seven o'clock in the evening. By now it was dark and he'd been unable to find them. I sent another couple of men out to look. They came back a few hours later. They hadn't been able to find them either. By this time I was pretty concerned. Apart from the worry that they might be perishing, my fear was that they had driven, at speed, into a concealed creek crossing. When the mining mobs put in the seismic lines, when they came to a steep creek the 'dozers would cut the line right up to the creek bank. They would then find an easier crossing further up or downstream, and make a detour to take their equipment across. Once on the other side they'd do the same. Cut the line right to the creek edge, so that it would look like a straight road right through. I thought these two blokes, if they'd been travelling with a bit of pace, may have driven over the steep bank of one of these creeks.

First thing in the morning I sent out a couple of vehicles to look for them again, but there was still no sign of them. It was now about ten o'clock in the morning. They'd been missing well over twenty four hours. I rang the police in Derby. I told them I could probably get a plane down from GoGo to help with the search, but I couldn't get through to GoGo because it was a weekend and the telephone exchange in Fitzroy Crossing was shut. The constable said, "Don't worry about that. We'll ring the police in Fitzroy and they can then ring GoGo." which they did. We couldn't get the plane from GoGo immediately, because it had gone up to Kununurra for a service, but they sent it down later in the day. In the meantime we had been driving up and down cutlines looking for these two fellows. Once we'd checked that they hadn't driven into one of the creek crossings, the next big concern was that they were lost, broken down and maybe perishing.

My men were still out looking for them when the plane arrived from Kununurra. I went up with Max, the pilot, and we flew the seismic lines systematically from end to end, one after the other. While we were doing this we noticed a dust in the distance. We left the cutline we were following and flew over to where the vehicle was. We had a loud speaker in the plane and we were able to tell the driver to go straight back to the station, that it was urgent.

Max and I flew back to the homestead and waited for the chap to come in. When he arrived he had one of the lost blokes with him. The young inexperienced fellow. The chap in the vehicle had been snooping around where he had no business to be, when he had come upon the young fellow, so he was a fortunate boy. When asked he told us how he and Jeff had got lost the day before and had then run out of fuel. They had left the vehicle and walked to Middle Bore, where they camped the night. In the morning they had had a disagreement about which direction they should go. The big local fellow reckoned one way, which in fact was incorrect, and the little chap thought another, which was more in line with the way back to the station. When the trespasser, snooping around in his vehicle, had come across the young chap he was carrying two glass bottles he had found. He had tied the necks together with bits of wire and filled them with water from the bore where they had camped. As he lent against the vehicle to speak to the driver, the bottles were so old and brittle they disintegrated. But at least he had had the sense to carry some water with him, even though the containers were precarious. After talking to him we went out again, overland, in the direction the young chap indicated the older fellow had been heading. I drove, taking a man with me to help look. The fellow who'd been trespassing said he'd follow along behind me in his vehicle. This proved to be very lucky.

I went in front. I knew the roads and the shortcuts. The road Jeff was thought to be on was not a very well used road. It was more of a bush track. We were going from Geoff's Bore and heading towards Brandy's. I kept checking that there was a dust behind me and that the second vehicle was still following. We weren't going very fast because we were looking along the way as we went. We were about two miles from Geoff's Bore when I realised there was no dust coming behind. I slowed down and kept checking in the rear vision mirror. There was still no sign of a dust. I slowed down more, but still he didn't seem to be coming. I thought something must be wrong, so I stopped. I waited for about five minutes, but there was still no sign of him. I turned around and headed back the way I'd come, to see what was going on. He was pulled up on the track and he'd found my lost man. He was about to give him a drink of water but I stopped him. I said he could only drink a very little bit. The rest was to be poured over his head and clothes. Jeff was talking a lot of rubbish. He was semi delirious I suppose, and his eyes were rolling around in his head. It was his lucky day. If we hadn't had the two vehicles following one another we would have missed him. He would have probably perished within the next few hours. Although he had heard me drive past, he was camped under a big boab tree a long way off the track. By the time he ran out I was gone. I wouldn't have seen him in the rear vision mirror because of the dust cloud my vehicle was throwing up. What he should have done was put some green bushes out on the road, to alert us before he camped. To draw our attention that he was somewhere nearby. But he had done nothing. It was sheer good fortune that the other fellow came along a couple of minutes behind me and spotted him. That was the only reason he was saved.

We took him back to the station and he had to go into hospital. He was dehydrated, but was all right. Later on he reckoned he was some sort of hero. He was skiting about it and I don't think he had any idea how close he had come to not being with us. He was a local man who should have known better. The other fellow was a newcomer to the country and completely green, yet he had done the smarter thing.

## A roll over at Lakes

Bill was a bespectacled, carrot haired bloke who worked on Meda for a time, putting spears in on traps. He was 'on' with one of Willie Lennard's daughters, Kitty, and they lived in the old hut at the Claypan where Tex had once lived. Bill owned an F100, which was a bit of a problem for me, because he could come and go as he pleased and there wasn't much I could do about it. If he went into Derby through the bullock paddock and the Leprosarium, or up the new oil road, I wouldn't even know about it, because he wouldn't have to pass by the homestead.

One day Bill went into town and he picked up quite a few of the Morlumbuns, an Aboriginal family from Mowanjum, and they bought a lot of grog. He drove home through the bullock paddock with seventeen people on his vehicle. On the way they decided they needed some meat for tea and that they'd get themselves a killer. It was 'dry' time and there were cattle getting a green pick on the swamp at Lakes bore. They tried to shoot a heifer, from the moving vehicle, wheeling it around the flat as they did so. The F100, overloaded with people, eventually rolled. The passengers were thrown out of the back and Kitty Lennard's younger sister, Barbara, was crushed by the vehicle and killed.

It was a Saturday. Janet, the children and I had been to Derby to visit my parents. We were on our way home late in the evening, when we met the police coming out of Meda. They told us what had been happening in our absence.

The next day it was reported on the news that a thirty year old woman had been killed on Meda, when a four wheel drive vehicle rolled. Janet was thirty at the time. People who knew us were ringing up, very concerned. If only they had given out a few more details, such as 'an Aboriginal woman' or 'a vehicle carrying seventeen people', it would have given our friends a hint that it wasn't Janet. But they weren't allowed to be racist, so it caused a lot of worry for a lot of people.

The driver was later acquitted of manslaughter, but the death of Barbara was not the only tragedy endured by her parents, Willie and Roslyn Lennard. A year or two later Kitty was murdered in Darwin and in subsequent years several of their offspring died, mainly as a result of alcohol.

## A bloke called 'Bull'

On stations you sometimes got people who were a bit strange, but if they could work I'd put up with them and their antics, up to a point. 'Bull' was one of these blokes. He was a tough fella, a good worker and strong as an ox, which is how he earned his nickname. I rather liked him, but he was definitely strange. I think his childhood had buggered him. Apparently he used be locked in a cupboard, as a kid, while his father bashed his mother up. It was 1983 when he came to work at Meda. One day we were mustering off the ridges, between Bobs Bore and Macaulay's, where we had a portable yard set up. We'd put up a series of hessian wings, which acted as funnels into the portable yards and we got a big mob of cattle. There were a good lot of big bullocks amongst them too. When we were drafting these cattle 'Bull' was in the pound, hunting them up. A cow came into the pound. A toey, shitty livered looking thing, so I said to this bloke, "You want to get the hell of there. That cow will nail you in a minute."

"Ah, no. I'll be right." he says. So I thought 'Oh, all right, you keep going then.' Next thing the cow went for him. This bloke was quick, I'll give him that. He went up and over the rails, but he missed his footing on the other side and slid down the outside of the fence. As he was sliding down the cow had a crack at him. She hooked him across the guts, leaving a livid red line across his belly, but luckily for him, her horns didn't penetrate. Another inch and she'd have dropped his guts clean out.

"Did you learn a lesson?" I asked.

"I learnt to jump higher and run faster John" he told me, but he was shaking.

This same fellow used to lift portable panels, single handed. We could all lift one on our own now and then, but he would lift them on his own all the time. We had a portable crush, normally a two, or three, man lift. 'Bull' would get the crush, shut the bale on it, put his neck through and flick it off the truck. He had exceptional strength and he didn't bludge, though he'd work on keeping himself fit and strong. He'd get a forty kilogram bag of horse nuts, hoist it onto his shoulders, then run around the billabong. He'd do this most evenings after he'd done a full and honest days work. The other blokes didn't give him any cheek.

One night we'd taken the Meda blokes into town for a Chinese. I'd made a deal to shout them tea at Lwoy's if we reached a certain number of branders for the season. When we got home Janet found we'd left some sprinklers on by mistake. We had a mob of day old chicks, in a pen on the lawn. It was flooded and the chicks, which had been sent up from Perth, were all wet and bedraggled. Janet was leaning into the pen and collecting up the wet chicks, putting them in a cardboard box to warm them up. 'Bull' came over and gave her a hand. I'd stayed at the single men's quarters having a few beers with the rest of the blokes. 'Bull' couldn't drink beer. If he did he went right off his trolley. He'd had a few during the evening, but not too many. I was still at the quarters when 'Bull' came back from helping Janet and he joined us for a drink too. I stayed there yarning with the blokes for a fair while and Janet had gone to bed well before I got home. Unbeknown to me 'Bull', having had a fair few beers by now, decided to go over to the main house. Janet heard the flyscreen door bang and thought it was me coming in late. But it wasn't. The next thing 'Bull' was in the bedroom. When Janet realised it wasn't me she slipped a cog and told him to get the hell out of the house. He said he'd just come to ask her to have a beer. Janet told him to get out, in no uncertain terms, and he did. She wanted me to put the skids under him after that, but he was a good worker so I didn't.

## A nose piercing

The old timber yards at Euringa were fairly big. A lot of yards were designed like that and I don't know why. Cattlemen must have known that it's hard to push cattle up out of a large yard into a small yard, especially if the gate isn't very big. But the Euringa yard was like that all my younger days.

One day we were at Euringa, trying to push the cattle up into a forcing pen for drafting. It was dusty and they didn't want to go in the gate. Cattle get to know not to go in there. The dust is really something. You can't see more than a few feet. I had some good smart young white fellas working for me on Meda at the time. One was an apprentice jockey from Bunbury. I was sitting on the rails watching. He was busy yapping and not really concentrating, though he was a lively lad. I said to him, "For Chris'sake shut up will you and watch those cattle? You'll get nailed in a minute."

"Not me Wellsy. I'll be right."

"OK, you keep doing what you're doing." You can't tell young fellas much. They think they're invincible. A moment later, out of the mob came about a two and a half year old half bred Santa Gertrudis bull, with horns about eight inches long and needle sharp. The bull was wanting to get out of the mob, away from the dust and the people. Epis went to run away. He turned one way to run, but the bull was going to turn that way to miss him. So he then turned the other way. But the bull had already turned that way, to get away from him. So then Epis turned around to face the bull. They both collided. One horn went up the young fellas nostril and came out at the bone. It slipped out again and the two parted company. The bull absolutely had Epis where he wanted him, if he'd wanted to kill him. But he let him go. I watched the whole thing. That bull never wanted to hurt the young bloke. When it was all over everything stopped for a while and we had a look at him. The wound was so neat you'd reckon we'd held him down and poked a scalpel blade up his nose and pulled it out again. There was no ripping, it just went in and out, clean as you like. Epis couldn't talk afterwards and he was the whitest white man I've ever seen in my life. He sat on a post for about two hours and we never heard boo out of him. I don't think he could physically open his mouth to talk if he'd wanted to, it had given him such a fright.

## Gila and a Yeeda bull

In latter years we employed a couple of girls in the stockcamp and I found them to be very good. Although they didn't have the strength of the men when it came to things such as shifting portable yards, or putting in rails, generally they were gentler on vehicles and machinery as well as stock. One of these young women was an American, called Gila, who came across from neighbouring Birdwood Downs.

We had a couple of Yeeda bulls running on Meda at the time. I suppose a flood must have washed them out to sea one 'wet' and the tide had brought them back onto Meda country, where they stayed. They were good looking Brahman bulls. I thought 'This is good. We'll keep these two bulls and get some calves from them.' We never did get any calves from them, because neither were any good. When we mustered we would pick them up and yard them with our mob. We found one to be a good, quiet bull. You could do anything with him and he'd go through the yard no trouble. But the other fellow wouldn't go into the forcing pen. When the numbers got less in the receiving yard, he'd start to chase somebody. It was just a fluke that the first time he pulled this caper he charged someone that was very frightened. They went over the rails and down the other side and he followed them, but he didn't stop. He just kept going, bush. He had jumped straight behind them, at the same spot, clean out of the yard and away. Once I'd seen him do this, if he was in the mob, I'd say to my workers, "Now if that bull charges you, don't just jump up onto the rails. You must jump up and over to the other side. Then run along the side of the yard and get out of his way, because he will follow you over the top."

One day we had him in the Claypan yards and he pulled the same stunt, this time charging the American girl. She was absolutely petrified. She jumped onto the top of the rails, but in her panic she fell. As she fell she turned over mid-air and was falling backwards. I ran and jumped up onto the rails a bit further along. As the girl was falling the bull went over the top of her. Gila landed on her back at the foot of the rails, a second later the bull landed, but he kept running. That's how close it was. After that I told Dennis to shoot him, which he did with his usual efficiency.

## Goose

Poor Goose. He was a very simple bloke, but he'd do anything you asked him, if he was capable of it. He had a good disposition and despite his difficulties, a very easy going nature. He was brought up by his grandmother and before he came over to us she rang up and asked what he would need. I said he would need boots and a hat. When he arrived he came with RM Williams boots and an Akubra. He couldn't ride a horse. He wasn't good with horses and cattle. He didn't belong to that sort of life. He couldn't really do a lot of things, but he was a good bloke nonetheless. Really you need someone like him in every stockcamp. He provided the entertainment. But his poor old grandmother, I think she must have had a hard time with him.

One time we were painting the station kitchen and Goose was giving a hand. He got the roller and he got the tray full to the brim with paint. In went the roller, up onto the wall. Paint dripping down the handle, onto his hands. He wiped the sweat from his face, streaking it yellow, as he shoved the roller up and down, flat out, across the wall. Onto the window, down the wall, onto the floor. Yellow paint was going everywhere. He was totally uncoordinated. You've no idea the mess, but he was willing. Always willing, to do anything, though sometimes it was better not to ask him.

Poor Goose, he got into some serious predicaments. One day he was filling up drums on the truck, from out of the tank. I was drafting, looking straight over in his direction. The truck had the crate on and Goose had the back door open. He had come over to the yards and backed the truck up to the trough. He was putting water into the trough out of the drums. He was up on the truck, in the crate, pulling the hose and walking backwards as he did so. I stopped drafting to watch him. He kept on walking backwards, straight out the back of the truck, flat on his back onto the ground. When I'd stopped drafting to watch Goose, the other blokes all looked over as well. We were all killing ourselves laughing. He was a big lump of a young fella and could have got badly hurt. But that was how it went, all the time. The bigger the danger, after a close shave, the more we used to laugh.

Goose completed the season with us and his grandmother wrote to me the following year and asked me if I'd take him back. But he wasn't really full value. I liked him. He made everyone laugh and enjoyed being the clown. I thought he was a good bloke, but as far as paying him wages, it probably wasn't economical. Well it possibly was, if not in productivity, in so far as keeping the other fellows amused and happy. But it wasn't my money paying his wages and although I would have liked to employ him again I knew I couldn't justify it. I got a lot of laughs out of Goose while he was with us, even though I knew I shouldn't really have been laughing at him. But he never seemed to mind, I think he even quite liked it. He had a fortunate attitude to people putting shit on him. Blokes could laugh at him and sling off and he'd crack jokes back at them. He'd never heckle up. He didn't have a bad streak in him and was a genuinely soft fellow. Goose was a nice, simple bloke and I have often wondered what ever became of him.

## 'Silly Pete'

I first got 'Silly Pete' in 1982 when an agency rang up and said they had a fellow looking for a job and could we fit him in. So we took him, but it turned out to be a big mistake. The fellow was absolutely useless, with none of the redeeming character traits we enjoyed in Goose. 'Silly Pete' was no longer young, though what age he was is hard to say. One day we were up at Poulton's Yard drafting and branding. We didn't have a calf cradle there so we were pulling the calves up to the rails, with the tractor and cutting, earmarking and branding them. 'Silly Pete' was driving the tractor. He'd be trying to pull the calves heads through the rails. He seemed to reckon the length of the rope was different everytime you went to pull up a calf. It was a wonder he didn't break their necks. In the end I put a log down, so when he went forward he ran against the log.

"Now, when the tractor wheel hits this log, that's the end of the rope, so don't go any further." I explained. You had to make things really definite for him. Everything went a bit better after that.

When we'd finished at Poultons, the stockcamp moved on to Orange Pool. 'Silly Pete' was driving the tractor and trailer, shifting camp for us. We had forty-four gallon drums for rubbish. We shouldn't have done this, but in those days you'd get all your tins and other refuse and chuck it in a gully somewhere. I said to Pete "Get these drums and tip them out into a gully and empty all the rubbish out of them. Then put the drums back on the trailer. Bring them and all the other gear along to the next camp, which is at Orange Pool." I was in the stockcamp at the time. When we were at Orange Pool we found that we were short of neck straps, there were no bloody hobbles, no ropes and no drums to put our rubbish in. I was a bit confused about this. We were fairly busy. We didn't need the ropes because we had a drafting yard at Orange Pool and also at Langoora, where we moved onto next. A few days later I had to go back home. I decided to go back around the way we'd come. When I got to Poultons there were the rubbish bins. All the rubbish had been tipped onto the ground and left out on the flat where we'd camped. A bag with the ropes, all made out of green-hide, along with bags of hobble straps and chains were left there on the ground as well. Silly Pete had been told to take the rubbish and chuck it in the creek, but no, he'd just emptied the bins where they were, then left the bins and all the other equipment lying on the flat. I couldn't believe it. I picked up all the gear and put it on the motorcar. I delivered the ropes, hobble straps and a few other things he'd left behind, to the stockcamp. I took the rubbish home. I really don't know what Pete thought he was doing. He didn't seem to understand the simplest things. With him, what was already on the trailer went with him and what wasn't, didn't. It just got left there. He was absolutely bloody useless.

We had a fire in the bullock paddock. I pulled all the blokes out of the stockcamp, back to the station. They got in at about three in the afternoon.

"We're going out to fight fires all night in the bullock paddock, so grab yourselves a feed at the kitchen now. Then I want you to get the truck, put on the forty-four gallon drums, go to the overhead tank and fill the drums with the hose. We'll need bags, rakes, shovels and matches as well. But grab yourselves a feed first." I told them. Silly Pete had not been with the stockcamp on this occasion, so he had eaten earlier. Having listened to what was going on, he went and got the truck, with the crate on and within the space of three minutes, had taken down a power line, run over a ladder and knocked the water filler off the overhead tank. I was fuming. I said to my blokes, "Don't ever let that silly bastard drive a vehicle on this place again." He was a real bloody worry, that bloke. I think there was something seriously wrong with him. At the end of the season when I sent the blokes on holiday I said to 'Silly Pete', "I don't need you to come back here next year."

Quite some time later, I was short of men. I went into Derby and went round the pubs asking if any blokes wanted a job. There were two who said, "Yeah. We want a job"

"Righto. I'll be back in an hour and pick you up."

I finished doing what I needed to and an hour later I went back to the Spinifex Hotel to collect them. Janet was with me. We picked them up and one of these blokes came round to the passenger side door and reckoned he was hopping in the front with Janet. I told him he could get on the back, where the other fellow had already gone. We drove to Elders and on the way Janet said, "Do you know who you've got?"

"No"

"That's 'Silly Pete' who you had working for you once before." So I thought 'Oh, shit'. I couldn't really tell him to get off, so I thought I'd better keep going with him and give him another try. But he was just as useless as ever and I was glad to eventually get rid of him. I feel sorry for him really. I think he was a bit simple, but he was too big a liability and of absolutely no value whatsoever.

A number of years later a bloke asked me if I knew 'Silly Pete'. I told him I did.

"He worked for you didn't he?"

"Yeah he did. He was bleep bleep useless."

"He's useless all right. We had him on Blina. He was employed as a grader driver. While he was there he went through a few gates and wiped out the struts and posts. Then he ran the grader over a big mob of building material we had on the ground. Eventually we got rid of him."

"Jeez. 'Silly Pete' driving a grader? That isn't a good idea. How come you employed him in the first place?" I asked.

"Well, I asked him a few questions, which he answered, then he said 'I've worked for John Wells a couple of times, on Meda.' When he said that I thought he must be all right, so I gave him the job."

"Well, you should have asked me before you employed him, not after." I told him, but I thought it was quite amusing.

## A place to call home

Meda, like any other Kimberley cattle property of the time, had the usual mix of station employees. From the young, lively, and mostly competent ringers, the handy, ingenious bush mechanics and windmillmen, the invaluable loyal native stockmen, down to the utterly useless poor bastards who blew in from time to time and who were generally sent swiftly on their way. But amongst the hotchpotch of humanity to be found in both camp and quarters there were always a few old derelicts, worn down by life, who pottered about doing odd jobs, only too pleased for a roof over their head, some tucker in their belly and some respite from the temptations of town. These old fellows were handy to have about the place, doing odd jobs, running errands and keeping an eye on things at the homestead. But they had to be heavily policed. They were cunning old devils and I kept tight rein of their alcohol intake. Their grog ration was two big bottles of beer a night, but they were devious and often tried to pry extra rations from us. They had no qualms about lying and would either tell Janet they hadn't been given it yet, or, if I was late getting home, would meet me as soon as I drove in to get a second ration, before Janet could tell me they'd already had it.

One such fellow was Jack Fox. He was an aggressive sort of bloke and a heavy drinker. He begged me for a job, to get him out of town and off the grog. He was getting on a bit, so I got him to do odd jobs around the homestead. Feed the chooks, tidy up, look after the pigs, that kind of thing. I'd get him to give the windmillman a hand if he needed it. Jack was too old and buggered to really do much, white haired and shelly, with the characteristically skinny legs of the hardened drinker. But he was quite useful to have around and he knew a bit about gardening which was a help to Janet.

Jack came to us soon after we got to Meda and Tex was working there at the same time. Tex had bought a horse off somebody, that was supposed to be next to Phar Lap, but wasn't any value whatsoever. He was a mongrel buck jumper and would unwind at any time. It used to give me the bloody horrors, because one man always had to be alongside it looking after Tex. This is called 'two men riding one horse'. It takes two men, but only one horse is working. It was a damn nuisance.

Eventually old Jack Fox bought this mongrel horse off Tex, as a race horse! I don't know why Jack thought it was so marvellous. It would have to have a bloody good jockey to stay on it. There was no way it was ever going to be any good to him and it certainly wasn't going to be a race horse. We had had another horse on Meda, called Frank. Frank was a good stock horse, but one year, after the 'wet', he came in with a big swamp cancer on him. We treated it, got the vet out to it and spent a fair bit of time on this horse trying to get him better, but it was no good. Eventually we had to destroy him. The mongrel horse that Jack Fox had bought off Tex also came in, at the end of one 'wet', with a big swamp cancer in exactly the same place as Frank's had been. From our experience with the good working horse I knew there was no point wasting our time trying to fix Jack's mongrel animal up. The kindest thing to do was put him out of his misery, so I got him shot. After a time I got a letter from a lawyer saying they were going to sue me for shooting Jack's horse without permission. Christ! It wasn't as if it had been a decent type of a horse. Nor was there any chance of it getting over the cancer it came in with. I couldn't believe Jack would be so damn stupid as to want to sue me. I'd been doing him a favour giving him a job at the station, to help him dry out, in the first place. This letter seemed a bit unreasonable. I decided to confront Jack about it.

"Look, I know you've been helping yourself to pigs, without permission, taking them into Derby for your mates, and making a good fellow of yourself. I think you'd better get onto these lawyers, Jack, because there are a fair few things I could tell them if I have to." I never heard another word about being sued after that.

One thing I will say for Jack. He was one these blokes who'd come to you for a bite, when he was pissed as a cricket. I used to think I'd never see that money again, but he'd always repay it eventually. I don't know how the hell he remembered, the state he'd be in when he borrowed it, but he'd never forget a debt, no matter how full he was.

## The one-eyed bandit

Another fellow of similar ilk was the one-eyed bandit. He too was a practical sort of bloke, ancient and somewhat snarly, but clearly a strong man in his youth. He had once been a panel beater and very good at his job too, but the poor bloke had the most terrible shakes, not just from the grog, but permanently. His hands shook so badly I don't know how he managed to do his job without hurting himself. To see him with a hammer was quite something. When he came into the station kitchen for smoko he'd pick up the big enamel teapot and wave it over his pannikin in an alarming way. We used to think he'd end up burning himself, but he had it down to a fine art. Having grasped the teapot firmly, he would take hold of his mug in the other shaking hand and slowly begin to pour. I don't know how the hell he did it, but somehow the teapot and pannikin moved in unison and not a drop would be spilled. If he left the mug on the bench and tried to pour out his tea the hot liquid would miss the cup and go everywhere.

Although the old man appeared devoid of humour he did give us reason to grin on a few occasions, the most memorable of which was during a thunderstorm. It was late in the day, during the 'wet' season. It was raining and there was a severe tropical storm about. Work was finished for the day and the men were milling about the quarters chatting, when all of a sudden there was a flash of lightening and instantaneously an explosive bolt of thunder. In itself, nothing unusual for that time of the year, except on this occasion a ghost appeared immediately afterwards. White as a sheet and stark naked, the one-eyed bandit emerged from the single men's quarters, shaking all over. He had been taking a shower when the storm hit. Thinking better of it he decided to step out of the shower and was leaning on the metal window ledge looking out of the louvres at the downpour. When the quarters were struck by lightening he was thrown backwards against the wall, but apart from shock, he appeared unharmed.

## Paddy the carpenter

He knew his trade and did a lot of good work during his years on Meda, but grog was a problem and I suspect had wrecked what family life he may once have had. The station became his home for several years and Paddy, shuffling about, his feet thrust into worn down thongs, stick like legs protruding from indecently wrunkled shorts, was a familiar part of the Meda scene. Paddy took a keen interest in our two young children, our daughter in particular and would buy clothes and presents for her when in town. The year Janet took us to England for Christmas Paddy bought a nice pink winter coat for her, which proved very useful, though how he'd made such a purchase in the tropics I don't know. Eventually we began to find his generosity disturbing, and his choice of gifts. The last straw was the purchase of several pairs of trainer knickers in lurid colours and slinky fabric, probably well meant, but inappropriate and worrying.

## Beef thief

There were a number of benefits in living close to town, but there were equally as many disadvantages. One of them was townsfolk helping themselves to killers. In an attempt to lessen the problem, I used to sell a bit of meat from the station and the money went into the station kitty. Sometimes the blacks would come and tell me what they'd seen, or what they knew. If they did I might give them a quarter of beef, if I had it in the cool room. But there were still a lot of people who preferred to come out of town to steal killers. It was a never ending problem for us. I always took a lot of notice of what kite hawks and crows were doing. I still do today, because they usually tell you what's where. One time I came onto a place where someone had got a killer. It was quite usual, if killing someone else's beast, to remove the ear with the earmark, so there was no proof of ownership should they be caught. The funny part about this killer was that, although they had taken off one of the ears, they had removed the clean ear and left the one with the earmark in it. Apparently they hadn't understood the reason for cutting off an ear, they just knew it was what one did.

One time a killer was shot, down in the bullock paddock. The bullock paddock was easily accessible from Derby. Would be thieves could come through the Leprosarium, or the oil road, without having to come past the homestead and it was the most common place to discover evidence of a theft. On this occasion the beast had been butchered out in the grass. I might never have seen it, had the thieves not dragged the beast across the only road going to the bores. To me this said 'Hey look! Follow this and see what we've got.' I found where the killer had been butchered. They must have got it early that morning or the previous evening, because what was left was still fresh. When I got home I rang the police and reported it. One of the coloured policemen said he'd smelt fresh meat on a couple of blokes in the pub. He went around to their place and sure enough, they had a fridge full of beef. So they got nailed.

It was the end of the year and there were only a few of us left at the station. Word was about that there was a lot of rain coming. We decided to go and get a couple of killers so we had plenty of meat. When the rains come you can't always get out to get a killer when you need one. I took Dennis, our mechanic, with me and we went down the bullock paddock. We were driving towards One Tree bore. There had been a lightning strike down there and a fire had burned a bit of country, but then gone out. I looked across at a burnt white gum tree. There was white stuff underneath it, but thinking it was ashes I didn't take much notice of it and I kept going. Dennis looked at me.

"Aren't you going to check that beast over there?"

"What beast?"

"Under that tree, there's a beast."

"No Dennis. That's only the ashes from that white gum tree that's been burnt." I told him.

"No. That's a beast." he insisted. We whizzed around and went back to see which of us was right. As we got closer I could see it was the gut of a beast. The meat had been taken off one side, and the gut was shining white. As we drove up a bloke stepped out from behind a tree. I knew him. I was a bit worried.

"Put a bullet up the breech of the rifle, Dennis, and when I get out and talk to this fella you look after me." I added, "Have it cocked." I got out and Dennis did too. This bloke walked towards me. As he did so another fellow stood up from where he'd been hiding, behind the belly of the dead beast. Dennis squatted down on his haunches, with the rifle pointing in the air, but he just had to drop it if they produced a rifle for me. I asked them what they thought they were doing.

"We needed some meat John. We were going to ring you up tonight and tell you we'd got it, then come out later and pay for it."

"Yeah?" I said sceptically. "There must be a lot of blokes like you around Derby." I noticed a vehicle parked about two hundred yards away, in the scrub. I said to Dennis, "You stay here with these blokes." I walked over to the car for a look. The meat was lying there on bushes, ready to load. I went back to our vehicle and said to these blokes, "Right, you can give us a hand now to put this killer in our vehicle. Is anyone else here with you?"

"No" So then we put all the meat into our vehicle.

"Righto. You can go, but when I get home I'll be ringing the cops." When I reported the theft the police asked me what the value of the beast was.

"It was a heifer that had been trucked down to Meda from GoGo for a breeder. She would potentially have had eight calves, so the value of them as well would be in the order of … "

"No, no you can't do that John. What was her value at the time she was shot?"

"Probably about $120." So the police went around and saw these fellas. Eventually they were fined and had to pay the value of the beast and do a bit of community service. Later the police told me that these blokes had wanted me charged for having a firearm and pointing it at them. Apparently the copper said to them,

"If you didn't know what you were coming up to, in those circumstances, wouldn't you have a firearm? You'll probably have a bit of trouble making the charge stick, especially as you were in the wrong. Anyway, I gather it wasn't actually pointing at you, but into the air." So that was the end of that and we had some meat for the station, without even having to butcher it ourselves.[10]

## Strike while the iron's hot

On all the stations I managed, I always prided myself for neat branding. As far as I was concerned it was one of the most important aspects of station management and I reckon my brands were some of the neatest and clearest in the Kimberley, although I did once put a brand on one horse upside down! We called her Topsy after that. Fossil Downs always had neat brands and some of the other Emanuel Stations were pretty good also.

On Meda the brand was CW7 and I'd put the year brand beneath, in a different position for each year. So in 1977 it might be CW7, with a 7 under the 'C'. In 1978 there would be an '8' under the 'W' and in 1979 the '9' would go under the '7' and so on. I also branded the year on the cheek, shoulder, ribs or down the hind leg a bit. If someone stole a killer, even with the brand removed from the rump, plus the ear gone, I could still find the year brand in one of these positions, to let me know it was a Meda killer and it's age. No-one else that I know of did this secondary year brand.

---

10    Dennis came out from Ireland, pretty much straight to Meda. He was our mechanic, a very good one, but if we ever needed extra men, he'd come out and give us a hand drafting. He was a good bloke and he was a crack shot. I knew this because of a few things I'd seen him do over time.
Once we were at Bob's bore. We'd been drafting cattle and had stopped for smoko. He and I were walking over towards the vehicle when a dingo ran past, about fifty yards away. Dennis raced to the front of the Toyota, got out the.243 and a bullet, then shot him.'Bang'.Straight behind the ears. Stone dead. So I knew he was a good shot and the right bloke to be watching out for me that day in the bullock paddock.
Mostly, if we needed a killer, we would go out to the back country, unless it was too wet, to find a bullock we couldn't catch. We didn't shoot 'money cattle'. Instead we'd go to the wild country, try to find a bullock out in the open and get him on the run. Dennis was usually the rifleman. I often wondered how and where he'd learned to be such a good shot.

## Dingoes

Dingoes were a constant problem on Meda, especially in our early years. I used to keep a bottle of strychnine in the glove box of the station vehicle and if I came across a calf that had been killed by dingoes I would poison the carcass. Sometimes when I saw a place where there was evidence of dingoes I would take out a hind leg of beef, wire it to a tree and poison that. We also did aerial baiting. Although I didn't like what it did to the birdlife, there was really no other choice. Dingoes usually work in pairs, though I have seen five working together to pull down a full grown bull, and later a pack of seven doing the same thing. Quite often a pair of dingoes will attack a cow and calf. When this happens the calf will usually run away. One dingo will follow the calf, while the other torments the cow until she is exhausted. Invariably they will kill the calf. I never 'let up' baiting for dingoes on Meda, even though in our latter years there we saw very few. If you don't keep 'at it' all the time dingo numbers quickly build.

## Bushfires

Bushfires were a constant worry on Meda, for the same reason as cattle killing. Easy access and close proximity to Derby made it a favourite hunting ground for townsfolk. Fishermen would come through the back roads into the bullock paddock and on to the saltwater reaches of the May River, which formed the northern boundary of the paddock. It was a popular fishing spot, frequented by many. The fishing itself was not a problem, but unattended or poorly extinguished campfires were. People who came out there fishing on weekends would light a fire and might put a ten foot log on it. They'd be fishing and having a good time. Then later they'd go back to town, leaving the end of the log sticking out into the grass. So about Tuesday a bushfire would start up. They would be big fires because it was big, open plain country with a lot of grass.

Bushfires were an easy means of revenge if I upset someone. Fishermen frequently left gates open along the way and if I 'chatted' someone about it, next thing the country was alight. One year we had fourteen bushfires on Meda, most of them deliberately lit. I think I must have upset someone, because I got lit up at each end of the bullock paddock, which made it very difficult to handle. Whichever way the wind blew one or other of the fire fronts would go. The wind blew the fire towards the homestead and I thought we were in big trouble. We had hoses out and were watering down the perimeter of the homestead area. I was very concerned about it, but because we had had horses and a few stud cattle around the house paddocks, it helped us. So we got let off.

At about the same time somebody was going up the road lighting spot fires every so often, off the edge of the bitumen. One day Janet was going into town and saw these newly lit fires. Our windmillman, Keith Bolger, was coming home from a bore run and also came across fires that had just been lit. None of them really got going that day, so we were lucky.

We had a trailer set up at the station, with a tank on it and a couple of 44 gallon drums. If there was a bushfire we'd take extra 44 gallon drums on the station vehicle. We'd also have hessian bags, matches and pipes with wicks at the bottom, which we'd put kerosene down, light, and drag along when back burning. We'd take bread, meat, tea and sugar with us, but nothing much else. Sometimes we'd be out for days on end fire fighting. Some blokes can stay awake for twenty four hours, others can't. I'm one of the ones who can't. But I could lie down anywhere, in the back of the vehicle amongst wet bags, bushes and hoses, or on bare ground, or on a dry billabong, and I'd go out like a light. Then after twenty minutes, or half an hour, I'd wake up and be able to keep going again.

## Norman Creek fire

One time we had a fire up towards the Blina, Debesa boundary, so I sent a crew out with two vehicles. Willie Lennard was driving one of them. They went in the evening, to fire fight in the cool of the night. We didn't think it was very big, or that it would be much of a problem. We'd often have to go across country fire-fighting and in the night it is easy to become disorientated. For whites, that is. The blacks always know where they are, if it's their 'home country'. But I'm not a bit surprised white people get lost at fires. When you're on open country, or in light scrub, white fellas often don't know where they are until the next morning. Whilst driving across country, there are ant beds, and stumps from fallen trees, to watch out for and in minneriche and wattle scrub, sharp stakes which can cause punctures. Somehow, during the night the two vehicles became separated. Willie and his mob kept fighting the fire, but the blokes in the other vehicle ran out of water and they got all four tyres staked. They took the wheels off and filled them up with spinifex, then drove back to Number Six bore. In the morning they had all 'had it'. They were exhausted and were waiting at the bore for somebody to come out from the station to help them. In the meantime Willie and his crew returned to the homestead, the fire having been put out. I sent Willie out again early next day, to find where the other vehicle was and to help them, but he couldn't find them. I was concerned that they and the vehicle might have been burnt. I asked Janet to find the telephone numbers of their next of kin, just in case. I also rang the police and notified them. Then I asked the manager at GoGo for the plane to come down to Meda and search for the missing vehicle. When the plane flew over, the country was all burnt. Eventually the pilot spotted the vehicle at the bore. The blokes were all lying around the bore, pretty much 'dilunk', but when they heard the plane they got a bit of life and started waving. Once they'd been located we went out and picked them up and we never had to phone their next of kin.

## Kimberley Downs goes into receivership

While we were at Meda the neighbouring station, Kimberley Downs, along with other ALCO properties, Louisa, Bohemia and Napier Downs, went into receivership. The receivers got onto Emanuel Bros Perth office asking to do a muster, because they thought there were a lot of Kimberley Downs cattle running on Meda at the time. Frank Mugford rang me to ask what I thought of it all. I told him I thought there were bugger all cattle, belonging to them, on Meda.

I knew in the recent past, Kimberley Downs had had managers who didn't brand anything. They only mustered to send off meatworks cattle, including breeder cows that had a bit of weight on them. Everything else was let go, unbranded. Unless a beast is branded it is not legally owned, so I was pretty confident there were not too many Kimberley Downs branded cattle running on Meda at that time. We decided to tell the receivers that they could come and muster on Meda, but they would have to do it themselves, using their own portable yards, and there would be a limited time in which to do it. Kimberley Downs had basically stopped using horses by this time, so they would have to use helicopters and muster straight into yards. After we had given permission for the muster to go ahead I hung around the area every day to see them do it, but in the end they decided not to go ahead with it. They probably realised we weren't messing around. If they had done the muster they'd possibly have got about two hundred head of Kimberley Downs cattle out of it. Not much at all and definitely not worth the expense they would incur. Presumably their change of mind was based on prudent economic probability, although there was no evidence of such sensible constraint when they appointed Bob McCorry as contract musterer, and his wife as station manager.

I knew Bob for a good many years. Although I never saw him on a horse, he had a reputation for being one of the best cattlemen in the Kimberley. He had a distinctive style, slouched posture, rolling gait, his hat pulled low over his brow, with a cigarette on his bottom lip. He invariably wore the typical garb of a Kimberley cattleman. Cuban heeled boots, his shirt collar turned up and a day or two's growth on his chin. He was generally a likeable fellow, dark eyed and affable, but I did not share the opinion of others in his ability with stock. Bob's style of cattlework was completely different to mine. He never tailed, or let cattle out of the yards with horses. When he drafted he just opened the gates and let the bush cattle go.

One time we were attending on the Meda, Kimberley Downs boundary. A portable yard was set up, not far from Poulton's Pool. I had gone out early and asked Janet if she would bring lunch out to us later in the morning, which she did. She parked the vehicle a short distance away and began walking across to the yards. She didn't realise when Bob drafted and called 'bush' he actually meant 'bush'. Bush cattle weren't drafted into a yard ready to be let out later, as we did on Meda. The gates were opened then and there and away they went, bush. Janet was halfway between the vehicle and the yard when out came a bull. I yelled to her, "Stand still. Don't move." She did as I said, thankfully. The bull didn't notice her and trotted away into the scrub. I didn't think it was a very good way of doing things. It saved time, but it wasn't the way to educate cattle. When we attended musters on Kimberly Downs we would take home six or eight decks of Meda cattle on a roadtrain, but when Bob came to get his cattle back from our boundary musters, he'd only get one DA15

Toyota truck load. Approximately sixteen head. I heard he once complained to the Ag. Department about this.

"Well, John Wells never lets a beast go without putting a brand on it. If you did the same you'd get more back." they told him.

Despite getting a good number of Meda cattle back from the boundary musters, we rarely got any calves. Because no 'mothering up' was done, the calves got left behind.

Bob's wife Sheryl was an amazing woman and a wonderful story teller. She was always immaculately dressed in well cut jeans and stylish shirt, beautifully manicured hands adorned with expensive looking jewellery. She was easily recognisable by her long, blonde, almost white, hair. She was a striking woman, no doubt about that. But it was the things she had done that set her aside from the ordinary woman. Sheryl has since become a best selling author.

One time we did a muster on Meda, out near Orange Pool. We had a helicopter, piloted by Peter Leutenegger, who later bought Napier Downs Station and turned it into a first class operation. This particular afternoon storm clouds started building up. We let the cattle into the trap paddock for a drink of water, left them to settle down, then yarded them up and started drafting. I was a bit worried about the cloud build up. It looked stormy. I asked Leutenegger, when he flew back to the homestead to pick up his gear, to tell the roadtrain driver to come straight out to Orange Pool that afternoon. We drafted off the Meda money cattle and when the roadtrain arrived I told Buddy, the driver, to take the cattle to Emanuels yard, unload them, then go back to the station. We stayed at Orange Pool, drafting till dark, then headed home. It was wet and pretty slippery by the time we called it a day, but the roadtrain had thankfully gone through before the rain came. We had almost finished the drafting. We had twelve Kimberley Downs bullocks in the mob, which we put in with our cattle, ready to be taken home later, the weather allowing.

Next day we waited till things dried out a bit, before heading back out to Orange Pool to finish off. Later Gordon Le Lievre's roadtrain came back out, picked up the rest of the cattle and took them to Emanuels yard. A day or two later we trucked our meatworks cattle down to Broome. There wasn't enough room to put the Kimberley Downs bullocks on, so we let them go in Emanuels paddock with our steers and spayer types. They would be sent to the meatworks the next time there was room on a roadtrain. A day or two later Bob McCorry telephoned. He asked me where his bullocks were.

"What bullocks?" I asked. I was intrigued to know how he knew about them.

"You know what bullocks."

"I don't know what you're talking about." I said, trying to find out if I had a spy in my camp.

"You know," he insisted. "And I know those bullocks went down to Midland."

"Is that right?" I asked.

"Yes. You know it's illegal to send bullocks to Perth. They have to go through the dip yards at Broome." He was pretty stirred up. I don't know where he got the idea from that his bullocks had been sent south. I wasn't very happy to be accused of something I hadn't done, or even contemplated doing.

"Is that right? You seem to know a lot about what's going on." I told him and I hung up.

While on Kimberley Downs the McCorry's suffered a terrible tragedy with the loss of their young son in awful circumstances. With a young son of our own and Adele only a couple of years younger than Kelly McCorry had been when he died, Janet and I felt nothing but sympathy for them. We wondered how they would overcome their loss, avoid the pitfalls of blame and recrimination and re-build their lives. They did, with dignity and stoicism and for that I admire them both.

## Touched by technology

Television had come to the Kimberley. I bought a T.V. for Dad who was frail, still living in Derby, but unable to do much. Janet and I thought he would enjoy watching David Attenborough documentaries, although we forgot Mum was a staunch creationist who disallowed such viewing. A year or so later we bought ourselves a television. A real luxury for us. Meda now had it's own telephone, no longer sharing a party line with Kimblerley Downs. Later on we even had a fax machine. A huge contraption that took up the entire desk space in the office.

telegrams became a thing of the past. We were slowly catching up with the times.

I had a brother in law, living down south, who had a microwave oven. I had seen it when we were on holidays. I was dead scared of it. I couldn't understand, when he took a cup of coffee out of it, how the liquid could be hot, but the mug cold. Whenever it was in use I always gave it a wide berth. After a time Frank Mugford decided to buy one of these gadgets for the station. I think this was partly due to me not eating until very late. Each evening Janet would keep my meal warm for me over a saucepan of hot water. I suppose Frank thought a microwave would save her the trouble, so up it came on Gascoyne Traders, in a big cardboard box. I didn't want to know about it and left it sitting on the back verandah for months. On one of his regular visits Frank spotted it still sitting there.

"Why is that still there?" he asked. After that I thought I had better get onto it, so when Frank left I asked Janet to ring the electrician in town and get him to come out and install it. She did.

The electrician was a nice bloke called Norm Rohringer. After Janet had told him what we needed and asked him when he could do the job for us, he told her in the kindest way, "Janet, you don't need me to install your microwave for you. Just open the box, take it out, plug it into the power point and turn it on."

## My last bull

We were out at Wallamore getting bulls. We had the DA15 truck there. Macaulay was in the bull buggy. He had a couple of smart men with him. I was in a brand new station Hilux, coming along behind. I don't think Macaulay knew I was there. I had a bloke in the front with me and several inexperienced blokes on the back. As we came out onto the flat two bulls ran onto the claypan. One went out onto open ground, the other was looking to duck away into the long grass and antbeds. Macaulay went after the bull out on the good ground. I watched for a bit, but the bull buggy didn't come back for the other, so I went after the second bull, trying to keep him from getting back into rough country. I kept trying to turn the bull into the open, but he kept propping and I thought I was going to lose him. Eventually I got him out in the open. The blokes I had with me were too inexperienced to put onto a full grown bull, so I jumped out of the vehicle to throw him. I'd run him around a bit by this time and thought he'd be knocked up, but somehow he got between me and the Hilux and he'd reached the charging stage. There were no antbeds or trees for protection, just bare open ground and he was wanting me. I was dodging him, ducking and diving this way and that, but I knew I couldn't keep it up. I called out to the young fellows,

"One of you blokes will have to get off that motor car and draw this bull's attention off me, so I can grab him." A game young fellow did as I asked and I was able to run in and grab the bull by the tail. Although he turned towards me as I wanted, I had a bit of a job getting him down. I was too knocked up from dodging him earlier and I couldn't catch my breath.

"One of you give us a hand here will you?" I called. They did and we got him down and tied him up, but I was absolutely 'had it'. I was really reaching for oxygen. It was a terrible feeling. I was totally buggered and felt crook for a week after. I knew then I couldn't keep smoking or it'd kill me. Janet wasn't very happy with me and she gave me a bit of a talking to. She didn't need to. I'd frightened myself enough to make sure it didn't happen again. That was the last bull I ever threw.

From then on I tried to give up smoking every way I could. I chewed gum till the sides of my cheeks and my tongue were raw. I mixed Nicorettes with gum. I tried acupuncture while on holidays in Perth. That made me silly. I was high and laughing one minute and down in the dumps the next. It took me years to finally kick the habit. Janet and the children were in England and I was alone in Derby when I eventually managed it. I went from a chain smoker to none and it was bloody hard. When I stopped I found I couldn't bear the smell of fresh meat or milk for a long time, because it all smelt off to me. Terrible. Eventually I came good and I haven't had a cigarette in twenty-five years. I wouldn't be here today if I'd kept going, I'm quite sure of that. Unfortunately my good friend Phil never managed to kick the habit and, sadly, he later paid the ultimate price.

## The 'barefoot bull catcher'

Emanuels told me once that I was not employed to break in horses, or to be in the stockcamp, only to manage the station. For me it didn't really work like that. I found it better to be involved and see that the job was done right, than stand back watching. I think my men respected me for hopping in and giving a hand. They knew I was capable of doing the work myself if need be. When the blokes were flagging, or getting sour, I'd crack some joke to lighten the mood, or if I noticed someone bludging, I'd get 'up 'em', or ask them 'if they were in love'. All round it made for a better working relationship, than me sitting on the top rail slinging orders, never raising a sweat.

We were building trap yards on Meda, which we worked at the end of the year when the natural waters dried up. We had a set of spears allowing cattle onto a trough in the yard, with another set of open spears to let them go 'bush' again. Once the cattle had got used to the set-up and were no longer baulking at going in for a drink, we'd close the gate going bush, so the cattle had to go through the yard into an adjacent trap paddock. The trap yards were set up so that the trapped cattle could still come in, from the trap paddock, through spears onto the trough to drink. When we were ready and thought we had trapped most of the cattle in the area, we would block them from getting back out into the trap paddock after coming in for water. This was done in the afternoon, so in the morning we would have a yard full of cattle which we'd draft, brand and earmark. The system worked well, there being no need for horses, or horsemen, at the hot dry end of the season, just a few able blokes to do the yard work. This practice enabled us, over time, to get control of a lot of bulls, bullocks and cleanskins which had previously evaded us whilst mustering. Because of our successful trapping programme, the number of 'out of control' cattle on Meda diminished significantly. I was surprised, therefore, when towards the end of one season, Emanuels instructed me to engage a contract bull catcher. It seemed strange to be spending money building trap yards, and also paying a contract bull catcher to catch bulls, which we would have trapped eventually for nothing. I simply couldn't see the sense in it, but these were the instructions I got from head office, so I did as I was told.

I decided to ask the 'bare-foot bull catcher' if he would do the job. He had earned himself the nick-name for obvious reasons and his feet were like leather. He was wild, a bit mad at times, and when he got excited his ice blue eyes would gleam, almost frighteningly, in his dusty face. With grog in him he was best avoided. One day, at the races in Derby, with a few drinks under his belt, the fellow had been slinging off about the number of bulls we had running on Meda. He was fairly vocal, insinuating that the place was overrun with them. This upset me a bit, so I was quite pleased when he came out to the station to look at the job and agreed he'd take it on. He brought Michael Bear, as his offsider, his own bull buggy, as well as his own truck to cart the bulls to the meatworks. I knew it was a bad idea to give a bloke a contract to catch bulls on your station, when he owned a property of his own between yours and the meatworks, but there weren't too many bull catchers to be had at the time. I knew the man could work like a demon and with Michael Bear off-siding for him I felt a lot happier about the deal, even though the whole idea was crazy. Anyway the 'barefoot bull catcher' came to Meda, but after only one month decided he didn't want the job anymore. He reckoned there weren't enough bulls to make it worthwhile. After him mouthing off at the races I thought this was a bit amusing. So that was the end of contract bull catching and we went back to working the traps we'd put in. Over time we cleaned up most of the wild cattle running on the station.

## Hit by a bolt from the blue

We had been on Meda nearly six years when an unexpected letter from Tim Emanuel rocked our world. He was going to sell out to the West Australian Government. We knew Tim had been unhappy with a few recent decisions made in high places. These included the reversal of the sale of Mount Anderson Station, from the successful tenderer, to an Aboriginal community, for seemingly political reasons. This prompted him to resign from the Lands Board. Ongoing difficulties and inequities with the BTEC programme (Bovine tuberculosis eradication scheme) also concerned him a lot. We realised there was a general perception that things were becoming unviable for Kimberley pastoralists, but we never saw this coming. It shocked us to the core and we felt as if our world was caving in.

Over coming days the picture became a little clearer and, in the short term, less desperate. It seemed that the State Labour Government had a fancy to re-structure the Kimberley pastoral industry. They intended doing this by resuming non compliant ALCO stations, purchasing the Emanuel properties, combining the whole for the purposes of improving, and re-stocking where necessary, then over time splitting the leases into smaller parcels of land. These would later be made available to long term Kimberley cattlemen, perhaps with the help of low interest loans, as owner occupiers. Their rationale seemed to be that they wanted to get away from absentee landowners holding vast acreages, and a desire to take control of stations not abiding by the terms of their lease, or of the TB eradication scheme, which was aimed to be completed by 1992. Although we thought that I might be one of the people eligible for a smaller lease under the proposal, the chances of me getting one seemed unlikely. I didn't trust politicians, even then.

We were heartened when Tim Emanuel came to visit soon after and told us that he wanted to retain Meda and sell only the Fitzroy properties. He explained to us what the government was proposing to do, if I would be applying for one of the smaller leases when they became available, or whether I would continue on Meda if he still owned it. He told us he had no desire to keep Meda unless I gave an assurance that I would stay on for the long term. He talked about some sort of a deal where I wouldn't merely be a paid manager. It sounded all right to me.

"If you keep Meda I'll stay with you. I don't want to go anywhere else." I assured him. Tim pointed out that Napier Downs was likely to be included in the carve up. He knew how rapt I was in Napier.

"I don't want to be left with Meda if you put in for a piece of Napier, John. I don't want you on my boundary." He joked. I had dreamed of owning Napier many times, but a lot had changed in my life since those days. Getting a piece of Napier seemed unlikely, besides Meda was my home. We had got on top of many of it's problems, it was secure and we liked working for Emanuels. It was close to Derby, where we now had two children going to school. It seemed foolish to move further afield, to go after a dream when we were perfectly happy with what we had. Again I assured Tim I'd stay with him and he left us, saying he would be in touch soon. Janet and I were overcome with relief. It seemed our world wasn't ending after all.

That lasted ten days, then late one Sunday evening Tim rang us up. He told us he had had a meeting with the Government, Brian Burke and his cronies. He said they'd told him if he didn't sell Meda they wouldn't be buying Cherrabun, Christmas Creek or

GoGo. It was all or none. Brian Burke said Meda must be included in the deal. It was an integral part of the plan, because they would have to re-stock Kimberley Downs and Napier at the conclusion of the BTEC programme and they would use Meda to do it.

"I've no choice but to sell. I'm sorry John." Tim told me. So that was that. It was all over and it seemed I was to be sold, for a third time in my career as a station manager.

Over the coming weeks, as the proposal hit the press, the Kimberley was abuzz with speculation. Tim tried to reassure us that all was not lost. He advised me to hang in and manage Meda for the government. To co-operate with Exim, give any advice they sought and stay put while the restructuring process went ahead. That way, he pointed out, I would be well positioned to apply for the block I wanted when the time came. It sounded like good advice, and really there was no other choice for us, other than starting again from scratch somewhere else. So we stayed.

*Janet and I outside the homestead during our first months managing Meda*

*The old timber yards at Euringa, where Epis had a nose piercing. 1985*

*Searching for clues near the Claypan after a shooting.*

*Meda shorthorns and a Brahman bull in portable yards at Euringa. circa 1986*

*Getting a killer, assisted by camp cook 'Thundercloud'.and station cook*
*Elaine Hassett. 1981*

*Steel spears into trap yard, showing spring mechanism.*

*Wattle spears into trap yard at Orange Pool. Photo courtesy of JJJ Wallace.*

# CHAPTER FIFTEEN

# EXIM

*The dust has settled on the rails, blood has stained the crush,*
*Still the choppers scan the scrub and piker bullocks flush,*
*Across the channels, through the creeks, on towards the wing,*
*Where hessian blows along the fence, they run the new mob in.*

## Press reports and politics

P ress reports stated that Tim Emanuel had approached the government with a view to buying his four Kimberley cattle properties. He had decided to put them on the market, because further massive investment was required to comply with the BTEC programme, at a time of ongoing uncertainty over pastoral leases. The proposal having been examined, on a commercial basis, by the West Australian Development Corporation went ahead.

Exim Corporation, the State Government's commercial arm, were appointed interim managers of the recently purchased Emanuel properties. Settlement for the acquisition of GoGo, Christmas Creek, Cherrabun and Meda stations was finalised at the end of April 1985. Their purchase had been made possible, in part, by a Commonwealth Government grant without which the deal could not have gone ahead. It was a 'specific purpose grant' with certain conditions attached. Namely the restructuring of the Kimberley Pastoral Industry in order to bring smaller more manageable areas within the financial reach of normal cattlemen, rather than entrepreneurial enterprise, and with an obligation to provide the Aboriginal community with cattle properties in the Fitzroy Valley equivalent to 25% of the area covered by the Emanuel leases. Bob Hawke was Prime Minister of the day and interestingly his son, Stephen Hawke, was heavily involved with the Kimberley Aboriginal community at the time, helping establish the Marra Worra Worra resource centre in Fitzroy Crossing. It was only to be expected that locals would speculate as to whether this had anything to do with the eventual outcome.

Responsibility for the project was placed in the hands of W.A. Livestock Holdings, a subsidiary of Exim, managed by Jim Coulthard and David Pentilow, with Jim Coulthard responsible for the operations of the four former Emanuel properties. It was planned that these be eventually split into at least eight smaller blocks and that the extensive Emanuel herd be used to re-stock the soon to be forfeited ALCO properties, Louisa, Bohemia, Napier and Kimberley Downs. An estimated twelve million dollars would be spent on developing and restructuring all properties concerned, with the eventual aim of returning the properties to private enterprise. That this was also the ultimate aim of Tim Emanuel cannot be doubted, although in his case the private enterprise he had in mind was singular. He was anxious to avoid the leases being handed over to someone who would, for commercial reasons, strip them. He wanted to ensure the future was reasonably secure for station employees, some of whom had worked for his family for three generations. These sentiments were publicly reported in mid October 1984. He had told us much the same thing privately and at this point Janet and I still believed we might one day benefit from such ideals.

Mr Brian Burke, then Premier of Western Australia proudly stated that his government had embarked upon the most exciting and long overdue restructuring of the state's pastoral industry ever undertaken. He may well have believed it, but history has shown that the sceptics can be forgiven for doubting the eventual outcome. Over time, it became clear that a key part of his proposal was unlikely to come to fruition, because acquisition of the ALCO leases, which were central to his far reaching scheme, became bogged down in legalities. Initially seeking to control the American owned properties through forfeiture, later resumption, the Government became involved in a legal battle and was challenged in the Supreme Court. As reported in The Western Mail, Weekend, July 1986 a deal was offered to

Carey Crutcher, who I knew of old as 'Hey Boy', that would enable him to keep two ALCO properties, Kimberley Downs and Napier and hand over the remaining two, Louisa and Bohemia, to the government. In addition to this swap he would be allowed to purchase Meda, from Exim, for up to two million dollars. When this newspaper report came out friends rang up to tell us. Apparently a confidential Exim report had been obtained stating the government could 'gift' Louisa Downs to the Aboriginal community with the 'minimum political backlash'. It sounded like a win/win situation for all parties, except us. The notion of Carey Crutcher buying Meda was about as bad an outcome as I could then imagine. I had already experienced the frustrations of working for ALCO and 'Hey Boy' and I had never seen eye to eye when it came to station management. If the deal went ahead we would be leaving Meda for sure.

Rumours were rife at this time and we never knew who, or what, to believe. Just three months later another story emerged. That Kerry Stokes and solicitor Jim McManus were negotiating to buy into ALCO. Over the course of time the ALCO properties had come under the management of a receiver-manager, Mr Peter Melsom, of Melsom Robson Co. Together with Carey Crutcher, the new Stokes and McManus owned company would offer to buy Meda, in exchange for Louisa Downs and a financial consideration, but in this instance Carey Crutcher would not have management control. It seemed 'the big boys' were coming out to play.

In May 1987 Peter Melsom placed a full page advertisement in the West Australian Newspaper in defence of ALCO against a proposed 'Special Legislation' by the State Government to acquire the ALCO properties. In June 1987 the Burke Government finally backed down. They struck a deal to buy two of the properties, Louisa and Bohemia Downs, allowing Crutcher to retain Kimberley Downs and Napier. But Carey Crutcher did not buy Meda, as had originally been suggested, though our relief at this news was short lived.

There had been much wrangling between the interested parties to reach this point. Once a settlement was reached it became clear that the reason for Mr Burke's insistence on purchasing Meda in the first place, namely to re-stock our ALCO neighbours, became irrelevant. Tim Emanuel could just as well have retained Meda, because in the end it never became part of the restructure Brian Burke was so proud of. A lot of taxpayers money would have been saved, our lives could have continued on as before and I might have remained managing the station I grew up on and loved, employed by the family for whom my father before me had worked for most of his life. The Emanuel family could have kept an interest in the Kimberley pastoral industry for future generations and the stench that subsequently followed the Government interference on Meda could have been avoided. But as it was the damage was done.

Meda was owned by Exim. A costly and extensive development programme had already been undertaken. Contractors engaged, yards erected, fences built and waters developed. W.A. Livestock Holdings continued as if nothing had changed. Indeed, we were repeatedly assured nothing had changed. Meda would still be divided into two or three smaller holdings, supposedly for the likes of me, and other long term Kimberley cattlemen to have a chance at. But the truth was the Burke Government's restructure programme was now focused on the Fitzroy properties. Meda was out on a limb. Janet and I still hoped that Exim would split the station into smaller units, especially given the enormous amount of work already undertaken to that end, but strong rumours were suggesting otherwise.

## Exim 1985 -1987

Having agreed to stay on as manager at Meda I soon found myself with a bevy of bosses. Pleased to still have the genial smile and sound, softly spoken advice of Frank Mugford, who was retained by Exim, gone was the friendly good manners and charm of Emanuel's head office and the feeling of being, if not quite part of the Emanuel family, at least of some interest to it. Times had changed on Meda and though money flowed freely, life was not the same under Exim. My immediate boss was a man called Jim, or Mr. 3% as he became known. He was based at GoGo and came down to Meda regularly. He was the front man, overseeing all the taxpayer funded improvements on the Exim properties during the 'restructuring programme'. He selected the contractors, negotiated the deals, ordered the gear and arranged for it's delivery to the station. My main role seemed to be ensuring the job was done properly by contractors I hadn't engaged, didn't pay and wouldn't have chosen. My authority being so undermined made things very difficult for me. I remember driving out to check on some fencing contractors one day, only to find them like dead men in their camp at ten thirty in the morning. They had been importing kava and were all out cold. They were not the good workers I'd had in the past, but included at least one known cattle thief. Mr 3% was employing men I wouldn't have had on the property by choice, but that's how it was and there wasn't much I could do about it.

My days were busy and different under Exim. Money was flowing and significant improvements were being put in. New steel drafting yards were built at Macaulay's, beyond Orange Pool, and at Bolger's, in the bullock paddock, where a new bore had been put down, windmill erected and a holding paddock built. A steel drafting yard was completed at Orange Pool, a Turkey Nest Dam constructed at Willie's and a trap paddock built. A concrete trough was erected at Rynne's flowing bore and numerous tanks, cement troughs and skirts were put in by contractors Keith and Barbara Edwards. In addition tanks were fibre-glassed and many miles of new fencing erected by three separate fencing contractors. Amongst them was a new fence put in from the Kimberley Downs boundary, through Orange Pool, to Macaulay's, Bobs, Geoff's and out onto the marsh. Mr 3% told me he didn't want the fence to go out onto the marsh. He wanted it to go to Meda Well, on the Meda River.

"No, I'm not doing that," I objected.

"Well I want you to." He told me firmly. I didn't like it. I knew it was wrong, but he was the boss and it sounded like an order.

"OK, but you put it in writing, telling me to do this, otherwise I'm not going to. If I do as you say the cattle will have no way of getting away from a flood." So the letter never came and I never did as he'd said. Instead we put the fence out onto the marsh, so the cattle could get onto higher ground if need be. Another fence was put in from Brandy's, along the Alexander Creek, then back onto the Kimberley Downs/Meda boundary. Another new fence was put in to Wallamore, running on the scrub side of Gum Hole, Big Springs and out onto an island on the marsh and beyond. In addition during 1986 Meda took delivery of close on a thousand head of Brahman cattle.

## Consultancy

As well as keeping an eye on all the contractors, I soon realised the main purpose for keeping me on Meda was so that Exim could 'bleed my brains'. Consultancy has become a highly profitable industry, for some, over the years, but for blokes like me sharing knowledge, having the know-how and giving advice when sought, has never paid. My nature is such that I don't feel able to ask for financial reward and people have no scruples about 'bleeding my brains' for free just because they can. In the case of Mr 3% the hefty salary he was on was probably justified in part by the knowledge he acquired during his frequent visits to Meda. Passed on to his even higher salaried seniors in Exim, no doubt they thought he was worth every cent. For my part I was simply telling him what I knew, glad to be earning a wage on a property I loved. In hindsight I suppose it was foolish of me to impart what I'd learnt from hard experience, older stockmen, aborigines and from being a third generation Kimberley cattleman, free of charge. But that is the Wells way and always has been.

## Steers to GoGo

Under Exim, Meda had to send all it's steers up to GoGo. These were from six months old, up to next year's bullocks. Only meatworks bullocks, bulls and spayed cows went directly off Meda to the abattoir. Even in Emanuel's time Meda steers had been sent to GoGo for finishing. Under Exim they went at a much younger age. Meda sent up an average of two thousand head a year to GoGo. Several times when I visited the Broome meatworks there were Meda steers in the yard ready for slaughter. I thought 'If they were going to sell them that young and light they may as well have gone straight off Meda. Why the hell pay to truck them up to GoGo, on the other side of Fitzroy Crossing, just to truck them back down to Broome before they were grown out.' It simply didn't make sense to pay the extra cartage on cattle too light to give a decent return. It was a constant source of frustration to me, having to send what were potentially Meda's money cattle into the care of another station, especially as I was often told that Meda ran at a loss, or didn't pay it's way. I had no way of knowing how many Meda steers were missed whilst mustering on GoGo. How many ended up in the station meathouse, or in someone else's coolroom, or how many perished through mismanagement, or tried to walk home. It was like putting money in a safe and leaving the door open. Meda's viability was potentially at the mercy of GoGo's management and the company book-keeper. If they wanted to show how poorly Meda performed financially there was no better way to do it than insist all it's male cattle be trucked elsewhere.

In the year W.A. Livestock took over, there were already a good number of Meda steers on GoGo. A further 2000 went up there during the 1985 season and a similar number the following year, so there were plenty of male cattle on GoGo from which Meda should have turned a profit if handled correctly. In addition, over one thousand spayed Meda cows had also gone to the Fitzroy Crossing property. Possibly my concerns were unfounded, but as manager I never once saw details of Meda cattle turned off GoGo, so I had no way of knowing how many actually went through the abattoir, or what their weights were.

After Meda was sold to Exim, in addition to the steers, we had to give working horses to GoGo. Some years earlier we had got control of the horse herd on Meda and since then I always ensured we had a good number of working horses and young horses coming on. I don't know why it was necessary for us to supply GoGo with horses, because in the days of Vic Jones and Frank Mugford they had heaps of horses there, running in a paddock called Big Dam. So I don't know what happened there, that they became short and needed to take ours.

## The year that took it's toll

It was a memorable year, 1985, but a difficult one. It was early January and the sale of the Emanuel properties was progressing. The Meda homestead was being renovated and on the third day of the year we had a visit from Emanuel's Pastoral Inspector Frank Mugford, Exim's Dave Thom, a Government representative and an auditor, who checked the station stocktake. Two days later, after finalising the stocktake, Janet, our two children and I, left to drive to Perth for holidays. We were away a month, during which time Janet chose curtain material and lino for the homestead and I made regular visits to head office. We drove back north in early February arriving at Meda in torrential rain.

The season began calmly enough with the usual early chores, cleaning, painting, various maintenance jobs and the arrival of boys, both native and white, who would make up this year's crew. Renovation work continued at the homestead, Janet made up new curtains throughout the house, the lino was laid, the children started school and in mid March a contract horse-breaker started breaking in.

April saw the start of mustering, the finalisation of Exim's purchase of the Emanuel properties and a visit from Janet's Swiss niece, Claudia. On 6th of May I attended a meeting at GoGo with Keith Gale, David Thom, Jim Coulthard and Frank Mugford, where W.A. Livestock Holdings outlined objectives for the year.

At the end of May Janet's seventy year old mother arrived from England. It seemed that with the change of ownership my in-laws now felt some urgency to visit us on Meda, perhaps realising there may not always be the opportunity if they left it too much longer. Nice though it undoubtedly was for Janet to have her relations to stay, it seemed to put an added strain on her. Her already busy days were made more hectic trying to show them as much as possible during the brief time they were with us. Added to this was a certain amount of anxiety, on her part, in trying to present her life in a way that would reassure them she was safe, well and happy. This was not always easy to do. On the day Meg arrived we had numerous visitors, including recently married GoGo pilot Max Ley, his wife Grace, Joe De Pledge from Mandora, teacher friends Rob McLarty and Meredyth Bolt, who were visiting from Kununurra, as well as a helicopter pilot called Giles. Janet was flat out looking after everyone. By the time Meg left Meda a fortnight later, any notion she might have had that station manager's wives led easy, leisure filled lives, drifting about the homestead, had been well and truly dispelled.

"I had no idea you were kept so busy." She kept telling her daughter.

## Cornish Wes

A week before Meg's arrival I had spent four days fire-fighting. It was the first of fourteen bushfires on Meda that year, many of them lit deliberately. Whilst I was out with the oil mob helping with the blaze a young pommy bloke rang the homestead looking for a job. Janet, recognising a distinctive West Country brogue, told him to come on out and see how he got on. His name was Wes, a nuggety little Cornishman who proved to be a good worker, tough, nimble and humourous. He was popular in the single men's quarters, amusing his workmates with stories of a hard farming life on Bodmin Moor and how he and his father managed to make ends meet, though not always by honest means. After Wes had been on the station several weeks he found himself in a spot of bother, having recently enjoyed a wild night out in town. He came up to the homestead telling me, somewhat sheepishly, that he needed to see a doctor. Unfortunately Wes, finding himself with an embarassing ailment, had asked his mates what he should do. Happy to help him out, they told him exactly what to do.

"First of all, don't be embarrassed. It can happen to the best of us." They told him. "You'll need to go into the hospital and see a doctor, but before you go you should shave yourself, down below, so it's easier for the doc to have a look at your old fella. Then when you walk in to outpatients you'll see a receptionist behind the front desk. Go straight up to her and tell her you've got a dose of the clap and you want to see the doctor. Don't beat about the bush mind. Just come straight out with it, bold as you like. The bolder the better." The poor young devil. He did as they said and when he came back they asked how he got on.

"I did as you said." He told them. "The chick behind the desk looked a bit surprised, but the doctor was good. He said something about a Brazilian but I don't know what he was talking about. She wasn't Brazilian I don't think. He kept asking who the girl was. I said I didn't know. It was dark. Then he said 'What was dark, the night or the girl?' Both, I told him."

## Meda 'Roadhouse'

Anyone who has lived on a station in the north will know that the cooler winter months from late May to early September will be punctuated by visits from southerners seeking to escape their cold, wet winters. It is a time when mustering is in full swing, interrupted only by a short break during the local race round. Friends from down south were welcome to visit at this time. It was always good to see them and their presence lightened the burden of long hard days out on the run.

One of our most welcome guests was Vi Burton, mother of my old school friends Harry and Max, with whom I'd played football in my younger days. During that time Vi, and her husband Curly, had treated me like a third son. They were always very good to me and I was pleased when Vi, now a widow and quite elderly, decided to visit us on Meda. One day a couple of young teachers from Derby were also at the station and I took our three guests down to the Claypan, where we had some cattle yarded. On the way we spotted a large king brown crossing in front of us at a point where the track traversed a dry, cracked billabong. We pulled up and tried to kill the venomous snake.

We threw various objects at it from the tray of the vehicle. Spanners, bits of wood, anything we could lay our hands on, but we kept missing. Being clear ground the snake was still in view, but getting further away all the time. The last item to come to hand was an axe. I picked it up and hurled it towards the snake in a last attempt to get it. The axe spun through the air like a Frisbee, the blade striking the king brown right behind it's head, severing it. My passengers couldn't believe it. It was an absolute fluke, but they seemed to think I was Crocodile Dundee!

About a week after decapitating the king brown I was driving Vi from Langoora towards the May River when I spotted a big bullock. I pulled up and had a good look at it. Vi was puzzled by my interest in the beast.

"What are you doing?" she asked.

"I was wondering where that bullock had come from, but I remember it now." I told her, adding, "We chased it with a chopper once."

"Did you get it?" The old lady asked. Janet and I were a bit bemused, because clearly we hadn't, or it wouldn't be standing out in the bush. Suddenly the penny dropped. Vi, being from a family of butchers had interpreted 'chopper' as a meat cleaver, not a helicopter. After my Crocodile Dundee act with the axe who could blame her.

Friends who visited the station during the cooler months sometimes brought along extended family, or other friends of theirs who we'd never met. Occasionally people with only the vaguest connections would call in and expect, accept and enjoy station hospitality. Often their company was enjoyable and the conversation of interest, but the arrival of a steady stream of uninvited guests put a heavy toll on the female of the house. During 1985 Meda saw a higher number of visitors than usual and we wondered whether the media coverage over the sale of the Emanuel properties had prompted the influx of tourists at the homestead. Or perhaps it was simply that the Great Northern Highway, having been sealed from Port Hedland to Broome in 1981, had made the road trip less onerous. It was now an easy drive for caravanners, who had previously been reluctant to pull on the four hundred and fifty kilometre stretch of corrugated dirt road. Either way the visitors kept arriving.

Early August saw the unveiling of a plaque on Meda, to commemorate Emanuel Brothers first pastoral settlement in the Kimberley. Located near the May River Crossing, it was erected by The Royal Western Australian Historical Society and Emanuel Bros and was unveiled on August 13th 1985 by the Governor of Western Australia. The memorial was constructed out of river stones by Keith and Barbara Edwards, with the plaque mounted on a large slab of rock taken from the May River. The official party arrived at the river crossing under police escort and included the Governor, Professor Gordon Reid and Lady Reid, Mr Tim Emanuel, Terry Burke, who was brother of the Premier and member for Perth, Harold Jones, Department of the Premier and Cabinet, Alan Ridge and Peter Standen, private secretary Government House, representatives from the WA Historical Society including Nan Broad and Norma and Jim Anderson, and Deputy Shire President Mr Allan Rees and Val Rees. Others present included Willie Lennard, Dave and Margaret Hewitt, three generations of the Wells family, Mr and Mrs George Wells, myself and Janet, as well as George and Adele Wells who presented Lady Reid with a bunch of Sturt Desert Peas. After the unveiling the party drove back to the Meda homestead where a formal afternoon tea was served.

Two days after this event Janet and I were thrust back into the reality of station life, when we were woken at two thirty in the morning by one of our newer station hands.

## A roll over at the Meda turn off

Exim, had employed three fellows who had come across from Queensland. The powers that be wrote to say that as these blokes were from Queensland we would have to pay them a higher wage.

To me that didn't make sense.

"I've got good experienced blokes here now. I'm not paying men I don't know, more than the good men I've already got and do know. I'll pay my three smartest men the money you want me to pay the new Queenslanders, and the Banana Benders can start on my blokes old wage, until they prove themselves." So these three blokes came and worked for us, but they weren't really worth feeding. One of them, a big handsome fellow, Cupid, was on with the station cook and he really thought he was something. One evening the blokes wanted to go into town. I said they could, but before they left all the gear was to be taken out of the back of the vehicle. Branding irons, axes, crowbars, wire and so on.

"Take it all out first, then seeing as you're wanting to use a station vehicle, you can go through the bullock paddock and check all the bores on your way in. Do whatever it is you're wanting to do in town, then come home tonight. The cook is to drive you. But make sure you take everything out before you leave." They said they would and off they went into Derby, via the bullock paddock, for the evening.

In the early hours of next morning Janet and I were woken up by someone calling out at the back door. It was Cupid. He had walked in to the station to tell us that the vehicle had rolled at the Meda turn-off on the way home from town. I got up and went down to the native camp to fetch Lorraine Lennard, one of Willie's youngest daughters and a crackerjack girl. She came up to the homestead to stay with our children for the rest of the night and to get them ready for school in the morning. Janet phoned the hospital and the police. We gathered up a bit of gear, sheets, blankets, torches and first aid stuff. We didn't know what we were going to find, so we took a fair bit of gear with us. When we got to the turn off the cook was lying motionless, her dress up around her ears. One young fellow, Lance, was also sprawled in the dirt, motionless. The others were crouching nearby, cold, frightened and sore. The vehicle had hit a large boulder, an antbed, and narrowly missed a tree. It had rolled over completely and was back on its wheels. Pipe, crowbars, branding irons, axes and other gear was strewn all over the place. I was annoyed to see they had never unloaded the vehicle before leaving the station, as I'd told them to. They were bloody lucky no-one was killed.

The ambulance came out from Derby and picked up the injured and took them in to hospital. Three blokes were hospitalised, as well as the cook. She had a dislocated elbow, severe bruising and a knock to her head. She had been drinking wine all night and was unable to drive home, so a bloke who wasn't supposed to, had driven instead. One young fellow had a broken pelvis. He was one of two passengers flown down to Perth for treatment. The driver ended up doing time for drunk driving as a result of the accident, and was put away for three months. The cook discharged herself from hospital and returned to the station, but she seemed highly emotional and her speech sometimes difficult to understand. We persuaded her to go to Perth for at least two weeks convalescence. This left us without a station cook and several men short. Janet did the homestead and station cooking once again. No extra pay of course. Winter visitors kept arriving, so some nights she had as many to feed at the homestead as in the station kitchen.

## Burn out

On the first day of September I sent Keith Bolger down to the bullock paddock to check the traps. He rang from Derby to say the trap paddock was burnt. Someone had set the bullock paddock alight in two places, five miles apart. One fire on the west side, one on the east. Whichever way the wind blew one fire front would get going. It was a Sunday and four of my blokes had taken their own vehicle and gone in to the session, Cupid amongst them. All other station hands were sent onto the fires. When the young fellows returned from the pub later that evening they too were sent out fire-fighting. Cupid ended up doing his quince and he beat up a fellow station hand, known as 'Red'. I sacked Cupid on the spot and told him to get going immediately.

"How am I going to get into town?" he asked me.

"The same bloody way you got into the session." I told him, so the young fellow who owned the car drove Cupid off the place. I was glad to see the back of him, but the night wasn't over yet.

We had our station grader out cutting firebreaks. The operator was an old man, Colin Wells, no relation of mine, who was another of those broken down but useful, rather worn out blokes, without whom stations would have been difficult to run. He got the grader bogged in Salt Creek. It was proving a difficult night. Another grader was brought out from Derby next day, which pulled ours out of the creek. 'Red' was taken into the hospital after his beating of the night before, for facial X-rays. Fire-fighting continued all day. We were helped by blokes from the Ag. Department, who left their fire fighting unit with us.

Day three saw the fire jump all cut lines until it was within a mile and a half of the homestead. Janet, who was still cooking, began hosing down, along the perimeter fence at home. The station was enveloped in a smoke haze, the light eerie as in an eclipse of the sun. The bushfire was visible for miles, with bursts of black smoke rising into the air as the flames caught dense patches of scrub. The oil mob from Blina, Home Energy, lent us a vehicle and our neighbours on Birdwood Downs also gave us a hand.

At four thirty in the afternoon a car load of visitors arrived at the homestead. We were expecting guests in a day or two, whom Janet had never met. Mistaking the new arrivals for those I knew, she welcomed them as best she could, whilst trying to prepare meals for seventeen in the station kitchen. At the same time a second vehicle pulled up. It was one of my more reliable hands who had driven a new station vehicle up from Perth, to replace the one written off in the accident. He had brought the cook back with him, as well as my fourteen year old son, Benn, a hitch-hiker they had picked up along the way and a crate of turkeys, which Benn had kept shaded and watered whilst travelling up in the trayback.

The approaching fire was finally stopped, at the last grid on the Claypan fence. Everyone involved was exhausted. Janet served the men their evening meal in the station kitchen, washed up and returned to the homestead. She fed the children, put them to bed and cooked for fifteen others, including the visitors, who she now realised were not who she'd supposed. All beds were occupied in the house and swags were spread across the wide polished floor of the front verandah. Neither of us were in a state to be hospitable, but tomorrow was another day. Another day that brought the next wave of visitors, this time the guests we had been expecting. The station cook was now back at work, and with the fire under control some of the pressure eased.

Two weeks later my sister-in-law arrived from Switzerland. Again Janet began pushing herself in an effort to give Tricia a good time. She took her up into the ranges, camping out at Poulton's, then down to Broome for a night or two. They booked into a hotel and I thought the rest would be good for her. It probably was, but our high spirited son, who disappeared whilst at the boat ramp beach, hiding amongst the rocks long enough to cause panic, inadvertently undid any beneficial effect. During the drive home my wife was taken ill, her sister took over the wheel, stopping off at Derby hospital before heading out to Meda. By the time they got home the roast dinner I had cooked for them was spoilt. Tricia took over. I was upset. The evening was not a success.

It was the end of September. Whatever ailed Janet was showing no sign of improvement. Several visits were made to the hospital and by the end of the first week of October she was ordered to have total bed-rest for a fortnight. She spent most of it sleeping. Towards the end of October the cook, still complaining of a painful elbow, asked to be taken to the hospital several times, before eventually being admitted. Janet visited her a day or so later to see how she was getting on. Because the initial elbow injury had been sustained whilst in a station vehicle, worker's compensation was a factor. When Janet asked for some details she was treated very hostilely by the nursing staff and told it was none of her business. It turned out the cook had nothing wrong with her elbow after all, but had had a much more personal problem which had now been dealt with in theatre. She resigned a few days later.

We limped towards the end of the season. Only a skeleton staff remained over Christmas, including our headstockman, who next season would become contract musterer, old Paddy the carpenter, Noel De Biasi our capable mechanic, windmillman Keith Bolger and one or two others. As always Janet cooked a traditional Christmas roast for all. One of our home grown turkeys, Christmas Pudding and all the trimmings. The meal was served at the house, followed by a lazy, relaxed afternoon on the front verandah. Five days later, on doctors advice, Janet and the children flew out of the heat, down to Perth for an extended rest. I remained at the station, seeing the new year in and waiting for sufficient rainfall before driving to Perth to join the family.

## 1986

When I returned from holidays I found a bespectacled young fellow, from GoGo, comfortably installed at Meda who, on my first day back, announced he was the assistant manager.

"Well you aren't." I told him bluntly. "There's only one boss here and that's me. You have no authority and you'll do as you're told." He was nicknamed 'Biggles' and he thought he was a pretty important fella, but really he was fairly useless. When I asked my 'gods' why I had got him they said they thought I would straighten him out, but I've wondered since if he wasn't sent down to be a spy. He stayed on Meda for a few months, but eventually I sent him back up to GoGo.

Improvements continued to be put in throughout the year. I was kept busy showing surveyors, line clearers, fencing crews and yard builders the work to be done, checking on contractors and ensuring the necessary materials were on hand for the job. As well, we had a contract musterer on Meda that season, John Macaulay, who had previously been our headstockman. The T.B. eradication programme continued, entailing extra handling of stock. At the end of June the Australian Bureau of Statistics conducted a nation wide census. Forms were delivered and later collected from the various contractors camps, mustering camp, station single men's quarters, cottages and main homestead, where as usual several visitors were staying overnight. Every individual on Meda on the night of June 30th had to be recorded. The nationwide census coincided with stocktake time, when odometer readings were taken, bulk store, workshop, station store, fuel, and so on had to be counted and recorded. Unlike other years, all the new work being undertaken on Meda at the time meant the stocktake was a far bigger job than usual. It took us several days to complete.

Throughout the year there was much talk and speculation over the probable carve up of the former Emanuel owned properties. Having remained on Meda, as Tim had advised, I was as aware as anyone of the significant improvements being put in place and I considered Meda to be one of the best properties in the Kimberley at that time. I was really hoping I would be one of the successful applicants when it came time for subdivision. A lot of people seemed to think I had a good chance. Even the blacks were coming to me and saying 'Shohn will you be get 'im station? You belongin' 'dis country and we know you belongin' dis country.' I thought this was encouraging. They seemed to think I ought to have a small cattle station of my own. If I got the opportunity to follow my dream of one day owning a part of Meda, I might have three or four hundred black fellas backing me.

## I smell a rat

At the start of 1987, during my annual break in Perth, I regularly called into Exim's head office to check what rainfall there had been on Meda. One day I dropped in and the office girl asked me if I was John Wells. I said I was. She told me someone there wanted to see me and that I would be shown the way to his office. I was taken up to another level and shown in to a room where the fellow was waiting for me. He was a tall man and as far as I could remember I had never met him before. He was very amiable and we started talking about this and that. After a while he offered me a beer. I said I didn't want one and we kept talking.

"So how good a place is Meda?" he asked.

"It's a good property." I told him.

He asked me a lot of questions, then again it was, "Do you want a beer John?" Eventually I agreed to have a beer with him. I stayed there all afternoon in his office drinking beer. I realised he was bleeding my brains the whole time. The questions went on and on. I thought, 'There's a rat here somewhere. Something isn't quite right.' At the end of the afternoon he told me he lived out near where I was staying in Nedlands, so he gave me a lift home to Clifton Street. The next time I went in to enquire about Meda's rainfall, we had to wire the rainfall readings down in those days, the same thing happened.

"Mr Soanso wants to see you." I was shown up to his office, given a friendly greeting, then asked a mob of questions. A short time later out came the beer. More questions, some were the same questions as before. Another beer, then he'd come back to the same thing, I suppose to see if I gave the same answer. All the time we were talking I was being offered beer and I ended up leaving there late. He gave me a lift again and when I got home I said to Janet, "I reckon they're going to sell Meda." I was sure I was right, so I got onto a friend of mine in the city, someone a bit savvy, who dealt with businessmen on a daily basis.

"I reckon Meda is coming on the market." I said. "It's not official. What about you see if we can get a syndicate together and buy it." He got onto it straight away. Things started moving fairly quickly. He got a bloke to go and see Exim, to find out what was going on with Meda and to express an interest in buying it. Although the meeting went ahead, nothing came of it.

"Sorry the station is not for sale. No, no definitely not for sale." He was told. "We're not deviating one inch off our original course." They insisted Meda was central to their restructuring programme. It was to be used to help re-stock other properties included in the scheme, which were to be de-stocked first as part of the BTEC programme. Despite Exim's denial our friend went ahead and got a syndicate together, amongst them a Singaporean with plenty of money. The deal was that I would stay on as manager, would have more say in the running of the place and there would be a couple of additional benefits in it for me, as well as better money. It all sounded quite promising. Another appointment was made with Exim. The syndicate representative again expressed an interest in purchasing Meda, but Exim hotly denied Meda was for sale.

"Well I'm under the impression that it is." The fellow persevered. "So if it ever does come on the market can we have first option on it?"

"Yes you can. But it won't be." Exim told him.

In the meantime I had gone back up to Meda to prepare for another season. A caretaker, appointed by W.A. Livestock Holdings, had been minding the station during my absence. This was unusual. In the past I had chosen who looked after things, but in hindsight I presume there was a reason why one of my men wasn't left in charge that year. Goodness knows who might have visited Meda while Janet and I were away. I knew someone was showing a close interest in the station, because on several occasions I noticed a plane flying very low over Meda country and I had no idea who it was.

## A new crew

Meda had a new contract musterer that year, Macaulay having moved on elsewhere. I did not approve of the new crew. Some of the stockmen were very hard on horses and before the end of May several already had sore backs and were unfit to work. Meda supplied the horses, so this annoyed me. I had made sure, over the preceding eight years, that we had a good number of working horses, as well as young ones coming on, but it didn't mean they could be treated poorly simply because we had sufficient replacements. The new contract musterer was well known to me. He was a likeable, cheeky rogue who was prone to be devious and scheming if the opportunity arose. I knew I would have to watch him carefully during the course of the season. Long term employee Keith Bolger had retired, although he still lived on the station. We now had a new windmillman, Reg Day, who proved to be a good, conscientious young fellow. Our mechanic Dennis had long since returned to Ireland and I now had an excellent local man doing the job. Despite being dyslexic, unable to read or write and with no formal qualification, Noel was as capable a mechanic as any. In many ways he was a station manager's dream. Engines were his life and he liked nothing better than fixing them. He knew every abandoned engine on every station rubbish dump he'd ever visited. If spare parts were needed Noel usually knew exactly where to find them. Whereas most mechanics needed new parts ordered up from Perth, Noel would often scavenge them, for free, from a rubbish tip somewhere. He saved us a lot of money, time and frustration. He loved his job, it was all he could talk about. It was his life. With Noel in the workshop things got fixed without the hassle of waiting for freight to arrive from Perth, or from over east. Two of my best men returned to Meda at the start of the year, to do some contract horse-breaking. Ronnie Palmer, who first came to work as a stockman on Meda at the age of fifteen, was assisted by Sneezy, who'd commenced with us aged fourteen. Over the years both young men had worked and played hard and were now two of the smartest ringers in the country.

## A close shave at Macaulay's Yard in May 1987

Mustering started towards the end of April and in early May we commenced mustering at Macaulay's, where we now had a big new drafting yard. I was on the drafting gate as usual. We had a bull and a couple of bullocks, big, old wild fellas, in the forcing pen, to go into the pound. We had to split the bull off from the two bullocks. They were all very aggressive. The bull went into the pound and I shut the gate. One bullock then came in behind the protection rail, where I was. I jumped up on the rail, between the forcing pen and the bull yard. The bullock came for me. I was frightened of this bullock. Then the second bullock came for me also, from the forcing pen, so I had one on either side. I hung onto the rail, two inch pipe, with my feet locked under the rails of the protection panel. I hung on as long as I could. The bullock hit my finger with his horns, splitting my finger right under the nail. I let go and I fell. As I had my feet locked in the rails, I fell down backwards and upside down. I was hanging, like a bit of meat in the cool-room. My chest, throat, head, my whole torso was exposed to the bull yard. I was in deep shit. I had one bullock behind the protection panel, one in the forcing pen and the bull in the bull yard blowing snot at me. Three trying to get me at once. I tried to get up, but I couldn't quite get there. I didn't have the strength from the position I was in to get the last bit. The bull in the bull yard wasn't quite game to come all the way, but he was still thinking about it. Usually a bull will leave you alone and rejoin the mob, once he's had a go at you. This one didn't. A young fella ran up alongside the rails in the bull yard, to draw the bull away from me. Another bloke, who was working the bull gate, ran past me and gave me a push up. That's how I got up and out of it, but my ticker was fairly going.

## Rumours, denials and the truth

A couple of days after my close shave at Macaulay's Yard Janet received a phone call to say newspapers were reporting that Meda had been sold. I was putting the skids under a new cook at the time, who had been giving trouble since she'd arrived just a week earlier. Janet tearfully gave me the news when I returned to the house. The following day we received a visit from Mr 3% to explain what was going on. It appeared the newspaper reports were true. Within months of Exim's emphatic denials it seemed Meda had been sold. It was Adele's eighth birthday, but the tea party we held for her, after our visitor left, was a subdued affair. News of the sale was cleverly done. Purchased by a group of businessmen, including entrepreneur Kerry Stokes, Vox Adeon's Brian Coppin, and Bill Hall, outrage was averted by the inclusion of Broome based businessman Peter Murray and cattleman Robin Finger in the syndicate. It was the latter two men who's names invariably preceded those of other financially hefty syndicate members, with the sale projected as being completely in line with the ideals of the restructuring programme. Namely to include Western Australian cattlemen, involved locally in the industry, not absentee owners, or overseas investors, smoothly overlooking the unfulfilled promise to subdivide Meda as intended. From our point of view the premature disposal of Meda, the station now rich in government funded improvements, looked to be something of a gift to the new owners.

Once the news broke, any hopes we had harboured of one day getting a piece of Meda were gone forever. Gone also the hope of a sale to the syndicate who had been promised first offer, that would have meant a secure future for us on the station we loved. It was becoming difficult for us to believe anything any more. It seemed ironic that, yet again, a station I was managing and had strived to improve over the years, was once more sold from under me. It had happened on Napier when Rowell and Maxted sold out to ALCO, again when Frazier was sold to the La Grange Aboriginal Community. When we first came to Meda we had felt secure. Meda had not changed hands in one hundred years. But again, during my tenure as manager it was sold to Exim. Now it had been sold again before being subdivided. It was the fourth time I had experienced a change of ownership whilst managing a property and I knew, from experience, it was usually difficult to adjust. Would I be able to do it again? Would it end badly as it had before? Would we even be asked if we wanted to stay on, and what were we going to do if we didn't? Only time would tell what lay ahead for us, the station, it's stock and it's staff.

## I'm put in my place

Whilst the general opinion was that I would be kept on as manager, I had my doubts. This was because of an incident that occurred a year or so earlier during a visit to Broome. I had gone down to watch the kill at the meatworks and later ran into Peter Murray at the Roebuck Hotel, which he then owned. I was sitting down having a beer when Peter walked in. He was standing alone at the bar, so I got up and went over to him, "G'day Peter. How're you going?" I asked. I'd known him for a lot of years and Janet and I considered him a friend. There was a story circulating at the time which I thought he would find amusing and I decided to share it with him.

"Do you want to hear a funny story Peter?" I asked.

"Yeah, righto Wellsy. What is it?"

"Well the latest rumour going around is that Peter Grey is leaving Leopold." Peter Murray owned Leopold Downs at the time.

"And the funny part of the story is that I am going to manage it." Well you should have seen him. He huffed and puffed and blew his chest out. He said, "Hmmph, well I can assure you Johnny Wells that that day will *never* come." I was surprised he bit so quick. I'd thought the rumour was a joke, but clearly Peter didn't. That incident taught me a lot. It told me exactly what the man thought of me, that I didn't have any ability and wasn't worth employing. If ever I had any doubts as to whether the big man intended the affront that day, they were dispelled some time later when I attended a cattle sale at Camballin. I had taken over three fat spayed cows from Meda and two bullocks, for which I hoped we'd get good money. Before the sale started I was talking to a lot of people and I ended up talking to Peter Murray. He and I had pretty much finished our conversation when it was announced that the auction was about to begin. Murray said he needed a leak. I did too, so we began to walk over to the facilities together.

"So are you going to try and get one of these blocks when the government cut them up Wellsy?" Peter asked.

"I've got an iron in the fire." I told him.

"Hmmph. If you got one of these joints Wellsy you'd either fuck it away, or you'd piss it up against the wall." he retorted. Well, the blood pressure fairly lifted and my heckles went up. I let him walk on ahead of me and I thought 'Jeez, I should give you a flogging for that.' There was no-one else around when I got to the loo. Murray was a big man, but I reckon I could have decked him I was that wild. I had to have a serious talk to myself. 'John don't do this, don't do this.' I kept telling myself. I didn't, but I was bloody fuming for the rest of the day. It was a bugger of a turnout all round, because the cows were sold dirt cheap in the end, to the butcher from Halls Creek. We could have got more for them if I'd sold them in town, so by the time I got home I was ropeable for several reasons. After these two incidents, now Peter Murray was a part owner of Meda, I had little confidence he would be keeping me on as manager there.

## We sit tight and hold on

After news broke of the sale Janet and I had one week to absorb the meaning of this latest development before we received a visit from Peter Murray and Robin Finger. During it we thought long and hard about what we might do. Other than leave the district altogether there seemed little choice for us, for there were few places not directly affected by Burke's restructure programme, other than those in which Peter Murray already had an interest. Napier and Kimberley Downs were clearly not an option for us, Frazier Downs was Aboriginal owned and a sad show, Myroodah I loathed. Meda was home. I'd done everything for that place. Even if it was mine I couldn't have done any more. I didn't care what was said about me, I knew I had pulled Meda up, from being in a pretty sad position when I first took over, to being one of the best run places in the Kimberley. We'd built trap paddocks and better fence set-ups. I'd got the horses back in control, to a point where we were now supplying other stations. We had improved the cattle herd, not only with bought Brahmans but with an ongoing spaying programme that rid the station of it's undesirable shorthorn cows. Watering points throughout the property were brought under control and we had a workshop full of properly maintained equipment to fall back on, if the need arose. Why would I want to move elsewhere and start all over again after so much had been achieved? I didn't. Our minds were made up and by the time Robin Finger and Peter Murray arrived at Meda, the following week, we had decided to stay put if we possibly could. To our relief and in my case, surprise, we were asked if we would stay. We accepted.

It was a strange time. Although we were aware that Meda had been sold, some confusion seemed to exist. W.A. Livestock Holdings were still our official employers, although Peter Murray was enjoying acting as our boss. Revelling in his new status, he was bringing a never ending stream of people to view the property and discuss it's future direction. During this time Janet and I attended a bull sale at Leopold Downs, one of Murray's properties. We were somewhat mystified when, during the day, Mr 3% purchased some Brahman bulls for Meda. These later became the subject of an amusing incident, whilst at the time highlighting the extraordinary state of uncertainty over who was actually in charge of Meda at that point.

Early in June we had a visit from the leader of the opposition, Mr Richard Court and the shadow minister for the Environment, Lands and Aboriginal Affairs, Mr Barry Blaikie, the Member for Vasse. Following this visit questions were raised in

Parliament. Mr Blaikie addressing the Assembly on June 18th said,

> *... We asked the Government whether there had been any moves to sell Meda Station. We may have worded the question wrongly and directed it to the wrong Minister because the answer we got was that the sale was not on. However, when we were in the Kimberley we were told a number of times that Meda Station was under some form of option for sale to a Peter Murray. Apparently the option ran out on the Tuesday or Wednesday after we were there. Either the Parliament has been sold a bum steer or all of the pastoralists in the Kimberley area were sold a bum steer. I believe that either we did not ask the question properly or we were not told the facts.'*

For us, work continued on Meda as if nothing had happened. I continued to keep a close eye on the contract musterer, a new fencing contract was begun for which Janet and I collected four hundred standards from Derby, and hay making began in the bullock paddock. Then abruptly we found ourselves in the midst of a Kimberley wide man-hunt for a crazed gunman.

## The German gunman June 1987

One evening, while Janet was showering the children, the phone rang and it was the police. They told me that a bloke in a yellow fore-runner was thought to be heading our way, down the Gibb River Road. They said he might come into the station looking for fuel. He had a dog with him and was considered extremely dangerous. The police told me if this fellow showed up at the station, we were to give him whatever he wanted, fuel, stores, whatever. They told me to warn everyone on the station. I asked them what the bloke had done, but they said they couldn't tell me. Two men had been murdered the previous week in the Northern Territory. They'd been shot whilst fishing at Victoria River. We wondered if it had something to do with that. While Janet gave the kids supper and put them to bed I had a shower, then went over to tell my blokes what the police had said. I sent someone down to the Claypan to let the stockcamp know what was going on also. That evening one of my men was crook and needed to be run into the Derby hospital. I made sure the blokes taking him in knew what was going on before they left. When I got back to the house Janet and I listened to the news. Three people had been found murdered at Pentecost Crossing, on the eastern end of The Gibb River Road. It explained everything. We decided to park our private vehicle, an old Holden Kingswood, at the back of the house, just in case someone did drive in during the night. This was so that Janet could take Adele and George through the back sleep-out, to the car. The plan was that she'd drive down to the Claypan and stay in the stockcamp for the night.

Later that evening the blokes who had taken the sick man into hospital rang up, from Derby. They told me they'd passed a yellow Hilux, similar to the one described by the police, turning into Meda and it had a white dog in it. This information caused a fair bit worry. We decided to turn off the lighting plant, so the homestead was in darkness, and I made sure there were a couple of firearms handy. Because of this new development, I thought it would be best if Janet took the children and left the house straight away. She went to their room, woke them up and told them to be very quiet. George was six, Adele had just turned eight. They were as good as gold. They never asked any questions, there wasn't a peep out of them. They just took it in their stride. I was very proud of them as they climbed silently into the back of the car. I told Janet not to turn the headlights on until she was at the far end of the airstrip. Away she drove, down to the Claypan. Once she got there and pulled up alongside the camp, there was a sense of relief amongst the men. They'd seen the lights coming and had thought it was the vehicle they'd been warned about earlier. Everyone was feeling fairly toey. Janet and the children slept in the stockcamp that night. By this time George thought it was a great joke. He sat up at the camp-fire with the men, listening to all their stories until late into the night, before finally curling up on the back seat of the car and going to sleep with Adele. I'd told Janet not to come home in the morning, but to wait until I came down to give the all clear.

"Don't worry about school." I told her. "I don't want you rolling up at the station, if we're in the midst of trouble. You just stay put until I let you know everything is OK."

Once Janet and the children were safely gone I felt better able to deal with whatever eventuated at the homestead, but I still spent an anxious night. I guess we all did. The station was in darkness, eerily silent with the generator turned off, but it was easier to hear any unusual sounds and my senses were on high alert all evening. When it was bedtime I brought our blue heeler, Goggles, indoors. He'd never been allowed in the house before, but I knew he'd let me know if anyone was about. He'd go for them too, if need be. I felt more secure having him there while I slept, not that sleep came easily, despite having a loaded .303 under my bed and the .22 alongside me.

Morning came without incident and with it a reassuring explanation for the vehicle sighting of the previous evening. Far from being a serial killer, it turned out to be Gerry Ash, who had come to visit my retired windmillman, Keith Bolger. They used to be part owners of Mowla Bluff, together with another friend of mine, Alan Lyons and had been mates for many years. Gerry owned a white bull terrier and a yellow Hilux, so my blokes had had good reason to raise the alarm, despite it turning out to be false.

I drove down to the stockcamp and gave the all clear. Janet and the kids came home. They had missed the school bus, so after some breakfast, with lunch boxes packed, Janet drove them into Derby. She went to see the headmaster, telling him that the children were not to be sent back to Meda on the bus that afternoon, but would be staying in Derby with their grandparents. She told him we had arranged for Adele and George to stay in town until the emergency was over, and she told him why. He didn't believe her. He laughed, thinking it was a joke and that Janet was being unnecessarily dramatic. By that afternoon news was all over the country about the Pentecost Crossing killings. The school principal, Max Clarke, no longer thought it amusing. One of the victims was from Derby, his children were pupils at the school and in the swimming club, of which Max was the coach. The dead man was the cousin of a friend of ours, his widow treasurer of the school P&C.

Important visitors were due at Meda that day, so Janet had to come home, though I would have preferred she didn't. Before she left town she rang the station. We had made up a coded message which we could use if something was wrong. If there was trouble we were to say 'Sorry we haven't got any turkeys for sale this year.' But all was calm on Meda that morning, so she drove the thirty miles back out to the station. We knew there was some danger in doing this and when she pulled up at the gate I watched her carefully from the window. I wanted to make sure she was behaving normally, that she hadn't been waylaid on the way out. That the bastard wasn't hiding in the car with a gun pointing at her. When I was satisfied everything was all right I went outside to meet her.

Meda was in the process of changing hands and we had a lot of visitors coming at the time. It made things very awkward. If possible Janet would drive into Derby and sleep at Mum and Dad's place. In the morning, after the children had gone to school, she would drive back out to Meda, to get on with whatever had to be done. It was not a good idea to be driving alone up and down the Gibb River Road at that time, so I'd always be watching through a window, with a rifle, when Janet got home. It was really a very dangerous time. Lots of people were feeling edgy. You didn't go anywhere without a loaded firearm, just in case. Going over the May River Crossing was particularly worrying. It was just the sort of place the gunman seemed to favour. I had contractors working out bush, who I had to check on, so whenever I went out that way I'd take our mechanic with me. Dennis was Irish and a crack shot. He'd sit in the passenger seat with a loaded firearm at the ready. People were living like this throughout the Kimberley during that period. It's a wonder some poor innocent bastard wasn't shot by mistake. It could have happened a couple of times on Meda, let alone on all the other isolated properties.

One day a bloke rang up to say he was coming to have a look at Meda on behalf of an Asian syndicate, despite strong rumours that Meda was already sold. I told him it would be all right, but that he was not to come into the station early in the morning because, if this bloke was around, he could get shot. Bugger me dead if he doesn't roll up just on daylight. He did exactly what I had told him not to do, so he copped a blast from me. Another day Father Chris Saunders, who was at Kalumburu at the time, pulled up at the gate. It was well after sundown, pitch black, and I didn't know who it was who had arrived. He got out of his car, in the dark and called out, 'Is that Bloody John Wells around here?' My ticker went like hell. Then I realised it was Father Chris. Very dangerous. He could have got a bullet whistling past him the way things were at the time. He thought it was a great joke. We were good friends, but he copped a blast from me as well. He went on to become the Bishop of Broome, so it's lucky I didn't take a shot at him.

By this time we had every journalist in Australia up in the Kimberley, all trying to justify their presence. No-one had any idea where the gunman was and rumours abounded. The main search was centred around El Questro, then people began to talk about him cutting across through Mornington, or perhaps through Windjana and Tunnel Creek onto Leopold. But nobody had any idea. It was all pure speculation. Mum rang up each day, morning and evening and if anything was wrong we were to give the coded message to her. Adele and George were still staying with her and had been for almost a week.

One day Peter Murray and his wife Ann, brought visitors from the Eastern States to Meda. The couple's son was one of Australia's best known country and western singers at the time. The visitors arrived late, so Janet didn't go back into town that day. She cooked an evening meal, and made up the spare rooms for Peter and Ann Murray and the Blundells. After coffee had been served Peter Murray decided it was time to leave. He said he was going to take his guests up the road camping and he did. I couldn't believe he would be so stupid. They had no idea where the gunman was, if he was alone, or had an accomplice. Everybody else was dead scared and we were all being told not to take unnecessary risks. But there he was, driving off in the dark, headlights on, to pick a camp site. I pointed out the foolhardiness of what he was doing, but Peter said in a very offhand manner, "We'll be right, John. We'll find a gravel pit somewhere." I felt really cross with him. It was utterly irresponsible. If he wanted to play the hero, that was one thing, but to take his guests into a situation like that, was extremely foolish. They could be camped right alongside the maniac and they wouldn't have a clue. If they lit a campfire it would be a beacon for the bloke, torches the same and in the silence of the bush at night, their voices would carry. I told Peter all this, but he said they'd be OK, he had a gun! 'What good would that be?' I thought. The madman could be anywhere. Everybody was on a high level of alert and there were loaded guns all over the place. They could even be shot at by some fearful Kimberley resident mistaking them for the killer. There was no talking him out of it and off they all went, into the night.

The tense situation in the Kimberly lasted a week before there was a break through. A helicopter pilot, Peter Leutenegger, was mustering horses for the forthcoming Fitzroy

Rodeo. One or two horses broke back and when he went to get them he spotted a camouflaged vehicle at the back of the paddock. He flew the chopper into Fitzroy Crossing, landing it right outside the police station. The tactical response group were still searching remote country near Pentecost Crossing when news of the sighting came in. Three police aircraft flew them down to Fitzroy, where the airport had been sealed off. The gunman was shot dead by police and was later identified as Josef Schwab, a West German from Bavaria. With the drama over and local residents breathing sighs of relief, journalists from around the country were left milling about the Kimberley looking for suitable stories to put in their magazines and newspapers. Many station folk in the region found themselves being interviewed by reporters who had little understanding of the lifestyle we led. Janet and I were amongst those whose story was sought, both by the Sydney Sun Herald and Woman's Day magazine. Because Janet was so obviously English, whilst I was regarded as a true Australian bushy, complete with drawl, these city bred journalists found us an unlikely couple worth writing about. Whilst it was amusing, at the time, to be interviewed in this way, the subsequent articles were infuriatingly inaccurate. In one I was described as being able to ... *throw a beast with a flick of my arms and break a wild horse faster than anyone'*, whilst Janet was said to have ... *been appalled by the behaviour of outback men*. But there was little time for ... *the poet who married the legend of the Kimberley* to dwell on the ridiculousness of the articles. She was being kept busy closing the books in preparation for the handover of Meda to the West Australian Cattle Company. A job she was asked to do more than once, before settlement finally took place on June 30th 1987, or so we were told.

*L-R Adele, Janet and me at Claypan Yard, Meda. September 1985*

The new circular drafting yard at Macaulays. 1986

Macaulays Yard is put to use for the first time.

*My mother in law, Meg Wallace, at old Euringa Yard. Meda 1985*

*The memorial plaque at the May River Crossing on Meda erected in 1985 to commemorate the first pastoral settlement by Emanuel Brothers a century earlier.*

*Haymaking in the Meda bullock paddock assisted by our neighbours, Birdwood Downs.*

*I watch as the Meda horses are brought in.*

# CHAPTER SIXTEEN
# WACCO 1987 TO 1989

*Willie you shine like a beacon, in a deep and dark rushing tide,*
*While your race sail the ship of destruction,*
*As we watch from the windward side.*
*Willie, you glow like a lantern, hung high on a clear moonless night,*
*While your kinsfolk blunder on blindly, unaware of their desperate plight.*

On July 1st 1987 we had a visit from Mr Brian Coppin and Peter Murray. During the morning Janet received a telephone call from John Barnett from the ABC Country Hour. He wanted to speak with Peter Murray about the purchase of Meda. I had taken the two men to the Claypan and when we got back we sat at the dining room table for an hour and a half while the two men told us, as Mr 3% had the previous day, that settlement was finalised. Peter Murray would be our immediate boss, working out of a Broome based company office.

Janet served lunch and the telephone rang at the appointed time. It was John Barnett and Peter Murray took the call as arranged. It was live on radio. We listened with interest as he was asked to confirm whether or not the rumours were true and he had indeed bought Meda Station. We were astonished to hear him emphatically deny it.

The station did change hands, as was publicly acknowledged a few days after, but the bare faced lies of that morning have stayed with us over the years. How Peter Murray could tell us one thing, and in the same hour, within our hearing, tell John Barnett another was a revelation. For us, from that point on, there was always a level of mistrust.

Meda, or 'Beaten Downs' as I should now call it, became part of the West Australian Cattle Company, a newly formed company that included seven stations and a farm in the Chapman Valley, near Geraldton. The stations included Mt. Hart, Leopold Downs, Fairfield, Wallal, Nanutarra, Yinnetharra and Meda. Those involved in the company were businessmen Kerry Stokes, Brian Coppin, Bill Hall, Peter Murray and Robin Finger. WACCO would later add Blina, Ellendale, Calwynyardah and Brooking Springs to their impressive list of assets. So much for the governments desire for diversity of ownership, smaller acreages and owner occupiers on West Australian pastoral leases. It was a joke.

In September all company station managers and their wives were summoned to Broome for the first of a series of manager's meetings. We were accommodated in the re-vamped Roebuck Hotel and were well looked after. The meeting ran for two full days when company policy was discussed, running costs estimated and branding numbers and sales figures projected. As well there were various presentations given, including one from veterinarian Dr Brown Bezier, who was to be involved in an embryo transplant programme at the Chapman Valley farm. It was all very amicable and at times entertaining. Peter Murray chaired the meeting and clearly relished his role. Peter was a funny man. He could be highly amusing, was often generous, had a big ego and was at times very likeable. But he had an air of self importance and I always felt he looked down on me. There was no doubting he was successful. He was often brash, full of bravado and he carried it off as well as any man. But I had been told things about him that somehow rang true and despite everything I have never felt I was his inferior. Sometimes I'd get a good rev at the WACCO meetings for using too much fuel, although our fuel consumption on the station hadn't increased in years. I'm a bloke who believes in going 'drive-about' to keep an eye on things. I have always found it worthwhile and I didn't miss much. I think it is an important part of good station management. Peter Murray suggested we put in airstrips at all the windmills and leave drums of fuel there, so aerial bore runs could be done, instead of me driving around. It was a crazy idea for a place like Meda, only a handful of kilometres from Derby. With every Tom, Dick and Harry driving through the place we were already having problems with fuel being stolen from engines on bores, without leaving forty four gallons drums out bush at airstrips, just waiting to be nicked. It wouldn't have been practical either, because the strips would need to be a fair way out from the bores to avoid cattle pads made by the stock coming in to water. How far did Murray expect the pilot to walk in the heat? It might be alright on the Barkly Tableland, with no town for miles and great turkey nest dams you could fly over, but it wasn't a good idea for us.

Although he was often jovial you couldn't read it with Peter Murray. Sometimes, without warning, he'd get hot under the collar about something. He had some strange ideas and did some silly things at times. We might be discussing something, having a few beers and he'd be sucking hard on his cigarette. Then, without warning, he'd get up from the table and walk out. He'd pace about on the lawn for a while, puffing away at a few more cigarettes. Then he'd come in and say, "I think I'd better go now!" I'd be thinking to myself, 'Thank Christ for that.' It used to really put me on edge. Then on his next visit he'd say, "I've thought about that, John and we'll do what you said." Nice as anything. One time he brought cattle down from Leopold and Fairfield. For some reason he decided to unload one deck of shit bullocks at Emanuels Yard and put on a deck of better Meda cattle, to take on to the meatworks.

"What am I going to do with these ones you're leaving behind?" I asked.

"Oh just put them in the horse paddock for now. When I need them I'll come back and pick them up." He told me. The horse paddock was for our mustering horses and pretty well eaten out at that time of the year. The rubbish bullocks would hang in corners, wanting to get back to where they came from. There was the risk of them getting out and if they did they'd head back to Leopold Downs, which was miles away. So they were a bit of a worry. Some time later, Murray rang up to tell me he was sending a roadtrain in next day to pick the Leopold bullocks up. We had to stop what we were doing, get men and horses up to Emanuels, muster the paddock, yard up and be ready for the roadtrain to pick them up. Because they weren't our cattle we didn't know what class of bullocks they were, whether they'd be easy to handle or not. It caused us a lot of messing around. But that was Murray. Impetuous at times.

## Meda starts bleeding. July to October. 1987

As I had feared, it wasn't long before I saw station assets going off the place. Steers, those that were left, went to Wallal Downs, south of Sandfire Roadhouse. So too did pipe, mesh and steel, previously earmarked for a trap yard around Bolger's Bore, in Meda's Bullock Paddock. Spare engines were taken from the workshop, for use on other WACCO properties who'd run into difficulties with their own. The kite-hawks were swooping. It was a case of 'Wellsy has got plenty. Go grab what you need from Meda.' Worst of all was the day Murray rang at eight in the morning to tell us a truck would arrive at midday to take Willie Lennard's house away. It was going down to Broome, to be used as quarters for WACCO's roadtrain drivers. Janet and I were appalled.

Willie was one of my best and most loyal men. From the age of fourteen he had spent much of his working life on Meda. Twenty years while my father was there, also for Frank Mugford when he took over. Later he stayed to work for Dave Ledger for a while, though this ended badly. One day Willie had got drunk. Ledger called the police and Willie was taken off the place, tied to a ring in the back of the police wagon, like some mongrel criminal. After that Willie gave up alcohol completely, but he never went back to work for Ledger. Instead he came and worked for me at Napier. When I left the Kimberley at the end of my marriage, Willie went up to Pantijan for a time with his own people, but he returned to Meda again when I took over, and had been there ever since. He was the most loyal, dependable and dignified of men, born into an impossible situation, but he made the most of life. Both he and his wife were teetotal, quiet, gentle and utterly reliable. They never gave us any trouble of any kind. Now, under new ownership, his home had been taken away without warning. He had nowhere to live. I couldn't believe what had been done. Left with no choice Willie and Roslyn moved into Derby to live at Karmalinunga, an Aboriginal Reserve on the edge of the marsh. Here they endured a miserable existence amongst the fighting, the alcohol and the hopelessness of town life. For a time Willie drove out from Derby, to work on Meda, but eventually it became too much for him to do on a daily basis, though he continued to come and help out when needed right up until I left.[11]

---

11    In Mary Ann Jebb's book, Blood Sweat and Welfare; A history of white bosses and aboriginal pastoral workers, published by the University of Western Australia Press in 2002 it states that
'In 1989 Willie Lennard and his family had only just arrived from Meda station
after around fifty years of work there. The new manager burned down the house
and sent them to town.'
I don't know how this story came about, but it is utterly incorrect. It is a good example of how history can be distorted and inaccuracies recorded, in print, for all time.

# Lorraine Lennard

One of Willie Lennard's younger daughters worked for us at the homestead. Lorraine was a good, clean and intelligent girl who, like her father, was reliable and trustworthy. She helped Janet in various ways and was good with the children of whom she was fond. She didn't drink and she confided to Adele and George that she was afraid of her alcoholic siblings. After the removal of Willie's house Lorraine did not want to go into Derby to live with her parents. She preferred to remain out on the station, rather than be exposed to the difficulties of the town reserve. It was unusual for an aboriginal to want to stay on their own, but Lorraine was an exceptional girl. She was a good reliable worker, who saved her money in a sensible and responsible way. Because she had money she knew her siblings would humbug her for it and make her life Hell. She knew she would not be able to endure life in town. Fortunately we were able to set up a small caravan for her to live in at the homestead and Lorraine remained working for us until we left.

Lorraine had two children whilst on Meda, to our mechanic Dennis. A daughter, Leanne and a son, John. Dennis returned to Ireland with the young children one wet season. He asked Lorraine to go with him, but she declined. While he was in Ireland his mother became sick. Dennis, being the eldest of a big family, remained in Ireland to help, never returning to Australia. The two children stayed with him.

After we left Meda Lorraine had no choice but to move into Derby. It was only a matter of time before the pressures of town life wore her down and she too turned to drink. In only a few short years she became a hopeless alcoholic and eventually died of liver failure. Janet visited her while she was being treated in Fremantle Hospital, five short years after leaving Meda. Lorraine was ill and very frightened. Janet arranged for a television to be set up in her room as a distraction for her. During the visit Lorraine vowed not to drink again, telling Janet she'd been told if she did she would die. A few weeks after returning to Derby she did, both drink and die. She was still a young woman.

Lorraine Lennard's death affected us deeply. It epitomised the hopelessness of life for our indigenous people. Even for the more intelligent and sensible amongst them, the odds are stacked too heavily against them. Decisions are made by well meaning people who simply do not know them. Some say it was the tragedy of losing her children that ultimately caused Lorraine to turn to drink, but I don't think so. Lorraine had another daughter a good while after Dennis had left. Whilst I'm sure she always mourned the loss of her two older children she showed no signs of weakness, or inclination to drink grog whilst on Meda. I fully believe, if we had remained on the station Lorraine would have stayed too, and that she would be alive today.

Many years later, after we had left the Kimberley, Lorraine's children Leanne and John visited Australia from Ireland. They travelled to Derby and met Lorraine's extended family and their half sister. Janet and I drove to Perth and met with the pair before they flew back to Ireland. They were both fine young people. Their mother would have been proud of them and we took the opportunity to tell them how proud they should be of their fine mother.

## Dinner with a pollie

Early in May 1988 Janet and I, together with a few other station people, were invited to a dinner at the Boab Hotel in Derby hosted by the Ag. Department. The guest of honour was the then Minister for Agriculture Julian Grill. During the course of the evening there was a vigorous discussion regarding the future direction of the Kimberley pastoral industry. The Minister obviously held very different views to most of us. It proved an enlightening experience. During the meal, in response to a question from one of the guests, Mr Grill replied that he did not believe people like ourselves were entitled to land in the Kimberley, saying the Aboriginals now owned many pastoral leases, and whether we liked it or not they were doing better than we were. Surprised by this retort Janet pointed out that the pastoral leases were given to the Aboriginal communities, together with Government funding to run them, whilst white pastoralists purchased their leases and funded the running costs themselves. She went on to say that after three generations of managing cattle stations in the Kimberley the Wells family were no nearer to obtaining a lease of their own than when they first came in 1900. Despite decades of hard work, there appeared to be no future in the industry for them. In our opinion, this was the reason why a large number of good, experienced cattlemen were leaving the industry to seek work elsewhere.

"If you are honest, no matter how hard you work, it is impossible, to get ahead."

we told him. His reply was that 'no-one gets ahead nowadays by being honest', saying we were the only people who could help ourselves. Janet and I were left speechless.[12]

## A bank manager visits

Peter Murray and I were driving round the run one day when he spotted a Brahman bull.

"That's not much of a bull. Where did you get that bull from?" he asked.

"He was one of a mob bought off you at your Leopold bull sale." I replied.

"Oh? What mob did that come in?"

"I don't know, but we got about twelve."

"Well that's a terrible ugly bull. I could've got you better than that." He said scathingly.

"You sold it to us, Peter. I had no say in it. This is just what I got."

"How much did you pay for it?"

"I think Exim paid about a thousand dollars a head."

"Hmmph. I could've got you one for $500." He snorted. I felt a bit annoyed with him. We drove on further down the bullock paddock.

A year earlier Exim had bought a mob of heifers, half breed Brahmans, from Doongan. Never been tailed out or anything. Chopper mustered, drafted, put on a roadtrain and sent down to us. We'd cross branded them and fed them hay, in the yards, for a week. We had put horses in with them, not with very good temperaments, to boss them and teach them a bit of respect, because these Doongan cattle had never been worked with horses. The day before we were going to let them out we didn't feed them. Then next day we put hay outside the yard, in the hope that, being a bit hungry, the cattle would pull up to eat the hay once they were let out, instead of taking off on us. We only let a few out at a time, so it was easier to handle them.

---

12   Julian Grill, together with Brian Burke, later gained considerable notoriety as lobbyists involved in questionable activities resulting in a number of court appearances over several years. It was simply our misfortune that these two men were in a position to make decisions that could wreak such havoc on our lives, and the lives of many others in the pastoral industry at that time.

Once they were all let out of the yard we tailed them for a bit, then with horses, walked them down to the bullock paddock. By the time Peter Murray and I went 'look-about' that day, a lot of the Doongan cows had calved. When Murray saw them he said, "I don't want you to cut any of these bull calves here, John. I want every bull calf, with a bit of Brahman in it, kept for a herd bull." I was surprised to hear this, because some of the cattle were all colours and pretty ugly.

"Everything?" I questioned.

"I just said 'everything' didn't I?"

"All right." I agreed. We drove down the track a bit further and came across a black and white beast that looked like it came out of the jungles of Africa.

"So that bull calf there, do you want me to keep that for a bull?"

"I just told you that." Murray growled.

"Right'o." I'd got the message. We drove on and had a look at a few other things, then returned to the homestead. On the way home Peter started talking about what a good wage I was on.

"I don't think I am." I told him. "I'm the manager here. I'm also the bloody social service officer. The fighter. The doctor. The nurse, policeman, vet. I'm every bloody thing. I'm called out at all hours of the night. You don't have long weekends or Easter holidays in this job. If I got a government job in town, I'd probably get a government car, air conditioning subsidy, return airfare to Perth for my wife and family, four weeks holiday a year and the bloke next door could cut his Missus' throat and I wouldn't have to know about it." Murray didn't say anything, but the next time he came to Meda he gave me a good pay rise!

The morning after our drive-about a bank manager, called Fred, came out to Meda. Peter Murray was still there and away we went, on the same trip we'd done the day before. At about the same time of day, under the same bauhina tree, was the same bull we'd seen the previous morning. Murray told me to drive over to it. I did and the bull stood up.

"What do you reckon to that bull Fred? Not a bad sort of a young Brahman bull, is it?" Murray asked the visitor. I thought it was quite amusing because Fred wouldn't have known if it was a good bull or not.

"We paid $5000 for that bull." Peter told him. I couldn't believe my bloody ears. We continued on our way. We drove here, there and everywhere, looking at this and that and all the while more bull shit. Murray who was trying to impress Fred, was full of it. Later, when we were on the way home Fred asked, "How long have you had the Brahmans here Peter?"

"We've brought them in since we bought the property."

I looked at Murray. He could see I wasn't pleased with him. He looked at Fred and after a moments hesitation added, "Aah, well, John had a few Brahmans here before we bought the place." Golly, just absolute dysentery flowing out of him. Nowadays it seems to be the norm' for people to talk crap, but in those days, well ----- I couldn't really believe it.

## The bullock paddock

The bullock paddock on Meda was extensive, being twenty miles or so in length and maybe ten or so wide and mostly good open plain country, but it was not easy to police. It was made up of two paddocks, with gates at each end, but you couldn't keep the paddocks separated because everybody used to come out there fishing. The blacks would go home on dark time and blacks are frightened of the dark. Kids especially. When they came to a gate a kid would have to open it. That was all right, while the headlights were shining on the gate, but once the vehicle had driven through, because it was dark the kid would be shitting himself. He'd jump back on the vehicle as quickly as he could, leaving the gate open. This was on all the time. On the marshy country, because it was salt, we used fibreglass pickets. The fishermen would get there, lie the fence down, drive over it and leave it.

Another thing about the Meda bullock paddock was that certain cattle had learnt to cross the saltwater, but only on certain tides. Although the May river was fenced off, with the problem of keeping gates closed our stock would quite often get through. If it was low tide and no water, it was too boggy for the cattle to cross. If there was too much water and flowing strongly, they might try to cross, but would be forced to turn back. Some cattle knew when to cross over. At certain times and on certain tides there would be enough water for them to swim over without getting bogged, or washed off course. I knew this because I'd see a beast down in the bullock paddock one week and it would be over at Euringa the next. Because of the problem with the fishermen and the gates, we had our good Brahman cows mixed up with our shorthorn and second grade Brahmans, so the whole show was a bit of a circus. Peter Murray had seen this, and when it came time to muster the bullock paddock he said to me, "You've got a bit of a mess down there John. You'll have to get it sorted out." I already knew I had a bit of a mess down there, but there wasn't a lot I could do about it and I said so.

"How do I stop the blacks, who've been fishing there for years, from leaving the gates open?" I asked.

"Put locks on the gates." Murray suggested.

"Yeah? Then they'll cut the bloody fences. If I front them, next thing the country is set alight. I've been up against this for a good many years Peter. It's not that easy."

"Well you need to get it sorted out." He told me bluntly.

Mustering in the bullock paddock came to an abrupt end one morning, at the end of May, when the helicopter suffered a snapped clutch cable. The chopper came down, from a hundred feet, into thick scrub two miles south of Lakes Bore. The machine was a right-off. Karl, the pilot, came out of it bruised, scratched and shaken, but with injuries no worse than a sore neck and shoulder. He was able to walk out to seek help from the stockcamp. He then drove himself back to the homestead in the bull buggy to report the incident to the authorities. Two officers from the Department of Air Safety flew up from Perth the following day to investigate. It proved a busy day for us. Peter Murray, Robin Finger, Malcolm Seaward and another man, unknown to me, arrived at Meda, purportedly so Murray could teach me how to draft, while the others watched. I felt very edgy and wasn't sure I'd be able to hide my irritation at this insult. Ann Murray was due to fly in at noon, with three more guests and a pilot. Janet had been instructed to make packed lunches for eleven people, told to meet the plane when it landed at the airstrip, then drive the party of visitors down to the stockcamp, where they too could watch me being shown how to do my job. The Air Safety officers were left to fend for themselves.

As it turned out I kept my cool. Murray was happy playing the cattle baron in front of his select audience, particularly so when he had one hundred top Brahman weaners drafted off and set aside to be trucked away. The day ended without incident, the visiting party left and life resumed it's normal pattern, for a while.

A month or so later we had another influx of guests, amidst a flu epidemic. My brother-in-law and his two youngest children were visiting and as usual Janet was extra busy trying to fit in as much as she could while they were there. She had taken them up the Gibb River Road on a camping trip for a few days, as well as an overnight visit to Broome. Then having caught up on station chores, an outing to Poultons Pool was planned for their last day with us. That was before Murray rang early in the morning to say he, his wife, Brian Coppin, Mrs Coppin, Kerry Stokes and his current wife, as well as four children, were coming to Meda that day. All other plans were abandoned. By now we had become used to turning on hospitality for the Murray's endless guests, at a moments notice. Long gone were the days of Tim and Sally Emanuel's handwritten letters asking if a visit would be convenient. How times had changed.

## Draft Doongan cattle out on the flat

We were down in the bullock paddock mustering the Brahman cows from Doongan for the first time. By now some of them had pretty big calves, plus another little calf on them, and all in the same mob. These were the wild, chopper mustered cattle we'd tried to educate before letting them go. We managed to muster them OK and Murray told me, over the phone, how he wanted them drafted.

"Draft into meatworks cows, first grade shorthorns, and first grade Brahmans." He said, "Then I want all the yearlings separate. I want it all open draft, out on the flat. Not through a drafting yard."

I thought 'Jeez. This isn't going to be too bloody good. Some of the cows with last years calf and with a new calf on them as well.' I was pretty worried about it. I thought 'This can't be done. Not out on the open. There's no way.' I thought about it for a while, then I rang him up.

"Look, what I'm ringing you about is this five way draft of cattle you want and you wanting them all drafted out on the flat. For starters, I haven't got the men with the ability. These cows aren't really that pliable. They'll just take off and leave their calf. Then the yearling will want to go too. We'll end up getting somebody killed. These cows are still bonded with their last years calves, not sucking, but still mated up. If their mum has got to go into one mob, then they'll reckon they've got to get over there too. We need to draft these cattle through the yards Peter." Oh Jeez! Did he go off.

"Do you mean to tell me there's no bloody good stockmen in the country anymore?" He exploded.

"That's exactly what I'm telling you." I replied. Afterwards I got onto Robin Finger and explained my predicament.

"Look, what Peter is wanting is hopeless. It can't be done. This isn't what you do with this class of cattle. Someone will get badly hurt."

"I told him that, but he won't listen." Robin sympathised.

"Well I'm not prepared to do it how he says. We've got the new yard at Bolger's Bore. I won't be drafting them out on the flat. They'll be drafted through the yard." That's what we did and nothing was said about it.

We drafted three lines of cows, good Brahman cows, good shorthorn cows and then second grade Brahman and shorthorn cows, plus a line of rubbish cows for the meatworks. The yearlings were separated and all the bull calves, with any Brahman in them, were kept, ugly or not, as had been instructed. These were later taken out to Daley's Bore and eventually dispersed throughout the herd.

I drafted all the best looking cows into one mob. If there was a good looking calf, it went in with that same mob. All the 'uglies' went into another yard. We had two paddocks there, with a gate at each end, to go into either paddock. We lifted the gates up, so that the calves could swap over. Only two calves died out of the whole deal, everything else sorted itself out.

When I rang to order the WACCO roadtrain, to cart the meatworks cattle to Broome, Murray's transport manager said, "But it's a weekend John. I can't expect the roadtrain driver to work on weekends. I'll have to hire someone else to do the job." I felt a bit annoyed. At the manager's meetings we were constantly being told we needed to make more money and cut costs. My stockmen and station hands worked on weekends and had done for as long as I could remember. I didn't see why other company employees couldn't be expected to do the same, when necessary.

## Old cows to Wallal

It was getting towards the end of the year. We had a mob of cows put together ready for the meatworks. Some of them were in calf, but they were poor and wouldn't see the wet out. I wanted to send them in to the abattoir and get a dollar for them while we could. On one of his visits to Meda Murray saw them and he told me to send them down to Wallal.

"That's not a good idea. They're too poor to truck, be dipped at Broome, then trucked on to Wallal. Even if they survive the journey, being on new country, they'll walk the fences and lose even more condition." I explained.

"No, no Wellsy. They'll be right. We'll take them, get a calf out of them, then send them to the meatworks next year." Murray insisted. I didn't like it. It was extra punishment for the cows, as well as an additional cost to the station, with no guarantee of any return.

"Look, Peter, you're better to grab ninety bucks a head now and call it quits. You've got to pay yard fees, trucking fees, cartage to Wallal and when they get there they don't know the country. They don't know the feed down there. You'll lose a lot of them and get nothing at all for them. You're much better to send them to the abattoir now." But he was determined. He took them anyway and I heard later that a fair few of them died on Wallal, as I'd feared they might.

## Contract musterer 'drops the can'

Back on Meda the roguish contract musterer was finishing off his season in a very lackadaisical manner. The annoyances, for me, were mounting. One of them was his habit of filling forty-four gallon drums from the delivery pipe to the tank at bores. Then, instead of putting it back, it was being left to run on the ground, making a bloody wet mess and undermining the moundring of the tank. Fishermen tended to do this also, using delivery pipes to shower under on their way back from the river.

As time went on there was less and less co-operation from the contractor. Miscounting, incorrect loading of cattle and a failure to fix up opened fences. Omitting to tell me when a bore had stopped pumping and the tank was dangerously low, finally brought things to a head at the end of October.

A renowned womaniser the contract musterer had, by then, taken up with our station cook. After a final disagreement over cattlework both he and she pulled out, within a day of each other. His job was incomplete. With work still to be done before the wet, I contacted my two good men, Ronnie and Sneezy. They were at Quanbun building troughs at the time. They agreed to return to Meda and step into the breach. I asked them if they could pick up a few blokes in town to give us a hand. They did. One was a clerk from Perth, two were Pommy tourists and one was a really good native boy called Johnny Butt. Johnny Butt had worked for me, on and off, many times since my days at Napier and I was delighted to have him back on the books. Meanwhile Janet again took over as station cook, unpaid as always, until a replacement was found.

## We get a big mob at Gum Hole

The first task for Ronnie, Sneezy, Johnny Butt and the three new blokes was to set up portable yards near Big Springs. It was the first week of November. The build-up to the wet had started, it was humid and very hot. Gloves were needed to move the steel panels. The English lads and their clerical colleague didn't know what had hit them. They only managed to move a couple of panels each, before collapsing in the shade, absolutely knackered. With the new chums unable to hack the conditions, my three experienced blokes basically built the yards alone. We were trapping at Orange Pool at the time, so the following day, once the portable yard was finished at Gum Hole, chopper pilot, Peter Leutenegger, came late in the afternoon to yard the Orange Pool trap cattle. We drafted them next morning, then Leutenegger yarded up at Langoora. The Langoora trap cattle were drafted on the Saturday morning before we turned our attention to Big Springs. Big Springs is an area of marsh country some forty-five miles from the homestead, up towards the Oobagooma boundary. Many years ago, before my father's time, a bore was put down out on the marsh. It was a flowing bore. Although once controlled, it has for many years flowed freely and over time an area of 'tropical rainforest' has developed. A unique and unexpected ecosystem in an otherwise desolate landscape. This place is known as Big Springs. Amusingly it was 'discovered' by a team of excited botanists a little over twenty years ago. It has been a favourite haunt of mine all my life, my fathers before me. It now extends over a kilometre or more in length and is a couple of hundred metres wide. With an abundance of fresh water it is an island of lush vegetation, of huge ficus trees, ferns, vines, and pandanus palms rising out of the surrounding, seemingly endless salt marsh. It provides a unique habitat to many bird species, including pheasant coucal, restless flycatchers, known locally as scissors grinders, heron, swamp hens, owls and numerous others. Cool, shady and with plenty of fresh water it is an ideal place for cattle to live. Dotted across the marsh are other smaller springs and pockets of pandanus. The area and surrounding scrub, was home to a lot of wild, ugly looking cattle.

We had two helicopters mustering that Sunday, from the Meda/Obagooma boundary, towards Gum Hole and out across the marsh, flushing cattle from Big Springs and the surrounding area. At the end of the day we yarded over four hundred head, amongst them a few big old bullocks, a lot of cleanskin bulls, mickies and mongrel spayer type cows. Because there was no water in the portable yard we decided to truck all the cleanskins, except for 'wet cows' and their calves, to a drafting yard at Geoff's bore, about fifteen miles away. A quicker turn around than carting them all the way back to the station first up. At Geoff's we would brand, earmark and tip them before trucking them back home to the Claypan. At the end of the year, if cattle were a bit weak, we didn't castrate them.

With the number of cattle in the portable yards at Gum Hole it was dusty as hell. You couldn't see a thing. The roadtrain had arrived and was at the portable ramp. Sneezy was down the back pushing up cattle ready to load. As he went to shut the heavy gate on the forcing pen, a bull came out of the dust hitting the top rail. It hit it that hard it bent a star picket, the gate hit Sneezy across the chest and he went down. The bull got stuck 'into him' straight away, hooking him from the feet up to the crotch. Then it came around the partially opened gate and started on his upper body. Johnny Butt, seeing what had happened, came off the top rail, landed on the bull, drew it's attention and got it off the man. Sneezy was a lucky bloke. He had livid, red marks all over him, but apart from shock was relatively unharmed. Afterwards over a cup of tea and still shaking he talked of the incident.

"He just came out of nowhere. I thought I was cactus."

"Yeah. I heard you squealing like a little girl." Ronnie teased. "Wellsy said 'what's that noise and I said 'It's probably just Sneezy dyin'" and so ended another 'close shave' with the usual laughter, friendly banter and high spirits, brought on by a cocktail of relief, a recent burst of fear, and adrenalin.

We had almost finished at the yard, when Peter Murray rocked up. Seeing all the big mickey bulls he asked what I was intending to do with them. I said I was going to truck them back to the Claypan, where we had a paddock, Bull Paddock, suitable for that class of cattle. They would be locked in the Claypan yards, on water and fed for a week, before being let go in the paddock. It worked quite well for me because if ever I was short of cattle I could set the trap at the Claypan in the afternoon and by next day I'd have ten, or fifteen meatworks cattle ready to truck away. It was a good set-up. But having seen them, Murray wanted them and he wasn't happy with the arrangement.

"No John. Don't take these cattle back to Meda. I'll organise for a roadtrain to come and pick them up and we'll take them straight down to Wallal." Again it was a case of cartage and dipping costs, taking cattle down onto strange country and new feed. But that is what happened.

I heard later, from reliable sources, that those cattle remained on Wallal for a long, long time. It was several years before they were able to regain control of them and finally sell them. Murray would have had a much quicker turn-over if he had let me do as I suggested. But then again, as things turned out, perhaps not.

## 'Peter the Painter' comes to caretake

With trapping finished, the season ended, and whilst we waited for another 'wet' to begin we started thinking about going down to Perth for our annual holidays. But before we could leave Peter Murray had a job for us. He asked us to go up to Mount Hart and care-take, for a couple of weeks. We did and apart from a niggling concern that if the rains came we might find ourselves stuck there for two or three months, it was actually quite enjoyable. Peter Murray had owned Mount Hart for a good while and Ann had developed a lush garden on the banks of a creek. The homestead was of the old style. Solidly built with the inside rooms surrounded by wide verandah rooms, where fireflies blinked at night and geckos hunted by day. There was no one, other than Janet, myself, Adele and young George on the place. Nobody to cause any grief or irritation. Nobody to give stores to, or feed. No-one needing fuel or wanting to be pulled out of a bog, and there was no telephone. Being so much further out of town had huge benefits and the never ending demands of life on Meda seemed a world away. Although we watched towering thunderclouds build up most evenings we had little real rain while we were there. After a fortnight of George happily fishing in the creek, Adele playing with her flower-press, Janet writing poetry or dabbling with her watercolours, or me taking them off to explore the nearby creeks and ridges, we left Mount Hart behind us and successfully negotiated the sixty kilometre long track back out to the Gibb River Road and drove through the King Leopold Ranges back home to Meda.

I was given no choice about who the 'wet season' caretaker should be that year. Murray had already decided to leave 'Peter the Painter', a WACCO maintenance man, in charge. I had no idea what the fellow knew about stations, or whether he had any experience. I wasn't particularly happy about the arrangement, but as with so many other things, I just had to wear it. We were sitting having smoko with the 'caretaker' one day when our turkeys began making a bit of noise at the front of the house. We took very little notice. A moment later 'Peter Painters' dog let out a yelp. A big dog, part Alsatian, it had been asleep on the cool cement verandah at the rear of the homestead. It leapt up and raced around the garden, absolutely flat tack, then shot out of the gate and across to the cottage where the painter was staying. By the time we walked the short distance over to it the dog was dead. It had been bitten by a seven foot king brown which we later killed. A day or two later Janet, the children and I left in a short wheel base Toyota for the three day drive to Perth. I was concerned about leaving 'Peter the Painter' to look after things on Meda while I was away, so I asked Keith Bolger, the retired windmillman, to check up on everything for me once he got back from his break. He did, but by then it was too late. Thirty or forty head of cattle had perished at the Claypan. I was not aware of this until I got home, when Bolger told me what had happened. He had been heading down to the bullock paddock, to check the bores, when he came across the dead cattle. He had found the windmill not pumping, the tank and troughs empty. They were trap cattle, tipped, branded and earmarked, but they hadn't been castrated. They were in the Bull Paddock where the windmill controlled everything. The paddock where I was going to put the Gum Hole mickies, had Murray not taken them to Wallal. When I heard what had happened I was not impressed. The Claypan was the closest bore to the homestead, but it seemed that 'Peter the Painter' hadn't even been that far to check on things. If only someone had seen that the windmill wasn't pumping, they could have cut the fence and let the cattle into the next paddock, where there was a billabong. It was a big loss. Not only in dollar terms, but also in effort. A lot of risk and hard yakka had gone into getting those bulls and bullocks, and all for nothing. Fortunately I knew none of this until after I got back from our holiday, but it once again highlighted to me the importance of leaving someone competent to caretake during the 'wet'.

Ronnie and Sneezy returned to the station at the beginning of the 1988 season. Ronnie had broken in a few colts for us, but by now we had a good supply of horses on Meda and breaking in wasn't the huge job it had once been in the early years of my management. Murray was needing a horse-breaker on Leopold and although Ronnie was going to run the stockcamp for me that year, we were not yet ready to start. I said it would be OK for him to go, if he agreed, with Sneezy as his offsider. It was about this time when Murray first saw Ronnie and he said to me, "Tell that bloke to get a haircut."

"You can tell him to get a haircut if you like, but I'm not going to" I replied "He's a really good, smart man and how he chooses to wear his hair is nothing to do with me, and it has got nothing to do with his ability." Whether Murray ever did speak to the man about his flowing mane I don't know, all I do know is that Ronnie never got his hair cut. By the time the pair came back from Leopold the weather had cooled and the country dried out. Conditions for man, horse and beast had improved enough for mustering to begin. I thought it was really good having some of my best ringers back working for me. They knew my style and how I liked things to be done. Everything went pretty well for quite a few weeks. But I had a stockcamp cook who was troublesome. Bob was an older bloke, who I later discovered was not only cooking and earning a wage on Meda, but also collecting the dole in town and spending it on grog, which he later took out to the stockcamp.

## A second chance

The stockcamp had been out for some weeks mustering, when one day a striking looking chestnut filly, ridden by Johnny Butt, got gored near Number Six bore. Johnny took it upon himself to truck her back to the homestead for treatment, later driving the DA15 Toyota back up to Emanuels yard where the stockcamp was then based. Neither Ronnie, Sneezy nor I, had ever seen Johnny Butt drive a vehicle, in his life. Let alone a truck. To my knowledge he had never held a driver's license and he certainly didn't have a truck licence. But such things didn't bother him. The horse had been hurt and she needed help. The truck was there, no-one else was available to drive it, so he just got on with it as best he could. That was all there was to it. The same day, Bob, the camp cook had been into town. He arrived back late at the stockcamp with a cargo of grog. Bottles of rum, cartons of beer, the lot. The ringers had had a long hard day, with a man short, a horse gored and a late finish. They hadn't seen a beer for six weeks. It didn't take much for them to become rotten drunk. By the early hours of the morning, thoroughly pissed, they decided it would be a good idea to take the station vehicle, drive into town and visit their girlfriends. They headed off down the Gibb River Road towards Derby, but when they reached the Leprosarium turnoff, just a few kilometres from town, they thought better of it. They did a 'U' turn and set off back up the road in the direction from which they'd just come. There were two of them in the vehicle, a Toyota Hilux and it was travelling at speed. It had been a long hard day, capped off by a night of heavy drinking. The driver kept nodding off. Jolted awake by his passenger several times, he somehow kept the vehicle on the road, until they reached Millard's Soak. Then leaving the bitumen it careered across the hard shoulder, over the windrow, flipped and rolled several times. The cab was totally crushed on the passenger's side. The passenger was thrown under the dashboard, the driver wrapped around the pedals. The vehicle was a right-off. Somehow neither man was seriously hurt.

When I reported this incident to Peter Murray he was, understandably, not impressed.

"So you've sacked them."

"I won't be sacking them." I told him.

"They've taken a station vehicle without permission, driven it while they're drunk, written it off and you're not sacking them? You must think pretty highly of them if you won't sack them for that." he was right, I did. He wrote me a letter telling me what he thought, saying that the pair were to pay two thousand dollars excess on the vehicle insurance. Murray was huffing and puffing, so I got Janet to write out a letter stating the case as I saw it. Something along the lines of 'These two blokes were very good workers and able stockmen. They had been with me for a good many years. I had taught them from young fellows, they knew the station, they knew how it all worked, they were quick, smart and usually dependable. Even though they could be wild young fellows at times, good ringers were becoming hard to find.' Then I reminded him that it was these two who had got us out of trouble at the end of the previous season, when the contractor had pulled the pin early. That it was this pair who had gone to Leopold horse-breaking when he needed them and done a good job. I told him I gave all my blokes a second chance and that I was giving these two their second chance.

In the meantime the two young men, realising they'd mucked up badly and would probably lose their jobs anyway, decided they had better leave of their own accord. They were waiting in Derby to hear what other consequences there might be. I took the letter to town and posted it. Then I took a copy of it to the pub where the young fellas were hanging out. I gave it to them to read.

"Don't send this off." They told me.

"Too late, I already have." I replied. "Now you'd better get back to work." I was pretty damned annoyed with them, but everyone I employ, who is any good at all, is given a second chance. That is how I've always operated and I think it is only fair. These fellows worked long hours, for weeks on end, doing a high adrenalin job a fair bit of the time, for not much pay. It was only human for them to make mistakes sometimes. I'd made more than a few in my time. My policy was, a second chance was reasonable, one error should be forgiven, but the next time it was the sack. The pair came back to work and did the job well for another month or two, then they blew their second chance and that was the end of them.[13]

## The flying stockcamp

After my men had run out of chances, Murray sent what he called his 'Flying Stockcamp' to do some contract mustering on Meda. I didn't like the arrangement much. Because they were employed by Peter Murray they treated him as the boss. I was just the shit kicker. I was constantly running around after them. It seemed I was their store deliveryman, fuel man, tucker man and gas bottle man. The latter because they had their own chuck wagon, which was fortunate in a way, or they'd probably have wanted me to supply them with wood as well. They were supposed to be contractors looking after themselves, but it didn't seem to work like that with WACCO. The other thing I didn't like about the 'Flying Stockcamp' was that men were employed who I didn't want, either on the station, or riding station horses. I had employed some of them in the past and knew them to be horse bashers, bad tempered bastards or plain useless. There were two or three in particular I was very unhappy about having on the place. One was a local coloured fellow. He had some ability, but a bad character. I'll call him Kimberley. Things went all right for a while, then one day an argument broke out between Kimberley and another fella, while they were heading out mustering. Kimberley rode alongside the other bloke, hit him on the jaw and knocked him clean off his horse. The headstockman sacked him for his efforts, then asked me to run him back into town. I didn't think this was right. I'd sacked the bloke twice, years earlier, when I had employed him, but this time he wasn't my man and I didn't see why I should do the dirty work. Anyway I did run him into Derby, but I didn't like it.

---

13    These same two young blokes, Ronnie and Sneezy, although they played hard in their youth, both worked as well as any man I've ever employed. Eventually each of them met and married good, capable young women. Both have successfully raised large, happy families. Having come to us in their early teens, they are now approaching fifty. Good husbands and fathers, neither ever out of work. The success they have made of their lives is a credit to them.

## Shortcuts don't work

It makes it very hard to run a cattle station when you've got blokes ignoring what you're telling them, or doing what someone else is telling them. You are ultimately responsible, but you lack the authority to see the job is done right. This is what happened with the 'Flying Stockcamp' and it was very frustrating. The first muster they did in the bullock paddock was at Bolger's Bore. They had got a fair mob of cattle together and I spoke to the man in charge and explained the set up to him.

"When you come to yard these cattle, don't try to walk them straight up and into the yard. Take them further down the fence, undo the wires on a strainer post, pull out a couple of star pickets and take the wires back onto themselves. Keep the cattle moving. Walk them a bit to take the sting out of them. When you've done that, bring them round wide, line them up for the gate and they should yard up all right. If you do it like that they'll think they're going back to country they've come off and it should make it a lot easier for you."

I left them to do this and drove on down to check One Tree bore. When I got back, some time later, the mob were two or three hundred metres from the yard, heading from the direction of the plain, where they'd been picked up. This was the opposite way to my instructions. When I saw this I wasn't very pleased. I parked the vehicle and watched. When they got close to the yard the cattle busted. They went every which way while the men tried briefly to put them together. I had three of my own men working with the 'Flying Stockcamp' at the time, one of them being Johnny Butt. After only a couple of minutes of trying to regain control, the 'Flying Stockcamp' men pulled up, whilst my three blokes tried to wheel the cattle out onto the plain, to get them in hand again. But the task was too great for them on their own. While the others just sat and watched, we ended up losing the lot. I couldn't believe the other horsemen hadn't moved or tried to help save the situation, which had been of their making in the first place. For they had not done as I'd said, not opened the fence and chosen instead to take the shortcut method, of taking cattle away from their country, instead of towards it when yarding up. Except for really quiet cattle this never pays. My way takes longer, but it's worth it every time.

Having lost the cattle the other men should have left the open side and backed up my three blokes, leaving just a couple of men on the tail, pushing them along out onto open country. Then when they had them out in the open, tried to wheel them round onto themselves, so that they started ringing in a wide circle. At that point the horsemen should back off a bit and give the cattle more room, minding them until they settled down. With a combined effort, and some perseverance, they could have got control of them and later tried to yard them up using the proper method.

A day or two later I was driving through the bullock paddock and I saw a mob of crows. I went to investigate and found a good Brahman cow with a broken leg. She had been shot and left to rot. No meat had been taken off her, she was just straight out waste. I had noticed previously that if the 'Flying Stockcamp' accidentally killed a beast with the bull buggy, they still went to the yards to get themselves a killer, rather than butchering the one they'd just 'despatched' by mistake. This wasn't my way of doing things, but this mob weren't employed by me. They were an independent WACCO outfit who were prone to please themselves whilst on Meda. I was pleased when they were moved on to work another company station.

## Buddy rolls the roadtrain

One Sunday Janet and I were having a siesta when young George, then aged seven, came running into the bedroom to say there was a fire. We went outside to have a look. There was a plume of black smoke up towards the main road. I knew straight away it was a vehicle. A moment later someone else came along. They told us a truck had rolled over, near the turnoff, with cattle on and that we might need to take a firearm with us. We left Lorraine minding the children and took off up the access road. As we approached the scene of the accident I recognised the truck. It was on fire. The driver was known to us. The crate was on it's side, the cab burning fiercely. I thought 'Jeez, if Buddy's trapped inside there I'm going to have to shoot him.' It was a pretty terrible moment. We couldn't get near the truck to get him out, so I thought we would have been doing him a favour. But when we got closer the cab appeared to be empty. We looked around and spotted Buddy up a bloody boab tree. Adrenalin must be mighty stuff, because I don't know how the hell he ever got up there. He wasn't a young man, nor a fit one. He had a big paunch and you wouldn't reckon he could move very fast at all. Here he was, up a boab tree that had no low branches at all. I couldn't have got up it, even when I was a super fit, athletic young man. How the hell Buddy got up there I'll never know.

As I've got older I've come to realise that fear can do two things to you. It can either make you an Olympic champion for one mighty effort, giving you a burst of super human power sufficient to save your life, or it can be the death of you by rendering you incapable of movement, with limbs turned to jelly. For Buddy, who was in his sixties, apparently it was the former. He had got himself out of the burning cab, only to be charged by a fear crazed bull which had escaped from the toppled crate. With nowhere to hide, Buddy had run and scaled a lone boab tree, shinning up the trunk to a height that was impossible to get down from, without the help of a vehicle parked beneath. I still find it hard to believe he managed it. The cattle truck belonged to Gordon Le Lievre. It was completely burnt out. There were dead cattle lying around, some were crippled and had to be destroyed, others had got away and gone bush. They were from Mount House Station. The driver came out of it unscathed.

## Verifying herd numbers

The WACCO office in Broome wanted a break down of the herd on Meda and sent up some paperwork for me to have a look at and sign. I had worked for Emanuels for six years, two and a half years for Exim and at the time, about a year for Peter Murray. I reckoned I had a fair idea how many cattle were on Meda. When the paperwork came I had a quick look through it. I'm not particularly smart with figures, but I couldn't believe the cattle they reckoned were on the place. I thought 'Jeez, this can't possibly be right.' We had run a spaying programme pretty much since I first went there, the spayer being Graham MacArthur, or 'The General' as he was known. The first year we had spayed nine hundred and fifty cows, eight fifty the next year, seven hundred and fifty the next and a hundred less each subsequent year. Over time we had spayed all the pie bald stuff, and the shitty livered stuff which was too young, or lightweight, to sell. The cows we spayed would, by now, have gone through the meatworks. When calculating herd numbers, you're supposed to take 10 % off your herd every year for stock losses. But by Jeez, looking at their figures we had a place that was overflowing with cattle. I knew it wasn't correct, so I got on the phone to Murray pretty well straight away, once we had read it.

"I can't sign this for you." I said.

"Why is that?"

"Because these cattle aren't here."

"Well I bought the place with those cattle on it." Murray told me. I couldn't let that go unanswered.

"I never ever saw you come and have a look here, or ask me any questions about herd numbers. The first I heard was that you had bought the station. The deal was done by the time I knew anything about it." I said. "But the point is, these figures aren't right and I'm not signing."

"In that case, you'd better send me a break down of what you reckon the herd is."

"No worries." I told him. Janet and I sat down and worked it all out, taking into account branders, spayers, steers to here, there and everywhere, meatworks cattle sent off, Brahmans bought in and a ten percent mortality rate for each year. When we'd finished we faxed it down to the Broome office. The phone rang immediately.

"This can't be right. There have got to be a lot more cattle there than this." Peter Murray was fairly unhappy about it.

"It's right all right." I told him and I wouldn't budge.

## Cleanskin heifers get a CW7 brand

The Flying Stockcamp had left Meda and gone on to one of the other WACCO joints. I had a few aboriginal stockmen doing the mustering for me, with one, Lee Thompson, running the camp. We were going back to muster in the bullock paddock, where we were beginning to get quite a few better looking Brahman calves coming on. When I told Peter Murray what we were doing he said, "When you're ready to draft give me a ring the day before and I'll come down." When we'd got all the cattle together I did as he said. The next day he came down to the bullock paddock and he had a bloke with him. Even when we had a contract musterer on the place I nearly always did the drafting. As far as I'm concerned that's my job, to be on the drafting gate. This particular day Murray gave the orders.

"Wellsy you can get on that gate there, such and such, you, on that gate." He took over and he drafted all the heifers off. He wanted them drafted into red heifers and grey heifers. These were the first lot by the better Brahman bulls. They were good looking heifers.

When we'd finished Murray said, "Now Wellsy, keep these heifers in the yard. I'll have a truck here tomorrow morning and they'll go off to Ellendale. And I don't want them branded or ear marked." he added. When I heard that I thought, 'John, your time here is finished!'

After Murray took off we sat down and had a very long lunch. I waited until the dust was gone, then we sat around for maybe another hour. When I was quite sure he wouldn't be back I said to the blokes, "Righto, light the fire and put the brands in." and we branded and earmarked every one of those heifers CW7. They went off to Ellendale next morning with a Meda brand emblazoned on them and Murray never said boo about it. Apart from it being illegal to truck cleanskins, I realised what Murray was aiming at. I was managing 'Beaten Downs' all right. Everything was being taken off the place, horses, engines, transportable houses, yard materials, and now the best of the Brahman heifers. He'd even tried to get them unbranded, so Meda wouldn't have been paid for them. What a good lurk! How was I ever supposed to turn a profit from the place, or improve the herd, when he took the cream off it. It was hopeless. I thought 'Bugger it. This is my last season here.' When I went home that night I said to Janet.

"I'm leaving at Christmas time. I'm just getting screwed here." She asked me what had happened and I told her. She realised it was the last straw.

"It will take the rest of the year to get my head round this, so I'll see the season out. We'll leave when the 'wet' comes." I told her. "I can't up and leave now. It's too hard." I wrote a letter to tell Murray I was pulling the pin. He rang me up and asked me to reconsider. I said 'No.' About a week later he rang up again,

"So you won't change your mind John?" I said I wouldn't.

"You've had a hard year on Meda this year. Look, I'll pay an airfare to Perth and back for you and your family, plus I'll give you $2000 spending money. Now will you stay?"

I said, "No". I'll admit Murray did do his best to persuade me to stay, but I knew it was no good. The sucking the station dry would only continue. I wasn't going to drop my pants and I wasn't accepting what I considered his bribes. He'd think if I can be bought once I can be bought twice. Much as I loved Meda I wasn't going to back down. Scotch College had taught me that. Backing down was something I didn't have in me.

Once I'd given notice and Murray had finally accepted it he asked me about Willie Lennard. Willie was still living in town, but coming out to Meda to work for me if I needed him to. I paid him wages and I gave him fuel for the trips in and out of Derby.

"Do you reckon Willie Lennard will work here after you've gone?" Murray asked.

"I don't know. You'll have to ask him." One day while Willie was working down at Pindan bore Murray did ask him. Willie just looked at him, then he walked away. Peter Murray came back complaining to me about his attitude.

"Well what do you really expect?" I asked. "You took his house away, with no warning. You can hardly blame him."

## Moving on

In December Janet got a job at Derby Regional Hospital doing after hours clerical work and holiday relief. I was looking around for a job in town also and eventually applied for a position as Shire Ranger, which I got. Once the rains came, early in January 1989 I left Meda and station life behind me. I was forty-five years old. For thirty two of those years Meda had been my home. It was one of the most heart wrenching days of my life.

*Roadtrain at Claypan Yards, Meda Station.*

*I check all is well before the double decker leaves.*

*Bull catching near Big Springs. L-R Philip 'Sneezy' Ah Chee, John Macaulay in the bull buggy, me and Mark Orme. Waiting for the truck to come.*

*Preparing to load a bull. It's legs are tied and horns tipped. L-R Stuart Mear, Sneezy Ah Chee and Roger Barker.*

*Bull being loaded into truck using bull buggy on the right. I wait on top of the crate to remove the chain once the bull is loaded.*

*Willie and Roslyn Lennard outside their Karmalinunga home in Derby.*

*The burnt out roadtrain at Meda's turn-off from which Buddy luckily escaped. Some cattle were less fortunate.*

*Ronnie Palmer breaking in at Claypan yard, watched by Michael Bear.*

*Sneezy Ah Chee and Ronnie Palmer branding cattle at portable yards on Meda.*

*Our first crop of good Brahman heifers, in Bolgers Yard, Meda bullock paddock. 1988
Destined for Ellendale, but with a CW7 brand on their hides, the loss of these heifers
was the catalyst for my leaving Meda.*

# CHAPTER SEVENTEEN

# COLLAPSE OF A COMPANY

*Meda! - I weep for Meda, but for more than her I cry,*
*I ache for the breaking heart of the man that I call 'my'.*
*'My man', whose life was Meda, who came here when just a babe,*
*Who's lived and grown and worked it, for him I'm so afraid.*
*Meda! - I weep for Meda, and the man who loved to roam*
*Over her plains and ridges, and loved them as if his own.*

In June 1989, just six months after we left Meda, The Australian newspaper reported that WACCO were seeking a partner for it's forty million dollar empire and it later transpired that Kerry Stokes and Brian Coppin had sold their 50% share in the company the same year.

I was not travelling very well during this period, being in a state of bereavement, or so I was later told. Nothing was important to me and all I could think of was Meda and what had happened there. People would come into Derby and tell me stories about what was going on at the station and some of the stories I didn't like hearing. Somewhere amongst the gloom of that time I was aware there were rumblings of financial instability for Peter Murray's company. Also that the last of the Exim properties were being sold by private treaty. Exim was now defunct and the WA Development Corporation was selling off Christmas Creek, Gilgie Downs and Beefwood Park.

The final outcome of the restructuring programme was far from what was originally intended. Certainly, so far as Meda was concerned it was a disaster. For one of the Emanuel's managers it proved to be of benefit, when Bulka, formerly part of Cherrabun, was bought by Jim and Joy Motter for an estimated $150,000. Newly formed Larrawa was also purchased by a genuine Kimberley cattleman, Kevin Brockhurst, for approximately $105,000.

In the final carve up, the Fitzroy Valley Aboriginal community got the former ALCO leases of Louisa and Bohemia Downs, as well as Mt Pierre, a newly created lease from an Emanuels property. The former Emanuel's flagship station, GoGo, was sold to the Harris family, from New South Wales, for a reported $12.5 million. Lawson Klopper, owner of Klopper Transport, bought Christmas Creek Station. The newly formed 184,000 hectare Beefwood Park lease was purchased by Danny and Ruth Webb-Smith, whilst the 275,000 hectare, Gilgie Downs, formerly part of Cherrabun, was also taken up.

In August 1990, after failing to find an equity partner, the West Australian Cattle Company, by now the biggest private cattle holding in the state, announced it was putting some of it's properties on the market. This followed an agreement made with Elders, that should a world-wide search for a partner prove fruitless the company would be split up and individual buyers sought. Interestingly Meda was not amongst those stations being offered for sale. By January 1991 none of the six properties offered had been sold and WACCO went into receivership. Gary Trevor of Ferrier Hodgson was appointed receiver manager in order to secure an Elders Rural Finance debt estimated at $20 million. According to newspaper reports the debt was incurred when Peter Murray absorbed the interests of former partners Kerry Stokes and Brian Coppin back in 1989. With the high interest rates at that time the debt was ever increasing, and by May 1991 eight WACCO properties were put up for tender. This time Meda was one of them. Janet and I pricked up our ears. It was two years since we had left Meda, but the wound was still raw. Nothing would have made us happier than an opportunity to go back to the station, if we could, on our own terms.

A glossy prospectus was circulated which we read with interest. Meda was said to have an estimated 13,000 to 18,000 head of cattle. 140 horses. Nineteen main paddocks, thirty two holding paddocks and ten sets of drafting yards. Whilst we knew we couldn't believe everything we read, we did know, first-hand, that Meda was one of the best improved properties in the region. We began to dream. I got in touch with Frank Mugford and Tim Emanuel. After several serious phone conversations Tim asked me to go and talk to the Agricultural Department in Derby, to find out what I could. I did, but they wouldn't tell me a bloody thing. I was told to write a formal request for any information I needed. I did that too, writing to Brad McCormack in mid August 1991. I requested information on the TB status of the herd, the estimated size of the herd, with a break-up of age, sex and breed of cattle. The number of bulls, whether Brahman, Santa Gertrudis or Shorthorn. Details of TB infected areas and what cattle were estimated to be in each area. I emphasised the importance of obtaining such information, especially in regard to the TB eradication programme, before a decision could be made whether to proceed with a tender for Meda or not. But it seemed I wasn't to be taken seriously.

In the first week of September Tim Emanuel flew up to Derby, bringing Frank Mugford with him. When he arrived he went in to the Ag. Department himself and spent four hours there. One day he flew Frank Mugford and I over Meda to have a look at the station from the air. He then rang the manager to ask if we could drive out next morning for a better look. It was arranged that we be there at eight o'clock. When we pulled up at the homestead the manager had already gone. Frank and Tim went into the house to talk to the manager's wife. She told them her husband was down in the bullock paddock, adding, "John Wells knows the way." I don't think she was particularly polite because later they commented on the reception they got and her attitude. We went down to the bullock paddock, but the manager wasn't there. We met a station hand who told us he was out at Macaulay's yard, so we back tracked. We crossed the May River and drove out beyond Orange Pool to the new circular yard, which Tim had never seen. The yard was full of cattle and the manager was there. Tim and Frank had a bit of a talk to him. His name was John Forrester and he was the third manager to be appointed in less than three years. The first was Jim Ferguson, who left in September 1989, then a caretaker was put on the place. 1990 saw Bill Graham appointed as manager, and he was swiftly followed by John Forrester in 1991. Tim told Forrester that he would be putting in a tender for Meda and, if it was successful, I would be going to manage it. After this we left Macaulay's yard and drove to Orange Pool, and across to Bull Camp. We had a bit of difficulty looking around because several of the gates were locked. We looked at a few more bores, then headed back to Derby.

Conversation over dinner that evening, at the King Sound Hotel, was pretty serious. Tim expressed a fair bit of concern about a lack of income for the first few years, should our tender be successful. There were very few steers left on Meda and what there were, were very young. It would be some years before the property could produce any money cattle and start paying it's way. The station was unarguably rich in improvements, but it's recent history had left it's stock numbers depleted. Also discussed that evening was what share we would have in Meda. Tim made it clear he had no interest in proceeding further unless Janet and I had a financial interest. A ten per cent share, giving him the security of knowing I would be there to run it for the long term. I wanted nothing more, but Janet and I had very little money, other than a heavily mortgaged house in Perth. It was all a bit daunting, but a dream we had to pursue. The following morning Tim flew himself and Frank back to Perth.

It was a strange period for Janet and I. One of suppressed excitement and guarded optimism, tinged with a fear of heart-breaking disappointment. We waited anxiously while Tim and Frank did their sums. There was a lot of interest in the tendering process for the WACCO properties, Meda in particular. After Tim's visit some people got very twitchy. I suppose they felt he had a high chance of success, if he really wanted to win the tender. Having worked for Emanuel Brothers we knew Tim would make a measured decision. There was never any likelihood of him putting in a high tender if it was not economically prudent, however much he might have wanted to buy Meda back. It was just as well we knew this. It would save us from any undue shock or disappointment later. When Tim decided to put in a low tender, deducting the running costs for the next two years from his estimated value of the property, we were not surprised. We knew then, almost before it was submitted, that we wouldn't get it.

The successful tenderer was Hugh McLachlan, a wealthy sheep farmer from South Australia who already owned numerous properties around Australia. A newly acquired property, running at a loss for a couple of years, would not be a problem for him. Possibly the reverse. His cousin Ian McLachlan was a prominent figure in the country at the time and a member of the board of Elders IXL Ltd from 1980 to 1990. It is understood Hugh McLachlan's tender was in the region of three million dollars. We were not even close to the mark, but at least we had tried.

# EPILOGUE

After leaving Meda we lived in Derby for a little over five years where I did a variety of jobs including Shire Ranger and West Kimberley Fuel depot manager. It was a period of very high interest rates and I needed to take whatever work was going. I also worked the fuel pumps at a service station and did a stint as bottle shop attendant. Janet continued working at the Derby Regional Hospital in a clerical role, covering the hospital during weekends and public holidays.

Neither of us particularly liked living in town. As I worked weekdays and Janet worked weekends, we never had a break together when we could head bush and get away from town life for a while. It was a difficult time for both of us. Really we were existing, rather than living. Life off the station seemed very flat.

I kept pigs on a block a short distance from town, which gave me an interest after work. I also built up quite a flock of pigeons, which I'd let out each evening and at weekends. They gave me a lot of pleasure. We kept a few chooks in the backyard and grew a few vegies. None of it was enough to hold my interest, or enthusiasm, in the way station life had. I was an unhappy man.

My parents were still living in their little corrugated house in Neville Street, although during the 'wet' season they went to Perth for a couple of months each year. Dad was becoming very frail, but Mum was still fairly active and involved in the community. I saw Willie and Roslyn Lennard regularly and helped them out when I could with a bit of tucker, or warm clothes and blankets if we had a cold snap during the 'dry'. Life for them was a constant struggle, trying to prevent aggressive intoxicated young fellas from stealing their food and belongings. Eventually Willie's eyesight began to fail and Roslyn suffered from dementia in her latter years, though both lived for a good many years after we left the Kimberley.

We sent Adele away to boarding school for two years. George was due to start high school at the beginning of 1994 and we knew we couldn't afford two lots of boarding school fees. We decided Janet should move south, put both children in as day pupils and try to find work nearby. She rented a small house adjacent to the school and in January that year we packed up our belongings and drove to Bunbury.

Having settled the family, I returned to Derby where I worked for several more months. I continued to hear stories of what was happening on Meda and I knew I had to get away from the upset it was causing me. Once Janet had secured regular part-time work at the Bunbury Regional Hospital radiology department, I left the Kimberley behind me and drove down to re-join the family and start a new life in the south-west.

*I exercise my campdraft mare on a southwest beach. circa 2009*

# GLOSSARY

A doing—Given a difficult time, harassed.

Antbed—Commonly used when referring to termite mounds.

Arvo—Afternoon.

Avgas—Aviation fuel.

Babbler—Colloquial name for a cook.

Biddul—Aboriginal name for my father, George Wells (Snr.)

Blowflies—People who ask others for money. Also large fly attracted to meat.

Blown—Flyblown, no money, broke. Also as in blowfly eggs laid.

Blue—An argument or fight.

Calcutta—A pre-race raffle and auction.

Camp—Stockcamp, also native camp.

Coacher—Quiet, as in handled, horse or beast.

Cockies Gate—Wire and star picket opening in fence.

Condemns—Condemned beast, only suitable for by-products.

Crook—No good, also unwell.

'Dat—'That' as pronounced by natives.

Dilunk—Knocked up, or buggered up.

Dinner—In stockcamps usually meaning lunch.

Dinner camp—A lunch stop.

Dogger—Someone who traps and baits dingoes for payment.

Dunny—Outside toilet.

Gascoyne Traders—Trucking company that serviced the Kimberley at this time.

Greenhide—Untanned hide off a beast used to make ropes and hopples.

Guddia—Aboriginal term for white man.

Gutser—A fall, as in horse fall.

Half clumper—A horse of heavy build, as in half carthorse.

Hatter—A loner, or hermit.

Heart starter—Term used when in need of a drink when hungover.

Hides cracking—Alcoholics need for a drink.

Hobbles—Leather straps and chain put on horses front fetlocks.

Hook—Steal.

Horse tailer—Stockman who looks after the working horses in stockcamp.—

Into it—Buck, as in 'get stuck into it'.

Jad'un—'That one' as pronounced by natives.

Joordu—Aboriginal word for snake.

Killer—A beast that is killed for meat.

King Brown—Big bottle of beer, also highly venomous snake.

Koepanger—From Indonesian city of Koepang. Term used loosely.

Larraping—A work out.

Linguida—Aboriginal term for saltwater crocodile.

Looma—An Aboriginal community.

Mickey—A young bull.

Minneriche—Hardy native shrub, with reddish wood which tends to splinter.

MMA—MacRobertson Miller Airline.

Mob—Group of cattle of any number.

Moundring—The base upon which a tank sits.

Mowanjum—An Aboriginal community near Derby.

Myall—A bush 'black fella', or traditional uneducated Aborigine.

Nikki nikki—Stick tobacco, or chewing tobacco, popular with older natives.

Packs—Pack saddles and pack bags for carrying gear on horses or mules.

Pick up—To see. Also, collect or round up.

Piker—Old bullock past it's prime.

Poddy—A calf that has lost it's mother.

Pound—Small enclosure in a drafting yard, used for sorting stock.

Rats—Suffering from alcohol withdrawal. Delirium Tremens.

Ratshit—Useless, no good, not feeling any good.

Rev—A ticking off.

Rig—Term used for horse with one testicle.

Run—General term for station country. As in 'out on the run'.

Rush—A stampede of cattle.

Shelly—In poor condition, generally due to age.

Smoko—Morning or afternoon tea.

Spayer types—Poor quality cows, not suitable for breeding.

Spears—Pointed timber or steel rails used for trapping cattle.

Stag—Term used for a bull castrated late.

Stood up—As in a horse that stands still and faces up to be caught or handled

Surcingle—Leather strap that goes over a saddle.

Tailed out—Horsemen minding cattle being held out in the open, not yarded.

Tea—Term used for the evening meal.

Toey—Nervous, unsettled.

Tucker—Food

Turkey's nest—Large circular tank with earthen walls resembling a small dam.

Ute—Utility vehicle, as in van with tray back.

Wudul—Aboriginal term for 'boss'.

Lightning Source UK Ltd.
Milton Keynes UK
UKOW07f0404151115

262723UK00001B/8/P